THE ONE YEAR®

PRAYING THE PROMISES OF GOD

The One Year®

PRAYING
the PROMISES
of GOD

CHERI FULLER & JENNIFER KENNEDY DEAN

Tyndale House Publishers, Inc.
Carol Stream, Illinois

Visit Tyndale online at www.tyndale.com.

Visit Cheri's website at www.cherifuller.com.

Visit Jennifer's website at www.prayinglife.org.

TYNDALE and Tyndale's quill logo are registered trademarks of Tyndale House Publishers, Inc.

The One Year and *One Year* are registered trademarks of Tyndale House Publishers, Inc. The One Year logo is a trademark of Tyndale House Publishers, Inc.

The One Year Praying the Promises of God

Designed by Julie Chen

Edited by Susan Taylor

Published in association with the literary agency of WordServe Literary Group, Ltd., 10152 S. Knoll Circle, Highlands Ranch, CO, 80130.

INTRODUCTION: PRAYING IN THE LIGHT OF GOD'S PROMISES

WELCOME TO a devotional book written specifically to encourage your spiritual journey by praying God's promises. Those precious promises, of which there are hundreds throughout the Bible, are provided to stir us and inspire us to pray. Yet sometimes we fail to notice, believe, and pray these promises. British pastor F. B. Meyer said, "Though the Bible be crowded with golden promises from board to board, yet they will be inoperative until we turn them into prayer."

As you read this One Year devotional book, you have the opportunity to turn God's golden promises into prayer each day and experience the blessings of a praying life. As we pray God's promises, the starting point is the nature of God. The essence of God's character is, in itself, a promise: "[God] keeps every promise forever" (Psalm 146:6). Throughout the Scriptures, each time God reveals something of his nature, he is promising us that he will be true to that nature in any circumstance.

God has always dealt with his people by communicating promises to them. By promising first and then performing what he has promised, he awakens in us the faith, desire, and expectation that point us toward him and find their outlets in the prayer of faith.

We might illustrate that process like this. Recently, I (Jennifer) saw an ad in a magazine for noise-canceling headphones. Until I saw that ad, I had no desire for noise-cancelling headphones. But once I knew they were available, I began to notice how loud the world was and to imagine how much better it might be if only I had noise-canceling headphones too. Knowing they were available awakened in me the desire to possess them. And knowing where to find them motivated me to seek them out. God makes promises to us for much the same reason. He is letting us know what he has available if only we will ask.

Misunderstandings about Praying the Promises

Sometimes people have been disappointed when they prayed God's promises and didn't get the answer they hoped for. If you have experienced that, you're not alone. Let us suggest some things for you to consider and warn you about some misunderstandings to avoid.

First, remember that there is a difference between *believing in a certain outcome and having faith in God*. Sometimes we decide what God should do, then construe a promise so that it matches what we want. We might pray that promise with the subtext being *our definition* of the impact that promise should have on our situation. Over all the years that the Lord has had the two of us in his school of prayer, a lesson we continue to learn at deeper levels is how to let the Word of God speak without imposing our own interpretations and preconceived expectations on it.

Second, avoid thinking of the promises as tools to use to get your way with God. Some people pray as if God occasionally forgets his promises or tries to renege on them and is depending on us to remind him of them. The truth is, God made promises and bound himself to us in a blood-sealed covenant so that we would know exactly what we could expect from him. The purpose of his promises is to give us confidence and peace. Instead, sometimes we pray as if we are responsible for finding the scriptural promise so we can guarantee the outcome we want, and then taking that promise to God to hold him to his Word.

This kind of prayer treats God's Word as if it's a catalog. We decide what God should do, look through the Bible to find a verse that will match our plans, and order it. As we do in catalog shopping, we then skim over everything that holds no appeal for us. We pick and choose.

Remember, Scripture is not God's *words*; it is God's *Word*. Scripture is a whole and can't be cut apart and pasted together to match our agendas. Rather, the golden promises are for *God to use* to inspire faith and confidence within our hearts and to shape our prayers as we look to his Spirit to guide us.

How to Use This Book

We encourage you to use this book as a personal devotional or to read it with prayer partners or your family. It is also an ideal small-group resource. *The One Year Praying the Promises of God* is meant to be a companion book to *The One Year Bible*, so you'll find the readings move chronologically throughout the year. Each day is a devotional thought from either the Old Testament, the New Testament, Psalms, or Proverbs. As you read the pages ahead, we pray you'll be drawn closer to the Father through Christ, that you'll sense him speaking to your heart, and that you'll experience his love more and more.

If you are using this book with others—either in a small group, with your girlfriend, or with your spouse, you might want to underline thoughts that speak to you in specific ways. You can use the questions below as you think about, process, and discuss what you've learned.

What did you underline this week, and why was it significant to you?
What promise this week gave you a new perspective on something you are dealing with?
What action steps or active changes will you make because of something you read this week?

More discussion questions for each week can be found at www.prayingthepromises.org.

As you read these devotionals, may you be encouraged and strengthened. May your burdens be lifted as you cast your cares upon the Promise Maker. May you see over and over the Lord's faithfulness and be filled to overflowing with joy. Thank you for joining us on this journey through God's Word and his promises!

Cheri & Jennifer

JANUARY

FRUITFULNESS

THEY DELIGHT IN THE LAW OF THE LORD,
    MEDITATING ON IT DAY AND NIGHT.
THEY ARE LIKE TREES PLANTED ALONG THE RIVERBANK,
    BEARING FRUIT EACH SEASON.
THEIR LEAVES NEVER WITHER,
    AND THEY PROSPER IN ALL THEY DO.

Psalm 1:2-3

THE WORD of God is to your life as a river is to trees. And the trees to which the psalmist points us didn't just spring up naturally. They have been planted. Placed in that location deliberately so that they have direct access to nourishment and refreshment and the flow of life. They put down their roots where water is abundant.

The trees take in the water through their roots, letting it circulate to every cell and molecule. The water that once flowed in the river now flows in the trees. The fruit the trees bear season after season is the visible evidence of what we don't see— strong root systems.

We find another description of trees in Jeremiah 17:8:

SUCH TREES ARE NOT BOTHERED BY THE HEAT
    OR WORRIED BY LONG MONTHS OF DROUGHT.
THEIR LEAVES STAY GREEN,
    AND THEY NEVER STOP PRODUCING FRUIT.

A tree deeply rooted and continuously nourished will be fruitful even during times when the environment is brutal and deadly.

Today, sink your roots deep into the living and active Word of God. Let its truth circulate to every corner of your life. As it nourishes your soul, you will find yourself resilient even when the heat is on. The difficulties of life will just force your roots deeper and make you drought-proof.

Lord, let me drink deeply from your Word. Let it inform my life and transform my circumstances so that I will bear hardy fruit.

Jennifer

The trials of the saint are a divine husbandry, by which [God] grows and brings forth abundant fruit.

—**CHARLES HADDON SPURGEON** (1834–1892), English preacher and writer

2 FAITHFUL AND TRUE

THIS FULFILLED WHAT THE LORD HAD SPOKEN THROUGH THE PROPHET: "I CALLED MY SON OUT OF EGYPT."

Matthew 2:15

GOD ALWAYS keeps his word—*always*.

We all find ourselves in times when chaos seems to reign and our situations feel out of control. It must have seemed that way to Joseph—newly married under less-than-optimal conditions, away from familiar surroundings, and having to navigate the treacherous waters of intrigue and danger. He must have felt that all the experiences that recently had defined his life were sweeping him up in a tidal wave. Who could have planned ahead for a middle-of-the-night escape to Egypt?

But how events look and feel at the time is almost never the true picture. God knows every tremor long before a tidal wave forms. Things are never out of his control. He is shaping events in a way that will highlight his faithfulness.

Joseph followed God one step at a time and found himself in Egypt, a place he never thought he would call home. But he settled in and waited until the next summons came. Do you imagine that between the times when the guiding voice of the living God was clear and Joseph's faith was strong, Joseph wondered when and how, and even if? Do you suppose you might have looked at those circumstances and wondered, Did I make a mistake? Is God really guiding me?

Step back and see how God is telling the story. He is doing as he promised he would do. He spoke his intentions generations before and did not vary one iota from his plan. No matter how things might appear on the surface, God is always working out his purpose in his way, in his time. His promises will not fail. If your circumstances seem to be running on their own steam with no escape in sight, take another look through the prism of God's promises and know that everything is proceeding under God's careful management.

Lord, I believe that you are working everything out for your own good purposes.
I trust in your love for me and in your power to do all you have promised.

Jennifer

You cooperate with the immediate inevitable because you know that in and through things God's will is being worked out.

—E. STANLEY JONES (1884–1973), American missionary and theologian

WALKING WITH GOD

ENOCH LIVED 365 YEARS, WALKING IN CLOSE FELLOWSHIP WITH
GOD. THEN ONE DAY HE DISAPPEARED, BECAUSE GOD TOOK HIM.

Genesis 5:23-24

TUCKED INTO one of those who-begat-whom chapters in Genesis, we stumble across a statement about a man named Enoch. The statement reveals more about God than it does about Enoch. It gives us another little glimpse into the character of God, showing us a promise about how he will act in our lives.

As you read the chapter, watch the rhythm. "So-and-so lived . . . and then he died." Someone lived, and then he died. Over and over, generation after generation. Someone lived, and then he died. The drumbeat never varies—until Enoch. Enoch throws everything out of sync.

My late husband was very tall. His stride was much longer than mine. When we walked together, he would sometimes forget and be far ahead of me, talking to me as if I were right beside him. He had to be intentional about pacing his steps so that I could walk with him instead of behind him. He had to want to walk with me.

When I read that Enoch walked with God, the first thing that amazes me is that it means God also walked with Enoch. God was willing to calibrate his stride for Enoch's sake—to take into account Enoch's frailty.

So intimate was the relationship between Enoch and God that when the time came for Enoch to leave earth and enter eternity, his walk just continued. One last step on earth's ground, the next step in heaven's vast expanse. Death for Enoch was the natural extension of his life. He just kept walking with God. He received the promise early that came later to the followers of Christ: "He who believes in me shall never die."

Thank you, Father, for the gift of your presence. I am filled with wonder, amazed and awed, that you love me so much you actually desire my presence. Teach me more each day what it means to walk with you.

Jennifer

Forbid, O Lord God, that my thoughts be wholly occupied with the world's passing show. . . . Grant rather that each day may do something to strengthen my hold upon the unseen world.

—**JOHN BAILLIE** (1886–1960), Scottish preacher

4

CALLING TOWARD

THE LORD HAD SAID TO ABRAM, "LEAVE YOUR NATIVE COUNTRY, YOUR RELATIVES, AND YOUR FATHER'S FAMILY, AND GO TO THE LAND THAT I WILL SHOW YOU."

Genesis 12:1

GOD CALLS us to something, not just away from something. When he called Abraham to leave the land of his birth, it was so he could give him the Promised Land. When God called his people out of Egypt, it was so he could bring them into Canaan. He is always calling us to the place where his provision awaits us. God's commands are, in the end, always related to his promises. He commands an obedience that will clear the way for his promised provision.

Notice the structure of the command he issued to Abraham and the corresponding structure of the promise: in Genesis 12:1, "The LORD had said to Abram, '[1] Leave your native country, [2] your relatives, and [3] your father's family, and go to the land that I will show you.'" The command does not end with what Abraham must leave behind. It commands him to possess and embrace what lies ahead. "Let go of what is in your hand right now so that your hand will be ready to grasp what I am about to give you."

Now, look at the promises in Genesis 12:2-3: "[1] I will make you into a great nation. I will bless you and [2] make you famous, and you will be a blessing to others. I will bless those who bless you and curse those who treat you with contempt. [3] All the families on earth will be blessed through you." This was not sacrifice for the sake of sacrifice, but rather sacrifice for the sake of something more. When God's call comes, don't let yourself dwell on what you might be called to leave behind. Instead, fix your heart on what you will be receiving into your life.

Jesus, I eagerly follow you. Give me the wisdom to let go of the baubles in my hand and reach out for the treasures of the Kingdom. Help me to trust your promise when it comes wrapped in a call.

Jennifer

When Christ calls us by his grace we ought not only to remember what we are, but we ought also to think of what he can make us.

—CHARLES HADDON SPURGEON (1834–1892), English preacher and writer

BE WEAK TO BE STRONG

GOD BLESSES THOSE WHO ARE POOR AND REALIZE THEIR NEED FOR HIM, FOR THE KINGDOM OF HEAVEN IS THEIRS.

Matthew 5:3

THE WORD was out about a new rabbi on the scene. He had been preaching and teaching and healing and was drawing larger crowds each day. This was apparently his first substantive address, though he had been teaching in their synagogues. What would he say? What agenda would he push? Would he razzle-dazzle them? Would he scold and rant?

His first words were those of today's verse, above.

The word translated "poor" is a word that means destitute; it describes those with no ability to provide for themselves, those who are completely dependent on others to supply their needs. It describes a beggar. Jesus could have used a less stark word, one that would mean the working poor, those who barely got by day to day. Instead, he used a word that meant utterly impoverished.

The first thing he wanted to say was that the Kingdom belonged to those who recognized that they were incapable of providing spiritually for themselves. They brought nothing with them that would give them entrance to the Kingdom. They could do nothing that would give them stature in the Kingdom. They could possess the Kingdom only by receiving everything from the hand of another.

Our weakness is our greatest asset in the Kingdom. It is in our weakness that God meets us and displays his power most clearly. Only when we are confronted with our own helplessness can we experience the power of Christ in us. He promises his power in our weakness.

Let your helplessness and your weakness be the offering you bring to him. He is not waiting for you to be strong. He is waiting for you to recognize that you are weak.

Lord, I freely admit that, apart from you, I am empty and weak. Let my emptiness be the condition that gives you room to fill me with yourself.

Jennifer

Your helplessness is your best prayer. It calls from your heart to the heart of God with greater effect than all your uttered pleas. He hears it from the very moment that you are seized with helplessness, and He becomes actively engaged at once in hearing and answering the prayer of your helplessness.

—**OLE HALLESBY** (1879–1961), Norwegian pastor and writer

6

STEP-BY-STEP

ALL WHO LISTEN TO ME WILL LIVE IN PEACE,
UNTROUBLED BY FEAR OF HARM.

Proverbs 1:33

WE LIVE in tumultuous times. An economy once thought to be unassailable seems to be crumbling. The structures of our society have been exposed and revealed to be shaky and uncertain.

Yet God promises us an untroubled peace: "All who listen to me will live in peace." Where does our fearlessness come from? God's voice, speaking to our hearts.

We don't study a God who spoke only long ago. We live in relationship with a God who continues to speak today. He communicates the words of Scripture into our lives in real time. Clear your life of its noisy clutter and listen to him. Marinate your life in his Word. Believe what he promises, and do what he says. Listening means responding to what you hear. He promises peace to all who listen to him.

Some time ago I had a situation in my life that was disruptive and nerve racking. There was no escaping it, no way around it. I had to work my way through it. I could have easily sunk into worry and felt overwhelmed. Only one thing kept fear at bay: God's voice. Whenever fear inserted itself into my thoughts and demanded my attention, I deliberately turned to God and heard him speak to my heart: *Jennifer, I will never leave you or forsake you. Jennifer, you can do all things through Christ who gives you strength. Jennifer, Jennifer, I have redeemed you; you are mine.* I found that I could focus on each required step, not worrying ahead about the next one, and step-by-step work my way through the trouble.

When I face difficult situations, I can walk through them with worry dogging my every step, or I can do it with settled peace. God's voice changes the atmosphere of my circumstances.

Thank you for speaking peace into my life. I choose to live in untroubled peace by listening to your voice in my heart.

Jennifer

Come, and however feeble you feel, just wait in His presence. As a feeble, sickly invalid is brought out into the sunshine to let its warmth go through him, come . . . and sit and wait there with one thought: Here I am, in the sunshine of His love.

—**ANDREW MURRAY** (1828–1917), South African pastor and author

THE SECRET PLACE

WHEN YOU PRAY, GO AWAY BY YOURSELF, SHUT THE DOOR
BEHIND YOU, AND PRAY TO YOUR FATHER IN PRIVATE. THEN
YOUR FATHER, WHO SEES EVERYTHING, WILL REWARD YOU.

Matthew 6:6

JESUS DRAWS a sharp contrast between those who *perform prayer* and those who *pray*. Some people treat prayer as if its power lies in the petitioners' words—their eloquence or pitch or volume. Those who pray in public for the purpose of being seen and admired or who use public prayer as a platform from which to display their own great spirituality have the reward they seek. In many cases, they experience the admiration of others, just as they hoped they would. Their spiritual lives may well be applauded and admired. However, they will have settled for a cheap reward. They will not be rewarded with the presence of God. And theirs will be a perishable crown.

Jesus tells us there is a better reward, a higher pursuit. The reward God offers is himself, and that will be more than enough. When you pray, let the Father be your focus. In his presence we find everything we are looking for: "You will show me the way of life, granting me the joy of your presence and the pleasures of living with you forever" (Psalm 16:11). He will display his presence through our lives to those around us. What we experience in the secret place of his presence will transform every aspect of our lives. He keeps his promises, and he promises that private time seeking his face is not wasted time, but time that yields rich fruit. Time alone with God is time rewarded.

How do you take hold of his promised reward? Make time alone with God a priority.

*Lord, I crave your presence, and all my longings find their fulfillment in you.
You are my reward and my one desire. Draw my heart to the secret place of your
presence.*

Jennifer

With Christ, we have access in a one-to-one relationship. . . . In the Old Testament, it was more one of worship and awe, a vertical relationship. [In] the New Testament, on the other hand, we look across at a Jesus who looks familiar, horizontal. The combination is what makes the Cross.

—**BONO** (1960–), Irish musician and humanitarian

8

KINGDOM FIRST

SEEK THE KINGDOM OF GOD ABOVE ALL ELSE, AND LIVE RIGHTEOUSLY, AND HE WILL GIVE YOU EVERYTHING YOU NEED.

Matthew 6:33

IS ANXIETY leaching the joy from your life? Then let this promise infuse you with hope and comfort.

These words come on the heels of an animated teaching about God's provision. Jesus wants his followers to understand how carefully the Father watches over them and is aware of their every need. Imagine Jesus, out in the open, surrounded by his disciples and crowds of eager listeners. He sees a bird in flight. Sweeping his arm skyward, he says, "Look at the birds of the air!" He glances at the ground and sees one of the hardy lilies indigenous to the region. Pointing at one, or perhaps plucking it and holding it up for all to see, he says, "Observe the lilies!" He wants to frame a picture in our minds that will focus our hearts on the Father and take our eyes off our worries.

When we view our needs through the prism of the love and power of the Father, our view is transformed. Our needs become the platform for his power, his entry point, his opening into our lives. He created you with needs. By his design, you require food and water and clothing and shelter. He knows you need all these things.

What to do when need looms large and anxiety takes you captive? Seek his Kingdom and his righteousness. Take all the energy that would go into fear and worry, and turn it toward the Kingdom. Let the King rule in your situation, and put your attention on worshiping and serving him. Let him use the situation that could distract you from him to draw you to him instead. Let your anxious heart come to rest in the promise that "he will give you everything you need."

> *Father, thank you for providing for my every need. Thank you that I don't have to spend my days consumed with worry; I can be consumed with you. No need enters my life for which you have not already planned and provided. I choose to keep anxiety from cluttering my heart, and instead let it be filled with you.*
>
> *Jennifer*

Prayer is but the opening of a channel from my emptiness to His fullness.

—E. STANLEY JONES (1884–1973), American missionary and theologian

SHELTERED FROM THE STORM

THE LORD IS A SHELTER FOR THE OPPRESSED,
A REFUGE IN TIMES OF TROUBLE.

Psalm 9:9

THE LORD shelters the oppressed—the broken, crushed, disappointed, disillusioned, grieving. Life can be brutal, but God is our safe place. He stands between us and life, absorbing its blows on our behalf.

What's the first thing you do when you know a tornado is headed your way? Seek shelter! You know the storm is too big for you. You can't withstand its power. So you find a refuge and let the storm pass over you.

The news introduces us to people who have weathered killer storms. Observing the littered landscape, we are left to imagine the force that created such devastation. Yet people are still standing. The storm that leveled everything in sight somehow missed them. How did they escape the storm's power? They found a shelter. They found a place strong enough to withstand the force of the storm.

This is what God is saying to you right now: *I'm stronger than your storm.*

At some point in the depths of my grief at the loss of my husband, I asked the Lord, "If you bear my burdens, then why do I have to feel this pain?" I thought about an experience when my son Kennedy asked me to put my hands against his punching bag and hold it steady for him to punch. Big, strong Kennedy put all his power into the punch. On my side, it stung my hands just enough for me to say, "Ouch!" But it was nothing like the pain I would have experienced had the punch landed on me. I'd have been knocked out!

The Lord seemed to say to me: *I stand between you and any blows headed your way. If the pain you feel hurts, just imagine the pain if I had not absorbed the blow for you.* God does not promise life without pain. He promises to be a shelter from life's knockout punches.

> *Lord, I give myself to you in total trust. I believe that you are stronger than my storm.*

Jennifer

He hideth our unrighteousness with His righteousness, He covereth our disobedience with his obedience, He shadoweth our death with His death, that the wrath of God cannot find us.

—**HENRY SMITH** (ca. 1560–1591?), English Puritan preacher

10 HIS HEALING TOUCH

"Lord," the [leper] said, "if you are willing, you can heal me and make me clean." Jesus reached out and touched him. "I am willing," he said. "Be healed!" And instantly the leprosy disappeared.

Matthew 8:2-3

AS JESUS reveals who he is by what he does, we can see the promise he makes to us. The same Jesus who touched the leper—the unclean outcast—reaches out to touch us with his tenderness and his compassion. Imagine the scene with me:

As the leper struggled through the crowd, his bell announced his shame. "Unclean! Unclean!" The clean ones moved away, avoiding his pain at all costs. The leper worked his way through the religious throng to find Jesus.

Jesus looked past the man's rotting flesh and saw the hope that was sloughing away with every rejection, every head that turned away, every face that registered disgust and fear. Jesus looked past the decaying skin and saw the little spark of life, almost extinguished and crusted over with loneliness and hurt.

He heard the anguished cry, "If you are willing, you can heal me and make me clean." He restored the leper's disease-ravaged body, but more than that, he restored his shame-ravaged soul. The fearless, compassionate touch of the Savior clothed the man in dignity. Jesus gave him more than a reprieve from death. Jesus gave him *life*.

Do you feel hopeless and alone? Do you feel that if anyone could see you as you are, you would be labeled "unclean"? Hear the promise Jesus whispers to your heart today: "I am willing to reach into your life with my healing, cleansing touch."

You don't have to hide. You don't have to disguise yourself so you can be lovable. You don't have to pretend so you can be accepted. Jesus embodies the promise of restoration and wholeness. He acts in your life in accordance with who he is: the Life Giver, the Sin Washer, the Soul Restorer.

Jesus, I surrender my shame. I let go of my false sense of worthlessness. Hear my cry: "You can make me whole!" Touch my life.

Jennifer

The cross is the lightning rod of grace that short-circuits God's wrath to Christ so that only the light of His love remains for believers.

—A. W. TOZER (1897–1963), American preacher and author

LEANING ON HIS STRENGTH

DON'T BE IMPRESSED WITH YOUR OWN WISDOM.
  INSTEAD, FEAR THE LORD AND TURN AWAY FROM EVIL.
THEN YOU WILL HAVE HEALING FOR YOUR BODY
  AND STRENGTH FOR YOUR BONES.

Proverbs 3:7-8

GOD CALLS us to an obedience that will position us for the promise. He wants to protect us from the consequences of acting on our own, short-sighted opinions, which are dependent on only what we can observe and interpret. We have access to a wisdom that can see far beyond what we can see. We can tap into the wisdom of God, who can do far more than we can ever imagine. He wants us to act on his best idea, not on our own.

Earlier, the writer had put it this way: "Trust in the LORD with all your heart and lean not on your own understanding" (Proverbs 3:5, NIV). The words bring an image to mind: I'm coming to the end of an arduous hike. I'm tired, hot, thirsty. My shaking leg muscles won't hold me up for one more step. Just then, I come upon a boulder. It's cool and strong and immovable. What do I do? I lean. I lean all my weakness into its strength. Its coolness overcomes my heat. It holds me up when I can't stand on my own. I receive from the boulder what I cannot provide for myself. I just lean.

Trying to navigate life in our own strength, depending on our own wisdom, wears us down. The stress and uncertainty even take a physical toll because God has created us so that all the parts work together—physical, spiritual, emotional.

We learn to trust the Lord and his ways so completely that the only thing we fear is walking outside his ways. His ways are not restriction, but protection. Even when our own perceptions seem to point us in another direction, the way of full and abundant life lies in obedience. Don't lean on your own wisdom—fenced in by small thoughts and myopic vision. Lean all your weight on him, and let him carry you into his huge, unimaginable plan for your life. He promises that he will do just that.

> *Whenever I'm tired, discouraged, afraid, hopeless . . . I know these are the symptoms that highlight the places in my life where I'm depending on my own wisdom. Right now, I choose to lean on you. In this moment, I lean my weakness on your strength.*
>
> *Jennifer*

The time of business does not differ with me from the time of prayer; and in the noise and clatter of my kitchen . . . I possess God in as great tranquility as if I were on my knees.

—**BROTHER LAWRENCE** (1614–1691), French lay monk and writer

12 GET BY GIVING

> HONOR THE LORD WITH YOUR WEALTH
>   AND WITH THE BEST PART OF EVERYTHING YOU PRODUCE.
> THEN HE WILL FILL YOUR BARNS WITH GRAIN,
>   AND YOUR VATS WILL OVERFLOW WITH GOOD WINE.
>
> *Proverbs 3:9-10*

GOD'S WISDOM and my understanding are often diametrically opposed. Get by giving? That doesn't sound reasonable. Get by hoarding? Now that sounds right. Give God your leftovers sounds right.

But God doesn't do leftovers. Giving God the first of the harvest, dedicating the first-born son, and offering the firstborn of the herd were all requirements God placed on his people. The gift of the firstfruits was an acknowledgment that everything belonged to God. He calls believers a kind of firstfruits, his "prized possession" (James 1:18). He means that we have been set aside for him from among his creation. The firstfruits also represented a portion of what was to come. When Jesus rose from the dead, he was "the first of a great harvest of all who have died" (1 Corinthians 15:20); in other words, he was the first, and he stood as an assurance that many more would follow.

Giving God our firstfruits is an act of trust and obedience and an acknowledgment of his ownership. Unfortunately, it is our nature to cling to the firstfruits and then see what we might spare for God from what remains. That is the way our own wisdom would call it. We tend to reason something like this: "Let me make sure I've got all I need first."

But God's promise is that when we honor him with our firstfruits, he will honor our obedience with his provision. The firstfruits of our day belong to him. The firstfruits of our energy belong to him. The firstfruits of our financial resources belong to him. When we offer him our firstfruits, we are really saying, "Everything is yours."

If you want to honor God, to give worship that is more than mouthing words, and to see God's provision in your real-life experience, it's all about giving him the firstfruits.

Father, I offer you the firstfruits of my life. Everything I have is yours. It comes from you and is for your use. Surrendering my firstfruits is surrendering all that I am and all that I have to you.

Jennifer

Until you have given up your self to Him you will not have a real self.

—C. S. LEWIS (1898–1963), Irish novelist, literary critic, and essayist

MY INNERMOST BEING

THE LORD IS IN HIS HOLY TEMPLE;
  THE LORD STILL RULES FROM HEAVEN.
HE WATCHES EVERYONE CLOSELY,
  EXAMINING EVERY PERSON ON EARTH.

Psalm 11:4

MEDICAL TECHNOLOGY has come so far in recent years that it's now possible for magnetic resonance imaging (MRI) to slice images of the body wafer-thin and create three-dimensional models of organs and tissues to find abnormalities and diagnose disease. Functional magnetic resonance imaging (fMRI) takes the technology one step further. Instead of creating images of organs and tissues as an MRI does, the fMRI looks at blood flow in the brain and detects areas of activity. It allows doctors to get a physical representation of our mental processes. An fMRI might even be able to detect whether we're telling the truth.

Amazing! Doctors can see past the surface of our bodies into their deep and hidden places and discover problems not visible to the technologies of years past. What an advantage it is to be able to detect diseases and irregularities in the beginning stages or exactly locate a tumor or lesion for removal.

God says that he is able to see into our innermost beings. He sees the motives behind our words and actions and the wounds that fester inside and release their toxins into our relationships. He sees the scar tissue that has built up over areas of our emotions from our efforts to ward off the pain of exposure.

And then he pours out the healing balm of his Spirit on our inner wounds. He excises cancerous thoughts and memories with pinpoint accuracy to make us whole. The hidden hurts and secret sins may not be obvious at a glance, but they are nonetheless deadly. Our Father-King sees and knows before we become aware, and he is already in the process of healing: "I will answer them before they even call to me. While they are still talking about their needs, I will go ahead and answer their prayers!" (Isaiah 65:24).

Heal me from the inside out. Examine my heart and heal its ills. Pour yourself out in my innermost being.

Jennifer

The all-seeing eye of God beheld our deplorable state; infinite pity touched the heart of the Father of mercies; and infinite wisdom laid the plan of our recovery.
—**DAVID BRAINERD** (1718–1747), American missionary to Native Americans

14 PURE PROMISES

THE LORD'S PROMISES ARE PURE,
LIKE SILVER REFINED IN A FURNACE,
PURIFIED SEVEN TIMES OVER.

Psalm 12:6

THE PSALMIST paints a picture of silver purified beyond ordinary standards. He describes a process that will produce 100 percent pure silver. Every bit of impurity or residue gone. God's promises are unmixed with any untruth. They've been put through the fire.

David wrote, "Your promises have been thoroughly tested; that is why I love them so much" (Psalm 119:140). God doesn't want his promises to be theoretical; he invites us to put them to the test so we will know for ourselves how trustworthy they are.

When Scripture tells us how to know God, it uses "sense" words:

- How sweet your words taste to me; they are sweeter than honey. (Psalm 119:103)
- I pray that your hearts will be flooded with light so that you can understand. (Ephesians 1:18)
- The Sovereign LORD has opened my ears. (Isaiah 50:5, NIV)
- Our lives are a Christ-like fragrance rising up to God. (2 Corinthians 2:15)

Consider this: How would you describe the taste of a strawberry to someone who has never tasted one? You couldn't. Things that we know through our senses we have to learn firsthand.

So it is with knowing God. You can know him only by firsthand experience and the certainty of his promises. They have to be tested in your fire.

But you cannot trust promises on their own merit. A promise is only as reliable as the person who makes it. If you don't know the promiser, you have no way of knowing whether or not to rely on the promise. You must trust the Promiser.

Faithful Father, the more I know you, the more faith comes naturally to me. Trust is no longer a generic idea but is becoming instead a deliberate act as I learn to trust in you. Show yourself to me in the comings and goings of my life, teaching me that who you are ensures what you will do.

Jennifer

The promises of the Bible are nothing more than God's covenant to be faithful to His people. It is His character that makes these promises valid.

—JERRY BRIDGES (1929–), American author and conference speaker

DON'T BE AFRAID

WHAT IS THE PRICE OF TWO SPARROWS—ONE COPPER COIN?
BUT NOT A SINGLE SPARROW CAN FALL TO THE GROUND WITHOUT
YOUR FATHER KNOWING IT. AND THE VERY HAIRS ON YOUR
HEAD ARE ALL NUMBERED. SO DON'T BE AFRAID; YOU ARE MORE
VALUABLE TO GOD THAN A WHOLE FLOCK OF SPARROWS.

Matthew 10:29-31

ARE YOU a born worrier? Did you learn fear in your family of origin, as I did, or did you perhaps acquire the skill along the way as life's problems came in waves to crash your serenity? No matter what your income level or situation, your age or stage in life, worry can sneak in and squeeze the joy and strength out of your days. Maybe you were relatively calm, cool, and collected until you got a cancer diagnosis or your spouse lost a job when the bottom fell out of the economy, draining your kids' college savings and your retirement account. Or things went smoothly until your college-age daughter was in a car wreck that caused her untold pain and months in a rehabilitation hospital.

The truth is, we all have panic buttons. And precisely because we humans are prone to worry, God addressed this emotion and its cousins fear and anxiety hundreds of times in his Word—including today's passage from Matthew 10. After explaining that the Father's eyes are on even the seemingly most inconsequential little birds, that he cares for us so much that he knows how many hairs are on our heads, Jesus says, "Don't be afraid." Why? Because to the glorious Lord in charge of heaven and earth, "you are more valuable . . . than a whole flock of sparrows," and his care for you is eternally faithful.

When our son was serving in Iraq as a battalion surgeon under enemy fire and was working to save marines' lives, I wasn't able to see him for many months. But this promise reminded me that God saw my son and was present with him, even though my loved one was thousands of miles away, and I knew that I could trust my Father's care. As you meditate on this passage today, I pray it will bring a freedom from worry to your soul and a renewal of God's joy and peace.

Lord Jesus, thank you for your assurance that you didn't intend for us to live in fear and worry, that you provided a way out by sending us eternal promises from your Word. Help me to trust in your gracious, loving care each day of my life.

Cheri

It seems to be God's plan to allow all sorts of things to happen that would naturally cause fear, but to forestall them by the assurance of his presence.

—**AMY CARMICHAEL** (1867–1951), Irish missionary to India

16 HIS PROMISED REST

JESUS SAID, "COME TO ME, ALL OF YOU WHO ARE WEARY AND
CARRY HEAVY BURDENS, AND I WILL GIVE YOU REST. TAKE MY
YOKE UPON YOU. LET ME TEACH YOU, BECAUSE I AM HUMBLE
AND GENTLE AT HEART, AND YOU WILL FIND REST FOR YOUR
SOULS. FOR MY YOKE IS EASY TO BEAR, AND THE BURDEN I
GIVE YOU IS LIGHT."

Matthew 11:28-30

A PASTOR took some members of his congregation to New Orleans to help people whose homes had been flooded and their community ruined. Everywhere they saw devastation. On Sunday morning as he looked out on the faces of the dwindling group of people who hadn't left the city after the hurricane, he saw loss, grief, weariness, and despair. Many had been displaced and lost almost everything. These people carried tremendously heavy burdens.

But then on the way home, the pastor thought about those in his own church and realized that though his congregation was in a suburban area, they weren't that different from the folks in New Orleans. His church family, too, staggered into church, flooded by emotional hurts and spiritual pain. They hobbled in, displaced, sin sick, tired and worn, carrying heavy burdens—some that nobody else on earth knew about.

We all carry heavy burdens. But Jesus says, "Come to me, my children, come to me. I know that you've been carrying a heavy load, the weight of your pain, the burden of your sins, the load of all your worries. Here. Come here. I will give you a rest."

Blessed be the Lord! The pastor was exactly right, for each day, no matter how stressed we are, "He carries us in his arms" (Psalm 68:19).

Surely Christ's invitation to help carry our burdens is one of the most precious promises in the Bible. Whether you're a heartbroken mom with a son serving time in jail, your mother or sister has been diagnosed with Alzheimer's, you have marital conflicts, or carry other heavy loads, Jesus means this promise for you. Come to him, and he will give you rest.

What a matchless promise that you, Jesus, the King of kings and Lord of lords, would daily help us carry our burdens. In your infinite care you carried the burden of our sin on yourself on the cross. I thank you and praise you for your great compassion. May my lips sing your praises forever!

Cheri

The grace of God is given when we are yoked to Jesus and share
his burden to love and care for others.

—JOHN J. PARSONS, contemporary American teacher and writer

THE LIFE-CHANGING POWER OF HIS NAME

HIS NAME WILL BE THE HOPE
OF ALL THE WORLD.

Matthew 12:21

I LOVE to discover the meaning of someone's name, because that name often reflects the person's character or destiny. With all the baby-naming books parents buy when a little one is on the way, the meaning of most names is easy to find. However, my husband's name is Holmes, in memory of an uncle who died in World War II. His family didn't know the meaning, and I had always wondered about it until the day I met a research director at one of the country's best public libraries. She was kind enough to search in several different books and databases and later called me back with the news. Holmes means "safe haven," a "dweller near a tree with roots going into the river," which brought to mind Psalm 1. From that day on I began praying that psalm for Holmes, and I still do today.

As interesting as our names are, there is one name that is of utmost importance. It is *Jesus*—the hope of all the world, as we read in today's verse. One day, at the sound of this name, every knee will bow and every tongue will confess that he is Lord, for his name—Immanuel—is above every name. He is the Living Word. The Prince of Peace. Our Refuge. The God of Our Salvation. The Promised One who saves us from our sins. In his name, prayers are heard and answered. Lives are healed. In his name there is dynamic, life-changing power. And these are not just theories or nice thoughts, but some of the Father's most marvelous promises. Whatever burdens or sins are weighing you down, Christ came to save you, to free you, to redeem you, regardless of how deep a pit you are in. And not only that, but he desires to demonstrate his gracious love and faithfulness to you, right where you are today.

> *Lord Jesus, I glorify your name, for it is a strong tower, a shelter, and the hope of all the earth. Help me to focus on the wonder of your name and who you are, not on how big my struggles and trials are.*
>
> *Cheri*

How sweet the name of Jesus sounds
In a believer's ear!
It soothes his sorrows, heals his wounds,
And drives away his fear.

—**JOHN NEWTON** (1725–1807), English clergyman and former slave-ship captain turned abolitionist

18 A WONDERFUL INHERITANCE

LORD, YOU ALONE ARE MY INHERITANCE, MY CUP OF BLESSING.
YOU GUARD ALL THAT IS MINE.
THE LAND YOU HAVE GIVEN ME IS A PLEASANT LAND.
WHAT A WONDERFUL INHERITANCE!

Psalm 16:5-6

WHAT COMES to mind when you hear the word *inheritance*? Do you ponder what you hope to leave behind to any children you may have? What your parents or grandparents will pass down to you in the way of property or a trust? Scripture says that "good people leave an inheritance to their grandchildren" (Proverbs 13:22). In the Old Testament, *inheritance* often referred to land, as in today's verse from Psalm 16: "The land you have given me is a pleasant land. What a wonderful inheritance!" God spoke about that very land—the Promised Land—to Abraham hundreds of years before the Israelites actually entered it.

This "wonderful inheritance" also refers to the truth that the *Lord* is our inheritance and our home (see verse 5)—not only on this earth but also in eternity: "Together with Christ we are heirs of God's glory" (Romans 8:17).

There is yet another dimension of inheritance: the wondrous truth that through the death of Christ on the cross, we who were once separated from God have become the Father's inheritance. How incredible that God would make us his bride, his heirs, and shape us into vessels through which he can shine his light to a dark world!

> *Holy Spirit, may your grace enable us to walk in the reality that you are*
> *our promised cup of blessing and true inheritance. May we leave a rich*
> *inheritance of faith, hope, and love to those who come after us. Grant us deeper*
> *understanding of the riches of the glory and inheritance that you have in us,*
> *your saints. In Christ's name, amen.*

Cheri

You may not be able to leave your children a great inheritance, but day by day, you may be weaving coats for them which they will wear for all eternity.

—**THEODORE LEDYARD CUYLER** (1822–1909), American pastor and author

FACE-TO-FACE

BECAUSE I AM RIGHTEOUS, I WILL SEE YOU.
WHEN I AWAKE, I WILL SEE YOU FACE TO FACE AND
BE SATISFIED.

Psalm 17:15

ONE SEPTEMBER day two weeks before my mother died, I was sitting by her hospital bed holding her hand. Mama's strength was failing, and her breathing had become extremely laborious, yet in those moments as she spoke, her eyes shone with a hope and joy that defied the suffering she was enduring.

"Cheri, I have been praying for you and all my six children and twenty-two grandchildren for many years. But pretty soon I'm going to get to see Jesus face-to-face and get to talk to him about you all," she said with a smile. She closed her eyes as her head relaxed on the pillow, and I sat pondering those words. Sure enough, only two weeks later, Mama entered eternity, special delivery, wrapped up in love.

In the twenty-eight years since the day Mama spoke those words to me, I have never forgotten them. She knew as well as I that it isn't our righteousness that allows us to see the face of God; it is our right standing and relationship with the Father through what Christ has done for us. Nevertheless, we are promised that though we now see imperfectly, like looking at a poor reflection in a mirror, when we pass out of mortality into immortality, we shall see the Lord face-to-face and see with clarity, as 1 Corinthians 13:12 describes. We will know God just as directly and intimately as he knows us now. All the sorrow and pain of life on earth will pass away, and we will experience the privilege of seeing his glory, the glory of our one and only Lord and Savior.

Oh God, fill us with the expectation and assurance that the best is yet to come, that no matter what happens on this earth, you have eternal joy awaiting us when we see you face-to-face and worship you in perfect harmony with all the angels and saints. Maranatha! Come, Lord Jesus!

Cheri

Eternity will not be long enough to learn all he is, or to praise him for all he has done, but then, that matters not; for we shall be always with him, and we desire nothing more.
—**FREDERICK WILLIAM FABER** (1814–1863), English hymn writer and theologian

20 GOD OUR SECURITY

THE LORD IS MY ROCK, MY FORTRESS, AND MY SAVIOR;
MY GOD IS MY ROCK, IN WHOM I FIND PROTECTION.
HE IS MY SHIELD, THE POWER THAT SAVES ME,
AND MY PLACE OF SAFETY.

Psalm 18:2

THIS PSALM, written by David on the glorious day God rescued him from his enemies, including Saul, holds great promise for us today, for it reflects the truth that God is our rock, protection, and fortress. The Hebrew word translated "fortress" means a stronghold or refuge, a well-fortified place that we can run to when we are in danger. This is our God! He—not a castle surrounded by a moat, a giant fort with weapons stationed at every turret, or a team of big security guards—is our fortress and security. Because the Lord is our shield and our solid rock, in whom we find protection, we are safe in his presence, even when everything around us is uncertain or dark.

Corrie ten Boom experienced this truth when, following her release from a German concentration camp, she traveled around the world sharing the message of God's love. She was not a young woman; she was already in her senior years. Yet God gave her the strength to travel from country to country, sharing her testimony so that others would find life, forgiveness, and salvation in Christ.

Once, Corrie felt called to go to Japan. Though sometimes she had a traveling companion, on this ministry trip she was all alone. At first she found it difficult to be in a country where she didn't know a soul or understand the language. But then she remembered that God is our security and our rock. She meditated on the promise that through faith we are shielded by God's power. Corrie's ten months of ministry in Japan proved very fruitful. As Corrie trusted in the Lord, her security, doors were opened, and many Japanese people came to know Christ.

The same God who sustained Corrie ten Boom through her captivity and the loss of her family and sustained her into old age as she ministered around the world will be your strength and fortress.

Oh Lord, my rock and security when everything around me is insecure, help me
to trust you to carry me throughout each day of my life.

Cheri

My unmoving mansion of rest is my blessed Lord.
—**CHARLES HADDON SPURGEON** (1834–1892), English preacher and writer

LEAVING THE FLATLANDS

GOD ARMS ME WITH STRENGTH,
AND HE MAKES MY WAY PERFECT.
HE MAKES ME AS SUREFOOTED AS A DEER,
ENABLING ME TO STAND ON MOUNTAIN HEIGHTS.

Psalm 18:32-33

STANDING ON flat ground is one thing; standing on mountain heights is something altogether different. First, there's the journey. Getting to the mountain height is no small accomplishment. The way to the top of the mountain takes a kind of strength that doesn't come naturally. We are built for even, smooth roads and level land. As long as those conditions are in place, we can do just fine. The problem is that landscapes, like life, never stay safe. The road never stays smooth and easy. Our own strength finds its limits early.

We are born flatlanders but have a longing for the heights. Something in our nature knows that there are higher planes and more rarified atmospheres somewhere out there. We are designed with a chip that spurs us toward the heights and programs us to long for higher ground.

That very longing is the entry point for God. Apart from him, we will never become truly ourselves. He created us with a soul thirst that only he satisfies. He acts as a magnet on our hearts, pulling us toward him from the moment we first have the ability to desire. A newborn baby reaching out for human contact is the beginning of the longing designed by God to bring us to him. We were built to be dissatisfied in the flatlands and to yearn for the mountain heights.

Now, the secret. God is the one who provides the strength and stability the journey to the heights requires. We come predisposed to the longing but unequipped for the journey. We will have the courage to climb the mountain only if we know the Strength Giver. Each step is fueled by the faith that his strength will hold us, that we are not scaling the heights in our own might.

Are you staying put in the flatlands because you think you have to climb in your own puny strength? Or are you willing to take the first step upward and depend on the one who will make you as sure-footed as a deer?

Lord, I ask for your strength for the climb, one step at a time.

Jennifer

I have learned that faith means trusting in advance what will only make sense in reverse.
—**PHILIP YANCEY** (1949–), American writer and preacher

22 ENOUGH

THEY ALL ATE AS MUCH AS THEY WANTED, AND AFTERWARD, THE
DISCIPLES PICKED UP TWELVE BASKETS OF LEFTOVERS.

Matthew 14:20

TUCKED AWAY in the middle of a story about Jesus feeding a crowd with a few fish and a little bread is a sentence that encompasses what Jesus wants to reveal about himself. It's something we can count on in our lives. He takes "not enough" and makes it "more than enough." He not only meets our needs but also fills us to overflowing so we can reach out to others in need.

Jesus had been teaching the people and healing those who needed it. The disciples came to him and suggested that he send the crowd away to buy themselves something to eat. Imagine their surprise when Jesus said, "That isn't necessary—you feed them" (v. 16). The disciples had already taken stock of the situation, and they knew they did not have the resources to meet the need. So Jesus is teaching his disciples, "It's not what you have, it's who I AM that defines the situation."

He could fulfill his purposes in this world without you, but instead he chooses to do it through you. Why? Because his "power works best in weakness" (2 Corinthians 12:9). When his power operates in your weakness, there is no explanation left except that the power of Christ rests on you. The "enough" is not in what we bring him; the "enough" is in him.

Is there a situation in your life that you have been defining in terms of what you have instead of in terms of who Christ is? You've already inventoried what you lack. Start again. Now take what you have—little, inadequate, and not enough—and ask him to multiply it. Step out in obedience just as you would if you knew you were fully supplied, because you are.

Jesus, I am trusting that the "enough" is in you. I will walk in the faith that you will supply all that is needed—and even enough to flow through me to others.

Jennifer

We sometimes fear to bring our troubles to God, because they must seem small to Him who sitteth on the circle of the earth. But if they are large enough to vex and endanger our welfare, they are large enough to touch His heart of love. For love does not measure by a merchant's scales, not with a surveyor's chain. It hath a delicacy . . . unknown in any handling of material substance.

—R. A. TORREY (1856–1928), American evangelist, pastor, and writer

GOD OF GRACE

[THE LAWS OF THE LORD] ARE A WARNING TO YOUR SERVANT,
A GREAT REWARD FOR THOSE WHO OBEY THEM.

Psalm 19:11

ONE OF the ways that God pours out his lavish and unbounded love and grace on us is by giving us laws to define the boundaries within which we will find our full freedom. We sometimes mistakenly believe that law and grace are opposites. But God has never been anything other than a God of grace, showering his people with undeserved love and provision. The apex of his grace came into view at Calvary. There our sins were forgiven and washed away, and the plan of grace was fully executed so that we live as the recipients of the salvation Jesus accomplished on our behalf.

We may tend to think of a lawgiver as one with an attitude that says, "I'm the one with the power, so I'm laying down the law. You obey me, or else. I'm just waiting for an infraction so I can show you who's boss!" But that is not the heart of our Law Giver.

Our Law Giver says, "I created everything that exists. I designed you and created you. Because I love you so much, I'm going to give you the secrets that will allow you to live fully, fearlessly, and freely. I'm going to warn you about the dangers that can derail your life. I'm going to explain how to make the most of everything I have created. I could have let you bungle and bumble your way through the days of your life, but I love you too much."

When we go our own way and treat God's laws as if they were a demanding burden instead of a protective covering, we learn the hard way that obeying his laws brings a great reward. He promises that when we walk in his ways, we live in his freedom.

Father, thank you for the protection of your laws. Enable me to walk in your ways so that I can live in your abundance and freedom.

Jennifer

The golden rule for understanding in spiritual matters is not intellect, but obedience.
—**OSWALD CHAMBERS** (1874–1917), Scottish minister and teacher

24 HEART'S DESIRE

TAKE DELIGHT IN THE LORD,
AND HE WILL GIVE YOU YOUR HEART'S DESIRES.

Psalm 37:4

GOD HAS scattered this promise throughout his Word. He promises to fulfill your heart's desire, but you cannot know the desire of your heart unless you know the heart of your desire. Usually what we call the desire of our hearts is really a secondary desire orbiting around the true desire. What we think we desire is really the way we have imagined the true desire will be met. We think we are asking for the desire of our hearts, but we are really asking for the desire of the moment. Often, in order to give you the desire of your heart, God will withhold the desire of the moment. He says no as a prelude to a higher yes. Give him time—give him access—so that he can peel back the desire of the moment and show you the true desire of your heart. To the desire of your heart, there will always be a resounding yes from heaven.

I began to learn this one time when I was leading a conference, and my voice got raspier and raspier as the conference went on. By the time I had finished, I had no voice at all. I had to leave the next morning and fly to another location, where I would begin to lead another conference. On the flight I prayed, "Oh God, give me back my voice."

I began to sense the Lord speaking to me: *Why do you want your voice?*

I answered, "So I can lead this conference."

Why do you want to lead the conference?

"So that people can learn how to live in your power."

Why do you want people to live in my power?

"So you can glorify yourself."

Then, Jennifer, he seemed to say, *ask me for that.*

And so my prayer became, "Father, glorify yourself."

The tension left me. My soul rested. God helped me discover the desire of my heart and relinquish the desire of the moment.

> Lord, I relinquish the desire of the moment, and I receive your promise to fulfill the desire of my heart.
>
> *Jennifer*

Pray till prayer makes you forget your own wish, and leave it or merge it in God's will.
—FREDERICK WILLIAM ROBERTSON (1816–1853), English clergyman

GOD'S SOVEREIGN CONTROL

YOU INTENDED TO HARM ME, BUT GOD INTENDED IT ALL FOR GOOD. HE BROUGHT ME TO THIS POSITION SO I COULD SAVE THE LIVES OF MANY PEOPLE.

Genesis 50:20

IN THESE words, Joseph sums up the intervening years since his brothers had planned and carried out treacherous schemes with only one goal: to ruin him. But Joseph sees the story from another vantage point. He has lived out the promise that God never relinquishes control, no matter how the situation might look to us.

For God's perspective on the situation, look at Psalm 105. What is God's will for the Israelites? "I will give you the land of Canaan as your special possession" (v. 11). But when the Israelites first reached Canaan, they were "few in number, a tiny group of strangers" (vv. 12-13). God needed to give them a place to grow, prosper, learn skills, and reproduce safely. He needed to put them under the protection of a larger, more advanced civilization for a time. He needed them in Egypt.

"He sent someone to Egypt ahead of them—Joseph, who was sold as a slave" (v. 17). It looked as if Joseph's evil brothers had sent him to Egypt, as if God's will were being thwarted by bad decisions. God used seemingly adverse circumstances to position Joseph for receiving the promise.

How did God get the Israelites out of Canaan and into Egypt? "He called for a famine on the land of Canaan, cutting off its food supply" (105:16). He brought famine on the land, but first he prepared the Israelites' deliverance. It was waiting for them in Egypt. What appeared to be a disaster and a tragedy drove them to God's provision.

God's promise to us is that he is always calling the shots. As Jesus stood before Pilate, seemingly at the mercy of those who had staged his arrest, he said, "You would have no power over me at all unless it were given to you from above" (John 19:11). No matter how it looks at the moment, you are safely in God's hands, and he is working out his plan for you.

Father, I embrace my present moment, knowing that you are in control.

Jennifer

If there is a single event in all of the universe that can occur outside of God's sovereign control then we cannot trust Him.

—JERRY BRIDGES (1929–), American author and conference speaker

26 GOD WITH US

GOD ANSWERED, "I WILL BE WITH YOU."

Exodus 3:12

WHEN MOSES encountered God at the burning bush, he was not the same Moses who had fled Egypt forty years earlier. Then, Moses had been a man of power and influence. Stephen described him like this: "Moses was taught all the wisdom of the Egyptians, and he was powerful in both speech and action" (Acts 7:22), and when he happened upon an Egyptian taskmaster beating an Israelite slave, he took matters into his own hands.

Consequently, this once-important leader was reduced to the lowest rank—a shepherd of someone else's sheep. Much later, Genesis 46:34 tells us how shepherds were viewed in Egypt: "The Egyptians despise shepherds." Moses, once admired, was now despised. Having fled from his own land, he was exiled into the desert. Moses fell very far, very fast.

I wonder about Moses during those forty years. Did he assume he had lost his chance and that his time had passed? I think so. He certainly didn't seem to be expecting to have another shot at rescuing his people. (He had already failed at it miserably and publicly.) When God called Moses to rescue the Israelites, the Moses who once assumed his fellow Israelites would realize that God had sent him to rescue them now said, "Who am I to appear before Pharaoh? Who am I to lead the people of Israel out of Egypt?" (Exodus 3:11). That's a big change in attitude from "I'm the one" to "Who am I?"

Why should Moses expect to succeed where he had already failed? This time Moses would go empowered by the promise of the presence of God: "I will be with you." The contrast was so striking that Moses developed a desperate dependence on the presence of God. At one point Moses told God, "If you don't personally go with us, don't make us leave this place" (Exodus 33:15).

The same promise that God made to Moses—"I will be with you"—accompanies God's call in your life. Whatever God asks you to do, he promises his empowering presence. That will make all the difference.

Lord, teach me a desperate dependence on your presence. I believe that you will be with me, whatever you call me to do.

Jennifer

Return to the battle again, no longer trusting in the false and insufficient human resources which so foolishly we had taken into the battle, but now trusting in the limitless resources of our risen Lord.

—ALAN REDPATH (1907–1989), English evangelist, pastor, and author

WEAKNESS IS STRENGTH

[The Lord said to Moses,] "Now go! I will be with you as you speak, and I will instruct you in what to say."

Exodus 4:12

GOD WAS calling Moses to a task that was bigger than he was. Moses' immediate response to the call was to catalog all his inadequacies. He defined himself by his weakness. God was sending him to be his spokesperson, and Moses' one fear seemed to be that he couldn't speak well. God wanted him to do the one thing he felt most inadequate to do.

How does a man whose reputation used to be that he was "powerful in both speech and action" (Acts 7:22) become a man who describes himself as "not very good with words" (Exodus 4:10)? I think that in the forty-year desert training period, God weaned Moses from his self-confidence. God's purpose was not to leave Moses insecure and weak, but instead for Moses to transfer his confidence to God. When it comes to God's power, Moses' weaknesses and inadequacies were irrelevant. Moses wasn't the linchpin. The only thing to measure is the power of God, and the power of God never comes up short.

Look what God promises Moses and, by extension, you and me: "Whatever you need in the moment, I will supply." In this case, Moses needed the right words. But whatever we need for the task to which we are called, God will supply. He will give us what we need when we need it.

We don't have to worry ahead about whether we will know what to do or what to say because the Spirit of God, who knows the mind of God, lives in us. He has direct access to our minds and can make a direct deposit of the wisdom we need (see 1 Corinthians 2:10-16; James 1:5).

His promise gives us the courage to be on call every minute of every day, ready to respond to his command. There is no need to inventory our weaknesses when God's strength is the determining factor. When we transfer all our confidence from ourselves to him, what is left to fear?

Lord, I depend on you. I thank you that my weakness does not hinder your strength.

Jennifer

Before [God] furnishes the abundant supply, we must first be made conscious of our emptiness. Before he gives strength, we must be made to feel our weakness. Slow, painfully slow, are we to learn this lesson; and slower still to own our nothingness and take the place of helplessness before the Mighty One.

—A. W. PINK (1886–1952), English evangelist and Bible scholar

28 GOD IN PURSUIT

SURELY YOUR GOODNESS AND UNFAILING LOVE WILL PURSUE ME
ALL THE DAYS OF MY LIFE,
AND I WILL LIVE IN THE HOUSE OF THE LORD
FOREVER.

Psalm 23:6

IT SURPRISES me all over again each time I am reminded that God pursues me. His love is neither conditional nor passive. He desires. He initiates. He reaches out.

My role is to respond. My role is to say yes. My role is to receive.

I have a scene in mind. Imagine one of those swashbuckling, boisterous adventure movies that take the hero into the bowels of a cave. Suddenly a great body of water breaks loose, and the hero runs with all his might—breathing labored, sweat flying, face flushed—working as hard as he can to escape the relentless wall of water that is pursuing him. Finally the water picks him up and floods over him. The water takes over all the effort, sweeps the hero up into its mighty center, and carries him to safety. The hero is rescued by what he had put so much effort into resisting. Can you see it?

That's the picture this promise paints. God's goodness and unfailing love are chasing us down. All we have to do is slow down our self-effort and let them catch us up and sweep us along. Then the whole earth becomes the Lord's house. Wherever we are, surrounded and carried forward by the Father's goodness and unfailing love, we are in our Daddy's house. Safe at home under his rule. Secure in his love. Sheltered by his presence.

When you stop and let this knowledge wash over you, do you feel the restfulness it brings? Are you released from trying to figure out how and where to find God's love and goodness? Let his tenacious, determined, pursuing love catch you up and carry you in its flow.

Father, let the force of your unfailing love move me in its current. Submerge me in your goodness and mercy. I surrender.

Jennifer

Remember, it is not your weakness that will get in the way of God's working through you, but your delusions of strength. His strength is made perfect in our weakness! Point to His strength by being willing to admit your weakness.

—**PAUL DAVID TRIPP** (1950–), American pastor, author, and speaker

TRUE BEAUTY

MANY WHO ARE THE GREATEST NOW WILL BE LEAST IMPORTANT
THEN, AND THOSE WHO SEEM LEAST IMPORTANT NOW WILL BE THE
GREATEST THEN.

Matthew 19:30

MAY I TELL you about my Grandma Amy? She went to be with the Lord at age 102, and she was feisty and funny to the last. The earth has a lot more weeds and dust bunnies without her.

I think you'd call her the salt of the earth. She would do anything for anyone. She and my Grandpa Dick knew how to do just about anything. Between them, they never left a need unmet. They delighted in that. You didn't have to be a family member, or even a friend. If they heard about a need, you could consider it met.

I'm talking about the kind of need meeting that got you dirty. Down in the dirt, or under the house, or up on a ladder. That kind of need meeting. Nothing dignified about it. Taking care of sick people or rocking a tired mother's fussy baby.

Grandma Amy lived twenty years or so after Grandpa Dick died. She slowed down only in her nineties following bypass surgery, and then only on doctor's orders. Her slowing down looked like my getting busy.

She never owned anything impressive. House, clothes, cars—all modest. She had no formal education. She never had a career. She had nothing by which the world measures success. She never pretended to be other than exactly who she was. She said what she thought and never tried to dress it up. If you didn't want to know her opinion, then you shouldn't get within earshot.

Going through her pictures in preparation for her memorial service, I ran across hundreds of snapshots my grandfather had taken of her when they were young. One of those photos he had sent to his parents, and on the back it said, in Grandpa Dick's familiar scrawl, "Isn't she just as beautiful as I told you?"

I imagine her entrance into heaven. My mind's eye can see the crowds, jostling and standing on tiptoe to get a glimpse of her. Excited whispers can be heard, and people wait with bated breath. Then she comes into view on Jesus' arm, sparkling and young again. And Jesus shouts, "Isn't she just as beautiful as I told you?"

Jesus, teach me to see as you see. Teach me how true beauty looks and lift my aspirations toward eternity.

Jennifer

God sees hearts as we see faces.
—**GEORGE HERBERT** (1593–1633), English poet

30 CHOICE BY CHOICE

WHO ARE THOSE WHO FEAR THE LORD?
HE WILL SHOW THEM THE PATH THEY SHOULD CHOOSE.

Psalm 25:12

LIFE IS all about choices. Any given day is defined by the hundreds of choices you make about how to spend it. Every single action you take or don't take is a choice made, a path chosen. How precious is the promise that God will show you the path to choose. A reverent and worshipful heart—the fear of the Lord—will open your mind to his leading.

Life is a whole lot of "small." Have you noticed? Mostly minutiae and details and ordinariness, punctuated by some drama here and there. If most of life is made up of small moments, then most of obedience must be made up of small acts of obedience. The path of obedience is going to take us off the beaten path and lead us into adventures of faith.

Consider the lame man whom Jesus healed in John 5:1-9. Jesus was in Jerusalem for a feast—probably the Feast of Tabernacles. We find Jesus in a location called the pool of Bethesda, where tradition held that an angel would trouble the water and the first to enter it would be healed.

This location was likely not Jesus' destination. He is most likely to have cut through it on his way elsewhere. It was a location jam-packed with people in need, none of them seeking out Jesus. But Jesus showed up anyway. He was always alert for the Spirit's spotlight to fall on someone who just happened to be on his way.

A woman at a well in Samaria. A widowed mother on her way to bury her only son. A man with a palsied hand. A beggar who had been blind from birth. And the lame man at the pool of Bethesda.

They didn't call out to Jesus; Jesus called out to them. What made him notice these "invisible" lost causes?

Jesus answered that question for us: "The Son . . . does only what he sees the Father doing. Whatever the Father does, the Son also does" (John 5:19). He was obeying the Father.

Father, show me the right path. Minute by minute, lead me off the beaten path and into the ways of faith.

Jennifer

Faith, as Paul saw it, was a living, flaming thing leading to surrender and obedience to the commandments of Christ.

—A. W. TOZER (1897–1963), American preacher and author

MOUNTAINOUS FAITH

YOU CAN PRAY FOR ANYTHING, AND IF YOU HAVE FAITH, YOU
WILL RECEIVE IT.

Matthew 21:22

PRAYER HAS no limits. Nothing is too small to pray about, and nothing is too big to be impacted through prayer.

Some people think they shouldn't pray about small things. God has bigger things on his mind, they reason. But Jesus invites us to be in an ongoing prayerful relationship with him—to pray without ceasing. As we maintain a certain level of mindfulness that he is ever present in us and to us, every thought becomes prayer. That mindfulness will sometimes be more focused because the activity of the moment doesn't require much mental engagement, and other times it will be running in the background as we give attention to our activities. But it is always operating. All the details of life are topics for prayer.

Others think that some problems are too big and beyond prayer's scope, considering some things or people lost causes. Some even think that God has washed his hands of certain situations. May I remind you of what has led up to this promise that you can pray for anything? Jesus used the metaphor of a mountain: "You can even say to this mountain, 'May you be lifted up and thrown into the sea,' and it will happen" (Matthew 21:21).

What's more entrenched and immovable than a mountain? Jesus, in his typical teaching style, uses the familiar and known to introduce the unknown. He is saying that nothing is outside prayer's purview. Don't focus on the size of the mountain, but on the power of prayer. How much power does prayer have? I think we can answer that with another question: How much power does God have?

Jesus doesn't promise that everything you think God should do, God will do. You can't take this one statement and set it outside the totality of what the Scripture teaches about prayer. The promise he makes is that nothing in your life—big or small—falls outside the parameters of prayer. Prayer absolutely will serve as the conduit through which all the power of God will flow into the circumstances of earth, and the fact that those circumstances are mountainous makes no difference.

Lord, I leave my mountain in your hands. You can do with it as you will. My mountain is not too big for you.

Jennifer

Christ holds that prayer is a tremendous power which achieves what, without it, was a sheer impossibility. And this amazing thing you can set into operation.

—**A. J. GOSSIP** (1873–1954), Scottish pastor and college professor

FEBRUARY

POWER UP

"I HAVE PLANNED THIS IN ORDER TO DISPLAY MY GLORY
THROUGH PHARAOH AND HIS WHOLE ARMY. AFTER THIS
THE EGYPTIANS WILL KNOW THAT I AM THE LORD!" SO THE
ISRAELITES CAMPED THERE AS THEY WERE TOLD.

Exodus 14:4

THE ISRAELITES were only days into their escape from Egypt, having been enslaved for 430 years. No one in that generation had ever been free, nor had they ever known a free person among their people. They had not imagined ever being free.

As they left Egypt in the middle of the night, can you imagine the mix of emotions? Elation, fear, hope, fear, relief, fear, excitement, fear, expectation, fear.

They had been on this emotional roller coaster for some time now. Moses and Aaron had been making their case to Pharaoh, who had acquiesced several times, only to change his mind and keep the people enslaved. Hopes had been awakened only to be dashed. With several of those experiences under their belts, perhaps it had become harder for the Israelites to live with expectation.

Have you ever been afraid to hope? I think that's where many of the Israelites found themselves. Then came the night that would redefine their lives and would divide their history into before and after. The whole nation left slavery. They didn't sneak away with just the clothes on their backs. They marched out with all their belongings and their livestock and great wealth the Egyptians had given them as they left. It had to have been a sight to see—the glory of God on parade.

Then, suddenly, it looked as if God had led them into a trap. They were sitting ducks with no way of escaping. Hemmed in, with the Red Sea before them and Pharaoh's army closing in from behind, the Israelites felt their jubilation plunge into despair. Again.

But in retrospect, every dashed hope, every unexpected twist was part of God's deliberate plan. Everything was perfectly positioned so that the only explanation for what would take place was the mighty hand of God.

Are you in the place where the Israelites were? Is all escape cut off, all hope lost? Trust God and wait for him to display his power in your life.

Almighty God, I'm standing still and watching for your salvation. Show me your power.

Jennifer

The danger may exceed thy resistance, but not God's assistance.
—ABRAHAM WRIGHT (1611–1690), English pastor and writer

2 FEARLESS

THE LORD IS MY LIGHT AND MY SALVATION—
SO WHY SHOULD I BE AFRAID?
THE LORD IS MY FORTRESS, PROTECTING ME FROM DANGER,
SO WHY SHOULD I TREMBLE?

Psalm 27:1

AS DAVID penned this psalm, he was surrounded by enemies who were set on his destruction. His circumstances were grim. He had good reason to fear, yet he did not fear. He was realistic about his circumstances, but he could look reality in the eye and not blink, because he realized that his circumstances were set pieces on God's stage. He knew that God was directing the action. He defined his situation in terms of God's protection instead of in terms of his own exposure to danger. He had already learned what the New Testament writer of Hebrews would teach generations later: "We [run with endurance] by keeping our eyes on Jesus, the champion who initiates and perfects our faith" (Hebrews 12:2).

Your mind always needs a reference point to correctly see reality. For example, imagine that you see a photograph of an object, and the object fills the frame. It looks big. Then you see a photograph of that same object held in a person's hand. Now, with the hand as a reference point, your perception of the object's size changes. Or imagine that you are in a traffic jam and all around you are big trucks that obscure your view of the horizon. If the trucks begin to move, it will feel as though you are the one moving. When the horizon comes back into view, you will reorient and know that you are sitting still. The horizon is your reference point. Without a reference point, your perceptions are skewed.

Jesus invites you to make his presence your one and only reference point. When you get your eyes locked on Jesus, his presence is your reality. Nothing else seems quite so compelling or so worthy of attention. Jesus fills your frame of reference, and everything else begins to look smaller in comparison.

Are there circumstances that give you good reason to fear? Let the eyes of your heart come to rest on the God who shelters and protects you, who fights for you. Let him be your frame of reference.

Lord, I want to live in the promise of your presence.

Jennifer

Fear is born of Satan, and if we would only take time to think a moment we would see that everything Satan says is founded upon a falsehood.

—**A. B. SIMPSON** (1843–1919), Canadian preacher, theologian, and author

PRESSED TO HIS HEART

EVEN IF MY FATHER AND MOTHER ABANDON ME,
THE LORD WILL HOLD ME CLOSE.

Psalm 27:10

FOR A CHRISTIAN, the absolute certainty of the Lord's love is the glue that holds everything together. It is the one thing that makes sense of life, and the reality that defines all other reality. The promise of the Lord's unfailing love anchors the heart, no matter what.

David casts his imagination as far as it can go to find the most unlikely scenario. Who would be the last people he could imagine abandoning him? His father and mother. That's a most remote possibility. But even if that were to happen, still the Lord would hold him close. We find similar words in Isaiah 49:15, where God says, "Can a mother forget her nursing child? Can she feel no love for the child she has borne? But even if that were possible, I would not forget you!"

Here is the promise that can burrow into the depths of your heart and make a home there. The Lord will never forget you, abandon you, or fail you. You are so precious to him that you are never out of his thoughts; you are never left out in the cold.

The Lord will hold you close. He will press you to his heart.

Maybe you've been betrayed or abandoned by someone who was supposed to love you forever. Maybe someone you were supposed to be able to count on—your parents, a spouse, a child, or a trusted friend—let you down, and that betrayal has made it hard for you to believe that God will never let you down. Would you pour out your hurt and confusion and anger to God right now and ask him to speak his tender and sure love to your heart? The Lord will press you to his great heart.

Father, you are the only one worthy of my absolute trust and confidence. I know I will always be disappointed if I trust others with the faith that belongs only in you. Right now, I choose to trust you and your love for me.

Jennifer

Let your faith in Christ, the omnipresent One, be in the quiet confidence that He will every day and every moment keep you as the apple of His eye, keep you in perfect peace.

—ANDREW MURRAY (1828–1917), South African pastor and author

4

CLEAN INSIDE

FIRST WASH THE INSIDE OF THE CUP AND THE DISH, AND THEN THE OUTSIDE WILL BECOME CLEAN, TOO.

Matthew 23:26

THIS PROMISE is tucked in alongside a challenge that Jesus was issuing the religious elite of his day. They were scrupulous about certain outward behaviors that would make them look good to those around them, but they were unconcerned about the state of their hearts. Jesus was pointing out that their emphasis was in the wrong place. He was calling them to a higher standard—cleanliness from the inside.

Jesus states a principle that when the inside is clean, the outside will become clean. The outside can't ever get really cleaned up until the inner matters are dealt with.

Do certain behaviors and habits continue to plague you, no matter how often you try to stop them and resolve to do better? This happens to all of us. When we belong to Christ, we long for holiness in our outward behaviors because we have an inner barometer that is weighted toward righteousness. Sin unbalances us and makes us feel "off."

Each of the behaviors we so want to change is the fruit produced by unrighteousness on the inside. If the inner root were gone, the fruit of it would be gone as well. When we put all the emphasis on an outward behavior and don't think about the root of that behavior, we find ourselves chasing our own tails and repeating the same behaviors over and over again. Then we fall prey to the enemy's attempts to discourage us. Or, like the religious leaders to whom Jesus addressed these words, we compensate with outward forms and traditions and find satisfaction in the mere appearance of holiness.

Because Jesus comes to reside in us, he has the power and access to work on our sins at their root. From within he cleanses and purifies us—making the inside of the cup and dish clean. The more we surrender to him in obedience and look to him for guidance and strength, the more we will find old behaviors and thought patterns disappearing and being replaced with healthy expressions of the Christ who indwells us.

Lord Jesus, cleanse me from the inside out.

Jennifer

Give up the struggle and the fight; relax in the omnipotence of the Lord Jesus; look up into His lovely face and as you behold Him, He will transform you into His likeness. You do the beholding—He does the transforming. There is no short-cut to holiness.

—**ALAN REDPATH** (1907–1989), English evangelist, pastor, and author

STUBBORN PEACE

THE LORD GIVES HIS PEOPLE STRENGTH.
THE LORD BLESSES THEM WITH PEACE.

Psalm 29:11

THE HEBREW word translated as our English word "peace" is shalom. Shalom is a state of tranquility and fulfillment and contentment. In the beginning, before the man and woman sinned, the Garden was a setting without fear or shame or unmet need or unfulfilled desire. A place of shalom.

All the peace busters that sin ushered into our experience work against what God has designed. He wants to give us that supernatural peace that exists in spite of and in the midst of life's storms and upheavals. The peace that the Lord gives us has nothing to do with outward situations. It is a stubborn peace that settles in and won't let go.

The apostle Paul wrote, "I have learned how to be content with whatever I have. I know how to live on almost nothing or with everything. I have learned the secret of living in every situation, whether it is with a full stomach or empty, with plenty or little. For I can do everything through Christ, who gives me strength" (Philippians 4:11-13). Paul had learned a secret that let him live every moment of every day in a state of peace. He had learned that the unchanging presence of God satisfied him. It was the same when God allowed adversity in his life as when God supernaturally intervened to circumvent difficulties. Whatever happened, he was the same.

We are all busy trying to arrange outward events in such a way that they will produce inner contentment—a sense of safety, of being loved, of satisfaction. If this would happen, or if that would go away, or if this would change, or if that would stay the same, we think, then we would have inner contentment. But Paul had learned that it's not what God does but who God is that produces contentment. What happened on the outside of him did not add to or subtract from his inner peace.

Father, plant peace in my life. Give it deep roots, and let it flourish there.

Jennifer

So long as we are occupied with any other object than God Himself, there will be neither rest for the heart nor peace for the mind.

—A. W. PINK (1886–1952), English evangelist and Bible scholar

6 GOD SPEAKS IN PRESENT TENSE

HEAVEN AND EARTH WILL DISAPPEAR, BUT MY WORDS WILL
NEVER DISAPPEAR.

Matthew 24:35

THE FIRST thing God teaches us about himself in Scripture is that he is a speaking God, whose words are the instruments of his work.

When God says, "Let there be . . . ," atoms bond together into mass, molecules accumulate into matter, cells fuse, and things that were not suddenly exist. When the breath of his mouth rushes out to vocalize his word, even the tiniest neutrino is ordered into lockstep. "The LORD merely spoke, and the heavens were created. He breathed the word, and all the stars were born" (Psalm 33:6).

God's word is as powerful now as it was in the beginning. His word is eternal, settled, unshakable: "Your eternal word, O LORD, stands firm in heaven" (Psalm 119:89). His revealed Word—the Scriptures—is his sacred promise. Every sentence, every phrase, every clause is truth on which we can stake our lives.

But God's Word is not merely ancient literature, trapped in time and irrelevant today. It speaks in present ways into the nows of your life. It echoes into the present and the future and lands in our lives as if freshly spoken. Nothing God speaks is without power. And God never utters a throwaway line. Cling to the promise of his Word, and let your faith find its foothold there.

> *Father, that you—Creator, Sustainer, All-in-All—would speak to me leaves me speechless. What words could I form that would do other than dissipate into the air around me and be gone as soon as they leave my lips? I receive the wisdom of Solomon when he proclaimed that God is in heaven and we are here on earth. Let our words be few. So, In-the-Beginning God, would you speak to me, and then through me? May your Word teach me, and shape me, and saturate me.*

Jennifer

Let God's promises shine on your problems.

—**CORRIE TEN BOOM** (1892–1983), Dutch author, speaker, and concentration camp survivor

IS GOD LISTENING?

O LORD, I HAVE COME TO YOU FOR PROTECTION;
    DON'T LET ME BE DISGRACED.
    SAVE ME, FOR YOU DO WHAT IS RIGHT.
TURN YOUR EAR TO LISTEN TO ME;
    RESCUE ME QUICKLY.
BE MY ROCK OF PROTECTION,
    A FORTRESS WHERE I WILL BE SAFE.

Psalm 31:1-2

RECENTLY I MET a young Muslim woman at a conference, and after talking for a while about our lives and families, she asked me what writing project I was working on. When I told her it was about God's promises and included prayers for each day, she commented, "But in my religion, we are taught that Allah is too busy to listen to our prayers, and we pray five times a day, only at certain hours. Allah will not hear us other times." After sharing that she found prayer difficult and monotonous, she asked, "Do you think your God is really listening or wants to bless you?"

When I shared with her that through Jesus Christ's sacrifice on the cross the way is opened to pray to the Lord God anytime, night or day; that he listens and answers; and that we can enjoy a close relationship with him, she was surprised, to say the least.

The truth is, unless we believe that God wants to bless us, prayer is difficult for all of us. Since prayer involves relationship, how we come to God is closely related to how we perceive him and whether we believe that—as the Bible says and as the psalmist believed—the Lord is truly listening.

God invites us to come into his presence in Christ's name through prayer, to experience his love, and to pour out our hearts to him. The same Creator who made us and knows us is *never* too busy to listen. That's one of the reasons prayer is such a great gift: we find a Father who welcomes us, listens to us, always understands us, and provides protection for us under his wings and peace in the perspective of eternity.

> *Lord, it's amazing that part of the gift of prayer is your graciousness in listening to your children. Thank you from the bottom of my heart for caring about me so much that you invite me to call on your name.*
>
> *Cheri*

What if God does not demand prayer as much as gives prayer? What if praying means opening ourselves to the gift of God's own self and presence?

—MARTIN L. SMITH, contemporary American writer, retreat leader, and preacher

8 OUR BROTHERS AND SISTERS IN PRISON

"WHEN DID WE EVER SEE YOU SICK OR IN PRISON AND VISIT YOU?"

AND THE KING WILL SAY, "I TELL YOU THE TRUTH, WHEN YOU DID IT TO ONE OF THE LEAST OF THESE MY BROTHERS AND SISTERS, YOU WERE DOING IT TO ME!"

Matthew 25:39-40

IN THE LAST few years I have had the opportunity to visit women in prison. When I first began going into our state's maximum-security women's prison, I was very aware that I wasn't just "taking Jesus to the prison" but that he was already there, working actively in the hearts and minds of the inmates. When they come to Christ, as many do through the Bible studies and spiritual activities, they become our sisters in Christ. Not just criminals, aliens, or strangers, but part of God's family, with Christ at the head.

I wrote a course to teach mothers to reach out to their children from behind bars. Through our nonprofit ministry, Redeeming the Family, we began the Oklahoma Messages Project, which videotapes parents reading a book to their children and sharing a loving, positive message with them. We send the children the DVD Message from Mom or Message from Dad and a copy of the book read on the video. The children can watch these videos over and over and be reminded they are not forgotten and are deeply missed—and this makes a world of difference in the kids' lives. The prisoners who get to do a DVD message are motivated to become better citizens and parents. Through this project they also sense God's love for them and their children.

Jesus' promise in today's verses is that when we visit those in prison, *whatever we do*, we are doing it to and for him. What an honor and privilege to minister to those behind bars in Christ's name!

Jesus, thank you for showing us what really matters: caring for the sick, visiting those in prison, and feeding people who are hungry, and doing these things in your name.

Cheri

Feed on Christ, and then go and live your life, and it is Christ in you that lives your life, that helps the poor, that tells the truth, that fights the battle, and that wins the crown.

—PHILLIPS BROOKS (1835–1893), American minister and author

THE GOD OF SECOND CHANCES

PETER SWORE, "A CURSE ON ME IF I'M LYING—I DON'T KNOW THE MAN!" AND IMMEDIATELY THE ROOSTER CROWED.

SUDDENLY, JESUS' WORDS FLASHED THROUGH PETER'S MIND: "BEFORE THE ROOSTER CROWS, YOU WILL DENY THREE TIMES THAT YOU EVEN KNOW ME." AND HE WENT AWAY, WEEPING BITTERLY.

Matthew 26:74-75

ON THE NIGHT before Jesus went to the cross, he and his disciples ate the Passover meal together. Then as they walked to the Mount of Olives, he told his followers they would desert him that very night. Peter insisted that he would *never* do that. But Jesus knew Peter's heart and what was ahead, and he replied with the words of verse 75, above. Just as Jesus had predicted, Peter denied him.

A few days after the Resurrection, Jesus prepared a marvelous breakfast for his disciples and asked Peter three times, "Do you love me?" (see John 21:15-17). Jesus gave the disciple who had betrayed him so blatantly a second chance—and important work to do: take care of his followers and lead them in the right direction. Though Peter had failed miserably, Jesus didn't give up on him. Instead, he restored him, filled him with his Spirit, and trusted him with a vital mission.

This is not the only time God gave someone a second chance. The pages of the Bible resound with stories of God's second chances: Jonah; David, following his sin with Bathsheba; Hezekiah and his illness; John Mark, after he failed Paul on a missionary journey. Throughout history God has given second chances—to St. Augustine, John Newton, and in our time, Chuck Colson and Franklin Graham. Just as he offered a fresh chance to these people who made mistakes, he offers chance after chance to you and me. How many of us need a second (or third or fourth) chance in an area in which we mess up or make poor choices? Be encouraged—there's no pit so deep or sin so dark that the Lord's grace cannot reach us when we come to him with repentant hearts.

Thank you for your mercy and patience with me, a sinner, desperately in need of your grace.

Cheri

My God is a God of second chances. I am thankful that although I sin, Jesus' sacrifice has paid for my punishment. God has given me a second chance, and a third, and a fourth. . . . Can I do anything else but the same?

—UNKNOWN

10 THE HIDING PLACE

> YOU ARE MY HIDING PLACE;
>> YOU PROTECT ME FROM TROUBLE.
> YOU SURROUND ME WITH SONGS OF VICTORY.
>
>> *Psalm 32:7*

AS A YOUNG WOMAN I read the book *The Hiding Place,* by Corrie ten Boom—the Dutch woman who survived German concentration camps during World War II.

Corrie's true life story in *The Hiding Place* and the movie by the same title gripped my heart: how she and her sister, Betsie, were sent to the Nazi death camp for helping the Jews, how the Lord sustained them by his Spirit through months of profound horror. Betsie's forgiveness of her tormentors and killers in the midst of dying. Corrie's courageous tramp across the world following the war to share the ocean of God's love and forgiveness through Jesus Christ.

I never met Corrie ten Boom, but she is truly one of my spiritual mothers. When I see her in heaven, I will thank her because my faith has been strengthened by her words and life. From her I learned about forgiving my enemies, rolling my burdens upon the Lord, and how God can use my weaknesses. One of the most profound lessons is how she experienced God as her hiding place over and over: protecting her Bible when she and the other prisoners were strip-searched and everything was taken from them; causing a "clerical error" that resulted in her release one week before all the other women prisoners her age were killed in the gas chambers.

We may not experience the horrors of a death camp, but all of us who trust our lives to Christ are "hidden with Christ in God" (Colossians 3:3). As we walk through raging storms and the valley of death, the Lord will be *our* hiding place, just as he was for Corrie ten Boom.

> *Thank you, Lord Jesus, for giving us security in the midst of insecurity, peace in the terrifying storms of life, and a hiding place in your safe and loving arms. Amen.*

> *Cheri*

If we are hidden with Jesus in God, then peace remains. We are not afraid, even if the earth gives way and the mountains fall into the heart of the sea (Ps. 46:2). Even if it is night, we can experience the promise that "He who dwells in the shelter of the Most High will rest in the shadow of the Almighty" (Ps. 91:1). Hallelujah, what a sure security!

—**CORRIE TEN BOOM** (1892–1983), Dutch author, speaker, and
concentration camp survivor

AS ONE SPEAKS TO A FRIEND

As [Moses] went into the tent, the pillar of cloud would come down and hover at its entrance while the Lord spoke with Moses. When the people saw the cloud standing at the entrance of the tent, they would stand and bow down in front of their own tents.

Inside the Tent of Meeting, the Lord would speak to Moses face to face, as one speaks to a friend.

Exodus 33:9-11

IT WASN'T unusual for Moses to hear from the Lord. He was accustomed to talking with God in a two-way conversation. The Lord spoke through Moses and shared what he was going to do. Moses listened as God spoke to him face-to-face, *just as someone speaks to a friend.* Moses received the Lord's divine direction while they talked back and forth. But he also shared his thoughts and petitions with the Lord.

After discovering the people's idolatry when he returned from Mount Sinai, Moses heard loud and clear God's anger and his intention to destroy the people. So why would a mere mortal have the boldness to try to change the Almighty's mind? Because Moses had day-to-day conversations with God. On behalf of those who had rebelled, he pleaded with God: "'O Lord!' he said. 'Why are you so angry with your own people whom you brought from the land of Egypt?'" (Exodus 32:11).

Because Moses found favor, God would do what Moses asked and forgive the unruly, rebellious people. Instead of wiping them out completely, God called them to account by sending a great plague upon them.

We are not the patriarch Moses, but because of the new covenant in Christ Jesus, God has called those who believe *friends.* Friends who speak to one another in the day and in the night. Friends who share their hearts and listen to one another. How thankful we can be that God no longer calls us servants, but promises a forever friendship through Jesus Christ our Lord! (See Psalm 25:14; John 15:15.)

Lord, help me to listen to your voice as you reveal to me your love and guidance.

Cheri

When you are rightly related to God, it is a life of freedom and liberty and delight. . . . You decide things in perfect delightful friendship with God, knowing that if your decisions are wrong, he will always check. When he checks, stop at once.

—OSWALD CHAMBERS (1874–1917), Scottish minister and teacher

12 A GOD OF HOPE

WE PUT OUR HOPE IN THE LORD.
   HE IS OUR HELP AND OUR SHIELD.
IN HIM OUR HEARTS REJOICE,
   FOR WE TRUST IN HIS HOLY NAME.
LET YOUR UNFAILING LOVE SURROUND US, LORD,
   FOR OUR HOPE IS IN YOU ALONE.

Psalm 33:20-22

ONE SUMMER when the temperature rose to 100 degrees (it reached that for forty days!), I was out in the garden and spied my scraggly-looking zinnias. When I purchased them at the nursery, they'd been filled with vibrant, multicolored flowers. Now they looked almost dead.

I wanted to save those plants! So I went to great lengths in my plan to rescue them: I transplanted them under the oak tree to shield them from the blazing sun. I cut off the dead brown leaves and buds and trimmed the branches. I removed the weeds that had wrapped around the roots of the plants. Then I fertilized with the best plant booster, feeling optimistic about the balance of sun and shade in the new spot. With water and some tender, loving care, I hoped the zinnias would once again bloom.

Sure enough, within three weeks my zinnias had adapted to their new environment. The partial shade gave them a break from the heat, and the pruning I'd done paid off. For the rest of the summer and fall we had new zinnia blooms every day. Whenever I cut a few blooms to bring inside, I was reminded that one of the reasons we can put our hope in God is because *he has hope for us, too*. No matter how scraggly we are from the trials of life, God is everlastingly optimistic. He prunes away what is dead and removes the weeds in our hearts and lives. He feeds us from his Word and pours out the living water of his Spirit so we can bloom again. Sometimes he even transplants us to a healthier environment.

I encourage you to yield to the Master Gardener and depend on the one who is eternally hopeful about you and has bright plans for your future as you trust in him.

> *Thank you, Father, for protecting us and sustaining us in the hardest of times. Thank you for never giving up on us and for tending us as a careful gardener does his flowers.*

> *Cheri*

God is able to accomplish, provide, help, save, keep, subdue. . . . He is able to do what you can't.

—**MAX LUCADO** (1955–), American pastor and author

FREEDOM FROM FEAR

I PRAYED TO THE LORD, AND HE ANSWERED ME.
HE FREED ME FROM ALL MY FEARS.

Psalm 34:4

AS A CHILD, I learned many wonderful things in our home: obedience, how to read, how to love the Bible and church, how to get along with others, and a strong work ethic. But I also learned and internalized a lot of fear. Besides the fact that traumatic events in childhood (of which I experienced several) predispose a person to anxiety, I also had a precious mom who was afraid of storms, flying in an airplane, and many other things. Mom was so protective that she never took us to the zoo, afraid one of us might get away from her and be eaten by one of the animals.

After my father died, I kept busy studying and working hard in school, but inside I became more fearful. By the time I was a young mother, I was consumed by fears of losing someone I loved, of death, of whether God cared.

I'm not alone. Surveys show that the number one problem people experience today is fear and anxiety—resulting in stress, faulty thinking, sapped strength, and depleted energy. Fear also limits our potential, robs us of faith and joy, and sets us up for failure. That's why all through the Bible God says, "Fear not."

I'm thankful that as I began to read verses in Psalm 34 and got to know God better, I discovered that the Lord could actually *free* me of my fears—and amazingly, he did! You don't have to hold on to your fears, either. You can trade your worry for wonder and trust in the one who delights to deliver us from fear, fills us with faith, and helps us live life as a great adventure.

Lord Jesus, here are the things I'm anxious or fearful about: _____.
I lay these burdens and worries before you and ask you to exchange my fear for faith.

Cheri

God incarnate is the end of fear; and the heart that realizes that He is in the midst . . . will be quiet in the midst of alarm.

—**F. B. MEYER** (1847–1929), English pastor and evangelist

14 RECEIVING INSTRUCTION

FEAR OF THE LORD IS THE FOUNDATION OF TRUE KNOWLEDGE,
BUT FOOLS DESPISE WISDOM AND DISCIPLINE.

Proverbs 1:7

INSTRUCT THE WISE,
AND THEY WILL BE EVEN WISER.
TEACH THE RIGHTEOUS,
AND THEY WILL LEARN EVEN MORE.

Proverbs 9:9

RECEIVING INSTRUCTION or taking correction is a blow to pride or arrogance. Our natural impulse is to resist and to be a know-it-all. But those who are wise welcome instruction and are trained by correction.

God loves us too much to leave us in our ignorance or to let us stay on a plateau and become satisfied with less than all he has for us. As the model parent, he instructs us, his children, and trains us and challenges us to grow: "People who accept discipline are on the pathway to life, but those who ignore correction will go astray" (Proverbs 10:17).

Where is God giving instruction to you right now? Is it coming through a source whose influence you resent or resist? Is God calling you to lay aside pride or stubbornness to receive his teaching? When you find yourself in such a situation, you have a choice to make: do you choose to protect your pride, or do you choose to listen and grow wiser?

God promises that when we accept instruction we will "learn even more," and our lives will be richer for it. Only fools would sacrifice wisdom for the sake of pride.

> *Father, help me to accept your training, no matter how it comes. If I need to humble myself to receive wisdom, then may I quickly bow at your feet. Even when I think myself unfairly criticized, teach me to set aside my resistant pride and look for any kernel of truth in the correction.*
>
> *Jennifer*

It could be a sign of pride in your life if a word of reproof or admonition is not able to be received with the same grace, whether it be given by the poorest of saints or the most educated person.

—JOHN BUNYAN (1628–1688), English writer and preacher

GONE FISHING

Jesus called out to them, "Come, follow me, and I will show you how to fish for people!"

Mark 1:17

WHEN JESUS CALLS, his call includes a promise. His call to do is wrapped up in his promise to empower. The essence of his call is this promise: "When you follow me, I will transform you. You will be a different person from who you were before you chose me over everything else in your life. You will have power that surpasses your training and abilities. Follow me, wherever I go."

Not all of us are called to earn our living through a professional ministry position, but we are all called to full-time service. I think the important parts of the call are not to leave fishing per se but to leave what we look to for security, what we draw our identity from, and what occupies our thoughts and attention. Transfer all that to Jesus. Simon and Andrew were still fishermen after they followed Jesus, but they were different men.

The call to discipleship is a call to follow Jesus day and night, not just at a whim. His call is not to a task but to a relationship: "Jesus said, 'Come to me, all of you who are weary and carry heavy burdens, and I will give you rest. Take my yoke upon you. Let me teach you, because I am humble and gentle at heart, and you will find rest for your souls'" (Matthew 11:28-29).

He is calling you to cling to him, to adhere to him as if you were superglue. These days we have a new definition for the word *sticky*. We use it to describe a website with such engaging content that once you land there, you just can't leave. Do you know that Jesus is sticky in that way? Follow him, and he will engage you so completely in what he is doing that you will discover just how sticky he is. If Jesus is a fisher for people, then you will be a fisher for people too. The promise is that whatever Jesus is doing in your personal world, you'll find yourself smack-dab in the middle of it.

All to Jesus, I surrender. I choose to rest in you.

Jennifer

Looking unto Jesus is at the same time a looking away from everything else.

—ERICH SAUER (1898–1959), German theologian and writer

16

THE POWER TO CLEAN

SEEING THEIR FAITH, JESUS SAID TO THE PARALYZED MAN, "MY CHILD, YOUR SINS ARE FORGIVEN."

Mark 2:5

IMAGINE JESUS on the day he saw the paralyzed man. At the peak of his popularity, he was mobbed wherever he went. Jesus had generated a lot of buzz. The stories of his miracles had, in today's language, "gone viral." Everyone wanted to have the Jesus experience.

The word was out about this new rabbi who spoke with authority and taught with such power that people sat spellbound for hours. But the best thing—the thing that made people do whatever it took to reach him—was that he healed. On this particular day, he was teaching to a packed house.

Out on the edges of all this energy and excitement were five friends—one who was paralyzed and restricted to a mat, and four others who were determined to get their friend to the Healer. You may already know the famous story of their never-say-die plan to work around whatever stood between them and Jesus; how they dug through the roof and lowered their friend to Jesus' feet.

Jesus has a way of seeing past secondary problems right to the heart of a matter. The man had a bigger problem than his paralysis, and Jesus responded to the disease, not the symptom. I have heard some speculate that the man must have been very disappointed to have been expecting to be healed, only to hear that his sins were forgiven. But I believe that in those words, this man received more than he had imagined or thought to ask for. The healing of his legs must have seemed anticlimactic. Who would have imagined that Jesus could touch someone and wash that person clean on the inside?

A dear friend of mine came to know Jesus in her adult years. To look at her life, you would likely not have thought her awfully sinful. She didn't think of herself as very sinful. She was a good and kind person. I still can't understand how one day this seemingly together, in-control person had an encounter with the living Jesus that changed her completely, but I know that when she told me, through her tears, she said, "I just feel so clean." Before, she had felt self-satisfied and self-confident. Now she feels clean.

Jesus, scrub my heart and disinfect my thoughts.

Jennifer

Forgiveness is the answer to the child's dream of a miracle by which what is broken is made whole again, what is soiled is made clean again.

—**DAG HAMMARSKJOLD** (1905–1961), Swedish diplomat, economist, and author

HOME IN HIS HOME

YOU FEED THEM FROM THE ABUNDANCE OF YOUR OWN HOUSE,
LETTING THEM DRINK FROM YOUR RIVER OF DELIGHTS.

Psalm 36:8

THIS PROMISE draws our attention to the intimacy that can be ours with the Father. He offers us the abundance of his own house. The things that are his are ours. We are not distant acquaintances or guests passing through. We are his children. He brings us into his house and makes us partakers of everything he has.

The apostle Paul packs this rich truth into a few words: "Since he did not spare even his own Son but gave him up for us all, won't he also give us everything else?" (Romans 8:32). He has already given us his greatest treasure. Reason and logic tell us that if God gave us his own Son, there is nothing he would withhold from us.

Maybe you are experiencing a time when it seems that God is withholding exactly what you think you need. You pray and pray and believe and believe, but it seems to get you nowhere. May I make a suggestion—something I learned out of exactly that kind of experience? The problem is not in how God gives but rather in how I receive. I want it all at once, right now, just as I think it should be.

Then I learned to start with believing God's Word. He is feeding me from the abundance of his own house and letting me drink from his own river. He is giving me everything I need. Like his provision of manna for the Israelites in the wilderness, every day enough for that day. I began to thank him for his provision, even when it didn't look the way I thought it should. I began to say, "I receive today's daily bread with thanksgiving and praise. I trust your love, your wisdom. I trust you to give me everything I need, when I need it and in the way I need it."

Father, open the eyes of my heart and cause me to see your abundant provision
for me. Where I might be seeing you as withholding, please refresh the scene and
let me see all that you are giving.

Jennifer

The remarkable thing is, we have a choice every day regarding the attitude we will embrace for that day.

—**CHUCK SWINDOLL** (1934–), American pastor and writer

18 GOD'S YES

TAKE DELIGHT IN THE LORD.

Psalm 37:4

WHEN YOU take delight in the Lord, he *becomes* the desire of your heart. The word translated "delight" comes from a Hebrew word that means soft, moldable, or pliable. When you delight yourself in the Lord, you become pliable and moldable in his hands. He is able to fashion a heart like his. He is able to create desires that match his will. In fact, Paul writes, "God is working in you, giving you the desire . . . to do what pleases him" (Philippians 2:13).

I love the word *delight*. It is a joyful word. It speaks of an emotion beyond mere happiness. When something delights you, it allures you, draws you, beckons you. The more you delight yourself in God, the more he is able to make deposits from his heart to yours. The more access he has to you, the more you find your heart refashioned by his hand. Your heart's deepest yearnings become echoes of his.

But delighting in the Lord takes time. It calls for determined devotion—choosing him above all else. Many distractions try to lure you away from the one for whom your heart is designed—Jesus. Tasks and people and causes compete for the position that belongs to him alone.

Take delight in the Lord. Not just in what you hope he will accomplish *for* you, but in what he will accomplish *in* you. He—not just his gifts but his person, his presence—is the real allure.

Give me wisdom to sort the precious from the worthless. Give me the knowledge of you that causes me to cling to you and to desire you above all else. So fashion my heart that it reflects yours more each day. Here I am. Mold me into your likeness. You are the desire of my heart.

Jennifer

Faith does not grasp a doctrine, but a heart. The trust which Christ requires is the bond that unites souls with Him; and the very life of it is entire committal of myself to Him in all my relations and for all my needs, and absolute utter confidence in Him as all sufficient for everything that I can require.

—**ALEXANDER MACLAREN** (1826–1910), British preacher and Bible expositor

UNDERSTANDING

[Jesus said,] "Pay close attention to what you hear. The closer you listen, the more understanding you will be given—and you will receive even more. To those who listen to my teaching, more understanding will be given."

Mark 4:24-25

IMAGINE YOURSELF in a crowd listening to a message in a language you do not understand. Imagine that those around you are responding enthusiastically, applauding, even jumping to their feet in response. You can feel the electric atmosphere as the listeners thrill to the words of the message, but you are left cold. You are hearing the same words, but the words don't touch you because you can't understand them. You are locked out of their impact because you lack understanding.

Hearing is one thing, and understanding is another. When the Lord speaks, only the Holy Spirit can produce understanding. Jesus once said to his detractors, "Why can't you understand what I am saying? It's because you can't even hear me!" (John 8:43). He made that statement to men who were standing right in front of him. His words were falling on their ears, yet they could not hear him at the level that brings understanding. They missed the impact of his words because he was speaking a language for which they lacked an interpreter.

Jesus makes a promise in Mark 4:24-25. If we pay attention to what he says, he will give us understanding. He will make sure that we are never locked out of his Word's impact. If we listen closely to him, we will understand what he is saying, and our understanding will grow. The measure of attentiveness we give to his Word will be the measure of understanding we receive from his Spirit.

The Scripture is the present voice of Jesus speaking to your heart and life. Drink it in. Ask the Holy Spirit to unfold its riches to you. Before Jesus ascended into the heavens, ending his days in visible form on the earth, Luke reports that Jesus "opened their minds to understand the Scriptures" (Luke 24:45).

Jesus, let your words live in me in all their power. Deepen my understanding as I fasten my heart on you.

Jennifer

If you do not understand a book by a departed writer you are unable to ask him his meaning, but the Spirit, who inspired Holy Scripture, lives forever, and He delights to open the Word to those who seek His instruction.

—**CHARLES HADDON SPURGEON** (1834–1892), English preacher and writer

20 CALM IN THE STORM

WHEN JESUS WOKE UP, HE REBUKED THE WIND AND SAID TO THE
WAVES, "SILENCE! BE STILL!" SUDDENLY THE WIND STOPPED, AND
THERE WAS A GREAT CALM.

Mark 4:39

SOMETIMES A PROMISE comes as a demonstration. In this scene, Jesus demonstrates that no power of any kind can keep him from his stated goal.

This event opens with Jesus making a statement: "Let's cross to the other side of the lake" (Mark 4:35). Those are the words that set the disciples in motion. Jesus clued them in to his intention—to go to the other side of the lake.

Later, when their faith had matured and the Holy Spirit had come to empower them by living in them, they would understand that if Jesus said he was taking them to the other side of the lake, that is where they would end up. They headed out in response to his direction and found themselves almost overwhelmed by a storm. But it was the direction of Jesus—"Let's cross to the other side of the lake"—that could have been their focus, rather than the storm that threatened to blow them off course.

When following Jesus leads me into the eye of a fierce storm, I've learned to think through some questions: (1) What did Jesus say in the beginning that launched me? (2) Could the same Jesus whose words the winds obeyed when the storm was at its peak have prevented the storm before it started? (3) If he could have headed off the storm but instead stays with me in the boat, what can I deduce from that?

When the storm hits, I can let worry and fear take charge of the rigging, or I can steer straight for the shore, knowing that I'm just passing through the storm. In this incident, the storm was so immaterial to Jesus' goal that he slept deeply while it raged. I can learn to rest with Jesus when I'm in the middle of a storm. Don't let a storm draw you in.

Jesus, remind me that no storm can take you off course. Just like Job, I know that you can do all things and your plan cannot be thwarted.

Jennifer

Anxiety does not empty tomorrow of its sorrows, but only empties today of its strength.
—**CHARLES HADDON SPURGEON** (1834–1892), English preacher and writer

HOLY, HOLY, HOLY

I AM THE LORD YOUR GOD. YOU MUST CONSECRATE
YOURSELVES AND BE HOLY, BECAUSE I AM HOLY. SO DO NOT
DEFILE YOURSELVES WITH ANY OF THESE SMALL ANIMALS THAT
SCURRY ALONG THE GROUND. FOR I, THE LORD, AM THE
ONE WHO BROUGHT YOU UP FROM THE LAND OF EGYPT, THAT
I MIGHT BE YOUR GOD. THEREFORE, YOU MUST BE HOLY
BECAUSE I AM HOLY.

Leviticus 11:44-45

WHEN GOD commands, he also promises. He never gives us a command that he does not empower us to obey. He commands us to consecrate ourselves and be holy; therefore, we can assume that he will give us the power, the desire, and the ability to do as he commands. What he requires, he also provides for.

A call to holiness sounds awfully intimidating and unrealistic. On some level, perhaps even unappealing. You might have an idea of holiness as being stuffy and stern. You might imagine a life of trying hard to live up to an impossible standard and failing more often than you succeed.

But let's define holiness. It means to be taken out of common use and set aside for God's purposes. God set aside one day of the week as the Sabbath, taking it out of common use and designating it to be used differently—for him. Holy. He called out a nation from among all the nations of the earth and designated it to be his nation, set aside for his use. Holy.

He has called you and designated you to live for his purposes and no other. You are holy. He has declared you holy and appointed your life to be his. God has a design for your life, and he created you in every way so that his design is the best fit for you. Yours is not an off-the-rack, one-size-fits-all, generic life. You are holy. Precious. Fashioned in every detail to fulfill a specific plan.

Because you are holy, God is training you to be holy in your behavior and to pursue God's purposes for you. That is what will bring peace into your life—when your behaviors match your identity.

Father, I long to feel fulfilled and live with purpose and direction. I am set aside for you, and nothing else fits. Today, I turn away from all the other ways I have tried to make myself feel significant, and I bow to your plan and your design.

Jennifer

Holiness is the symmetry of the soul.

—**PHILIP HENRY** (1631–1696), English clergyman and diarist

22 SOLID GROUND

LORD, WHERE DO I PUT MY HOPE?
MY ONLY HOPE IS IN YOU.

Psalm 39:7

GOD'S GREAT, overarching promise is himself. He has given himself fully to us, and in any situation, at any moment, for any reason, he is completely sufficient. When we look around for other rescue, other supply, we come up dry. Everything else is flimsy and untrustworthy, but the promises of God are sure. We can confidently put our hope in him.

God is not only the foundation of hope but also the source of hope: "I pray that God, the source of hope, will fill you completely with joy and peace because you trust in him. Then you will overflow with confident hope through the power of the Holy Spirit" (Romans 15:13). As we turn toward him with all our cares and anxieties, he generates hope in us. That hope so fills us with joy and peace that our lives overflow with it. People around us are infected with it.

My mother is a woman of infectious hope. At age eighty-five at the time I was writing this, she said, "I've lived too long for worrying to make any sense." No matter what has come her way through the years, she learned long ago to praise God for who he is and place all her hope in him. I've observed her all my life and have witnessed what it looks like to put one's hope in God. I've seen her come through bruising difficulties unscathed. I've seen her weather heartaches and emerge stronger. She stands in these last years of her life as living proof that a woman can live a lifetime with God as her only hope and can be a real, genuine, honest-to-goodness human being living real life with all its difficulties and sorrows.

What are you facing today—big or little? Where is your hope? What if everything you had confidence in has proven unreliable? Try to identify misplaced hope, and deliberately transfer all your hope to God. He is safe and reliable and sure.

> *My only hope is in you, Father. Teach me what that means in the details of my life. Alert me when I have placed hope somewhere other than in you.*
>
> *Jennifer*

If you hope for happiness in the world, hope for it from God, and not from the world.

—DAVID BRAINERD (1718–1747), American missionary to Native Americans

WORD POWER

THE WORDS OF THE GODLY ARE A LIFE-GIVING FOUNTAIN.

Proverbs 10:11

I DON'T think I have to convince you what power words wield. When you think back to eventful moments in your life, there were likely words involved, either encouraging or discouraging. Those words had power. They perhaps changed your course. Words are amazing deadly weapons or great healers.

Words have to be managed carefully. Once spoken, a word can't be unspoken. Words take on lives of their own. If you let words fly in the heat of the moment, someone will have to heal from their impact. You can say, "I'm so sorry! I didn't mean that!" but the words are out, and they live on in the mind and heart of the person to whom you spoke them. No wonder the Word of God is jam-packed with warnings about using words prudently.

Words have the power to tear down, but they also have the power to build up. God can empower our words so that one small word can redirect the trajectory of a life: "The Sovereign LORD has given me a well-instructed tongue, to know the word that sustains the weary" (Isaiah 50:4, NIV). An instructed tongue. Not a wild, untamed tongue or a go-its-own-way tongue. A trained, disciplined, controlled tongue. God wants you to speak words taught you by the Spirit (see 1 Corinthians 2:13).

The Father wants to speak his healing, encouraging, strengthening, eternal, life-giving words through your mouth. He wants to instruct your tongue. The astonishing power of his Word will accomplish what he desires and purposes. Make it your goal to speak into others' lives such an abundance of uplifting, encouraging words that they will eventually tip the balance and move a life from discouragement to hope.

Lord, so fill my heart with your Word that it overflows from my mouth. Make my words healing. Edit out any hurtful or damaging words, and let my remaining words be a fountain of life.

Jennifer

Give my words wings, Lord. May they alight gently on the branches of men's minds bending them to the winds of Your will. May they fly high enough to touch the lofty, low enough to breathe the breath of sweet encouragement upon the downcast soul.

—**JILL BRISCOE,** contemporary British-American author and speaker

24 TREASURE HUNT

> MAY ALL WHO SEARCH FOR YOU
> BE FILLED WITH JOY AND GLADNESS IN YOU.
> MAY THOSE WHO LOVE YOUR SALVATION
> REPEATEDLY SHOUT, "THE LORD IS GREAT!"
>
> *Psalm 40:16*

GOD HAS made himself imminently findable. He created us with Godward longings and then positioned himself in full view.

When we begin seeking God, it is because he is seeking us. His pull on our hearts causes us to desire him: "'If you look for me wholeheartedly, you will find me. I will be found by you,' says the LORD" (Jeremiah 29:13–14). Look carefully at what he says. When you seek him—when you respond to his pull on your heart—you will, without a doubt, find him: "I will be found by you." He makes himself the subject—the doer of the action. He will do the "being found." God isn't playing hide-and-seek. He is standing in your path, waving his arms, and shouting in a loud voice, "Here I am!"

The book of Hebrews tells us that God "rewards those who sincerely seek him" (Hebrews 11:6). The reward of a search is finding that for which you are searching. For example, a person who is searching for sunken treasure would feel himself rewarded by finding sunken treasure. God rewards those who seek him. What is that reward? Himself. God said to Abraham, "I am . . . your very great reward" (Genesis 15:1, NIV). When he himself—not blessings by way of him—is the focus of our search, we are extravagantly, exorbitantly rewarded. When we find him, we find everything. He promises that when we find him, we will find the joy and gladness we so desire. David wrote, "You will show me the way of life, granting me the joy of your presence and the pleasures of living with you forever" (Psalm 16:11).

Lord, I crave you. More of you. All of you. Only you.

Jennifer

God, of Your goodness, give me Yourself; for You are sufficient for me. I cannot properly ask anything less to be worthy of You. If I were to ask less, I should always be in want. In You alone do I have all.

—JULIAN OF NORWICH (c. 1342–after 1413), English Christian mystic and writer

JOYFUL GIVERS

OH, THE JOYS OF THOSE WHO ARE KIND TO THE POOR!
THE LORD RESCUES THEM WHEN THEY ARE IN TROUBLE.

Psalm 41:1

IMAGINE TYING a promise to our care for the poor! What does that tell us about God's heart in such matters? Even a cursory reading of Scripture tells us that God's heart is very tender toward the poor and weak and that he charges his people to protect and care for them.

When he set up the government of his chosen people, whose role was to be the setting in which he worked out his principles, he made sure that the poor were cared for and protected. He made sure they could not be taken advantage of through exorbitant interest rates and greed by setting up the Year of Jubilee. Every fifty years, all debts were cancelled, and the economic climate was reset. What reason could there be for such a law except to protect the economically vulnerable? He instructs those with means not to gather everything they can get their hands on but instead to leave some behind for the poor (see Leviticus 19:10; 23:22).

He calls us to be on board with his agenda. He wants us, like him, to be aware of those who are weak or struggling. Is it possible that one of the reasons he gives such detailed and numerous instructions about how to treat the poor is that it protects those with resources from having their hearts overtaken by them? Is not generous giving to the poor the best inoculation against greed?

This promise tells us that when we learn to be generous to the poor, we will experience joy. He is so committed to seeing his people act compassionately toward the poor that he places reminders throughout his Word: "Those who oppress the poor insult their Maker, but helping the poor honors him" (Proverbs 14:31).

Give me a generous heart, Father. A heart that reflects your compassion for the poor. Never allow me to be owned by my possessions but instead to hold them in open hands, ready to serve you with what you entrust to me.

Jennifer

Social responsibility becomes an aspect not of Christian mission only, but also of Christian conversion. It is impossible to be truly converted to God without being thereby converted to our neighbour.

—JOHN R. W. STOTT (1921–2011), English minister and writer

26 LIFE GIVERS

If you try to hang on to your life, you will lose it. But if you give up your life for my sake and for the sake of the Good News, you will save it.

Mark 8:35

WHEN WE READ these words of Jesus, it seems he is talking about a kind of laying down our lives that refers to more than just our physical lives. Jesus expounded on his command to love as he loved by describing the highest expression of love: to lay down our lives for our friends. There are many in our world who live ready to lay down their physical lives for the sake of others: those in the armed forces, law-enforcement officers, and others whose jobs bring them into physical danger. But for most of us, physically laying down our lives for others is a remote possibility. Yet this command is to all of us.

Years ago the Lord began to teach me how this worked in my own life: time and time again he calls me to lay down my life. Not my physical life but my own self-interests, my own schedule, my own comfort.

The love to which God calls us is specific and active. It nearly always means setting aside our own interests, even if only momentarily. Rarely is it convenient. It will almost never fit into our schedules where we have a break. It will mean lots of rearranging. Daily there will be calls to love those around us the way Christ loves us. Calls to lay down our lives with our self-focused vision and actively love those around us, even when it is inconvenient.

The promise Jesus makes is that when we learn to give up our lives for his sake, we will have saved our own lives. We will have found the real meaning of life. Life lived with ourselves at the center is a continual drain. It wears us out and leaves us empty.

If your life is filled with hurt feelings, resentment, discouragement, and anger, start responding to the opportunities God presents to give up your life. When you give up your life for his sake, you are giving over your own life to his care. That is where you will find everything you are searching for.

Here is my life, Lord. It is yours alone.

Jennifer

In the total expanse of human life there is not a single square inch of which the Christ, who alone is sovereign, does not declare, "That is mine!"

—ABRAHAM KUYPER (1837–1920), Dutch statesman and theologian

LORD OF THE OUTCOME

ANYTHING IS POSSIBLE IF A PERSON BELIEVES.

Mark 9:23

JESUS MAKES a powerful promise: to anyone who believes, anything is possible. The question is, believes what? Does this mean that you and I can think up what we want to happen and then "believe" it into being? You probably already know that doesn't work. From my experience, if I could manipulate God into doing everything I could think up by believing really hard, my life would be a mess.

It might be that this promise, and others like it, have become stumbling blocks for your faith because your experience does not seem to bear them out. If so, you are not alone. But this is a precious and powerful promise, and maybe we can untangle some of the misunderstandings that have kept you from being able to grab hold of it in faith.

Jesus spoke these words to a distraught father who had brought his son to Jesus for healing from uncontrollable convulsions. The father also brought his desperation and hopeless situation to Jesus. His nearly suffocated hope gasped this last, dying breath: maybe Jesus has the answer. That's all the faith it takes. Just enough to let Jesus be Jesus in the midst of your all-hope-seems-lost situation.

Compare this to an incident Mark records just a few chapters earlier, when Jesus went to his hometown of Nazareth and the people he had known all his life rejected him. Mark reported that "many who heard him were amazed. They asked, 'Where did he get all this wisdom and the power to perform such miracles?' Then they scoffed, 'He's just a carpenter.' . . . They were deeply offended and refused to believe in him" (Mark 6:2-3). Notice that they acknowledged what he could do, but they refused to believe in who he was.

Do you see the difference? Jesus promises that anyone who believes in who he is—anyone who entrusts himself to the person of Jesus—will never encounter an impossibility. Jesus won't give a command performance in response to your expectation, but Jesus will be Jesus in your circumstances. We don't need to believe in an outcome but in Jesus, the Lord of the outcome.

Jesus, I trust you. Right now, right here, in this situation, I trust you.

Jennifer

O slow of heart to believe and trust in the constant presence and overruling agency of our almighty Saviour!

—ADONIRAM JUDSON (1788–1850), American missionary to Burma (now Myanmar)

28 KNOW THE TRUTH

ONLY BY YOUR POWER CAN WE PUSH BACK OUR ENEMIES;
    ONLY IN YOUR NAME CAN WE TRAMPLE OUR FOES.
I DO NOT TRUST IN MY BOW;
    I DO NOT COUNT ON MY SWORD TO SAVE ME.
YOU ARE THE ONE WHO GIVES US VICTORY OVER OUR ENEMIES.

Psalm 44:5-7

HOW DOES God's Word define our enemies? "We are not fighting against flesh-and-blood enemies, but against evil rulers and authorities of the unseen world, against mighty powers in this dark world, and against evil spirits in the heavenly places" (Ephesians 6:12). Our real enemies are not physical enemies but instead are spiritual forces operating from the unseen world.

Let's look at the facts. First, we have an enemy in the spiritual realm. That enemy is real and is working to undermine anything that God desires. Second, that enemy is not all-powerful, and in comparison to our Savior, he is puny and weak. Third, that enemy has only one weapon to use against believers, and that weapon is lies: "When he lies, it is consistent with his character; for he is a liar and the father of lies" (John 8:44).

Now look at the promise in Psalm 44:7: "You are the one who gives us victory over our enemies." We are not at our enemy's mercy. Our enemy is spiritual, and the weapons with which we have been supplied are spiritual (see 2 Corinthians 10:3-4). They are not weapons of this world. They don't break down or miss the intended target or become obsolete. We don't have to depend on our own best efforts to counter the lies the enemy presents to us. We have the one weapon that causes the enemy's lies to malfunction from the start: "You will know the truth, and the truth will set you free" (John 8:32). In this promise, Jesus is saying that we will know more than just the difference between true statements and false ones. He is saying that we know the one who is Truth embodied, and that Truth will set us free.

Jesus, let me be so mindful of your presence in me, and your word to me, that the enemy's lies never find an exposed target in my life.

Jennifer

As in all warfare, the two essential elements in victory are knowing your enemy and knowing your resources.

—**SINCLAIR B. FERGUSON** (1948–), Scottish preacher and theologian

MARCH

THE BURDEN BEARER

GIVE YOUR BURDENS TO THE LORD,
AND HE WILL TAKE CARE OF YOU.
HE WILL NOT PERMIT THE GODLY TO SLIP AND FALL.

Psalm 55:22

HAVE YOU ever had days when you felt like nothing more than a beast of burden plodding under the weight of your load? We were not designed to be burden bearers. When we try to carry our burdens on our own, we break down under them. Here's the good news: Jesus is the burden bearer. David wrote, "Praise be to the Lord, to God our Savior, who daily bears our burdens" (Psalm 68:19, NIV).

Are you loaded down with anxiety, guilt, others' expectations, unforgiveness, bitterness, worry, or feelings of inadequacy—the burdens life piles on? Listen to this invitation: "Come to me, all of you who are weary and carry heavy burdens, and I will give you rest" (Matthew 11:28).

Jesus offers rest. He offers his strength for your weakness, his fullness for your emptiness, his power for your inadequacy. He offers you himself and longs to take the weight from your shoulders. You can "give all your worries and cares to God, for he cares about you" (1 Peter 5:7).

He loves you, and none of his plans are for your harm. He is wise and can take into account the whole picture, from beginning to end. He has the power to do what you cannot. He is able to provide for your every need, and he delights in doing so. He is able to do more than you can think to ask, and he is always working behind the scenes to bring about a redemptive conclusion. Even when things look bleak and seem to be taking their own courses, God is in control and is working everything out according to his perfect plan.

What is weighing you down? In this moment, hand that burden over to Jesus, the burden bearer. As you do, let him remind you of the trustworthiness of his love for you, and experience the lifting of the burden, the transfer of the load from your shoulders to his.

Thank you, Jesus, for bearing my burdens. Teach me how to live so close to you that I never try to carry my burdens on my own.

Jennifer

He that takes his cares on himself loads himself in vain with an uneasy burden. I will cast my cares on God; he has bidden me; they cannot burden him.

—**JOSEPH HALL** (1574–1656), English bishop and satirist

2 THE HONOR OF SERVING

[JESUS SAID,] "WHOEVER WANTS TO BE A LEADER AMONG YOU MUST BE YOUR SERVANT, AND WHOEVER WANTS TO BE FIRST AMONG YOU MUST BE THE SLAVE OF EVERYONE ELSE. FOR EVEN THE SON OF MAN CAME NOT TO BE SERVED BUT TO SERVE OTHERS AND TO GIVE HIS LIFE AS A RANSOM FOR MANY."

Mark 10:42-45

HAVE YOU noticed how draining it is to always be in competition with others? These days we can watch in real time as the drive to be biggest and best diminishes and ravages the soul. Ask anyone who has ever been at the top of the heap. No one can stay there.

In this world, the measure of a person's worth is ever changing. Yesterday's mogul is broke and humiliated today. The rising star, fawned over and envied today, will be a punch line for comedians tomorrow. People fight and struggle to reach success, only to find it a demanding taskmaster impossible to satisfy.

Because you know your worth in Christ, you are free to be a servant: "Jesus knew that the Father had given him authority over everything and that he had come from God and would return to God. So he got up from the table, took off his robe, wrapped a towel around his waist, and poured water into a basin. Then he began to wash the disciples' feet, drying them with the towel he had around him" (John 13:3-5). Because he knew the highest place was his, he could take the lowest place.

Here is the paradox: seeking to be served wears you down. Serving others fills you up. How freeing it is to know that in Christ your identity is settled and you can serve without restraint.

Father, thank you for your promise that I don't have to be tyrannized by the need to be noticed. Give me the privilege today of serving others and so serve you. Master, whose feet may I wash today?

Jennifer

Immortal meek! who take the earth
By flinging all away!
Who die—and death is but their birth,
    Who lose—and win the day.
        Hewn down and stripped and scorned and slain,
            As earth's true kings they live and reign.

—HANNAH HURNARD (1905–1990), English poet and author

STEADY FAITH

GOD IS OUR REFUGE AND STRENGTH,
    ALWAYS READY TO HELP IN TIMES OF TROUBLE.
SO WE WILL NOT FEAR WHEN EARTHQUAKES COME
    AND THE MOUNTAINS CRUMBLE INTO THE SEA.

Psalm 46:1-2

HUMANS HAVE learned to control many things once thought uncontrollable—but not the weather. Earthquakes, tsunamis, hurricanes, floods, droughts. No one is rich enough or smart enough or powerful enough to control the forces of nature.

Listen to God's promise: "God is our refuge and strength." Now, notice how the psalmist frames this response to the promise: "We will not fear when earthquakes come and the mountains crumble into the sea." Because of God's promises, we don't have to live in fear of those things we can't predict or control.

A refuge is a safe place, a place that is stronger and sturdier than the storms that come against it or the enemies that assail it. When you have taken refuge inside a strong shelter, the winds that would have blown you about at will don't touch you. The storms that would have pummeled you don't come near you. The refuge takes the force of the blow. You live in the calm center.

During a recent crisis of my own, when my husband was diagnosed with terminal brain cancer and passed away quickly and unexpectedly, I found great comfort in the words of "Jesus Loves Me." The line I sang to myself over and over says, "[I am] weak, but he is strong." My weakness did not define the situation. I *was* weak—and helpless and useless—and I didn't have to pretend to be anything else. But one thing never changes. *He is strong.* He has been my strength and my refuge. I experience the reality of his promise every minute of every day.

Anything can happen at any moment, but I don't have to fear it. The circumstances of my life may be volatile and fluid, but I have a Refuge who never changes. He promises me himself.

Father, every moment that I breathe, you are my strength. My world might crack wide open, and my life may be shaken to its core, but you are my refuge. In the challenges and uncertainties of which this life is constructed, your unfailing presence is the most beautiful promise of them all.

Jennifer

You must learn to take the calm with you in the most hurried days.
—*GOD CALLING*, edited by A. J. Russell

4 SEEING REALITY

> MY WORDS WILL CERTAINLY BE FULFILLED AT THE PROPER TIME.
>
> *Luke 1:20*

THESE ARE the words the angel spoke to Zechariah after promising the old man that he would become a father. Zechariah could not quite believe it, but the Lord's angel assured him that God would stand behind his word.

I understand Zechariah. He heard the message, but what he could see—that he was old and his wife was also well along in years—seemed to render it impossible.

In this case, what he saw was not what he got.

When God's promise connects with faith, we have the ingredients necessary for a miracle. If our faith is a little slow in embracing a promise, God is patient and determined. He promises a reality that is hidden from our sight and calls our faith to grasp hold of his word. Then, when the time is right, that invisible promise becomes visible reality.

The time when Elizabeth could realistically hope to have a son was past. Ever since her days as a young bride, she had lived with an unfulfilled longing—one she at some point had probably accepted as hopeless—because her womb, as Sarah's womb had been, was "as good as dead" (Romans 4:19). With Elizabeth's womb dead, her hope died too.

What could be more final, more hopeless, than death? Yet for God, death is not a dead end. Death of a womb, death of a dream, death of a hope, or death of a body—in his hands any death is a prelude to resurrection. Death doesn't have the last word.

> *Even when my faith is tiny, weak, and hidden, your promises, Lord, can bring it out of hiding. I embrace your promises, though they may seem as impossible as an aged, barren couple having a baby, because you are the God who can create new things out of nothing.*
>
> *Jennifer*

Difficulties and obstacles are God's challenges to faith. When hindrances confront us in the path of duty, we are to recognize them as vessels for faith to fill with the fullness and all-sufficiency of Jesus.

—A. B. SIMPSON (1843–1919), Canadian preacher, theologian, and author

AS YOUR NAME DESERVES

As your name deserves, O God,
you will be praised to the ends of the earth.

Psalm 48:10

I WANTED to praise God, but I had run out of steam. As our financial situation grew dire, my anxiety also grew, and I couldn't muster up any faith or hope. I didn't see how I could praise God when I felt so discouraged and sad.

We had lost our savings after the financial crash of 1987. My husband was out of work and depressed, and we were living two thousand miles away from family and friends. Our family car had recently been hit head-on by a motorcycle, and we didn't know how we were going to move our furniture and family back to Oklahoma. Day by day, like ivy twining around a house and shutting out the light, discouragement wrapped around my soul.

Through a friend, I was introduced to an elderly missionary. I was amazed at her vibrant spirit. Anne was blind and disabled, but her spirit and sense of humor were alive and well. She was still living to make Christ known, in every appointment, with every person she met, just as she had during her many years of service in China and in a Japanese prison camp. When she asked me about our difficulties, she listened to my answer, but she urged me to praise God simply because he is worthy. She quoted the words of Psalm 48, reminding me that God's name deserves to be praised to the ends of the earth. "Trust the Lord because he is absolutely worthy of your trust, no matter how bad your situation is. No matter what's on your mind, roll it onto his shoulders and rest under his wings. Ask for the grace each day to praise him," she continued, "and he will give it to you. Even if tears are running down your cheeks, get out the Psalms and read them aloud to the Lord as your sacrifice of praise. His name is worthy to be praised."

In the years since that day, I have found that God is indeed worthy of our trust and our praise.

O Lord, give me grace to praise and thank you today.

Cheri

There are two reasons for loving God: no one is more worthy of our love, and no one can return more in response to our love.

—BERNARD OF CLAIRVAUX (1090–1153), French reformer and mystic

6

THE LORD SPEAKS

WHENEVER MOSES WENT INTO THE TABERNACLE TO SPEAK
WITH THE LORD, HE HEARD THE VOICE SPEAKING TO HIM
FROM BETWEEN THE TWO CHERUBIM ABOVE THE ARK'S COVER—
THE PLACE OF ATONEMENT—THAT RESTS ON THE ARK OF THE
COVENANT. THE LORD SPOKE TO HIM FROM THERE.

Numbers 7:89

GOD PROVIDED a special way to communicate with his servant Moses in the Tabernacle's Most Holy Place, or Holy of Holies, between the two cherubim. And for thousands of years, the high priests also had a special place to minister to God as they entered the Holy of Holies behind the veil of the Temple.

Today, because Christ has given his life on the cross, we are no longer left outside the Holy Place but are welcomed and given access to God, just as Moses was. One quality that marked Moses' service to God was his wholehearted attention when God spoke. Moses listened! Unfortunately, we often leave that part out of the prayer process. We can be so busy and attentive to our schedules that we neglect to wait and listen. Even in times of prayer, it's easy for us to be caught up in making so many requests that we don't wait to hear God's Spirit giving guidance or instructions to our hearts.

If we will listen for God's Spirit and learn from him, we can gain more wisdom than we could in a lifetime of doing life on our own terms. When we ask, listen, and wait on the Lord, he will show us remarkable secrets and bless us with his wisdom and perspective.

The Lord didn't speak only to Moses and the Old Testament prophets. He is still speaking today by his Spirit, but often we don't hear him because we're attached to our cell phones, our constant hurry, and noise. Let me encourage you to ask for a listening heart and to stay tuned in during the day. As you do this, your life will be blessed beyond belief. God's Word will light your path, and you will find God's presence your security and joy.

Father, forgive me for failing to pay attention to your eternal voice. Give me grace to listen and receive, in Christ's name. Amen.

Cheri

God has given man one tongue but two ears that we may hear twice as much as we speak.
—UNKNOWN

TRUE THANKS

I DO NOT NEED THE BULLS FROM YOUR BARNS
    OR THE GOATS FROM YOUR PENS. . . .
MAKE THANKFULNESS YOUR SACRIFICE TO GOD,
    AND KEEP THE VOWS YOU MADE TO THE MOST HIGH.
THEN CALL ON ME WHEN YOU ARE IN TROUBLE,
    AND I WILL RESCUE YOU,
    AND YOU WILL GIVE ME GLORY.

Psalm 50:9, 14-15

WHAT A GREAT PROMISE is contained in this psalm: if we will give God our sincere thanks and trust him in times of trouble, he will rescue us. Whether or not the Israelites had hearts that were truly thankful, they gave a great deal of attention to following the letter of the law with their prescribed sacrifices of bulls and goats. But God saw through their shallow motivations, and he didn't need their sacrifices for his survival or sustenance. Instead, what he wanted—and still desires from his people—is deep and heartfelt thanks.

God wants gratefulness and praise, which come out of a genuine trust that enables us to be thankful even when circumstances are overwhelming and we can't see the light at the end of the tunnel. It is easy to thank God when things are going according to our plans. But what about when our bank accounts are empty or we have lost our jobs? When our teenagers are out of control, or our spouses have disappointed us?

Whether our circumstances put us in the brightness of sunshine or in the darkness of shadow, we are to bring our thanks to God and proclaim his unfailing love and mercy. We are to get up in the morning thanking him for another day of life and go to bed thanking him for his faithfulness, even when we don't have the much-longed-for answer to our prayers. As we learn to be grateful in the best of times and the worst of times, we will experience great joy.

Lord, I confess that in difficult times I grumble more than I thank you, and I get stressed rather than look up and practice your presence. Have mercy on me, and fill me with deep thanks, today and every day.

Cheri

For three things I thank God every day of my life: thanks that he has vouched-safed me knowledge of his works; deep thanks that he has set in my darkness the lamp of faith; deep, deepest thanks that I have another life to look forward to—a life joyous with light and flowers and heavenly song.

—**HELEN KELLER** (1880–1968), American author

8 NOT BY MYSELF

[MOSES SAID,] "WHERE AM I SUPPOSED TO GET MEAT FOR ALL THESE PEOPLE? THEY KEEP WHINING TO ME, SAYING, 'GIVE US MEAT TO EAT!' I CAN'T CARRY ALL THESE PEOPLE BY MYSELF! THE LOAD IS FAR TOO HEAVY!"

Numbers 11:13-14

HAVE YOU ever felt all alone in the responsibilities you carry, sensed that the buck stopped with you and there was no one to help carry the load? That those you are trying to help are griping at you and demanding more? If so, then perhaps you can relate in a small way to what Moses was feeling when the children of Israel were weeping and crying out to him. They—not a few families but a few million people—wanted meat and expected Moses to provide it. No wonder he was at the end of his rope! He felt God expected him to carry these grumbling, angry people in his arms the way a mother carries her babies—all the way to the land God had promised them. Moses' strength was gone. He was done. He couldn't carry the load anymore or judge the people's many disputes with one another.

But God, as he always does, had a plan: Moses should gather seventy leaders of the Israelites, for God had decided to put part of his Spirit upon those men. He told Moses, "They will bear the burden of the people along with you, so you will not have to carry it alone" (Numbers 11:17).

Just as God understood Moses' limitations, he knows our breaking points. When we feel alone and burdened by the responsibilities and people we "carry," he doesn't want us to throw in the towel but rather to pour out our hearts to him and trust him to provide. There is no limit to his power and to what he can provide! The Lord will never fail or forsake us. Just as his presence went with Moses every day of his life, our faithful God will be with us.

Father, sometimes I forget that I don't have to carry everything and everyone by myself. Forgive my self-sufficient patterns of behavior, and keep me in your presence.

Cheri

Lord, help me remember that no matter what happens, nothing is going to happen to me today that you and I cannot handle.

—UNKNOWN

MY ROCK AND MY SALVATION

I WAIT QUIETLY BEFORE GOD,
FOR MY VICTORY COMES FROM HIM.
HE ALONE IS MY ROCK AND MY SALVATION,
MY FORTRESS WHERE I WILL NEVER BE SHAKEN.

Psalm 62:1-2

ARE ANXIETY, fear, and stress your constant companions? Does uncertainty dog your path? Are you plagued with feelings of insecurity? Is your soul in a state of turmoil? The Father wants to take you by the hand and lead you into his quietness and rest, just as he took the Israelites by the hand and led them out of Egypt (Jeremiah 31:32). God instituted a life of Sabbath for his people—a life of rest, completeness, fulfillment. He wants to teach you that Sabbath is not just a day of the week but a state of the soul.

He wants you to know the secret of living in a "soul Sabbath." That means much more than an absence of activity. It means a settled, deep stillness, a quiet relaxation in body and soul.

Sabbath for you and me means living our lives in absolute surrender and total trust in the finished work of Christ. Not only has he accomplished the work of salvation, but every need that comes into our lives has already been provided for, every dilemma has already been resolved, every question has already been answered. We simply need to place our lives in the flow of his provision and live where his power is operating. The Kingdom of God is a land where the soul has continual Sabbath rest.

Hear Jesus' invitation to your heart: "Come to me, all of you who are weary and carry heavy burdens, and I will give you rest. Take my yoke upon you. Let me teach you, because I am humble and gentle at heart, and you will find rest for your souls" (Matthew 11:28-29).

Jesus, I receive your promise of rest for my soul. Teach me. Show me how to rest in you and in everything you have available to me. Show me where I am struggling and missing the soul Sabbath you have for me.

Jennifer

The branch of the vine does not worry, and toil, and rush here to seek for sunshine, and there to find rain. No; it rests in union and communion with the vine; and at the right time, and in the right way, is the right fruit found on it. Let us so abide in the Lord Jesus.

—**(JAMES) HUDSON TAYLOR** (1832–1905), English missionary to China

10 I'M WITH HIM

Jesus said, . . . "You will see the Son of Man seated in the place of power at God's right hand and coming on the clouds of heaven."

Mark 14:62

JESUS, STANDING TRIAL in the hours before his crucifixion, boldly proclaimed this promise in response to his interrogators and accusers, and it stands firm until the end of time. He assures us of two certainties regarding his position: he will be seated at the Father's right hand, the place of power, and he will come back on the clouds of heaven.

Let's unpack the first part of his promise. His hearers will see him seated at the place of power in the heavenly realms. That promise has already been fulfilled. Paul describes the power of God that works in our lives right now: "This is the same mighty power that raised Christ from the dead and seated him in the place of honor at God's right hand in the heavenly realms" (Ephesians 1:19-20). Jesus is already seated in this place of power. "He is far above any ruler or authority or power or leader or anything else—not only in this world but also in the world to come" (Ephesians 1:21). The Father has already "put all things under the authority of Christ and has made him head over all things for the benefit of the church" (Ephesians 1:22).

What does that mean to you and me as we face challenges and opportunities that are too big for us? It means that God "raised us up from the dead along with Christ and seated us with him in the heavenly realms because we are united with Christ Jesus" (Ephesians 2:6). We are organically connected to Jesus through his Spirit—grafted into the Vine—and we operate from that position. We're already "with him."

When fear, anxiety, envy, insecurity, or any of the enemy's lies try to find an opening into your life, stand up, look it in the eye, point to Jesus, and say, "I'm with him." Let Jesus take it from there.

Jesus, teach me to rest in your power over anything that could possibly come my way.

Jennifer

How shall we rest in God? By giving ourselves wholly to Him. If you give yourself by halves, you cannot find full rest.

—**JEAN NICOLAS GROU** (1731–1803), French mystic and spiritual writer

GOD'S OPEN-DOOR POLICY

JESUS UTTERED ANOTHER LOUD CRY AND BREATHED HIS LAST. AND THE CURTAIN IN THE SANCTUARY OF THE TEMPLE WAS TORN IN TWO, FROM TOP TO BOTTOM.

Mark 15:37-38

AT THE VERY MOMENT that Jesus' earthly body died, the curtain in the Temple was torn and destroyed. In this carefully orchestrated episode, God was illustrating what was transpiring in the unseen realm that would change forever our access to the Father.

Every object in the Temple was a shadow or reflection of a solid reality that exists in the spiritual realm. The Temple curtain separated the Holy of Holies, where God's presence was, from the rest of the Temple. Only the high priest could enter that place, and then only once a year, on the Day of Atonement. The curtain hid the presence of God. The writer of Hebrews explains that Jesus' earthly body was the reality pictured by the Temple curtain. He wrote, "A new and living way opened for us through the curtain, that is, his body" (Hebrews 10:20, NIV).

The presence of God was no longer hidden. Through his death on the cross, shedding his own blood, Jesus opened the way into the presence of God for everyone who would accept his free gift and enter through him. He is the curtain. Access is no longer restricted.

The salvation Jesus purchased for us is so full-spectrum and extravagant that we can scarcely begin to comprehend it. Forgiveness of sins, eternal life, God's provision for our lives, peace, power, wisdom—the list never ends. But it all flows from this promise, portrayed in the Crucifixion's closing scene, that the way has been opened for us to live in the presence of God.

Father, teach me to be aware of your abiding presence. How would my attitude and thoughts change if I kept my heart open to you, minute by minute, day by day? I want to learn.

Jennifer

Do not lose yourself in your everyday work and activities. Rather, lose yourself in God. When you are doing work, let your innermost heart be centered on Him. Live in His presence and abide in Him. Then your work will follow you into eternity, and you will reap a rich harvest.

—MOTHER BASILEA SCHLINK (1904–2001), German religious leader and writer

12 THE PROMISE TO CARRY OUR BURDENS

GIVE YOUR BURDENS TO THE LORD,
AND HE WILL TAKE CARE OF YOU.

Psalm 55:22

WHEN I SPEAK at women's retreats, I often hear women say they desire to live closer to the Lord and feel his presence and love, but somehow they feel they are missing out. They describe feeling overwhelmed by all they have to juggle and, at times, disconnected from God—even though they attend church and go to Bible study.

Something Pastor John Piper says in his book *Pierced by the Word* sheds light on this issue. In examining several decades of church ministry, Piper found that the number one reason Christians don't experience intimacy with Jesus Christ is that *they don't let him carry their burdens*. Although we've laid down our burden of sin at the Cross, we self-sufficient people still try to carry our own load and do everything in our own strength. In the process we get burned out and crushed by the load.

Yet this verse tells us that *if* we will give our burdens to the Lord, sometimes even on a moment-by-moment basis, he will carry them for us. What a promise! What an invitation! We have a Savior who cares for us intimately and is thinking about us constantly. His power can make us able to cope with any situation. He who dwells within us by the Spirit is greater than the enemy who prowls about seeking to devour us. He will provide, protect, and shower grace in abundance as we give our burdens, the heaviness of our jobs or family situations, to the one who is eternally faithful and true. When we do, the Spirit will show us what is *our part*, what is *God's part*, and what is *others' part* so we don't try to do everything. As we give the Lord our deepest burdens, we will know him more deeply and grow in thankfulness. Then we will find rest for our souls.

Thank you, dear Jesus, that you provide a way for us to walk in freedom from worry rather than be burdened by the cares of this world. Forgive my attempts to do everything myself instead of accepting your invitation to carry my load.

Cheri

O what peace we often forfeit,
O what needless pain we bear,
All because we do not carry
Everything to God in prayer!

—"WHAT A FRIEND WE HAVE IN JESUS" BY JOSEPH SCRIVEN (1820–1886),
Irish-Canadian hymn writer

WE ARE NOT ALONE

MOSES AND AARON TURNED AWAY FROM THE PEOPLE AND WENT TO THE ENTRANCE OF THE TABERNACLE, WHERE THEY FELL FACE DOWN ON THE GROUND. THEN THE GLORIOUS PRESENCE OF THE LORD APPEARED TO THEM.

Numbers 20:6

MOSES AND AARON'S relationship was far from perfect, yet these brothers needed each other to accomplish their purpose. Just as the Lord didn't send Moses alone to Egypt to set his people free, we're not meant to be or to work entirely alone. God shows his faithfulness in sending people to work together as Aaron and Moses did. That's one of the reasons that each of us is a combination of both strengths and weaknesses; nobody is strong in every area. God planned it this way so we would need one another.

The New Testament bears witness to this truth: "Just as there are many parts to our bodies, so it is with Christ's body. We are all parts of it, and it takes every one of us to make it complete, for we each have different work to do" (Romans 12:4-6, TLB).

God also graciously gave us the stories of those who have gone before us in this journey. In Hebrews 11, the Hall of Faith, are men such as Noah, who believed God and built the ark as he commanded him; Abraham, who left his home and went far away to the land God had promised to give him; Jacob and Joseph; Moses; and other people of great faith. But look also at the lives of women in the Bible: Sarah, who because of her faith became a mother in old age; Esther, whom God had brought into the palace "for just such a time as this" (Esther 4:14) to save the nation of Israel; Ruth, who, though widowed at a young age, sought refuge under the wings of God. Deborah, Rahab, Mary, Elizabeth—all these women are part of the great cloud of witnesses who are cheering us on in this adventure of faith. Read their stories, and remember—you are not alone!

Lord, when I feel alone, remind me that you are near and your people are not far away. Connect and unite me with your body of believers, for Christ's sake.

Cheri

Be united with other Christians. A wall with loose bricks is not good. The bricks must be cemented together.

—**CORRIE TEN BOOM** (1892–1983), Dutch author, speaker, and concentration camp survivor

14 RECEIVING THE IMPOSSIBLE

NOTHING IS IMPOSSIBLE WITH GOD.

Luke 1:37

THIS PROMISE is part of the birth announcement of the Savior. The angel is telling Mary that she, a virgin, will conceive a son, and the angel punctuates this staggering pronouncement with the assurance that nothing is impossible with God.

God never promises to do anything that he does not have the power necessary to accomplish. Mary could not help but wonder how such a thing—a virgin bearing a son—could happen. The biological world did not offer a way. The usual process of procreation rendered such a thing impossible.

But where the world has no way, God has a way. He *is* the way. By the exercise of his power and his presence, what was not so becomes so. In Gabriel's words, Mary heard a declaration that the only things necessary to fulfill God's promise are his power and his presence. With God all things are possible.

He promises the impossible. He never speaks a word that does not carry his guarantee in it. He never speaks a word that is not fully backed up by his power. Whatever he promises, he performs. Why do I think I have to be able to see a way? He does not call me to a belief based on observable evidence; he calls me to believe things that are impossible.

What seems impossible to you today? God specializes in impossible. Do you find yourself in a situation that is bigger than you are? That's where God is at his best. Have you tried everything you know to do and still come up short? God is on the move. Have you run out of ideas? God will work far beyond your best idea. Nothing is impossible with God.

> Lord, I embrace your promises and rest all the weight of my life on your sure
> Word. Teach me to stop looking around for answers and, instead, look up to the
> Answer. God of the impossible, here I am.
>
> *Jennifer*

Faith sees the invisible, believes the unbelievable, and receives the impossible.

—**CORRIE TEN BOOM** (1892–1983), Dutch author, speaker, and concentration camp survivor

GESTATING A PROMISE

HE HAS SENT US A MIGHTY SAVIOR
FROM THE ROYAL LINE OF HIS SERVANT DAVID,
JUST AS HE PROMISED
THROUGH HIS HOLY PROPHETS LONG AGO.

Luke 1:69-70

THESE LINES are from the praise song of Zechariah as he rejoiced in the miraculous birth of his and Elizabeth's son, John, known later as John the Baptist. John was the forerunner of the promised Savior, the Messiah.

Zechariah's song reminds us that the promise that was about to be revealed in the person of Jesus had been spoken long ago. For generations, God's people had clung to the promise of a Messiah, in spite of circumstances and events that seemed to belie the truth of God's Word. God renewed the promise through his prophets generation after generation, awakening and sustaining hope and expectation and faith.

Mary was pregnant with the Savior; God's people were pregnant with his promise. It gestated in their hearts over generations, through wars and famine and victories and defeats and times of slavery and times of freedom and prosperity. And then, the due date arrived. The Promised One was born of a virgin, and the fulfillment of God's promise was revealed on the earth. Hope deferred was now fulfilled. God had proven his words true and had proven himself true to his words.

God never leaves us out of his story. He pulls us into the action by requiring faith in something not yet seen, something impossible. He encourages and upholds us as we walk that part of the journey, during which the promise gestates and what he has promised seems not to come. Time passes, and faith almost faints. Then, in the fullness of time, what he has spoken he performs.

Are you journeying through a gestating promise right now? Yield to the process. Let the promise do its work in you. Wait patiently for the fullness of time.

> *Jesus, you are the proof that God's promises are sure. When it looks to me as if you are neglecting your promises, let my heart see you, the Promise, lying incongruously on a bed of hay, transforming the ordinary into the holy. My soul waits for the fullness of time.*
>
> *Jennifer*

Faith is deliberate confidence in the character of God, whose ways you may not understand at the time.

—**OSWALD CHAMBERS** (1874–1917), Scottish minister and teacher

16 BEYOND THE GLITTER TO THE GLORY

SOVEREIGN LORD, NOW LET YOUR SERVANT DIE IN PEACE,
AS YOU HAVE PROMISED.
I HAVE SEEN YOUR SALVATION,
WHICH YOU HAVE PREPARED FOR ALL PEOPLE.

Luke 2:29-31

THESE ARE the words of a man named Simeon, who had been gestating a promise in his life. Luke tells us little about Simeon except that he was old, that he was righteous and devout, and that God had made him a promise. God had promised Simeon that his eyes would see the Savior.

When Mary and Joseph brought their little baby to the Temple courts, they had come to offer the customary sacrifices at the customary time in the customary way—an ordinary scene. Nothing outstanding or unusual was happening; nothing occurred to draw Simeon's attention to the family from Nazareth.

At Simeon's age, it is likely that his eyesight had faded. He probably could not see as clearly as many of those at the Temple that day. Yet Simeon saw and recognized in the flesh what his heart had been seeing in the Spirit for years—the fulfillment of God's promise. There it was, cloaked in the ordinary. Those who were focused on rites and ceremonies, those who were evaluating position and prestige, missed it. Though the fulfilled promise was right in their midst, they were blind to the presence. But Simeon, whose spiritual sight was sharp, saw clearly.

When he saw the Promised One, he proclaimed himself at peace. Simeon took Jesus up in his arms—and looked into the face of his Savior. What a moment that must have been. I imagine that tears flooded his eyes and tumbled down his craggy cheeks. He had to have felt that divine and eternal moment with his whole being. Simeon held his own salvation in his embrace and felt the Master's touch. He had gestated a promise and now saw it revealed on the earth. He could now say, "As you have promised."

Lord Jesus, let me see you in the ordinary. Let me recognize you in the comings and goings. Let me look beyond the glitter of the moments and see the glory of your presence. And I, too, will be at peace.

Jennifer

We must make the invisible kingdom visible in our midst.
—**JOHN CALVIN** (1509–1564), French theologian and pastor

THE LORD IS MY STRENGTH

WITH GOD'S HELP WE WILL DO MIGHTY THINGS, FOR HE WILL TRAMPLE DOWN OUR FOES.

Psalm 60:12

NOTHING WILL come against you that God is not ready, able, willing, and even eager to empower you to overcome. In his strength you are able to accomplish far beyond anything that is possible in your natural strength. Courageous living comes from knowing this as a life principle. You can face anything because you are not depending on your own strength.

Author Carol Kent and her husband, Gene, were thrust without warning into a nightmarish event that forever redefined their idea of normal. Their only child, Jason, who had been nothing but a joy in their lives, was arrested and charged with murder. Jason, fearing for the safety of his two young stepdaughters, had shot their biological father, whom Jason believed to be a danger to them. Carol remembers her heart sinking into her stomach, her entire body going numb, and the subsequent heartache and agony as Jason was convicted and sentenced to life without the possibility of parole.

But what could easily have been a story of defeat and disillusionment is instead one of courage, faith, and strength. Jason leads Bible studies in prison, mentors other prisoners, and leads prayer groups, having an impact in the most unlikely place. His influence is changing the lives of men whom he would likely never have encountered had his life not taken this turn. Generations will be different because Jason Kent has chosen to let God's strength sustain him.

Anytime I imagine the worst thing that could ever happen, my mind goes to Carol and Gene. I look at them and know that if the worst thing imaginable ever happened in my life, God's strength would be enough. Of course, there's no need to worry about all the terrible things that could befall us. We will have difficulties, and some of them will be major problems. Some of them will throw our lives into chaos and redefine our own ideas of normal. But God's strength will always be ours, and *he* will always be more than enough.

Father, I thank you that your strength makes me ready for any of life's challenges. No matter what comes my way, you can make me victorious.

Jennifer

Only he who can say, "The Lord is the strength of my life" can say, "Of whom shall I be afraid?"

—**ALEXANDER MACLAREN** (1826–1910), British preacher and Bible expositor

18 CLING

YOU ARE MY SAFE REFUGE,
 A FORTRESS WHERE MY ENEMIES CANNOT REACH ME.
LET ME LIVE FOREVER IN YOUR SANCTUARY,
 SAFE BENEATH THE SHELTER OF YOUR WINGS!

Psalm 61:3-4

UNDER HIS WINGS. God's Word often uses this image to describe his intimate and protective love for us. It calls to mind a scenario in nature with which his people were familiar—the sight of a mother bird gathering her chicks under her wings.

From there, pressed up against the mother, the little chicks are warmed and find shelter from both weather and predators. There they have no fear, kept safe from any danger.

David uses the same imagery in Psalm 63:7: "Because you are my helper, I sing for joy in the shadow of your wings." We find joy in God's embrace. We are to live under his wings; we are to make the shadow of his wings our dwelling place. He invites us to a life pressed close to him. David completes this thought with these words: "I cling to you; your strong right hand holds me securely" (Psalm 63:8).

I think the invitation to such intimacy—pressed against God's heart—is rightly met with David's response: "I cling to you." I love the word *cling*. It means adhere to, stick like glue, press against. It makes me think of static cling. Some kind of electrical attraction gets hold of something and it sticks to you. You can't unstick it. If you try to brush it off, it jumps right back on. It clings.

That should describe your relationship with Jesus. Is anything troubling you right now? Do you feel vulnerable or exposed or unprotected? Are there circumstances that seem threatening? Do you feel as if you are on your own? Cling to Jesus. Take refuge under his wings. Hear his heart. Let him warm you and cover you. Stop now and deliberately respond to his invitation: "Come, child. Let me spread my wings over you. Come into the shelter of my presence."

Jesus, pull me close to you as a hen gathers her chicks under her wings. You are all the shelter I need. You are all the refuge I seek. I sing for joy in the shadow of your wings.

Jennifer

O God, Thou has made us for Thyself, and our hearts find no rest until they rest in Thee.
—**ST. AUGUSTINE** (354–430), *Latin North African theologian and philosopher*

JESUS IS LORD

Let all that I am wait quietly before God,
for my hope is in him.
He alone is my rock and my salvation,
my fortress where I will not be shaken.

Psalm 62:5-6

MARY, MARTHA, and Lazarus were close friends of Jesus. He often spent time in their home. They knew him as well as anyone on earth knew him. They had seen him respond to needs over and over again. They knew what they could expect of him—or so they thought.

When Lazarus became ill, Mary and Martha sent a message to Jesus. It was simple and represented their absolute faith in Jesus to respond to their needs: "Lord, your dear friend is very sick" (John 11:3).

John, as he tells the story, sets the stage with these words: "Jesus loved Martha and her sister and Lazarus" (John 11:5, NASB). Why do you think he put that sentence in? I think it was because of what comes next:

"When He heard that he was sick, He then stayed two days longer in the place where He was" (John 11:6, NASB). John wanted to make it clear that when Jesus built a delay into the process, when he stayed where he was for two days more, it was in the context of his love for Martha, Mary, and Lazarus. His delay was loving, purposeful, profitable, and deliberate. It was necessary for accomplishing a bigger agenda.

How did the delay benefit Mary, Martha, and Lazarus? If Jesus had come to Bethany and healed Lazarus before he died, Mary's and Martha's prayers would have been answered. Their faith in Jesus would have been affirmed. They would have been more certain than ever that Jesus is Lord over illness. But they would never have learned that Jesus is Lord over death. The Father is always teaching us the lordship of Jesus in deeper, more experiential ways. "Jesus is Lord" is the truth that anchors everything.

Father, I believe that which I cannot see. I know that you are working. As I wait quietly for your work to be revealed on earth, I celebrate the work now in progress.

Jennifer

In Him the great clarification took place. When [the disciples] said, "Jesus is Lord," then everything in heaven and earth fell into place.

—E. STANLEY JONES (1884–1973), American missionary and theologian

20 FINDING SATISFACTION IN CHRIST

YOU SATISFY ME MORE THAN THE RICHEST FEAST.
I WILL PRAISE YOU WITH SONGS OF JOY.

Psalm 63:5

GOD HAS CREATED us so that only in him will we find true satisfaction. Ecclesiastes 3:11 says, "He has planted eternity in the human heart," and nothing temporal will satisfy. We might spend our lives searching for the missing piece that will finally make us whole or give us the contentment we long for. *If only I owned this. If only I could do that. If only my circumstances would change.* If we are not careful, we can live on a treadmill of elusive desires. Outside Christ, nothing is ever enough.

The Creator designed us with needs and desires. He built them into our blueprint so that they would be his entry points into our lives. He configured our needs so that they would be an exact match to his provision, as if the two were interlocking parts, fitting together like hand in glove.

We often take those God-designed needs and desires and try to find their fulfillment on our own, from something or someone other than God. God's promise to us is that he will satisfy every need and every desire with himself. We will never be fully satisfied on earth because earth is not our home. But we will find the contentment for which we were created when we let all our desires point us to him the way a magnet swings to true north. He is the polestar of our souls.

> *Hear the prayer I echo from the Psalms: "O God, you are my God; I earnestly search for you. My soul thirsts for you; my whole body longs for you in this parched and weary land where there is no water."*

Jennifer

If I am a son of God, nothing but God will satisfy my soul; no amount of comfort, no amount of ease, no amount of pleasure, will give me peace or rest. If I had the full cup of all the world's joys held up to me, and could drain it to the dregs, I should still remain thirsty if I had not God.

—GEOFFREY STUDDERT KENNEDY (1883–1929), English priest and poet

OBEY THE PRESENT VOICE

WHEN [JESUS] HAD FINISHED SPEAKING, HE SAID TO SIMON, "NOW GO OUT WHERE IT IS DEEPER, AND LET DOWN YOUR NETS TO CATCH SOME FISH."

Luke 5:4

SIMON PETER was an experienced fisherman from a line of fishermen. Fishing was what he knew. If a person had a question about fishing, Simon Peter would have been an excellent resource.

Simon had spent the night fishing. He had done everything right, used all his skill and all his training and all his experience. And he and his nets had come up empty.

Now right in the middle of Simon's emptiness, Jesus showed up. Our stories about Jesus seeking us out often use the phrase "It just happened." Simon had not been seeking Jesus out; Jesus sought Simon out. Jesus borrowed a boat to launch out from the shore so he could teach the crowds from a better acoustical perch. It "just happened" that the boat he used belonged to Simon. It "just happened" that Simon's failed fishing trip positioned him for an encounter with Jesus.

I imagine Simon—macho, proud, quick-tempered, passionate Simon—hearing this rabbi named Jesus, who knew nothing of fishing, tell him how to fish. The last thing he wanted to do after a night of disappointing effort was launch out again.

But Simon decided to do what Jesus was telling him to do, whether it made sense to him or not. Even if he thought it might well be a waste of time, Simon decided to obey Jesus' present-tense command.

In this encounter, we see the promise that Jesus makes in our lives as well. When we obey him in the present moment, it will change the moments that follow. When Simon launched out into the deep at Jesus' direct command, he accomplished what all his skill and training and experience could not. Every obedience to the present voice of the present Jesus opens our lives to his miraculous work.

Lord Jesus, open my ears to hear your voice in my now. I say with Samuel, "Speak, your servant is listening."

Jennifer

I have to get to the point of the absolute and unquestionable relationship that takes everything exactly as it comes from Him. God never guides us at some time in the future, but always here and now. Realize that the Lord is here now, and the freedom you receive is immediate.

—**OSWALD CHAMBERS** (1874–1917), Scottish minister and teacher

22 COMPLETE FORGIVENESS

THOUGH WE ARE OVERWHELMED BY OUR SINS,
YOU FORGIVE THEM ALL.

Psalm 65:3

OUR CREATOR knows what will cause us harm. He knows what will pile burdens on us that we are not meant to carry. He knows what will diminish us and steal our sense of destiny. He has given a name to any action or attitude or thought pattern that will tear us down instead of build us up—*sin*.

Our sins enslave us. First entered into freely, sin quickly causes a role reversal so that we who entered by choice now find ourselves shackled and captive. The Creator knows well the way sin's power operates. That's why he warns us to resist sin and, ultimately, covers us and takes sin's blows upon himself.

Sin will overwhelm us. Little by little, like a stealth disease that starts imperceptibly and spreads its destruction almost unnoticed, sin wears us down and destroys us. The entire Bible could be summed up in this one great promise: "Though we are overwhelmed by our sins, you forgive them all."

Are you feeling crippled by sin? Are you overwhelmed by the destruction sin has brought into your life and your relationships? Are you tired of trying and failing? Do you believe you have forfeited your hope of experiencing the cleansing, renewing touch of the Savior?

Listen to today's promise. God forgives *all* our sins. Every single one. He washes them away and leaves us clean and free and new.

> *Merciful Savior, I believe your promise. You forgive every sin. I reject the lie that my sins hold me captive. Your amazing work of love, accomplished at the Cross, is enough. I receive your forgiveness and cleansing.*
>
> *Jennifer*

Our Saviour kneels down and gazes upon the darkest acts of our lives. But rather than recoil in horror, he reaches out in kindness and says, "I can clean that if you want." And from the basin of his grace, he scoops a palm full of mercy and washes our sin.

—**MAX LUCADO** (1955–), American pastor and author

THE GIVING GENE

THE GENEROUS WILL PROSPER;
THOSE WHO REFRESH OTHERS WILL THEMSELVES BE REFRESHED.

Proverbs 11:25

THE RULES of the Kingdom of God are often in direct contradiction to the rules of the kingdom of this world. We tend to be so conditioned to the way things work in the world that the promises of God can seem unrealistic.

The world's rules for prospering are to hoard what you have, use your resources on yourself, measure carefully what you give away, climb over those in your way to get more. The world's rules for finding refreshment are to think always of your own needs, make sure no one takes advantage of you, and look out for your own interests above all else.

I'd like to tell you about a woman I have known all my life. She lives by the principle of Proverbs 11:25. She is well into her eighties, healthy and energetic, and financially secure. Though she has the resources to live extravagantly, that doesn't interest her. She is happy to live simply.

Nothing brings her more pleasure than helping someone in need, usually doing so anonymously. She delights in giving generously to her church and other ministries. Giving is what makes her tick.

When she was younger and in better physical condition, her giving went far beyond money. She would drop whatever she was doing instantly if someone needed her. She considered it an honor rather than an imposition. She seemed never to run out of energy.

Her grown children and her grandchildren are much the same way. She has passed on the giving gene.

I know many people her age, but she is the happiest, the most cheerful, most filled-with-zest-for-life person I know—of any age. What do you think is the secret to living long and well? What is the key to spending your last years happy and fulfilled rather than regretful and bitter? Could it be that she is the living demonstration of God's promise that "those who refresh others will themselves be refreshed"?

Lord, make me aware of every opportunity to be generous. Clean out my self-involved, self-protective, self-focused heart and make it available to you.

Jennifer

Want to snatch a day from the manacles of boredom? Do generous deeds, acts beyond reimbursement. Kindness without compensation. Do a deed for which you cannot be repaid.

—**MAX LUCADO** (1955–), American pastor and author

24 A FRUITFUL DESERT

THE LORD YOUR GOD HAS BLESSED YOU IN EVERYTHING YOU
HAVE DONE. HE HAS WATCHED YOUR EVERY STEP THROUGH
THIS GREAT WILDERNESS. DURING THESE FORTY YEARS, THE
LORD YOUR GOD HAS BEEN WITH YOU, AND YOU HAVE
LACKED NOTHING.

Deuteronomy 2:7

AS WE SEE in today's verse, God shows us who he is by what he does. We see his promises
worked out in the lives of his people and know that the same God is working in our lives.

Moses is reminding God's people of the ways God has been faithful and of how his
hand has been on them every step of their forty-year journey in the wilderness. Can you
relate to a wilderness journey? Life's path takes all of us into desert territory from time
to time. Sometimes the terrain is brutal and the sun scorching. We feel parched and desperate for a relief that seems not to come. And just like the Israelites, we can see God's
hand most clearly in retrospect.

When we are in the middle of a desert trek, God's hand seems absent, blinded as we are
by the glaring circumstances. But when we emerge from that leg of the journey, we can look
back and see that God has watched over our every step. The journey was hard and went on
longer than we thought we could bear. But here we stand. All the way through the desert,
just when we thought we couldn't last another day, God's mercy met us in some observable
way: a kind word, an unexpected provision, a "chance" encounter. The assurance of his presence always came.

The desert has things to teach us. We learn things there that we can't learn anywhere
else. We see the careful provision of our Father in a different light. His love stands out in
stark relief against the background of the desert's barren landscape. In the wilderness, we
come to the end of ourselves. We learn in new and deeper ways to cling to him and wait
for him. When we come out of the desert, the desert lessons stay with us. We take them
with us into the next stretch. We remember the God who led us through the desert, and
we know that he is with us still.

Lord, sanctify my desert times. Let them be fruitful in my life.

Jennifer

True contentment is the power of getting out of any situation all that there is in it.
—G. K. CHESTERTON (1874–1936), English journalist and author

ENJOYING GOD

SING PRAISES TO GOD AND TO HIS NAME!
  SING LOUD PRAISES TO HIM WHO RIDES THE CLOUDS.
HIS NAME IS THE LORD—
  REJOICE IN HIS PRESENCE!

Psalm 68:4

IT'S SO EASY to lose our enjoyment of God and his creation and to neglect rejoicing in his presence the way this verse describes. In fact, it is rare to find a person who truly enjoys God and finds delight in this relationship. There are so many demands on our time. So often our thoughts are focused on me-myself-and-I, work, worries about tomorrow, and what we need to finish today. That's part of being human, but over and over the Scriptures bring us back to meditating on how marvelous and mysterious God is: he rides the clouds; he provides rain and a bountiful harvest. We're encouraged to gaze at the clouds or the night sky.

When we lose our enjoyment of God, it's usually because we've gotten hung up in the brushstrokes of living the Christian life and lost the portrait of the life of Christ. We've directed our gaze downward to earth's cares instead of upward to God's wonders. If this sounds familiar to you, let me encourage you to take a walk in nature and get lost in the details.

Whether you walk in a rose garden in the spring, watch a sunrise and sunset, or look at a moonlit sky studded with stars, get away from the noise of the television, computer, cell phone, and ticking clock and enjoy the Lord in the beauty of his creation. "Through [Christ] God created everything in the heavenly realms and on earth. . . . Everything was created through him and for him" (Colossians 1:16). God made the vastness of space and the boundless and beautiful world for us to enjoy. He is glad when his handiwork causes us to rejoice.

Lord, I confess I've become "wonder impaired" about so much, even the miracle of each new sunrise that lights up the earth morning by morning. Restore to me enjoyment of you and your creation, that I might sing your praises and rejoice all the more. In Christ's name, amen.

Cheri

God is most glorified in us when we are most satisfied in Him.

—JOHN PIPER (1946–), American pastor

26 A PARENT'S PRIORITY

COMMIT YOURSELVES WHOLEHEARTEDLY TO THESE COMMANDS THAT I AM GIVING YOU TODAY. REPEAT THEM AGAIN AND AGAIN TO YOUR CHILDREN. TALK ABOUT THEM WHEN YOU ARE AT HOME AND WHEN YOU ARE ON THE ROAD, WHEN YOU ARE GOING TO BED AND WHEN YOU ARE GETTING UP.

Deuteronomy 6:6-7

WHETHER CHILDREN are ten months or ten years old, childhood is a prime time to hide God's Word in their hearts, to know God's love as expressed in the Bible, and to help them understand that the Bible addresses real life. Children may learn Bible verses at church or be exposed to God's Word at camp, Christian school, or vacation Bible school. But God's very clear instruction in this familiar Deuteronomy 6 passage is that *parents*—not the pastor or Sunday school teacher—are to teach their children God's Word at every opportunity—at the breakfast table, on the way to school, in the park, and at bedtime.

Exposing our children and grandchildren to Scripture in everyday living is a vital part of helping children develop a living faith in the living God.

In this passage, the Lord didn't make a suggestion to parents: "If you have time and feel like it, or if you've had seminary training, *then* teach your children my commands." No, it was a blanket command to all God's people: "Commit yourselves wholeheartedly to these commands. . . . Repeat them again and again to your children." Why? So they would love the Lord their God and obey his commands and he would keep his covenant for a thousand generations (see Deuteronomy 7:7-9). This command wasn't meant to burden parents but to bring blessing promised to every future generation that follows and obeys him. God's powerful Word is the key way for children to discover and know him. So let it happen, little by little, day by day, from high-chair devotions with your toddler to Bible stories with your first grader, and later as you engage in a discussion with your teen about a difficult decision.

Father, help me to hide your Word in my children's and grandchildren's hearts. Your word is eternal. Thank you for the privilege of sharing your love and nurturing faith in little ones' hearts and minds.

Cheri

There is no doubt that it is the job of us as parents—not the priests, kings, or prophets—to teach God's truth to our children.

—BRUCE WILKINSON (1940–), American teacher and author

PERSISTENT PRAYER

I keep praying to you, Lord,
hoping this time you will show me favor.
In your unfailing love, O God,
answer my prayer with your sure salvation.
Rescue me from the mud;
don't let me sink any deeper!

Psalm 69:13-14

ONE OF THE most important lessons I've learned in life is that perseverance makes all the difference. In this passage the psalmist says, "I keep praying to you, Lord" to rescue him not only from trouble but also from approaching death at the hands of his enemies. He desires that God act out of his mercy and love, but he indicates that this isn't the first time he has prayed for favor and help.

"I *keep praying* to you" indicates a verb tense much like what we find in Matthew 7:7-8, where Jesus tells us to ask and keep on asking, to seek and keep on seeking, and to knock and keep on knocking. The Lord didn't suggest that we ask just once and give up when we get tired of waiting or the answer we expect doesn't come. He was telling us to be persistent—to keep on praying, seeking, knocking, and asking, and then we will be given what we ask for. Keep on looking, and we will find. Keep on knocking, and the door will be opened. In these and many other verses throughout the Bible, God communicates the fact that it takes strong faith to be persistent in praying and encourages us to press on. There is great promise for us as we persevere in prayer and "keep praying."

The Bible contains many examples of people who prayed multiple times. Elijah prayed to God seven times before drops of rain began to fall from the sky (see 1 Kings 18:42-45). And Jesus told us to be like the widow who came to the unrighteous judge day after day to plead her case. Though the judge didn't fear God or man, he finally granted the woman's petition because of her persistent requests (see Luke 18:2-5). Receive the promise of persevering prayer, and P-U-S-H—**P**ray **U**ntil **S**omething **H**appens!

Lord Jesus, develop in my character perseverance and faith. Help me to never give up but to keep right on praying to you.

Cheri

Every single believing prayer has its influence. It is stored up toward an answer which comes in due time to whomever perseveres to the end.

—**ANDREW MURRAY** (1828–1917), South African pastor and author

28 ROOTING OUR LIVES IN GOD'S LOVE

WICKEDNESS NEVER BRINGS STABILITY,
BUT THE GODLY HAVE DEEP ROOTS.

Proverbs 12:3

MANY YEARS AGO I learned a great lesson from a godly woman I knew. We both loved gardening and trees, and one day she shared with me something God taught her in a storm. Flo was in a season full of troubles: her daughter and two grandkids were living with her in their tiny house. Her husband was unable to work because of severe depression, and Flo worked long hours, weekends, and holidays to support them all. Her strength was almost spent, and she wondered how long she could withstand the pressure.

Late one night a winter rainstorm raged. As the wind howled and lightning flashed, Flo looked out at her young peach tree being whipped back and forth. Would the tree last until morning or be broken by the violent winds? The next morning, to Flo's surprise, the tree stood tall, basking in the sunlight.

Seeing that her tree had survived, Flo knew that whatever happened or how harsh her trials were, God would provide the strength she needed, because she was rooted in his love and his Word. Though she might continue to be hit by gale-force trials, she would bend but not break.

Trees and people are created to bend with storms and bounce back—unless they are weakened by bitterness or improperly planted. We must be planted in God's truth. Then "the godly have deep roots" will be true in our experience. God did sustain Flo through that stormy, trying period of her life. He gave her strength and grace to deal with difficulties and eventually brought her into a season of joy and new fruitfulness. He can do the same for you.

> *Thank you, Father, for giving rest to the weary and peace to the storm tossed. Keep me free of bitterness; sink my roots deep into your truth and love through Christ Jesus.*

Cheri

The Bible nowhere indicates that God withdraws us from the troubles of life. In fact, we become more involved in life's troubles when we come to Christ. But he gives us power to go on with the battle.

—BILLY GRAHAM (1918–), American evangelist and author

UNSEARCHABLE RICHES

> MAY ALL WHO SEARCH FOR YOU
> BE FILLED WITH JOY AND GLADNESS IN YOU.
> MAY THOSE WHO LOVE YOUR SALVATION
> REPEATEDLY SHOUT, "GOD IS GREAT!"
>
> *Psalm 70:4*

GOD WANTS to use our lives as platforms for displaying his power. He wants to work in our lives in such a way that we become trophy cases for his victories. When God works his wonders in our lives, those watching will be filled with wonder and shout, "God is great!"

Consider the story of Lazarus, whom Jesus raised from the dead. When Lazarus became ill, his sisters Mary and Martha sent a message to Jesus. Their message was simple and represented their absolute faith in Jesus to respond to their needs. "Lord, the one you love is sick." They expected him to arrive in time to heal their brother, but Jesus had bigger plans.

Imagine that Jesus had arrived at Bethany in time to heal Lazarus. Who would have seen his glory? Read John 11:19: "Many Jews had come to Martha and Mary to comfort them in the loss of their brother" (NIV). Why were people at Mary and Martha's house? Lazarus's illness would not have brought them. What did it take to bring them? It took Lazarus's death.

What happened because the Jews from the area had come to mourn Lazarus's death? They were positioned to see Jesus prove his mastery over death in raising Lazarus from the dead. Now look at John 11:45:

"Therefore many of the Jews who had come to visit Mary, and had seen what Jesus did, believed in him" (NIV).

Jesus is engineering our circumstances so that his power and glory will be on display. When God builds a waiting period into the course of your affairs, it means that what he is doing requires it. His apparent delays are loving, purposeful, and deliberate.

> *Thank you for experiences teaching me that your ways are higher than mine.*
> *Father, use my life to display your power.*
>
> *Jennifer*

My Master has riches beyond the count of arithmetic, the measurement of reason, the dream of imagination, or the eloquence of words. They are unsearchable! You may look, and study, and weigh, but Jesus is a greater Saviour than you think him to be when your thoughts are at the greatest.

—**CHARLES HADDON SPURGEON** (1834–1892), English preacher and writer

30 WHERE IS YOUR FAITH?

A FIERCE STORM CAME DOWN ON THE LAKE. THE BOAT WAS
FILLING WITH WATER, AND THEY WERE IN REAL DANGER.
THE DISCIPLES WENT AND WOKE HIM UP, SHOUTING,
"MASTER, MASTER, WE'RE GOING TO DROWN!"
WHEN JESUS WOKE UP, HE REBUKED THE WIND AND THE
RAGING WAVES. SUDDENLY THE STORM STOPPED AND ALL
WAS CALM. THEN HE ASKED THEM, "WHERE IS YOUR FAITH?"

Luke 8:23-25

MY HUSBAND and I once were passengers in a double-decker boat called *Balmy Days* off the coast of Maine. The brochure had promised a quiet ride to Monhegan Island, but our excursion was anything but that. The boat pitched and rolled, and I thought each wave that hit the boat would wash us into the frigid depths of the Atlantic Ocean.

As I held on for dear life, I recalled the cry of Jesus' disciples: "We're going to drown!" and quietly prayed: *Jesus, you made the wind and the waves; surely you could quiet them the way you did for the disciples.* I followed this persuasive line of reasoning for a few minutes, but the boat only heaved more. When I got quiet and started listening, what I heard God say to my heart surprised me—he wanted me to enjoy the ride! I focused on the horizon and gave my fears to him, and a sense of peace filled me. The waves didn't calm down, but I realized that the Lord had done something just as amazing—he had calmed the storm in my heart and mind. The Christian life is rarely a calm ride. It's more like an uncertain excursion with huge waves and a bumpy ride. But I've discovered that when God doesn't quiet the storm that's raging around us, he is able and willing to quiet our hearts with his peace.

Lord Jesus, thank you that inherent in the storms of life is your promise of peace. Not peace that is the absence of trouble, but peace that eclipses circumstances. Incline my heart to yours that I may experience more of your peace in every storm I face.

Cheri

The night and storm look as if they would last forever; but the calm and the morning cannot be stayed; the storm in its very nature is transient. The effort of nature, as that of the human heart, ever is to return to its repose, for God is peace.

—**GEORGE MACDONALD** (1824–1905), Scottish author and minister

PRAISE HIS GLORIOUS NAME 31

PRAISE THE LORD GOD, THE GOD OF ISRAEL,
   WHO ALONE DOES SUCH WONDERFUL THINGS.
PRAISE HIS GLORIOUS NAME FOREVER!
   LET THE WHOLE EARTH BE FILLED WITH HIS GLORY.
AMEN AND AMEN!

Psalm 72:18-19

THERE IS no greater privilege than knowing God. The Father gave his precious, only Son that we might know him, not in a nominal, disconnected way but in an intimate way. While Scripture says that the people who know God are strong and able to resist evil (see Daniel 11:32), those who forget God or turn from him experience confusion, pain, and emptiness. Those people who revere the name of the God of Jacob are set securely on high and are sent help and support from heaven (see Psalm 20:1, NASB). Most of all, they find life, and life abundant. Yet those who rely on their own understanding and live without God inevitably head down a path of destruction rather than life. They boast in their own "chariots and horses," in our day equating to accomplishments and wealth, but we are to "boast in the name of the LORD our God" alone (Psalm 20:7) and bless his glorious name forever.

But how can we praise his glorious name if we do not know God as he really is? Fortunately, the Lord didn't leave us to our own devices to figure out who he is. He provided his Word, his wondrous deeds, and especially his many names revealed throughout the pages of Scripture to help us.

We are to bless *Elohim*, the Creator of heaven and earth; *El-Shaddai*, the God Almighty of Blessings; *Adonai*, our Lord; *Jehovah*, the Completely Self-Existing One, always present, revealed in Jesus, who is the same yesterday, today, and forever; and *Jehovah-Shalom,* the God of Peace, who in Christ is our peace in all situations and seasons until we see him face-to-face. Bless the Lord God, and praise his glorious name forever!

> *Oh God, lift our thoughts and hearts this day to your glorious names and manifold nature. Though we will never plumb the depths of the glory of your being, may we exalt, worship, and adore you, blessing your glorious name forever.*
>
> *Cheri*

God reveals himself unfailingly to the thoughtful seeker.
—**HONORÉ DE BALZAC** (1799–1850), French author and philosopher

APRIL

STRENGTH FOR ALL YOUR DAYS

About Asher [Moses] said:

"Most blessed of sons is Asher;
  let him be favored by his brothers;
  and let him bathe his feet in [olive] oil.
The bolts of your gates will be iron and bronze,
  and your strength will equal your days."

Deuteronomy 33:24-25 (NIV)

FOR WEEKS my friend Glenna had been feeling exhausted. "I'm so tired," she said. "I'm seventy-six and have no energy. I don't know how I'm going to keep up the yard work and household duties all alone. Will I have enough strength in days and months ahead?"

One morning, feeling as tired as ever, Glenna opened her Bible, and the reading for that day was in Deuteronomy 33. As she read Moses' blessing on the tribe of Asher, she felt as if God had spoken his promise into her spirit and said, "Glenna, your strength *will equal your days*. Praise me as your strength instead of focusing on your lack of energy or recounting the tasks to be done."

Glenna knelt and began to worship the Lord for his great promise, assured that he would support and sustain her. As she prayed, renewal began in both her spiritual and physical being; she felt a vigor she hadn't experienced in a long time. She realized she didn't have to worry about the possibility of being more exhausted in a year. God's strength would match the length of her days then, too.

It's easy to be downhearted when we wake up exhausted or don't feel up to the demands of life—household work, jobs, and caregiving. And when we're worn out because of ill health, old age, or crushing burdens, it's hard to keep going. But throughout the Scriptures is the theme that the Lord can renew our strength. When Glenna shared this promise with me, I was encouraged. Now I pass it on to you, believing that this blessing is not only for the tribe of Asher, but for all of us who are in Christ.

Lord, when we don't know how we will go on, you have an answer. Thank you, Father, that all your promises are yes and amen in Christ. Thank you for supporting us and providing strength for our days.

Cheri

The weaker we feel, the harder we lean on God. And the harder we lean, the stronger we grow.

—**JONI EARECKSON TADA** (1949–), American author, artist, and advocate for the disabled

2

HEART WIDE OPEN

These were [Jesus'] instructions . . .: "The harvest is great, but the workers are few. So pray to the Lord who is in charge of the harvest; ask him to send more workers into his fields."

Luke 10:2

WHEN THE SCRIPTURES instruct us to pray, we can consider that instruction a promise of what God is willing and able to do in response to our prayers. What can we learn from this call to prayer? That the harvest is great.

Everywhere your life takes you, you can be sure there are hearts ripe and ready to be harvested for the Kingdom. The Holy Spirit has already been working. He has plowed the ground, planted the seed, and nurtured and protected it as it took root.

I have discovered, first, that sometimes the one whose heart has ripened may be the last person I would assume to be ready. Where I worked years ago, I sensed the Lord impressing me to start a prayer group. I didn't want to put myself out there quite that far, so I thought I would privately contact the people I assumed would be interested. But the feeling persisted that I should put the invitation in the office communication, and I hesitantly did so. No one responded. I feared no one would come. When the time came, none of those I thought might be interested showed up, but others I would never have imagined contacting were there. Each had a story about crying out to the Lord and asking for some way of knowing him.

The second thing I've learned is that God will send workers in response to prayer. He knows how to call his own and direct them to the very places where he is working. He engineers divine appointments and initiates strategic conversations that lead to harvesting hearts.

You are where God has placed you because the harvest is great and you have been called. Trust the God of the harvest to lead you and to give you wisdom and sensitivity in the field to which you have been appointed. Be prayerfully alert to the Spirit's nudging, and live with a heart wide open to those around you.

Here I am, Lord. Send me.

Jennifer

The Son of God is spreading His love, His lifestyle, and His life-saving message across this planet and you know what? He has summoned you to join Him in His glorious Administration. Don't settle for anything less.

—**RON HUTCHCRAFT,** contemporary Christian communicator and author

GOD WITH US

WE THANK YOU, O GOD!
WE GIVE THANKS BECAUSE YOU ARE NEAR.
PEOPLE EVERYWHERE TELL OF YOUR WONDERFUL DEEDS.

Psalm 75:1

THE MOST ASTONISHING promise of all is that God is near.

Jesus, Immanuel, "God with us." I cannot grasp the fullness of it.

God the Son voluntarily left his rightful place on the universe's throne, left the riches and the unimaginable glory that were his, left the sound of unending praise and worship that surrounded him—left it all to be with us.

What must that moment have been like? When heaven's great Treasure shed his kingly grandeur and donned the clay of humanity, did the angels for a moment hold their breath and look on in astonishment? When he who was from the beginning took the form of a servant, did the eternal realm stand speechless with wonder? When the King of kings exchanged his majestic robes for swaddling clothes, surely it was one of the most beautiful, awe-inspiring moments in all eternity.

God *with* us. Can that little word *with* capture the meaning? Does it mean "with me," like next to me? No, nearer than that. Does it mean "with me" like someone holding me in a tight embrace? No, nearer than that. "With me" like the blood in my veins? No, nearer still. "With me" like the beat of my heart? No, nearer, nearer.

"It is no longer I who live, but Christ lives *in* me" (Galatians 2:20, emphasis added). *With* me becomes *in* me. When *God with us* was born, he opened the way for heaven to invade earth and for earth to experience heaven. It was the first step in the grand, eternal plan that would make it possible for Jesus to be Christ in me.

Jesus, you are no faraway deity waiting for us to find you. You are God with us.
May your Spirit so align my life with your willingness to embrace humility that
this same willingness becomes the evidence of Christ in me.

Jennifer

He so loved us that He was created from a mother whom he had created, was carried in hands he had made, was nourished at breasts He had filled; that He, the Word without Whom all human eloquence is mute, wailed in a manger in mute infancy.

—**ST. AUGUSTINE** (354–430), Latin North African theologian and philosopher

4

ASK, SEEK, KNOCK

[JESUS SAID,] "I TELL YOU, KEEP ON ASKING, AND YOU WILL RECEIVE WHAT YOU ASK FOR. KEEP ON SEEKING, AND YOU WILL FIND. KEEP ON KNOCKING, AND THE DOOR WILL BE OPENED TO YOU. FOR EVERYONE WHO ASKS, RECEIVES. EVERYONE WHO SEEKS, FINDS. AND TO EVERYONE WHO KNOCKS, THE DOOR WILL BE OPENED."

Luke 11:9-10

PRAYER IS not for quitters. It doesn't work like a vending machine—put in a prayer, take out an answer. God has much more to accomplish through our prayers than just giving us "stuff." When we pray, he engages us in such an intimate, heart-to-heart process that we can't pray and not be changed.

He has established prayer as the conduit through which the power of heaven changes the circumstances of earth. He designed prayer deliberately so that we are pulled into the desires of God, and our hearts are transformed until his desires become ours.

Jesus tells his disciples to keep on asking, keep on seeking, and keep on knocking. Three levels of prayer, each requiring perseverance. *Ask* with unpretentious faith, like a child asking a parent. Simple and trusting. *Seek* with determined faith. Seeking prayer puts us in a learning mode. We are open, alert, observant. *Knock* with persistent faith. Knocking implies an intention, a certainty that you want entrance to a particular door. You want to gain access to the person behind the door. No one else will do. You will knock and keep on knocking until you have met that person face-to-face. Knocking is the kind of prayer that seeks the *face* of God rather than the *hand* of God.

Every form of prayer takes persistence. Not because God must be worn down or won over, but because he is working out a process in us that will wean our hearts from any desire except for God himself. We have his promise that our persistence will be rewarded.

Father, I thank you for my needs, because they lead me to your supply. Glorify yourself through my needs. Most of all, Father, use them to establish your Kingdom and your righteousness.

Jennifer

Bear up the hands that hang down, by faith and prayer; support the tottering knees. Have you any days of fasting and prayer? Storm the throne of grace and persevere . . . and mercy will come down.

—**JOHN WESLEY** (1703–1791), British minister and theologian

RADIATING CHRIST

IF YOU ARE FILLED WITH LIGHT, WITH NO DARK CORNERS, THEN
YOUR WHOLE LIFE WILL BE RADIANT, AS THOUGH A FLOODLIGHT
WERE FILLING YOU WITH LIGHT.

Luke 11:36

JESUS PROMISES us that if we are filled with his light, our lives will be radiant. They will reflect his light and bring light to the darkness. We can be so filled with light that we emit light.

Using the metaphor of light, Jesus is referring to a powerful scriptural theme that we can trace from God's first words in the act of Creation: "Let there be light." Light had to come first; then the rest of Creation followed. Why the need for light? Because there was darkness. Darkness covered the formless earth, and the only counterbalance to darkness is light. Is there any other way to dispel the darkness? Our first glimpse of the Creator in Scripture is as the one whose word lit the world. That is how he introduces himself—as the Light Giver. Darkness gave way to light in the beginning and does so every time light comes on the scene.

Jesus is "the one who is the true light, who gives light to everyone" (John 1:9). He said of himself, "I have come as a light to shine in this dark world, so that all who put their trust in me will no longer remain in the dark" (John 12:46). Every mention of light, starting with Creation, is pointing to the true light. The very nature of light as we know it in our world is a picture of the true light.

In today's verse, Jesus promises to be so present and powerful in his people that we become the transparent vessels through which he shines the light of his grace and truth into our dark world.

Lord Jesus, let me radiate your light. Teach me to be so available to you and so transparent to those in my world that you shine brightly in my life.

Jennifer

Men come and go; leaders, teachers, thinkers speak and work for a season, and then fall silent and impotent. He abides. They die, but He lives. They are lights kindled, and, therefore, sooner or later quenched; but He is the true light from which they draw all their brightness, and He shines for evermore.

—**ALEXANDER MACLAREN** (1826–1910), British preacher and Bible expositor

6

ANTIDOTE TO ANXIETY

WHAT IS THE PRICE OF FIVE SPARROWS—TWO COPPER COINS?
YET GOD DOES NOT FORGET A SINGLE ONE OF THEM. AND THE
VERY HAIRS ON YOUR HEAD ARE ALL NUMBERED. SO DON'T BE
AFRAID; YOU ARE MORE VALUABLE TO GOD THAN A WHOLE
FLOCK OF SPARROWS.

Luke 12:6-7

IN THESE VERSES, Jesus wants to drive home a point. He wants to make sure that we really see what he is promising. He wants to paint a picture in our minds that will stick with us: we don't have to fear anything, because God—Creator God, Ruler God, Power-over-Life-and-Death God—values and cherishes us.

We have great worth to him. It's so improbable a concept that Jesus adds some texture to the promise with a description meant to anchor it in our understanding.

When Jesus spoke the words above, he and his audience were outside. Maybe the marketplace was in view and they could see in the distance someone purchasing some sparrows, the cheapest and least-valued birds—the fare of the poor, for the most part. Imagine Jesus pointing in that direction, framing the scene in his hearers' imaginations and asking, "What is the price of five sparrows—two copper coins?"

Jesus emphasizes that God is fully aware of every single sparrow—creature of little value, cheap to buy. But if God watches over even the sparrows, then surely he watches over and cares for you and me.

We don't have to be afraid of anything, anytime, anywhere. God's protection and provision for us are so detailed that he knows how many hairs are on our heads. Nothing escapes his notice. Nothing gets past him. Nothing is hidden from his sight.

So, Jesus reminds us, we don't need to be afraid.

When anxiety tries to lay claim to my thoughts, when fear seeks a foothold in my mind, when confusion threatens to make a stand in my heart, I look to you; I seek your face. You are all the antidote I need to anything that might steal my peace.

Jennifer

The beginning of anxiety is the end of faith, and the beginning of true faith is the end of anxiety.

—GEORGE MÜLLER (1805–1898), German evangelist and orphanage director

A LESSON FROM THE TREES

CAN ALL YOUR WORRIES ADD A SINGLE MOMENT TO YOUR LIFE? AND IF WORRY CAN'T ACCOMPLISH A LITTLE THING LIKE THAT, WHAT'S THE USE OF WORRYING OVER BIGGER THINGS?

Luke 12:25-26

AFTER THE BIRTH of her daughter, Lynn felt God guiding her to leave her professional career of twenty years. She fretted over this wrenching decision, clinging desperately to her respectable income, her workplace friends, and lots of recognition in her job. To her, this was a *big thing*, and she worried that staying at home, deprived of interaction with colleagues and the meaningful work she had enjoyed for so long might cause her to become depressed.

One weekend as she walked in the autumn woods, she watched the colorful leaves cling to branches, struggling to hold on. With each gust of wind, as if by God's command, they simply let go. They pirouetted with abandon in the breeze.

At that moment, Lynn heard God whisper to her heart, *Lynn, let go!*

She gave her employer notice and committed herself to enter whatever "dance" God was choreographing for her. Yet depression, doubt, and loneliness ensued as she struggled to adjust to life at home with a baby and without her stimulating career. Again God spoke to her through nature. Like a winter tree, Lynn felt stripped of the lush foliage of professional purpose and friendships. But although a winter tree looks dead, life remains in the roots. Likewise, as Lynn rooted herself in God's Word, her life would become fruitful.

Trees don't fret, and neither do the birds that nest in their branches. The trees bloom in season, and in times of barrenness they raise their leafless limbs in praise to their Maker. Stripped of foliage, they behold the stars shining like brilliant jewels between their branches.

Lynn took a lesson from the trees. She decided to stop fretting and look instead for the stars twinkling between the branches of her life. And each day she discovered surprises, new purpose, cherished times with her child, and a host of blazing constellations of joy.

Lord, I, too, have a tendency to fret and worry. Help me to trust you more and not to bank my identity on a job description, knowing that I am valuable to you simply because you gave me life. Help me to be carefree in your care!

Cheri

Worry is an indication that we think God cannot look after us.
—**OSWALD CHAMBERS** (1874–1917), Scottish minister and teacher

8

WORK AS WORSHIP

WORK HARD AND BECOME A LEADER;
BE LAZY AND BECOME A SLAVE.

Proverbs 12:24

JESUS HAS TRANSFORMED work into worship: "Work with enthusiasm, as though you were working for the Lord rather than for people" (Ephesians 6:7).

When we work with our focus on Jesus rather than on others, our work can take on new meaning. The work God gives us to do, whatever the arena, becomes another setting in which he can reveal himself through us. We won't have to worry about getting proper acknowledgment or about being sure we don't have to do more than our share. We are not working for anyone or any purpose other than as an act of love and worship to the Lord.

We can't compartmentalize our lives into secular and sacred, because the Christ who lives in us lives in us all the time. Doing our work with integrity and discipline demonstrates the character of Christ. All work is then sacred.

God promises us that if we are diligent in our work, we will become leaders. We can't take that to mean that we are guaranteed the biggest salary or the grandest title. But we can be sure that if we work with rightly focused hearts, others will follow our examples and will be influenced by how Christ demonstrates himself through us. Not everyone will, but someone will. We will be leaders to someone.

On the other hand, if we neglect our work or do it poorly, we will become enslaved. Enslaved to others, and enslaved by the work. Have you ever neglected something that needed to be done? Did that neglected work hang over you and oppress you and steal your joy? Neglecting our work can rule our attitudes and our emotions.

So embrace the wisdom in this promise. Take that work that you are neglecting, for whatever reason, and do it as if you are doing it for the Lord. Offer it as worship. Stop letting it rule you.

In fact, start redefining all your work as worship. If your work itself seems to have little effect, don't worry. Your obedience is having great effect.

Lord, accept as worship the work of my hands.

Jennifer

We ought not to be weary of doing little things for the love of God, who regards not the greatness of the work, but the love with which it is performed.

—BROTHER LAWRENCE (1614–1691), French lay monk and writer

AN INSIDE JOB

[JESUS] ASKED, "WHAT ELSE IS THE KINGDOM OF GOD LIKE? IT IS LIKE THE YEAST A WOMAN USED IN MAKING BREAD. EVEN THOUGH SHE PUT ONLY A LITTLE YEAST IN THREE MEASURES OF FLOUR, IT PERMEATED EVERY PART OF THE DOUGH."

Luke 13:20-21

THE POWER of the Kingdom is so potent that a little goes a long way. Jesus told this parable of the yeast as part of a series of parables describing how the growth process works in the Kingdom. He is talking about the Kingdom of God that has come in the hearts and lives of his followers. If you are a follower of Jesus, then you are in the Kingdom, and the Kingdom is in you.

As usual, Jesus took a spiritual principle and placed it in a familiar setting: a woman making bread. In this parable, Jesus referred to a very large amount of flour. The Greek word refers to enough flour for about twenty loaves of bread—an extravagant amount. Even though the amount of flour is so great, a little bit of yeast leavened all the dough.

Yeast mixed into dough is not discernible to the eye. It becomes part of it. Once the yeast starts to work, it can't be separated from the dough; they become one, and once the leavening process has begun, it is irreversible.

Yeast works slowly and progressively. Working from the inside, it changes the texture, look, and taste of the dough. The flour and other ingredients do not expand and rise apart from the yeast. When it has finished its work, the dough has been transformed. In the Kingdom, God places no value on instant gratification. The process is as important as the finished product. Even when you can't see the progress, you can trust that it is occurring.

> *Lord, teach me patience as I look for evidence of your Kingdom's power in the situations of my life. Train me to live by what I know rather than by what I see. Let your Kingdom work in my life.*

> *Jennifer*

He is intangible and invisible. But His work is more powerful than the most ferocious wind. The Spirit brings order out of chaos and beauty out of ugliness. He can transform a sin-blistered man into a paragon of virtue. The Spirit changes people. The Author of life is also the Transformer of life.

—R. C. SPROUL (1939–), American theologian, author, and pastor

10 A CALL TO BE FEARLESS

THIS IS MY COMMAND—BE STRONG AND COURAGEOUS! DO NOT BE AFRAID OR DISCOURAGED. FOR THE LORD YOUR GOD IS WITH YOU WHEREVER YOU GO.

Joshua 1:9

JOSHUA WAS about to step into some big shoes. Moses had died and left his position of leadership to Joshua. The Scripture describes Moses like this: "There has never been another prophet in Israel like Moses, whom the LORD knew face to face" (Deuteronomy 34:10). We can easily understand that Joshua needed reassurance.

The same promise God made to Joshua he reaffirms to all his children throughout his Word. Jesus speaks the same promise in Matthew 28:20: "Be sure of this: I am with you always, even to the end of the age."

So many times his call is introduced with similar words: *Do not be afraid.*

Why would we be afraid? Because he comes to call us to tasks so big we could never accomplish them and would never dare to undertake them on our own. He comes to assign us a place in his plan. And with his command comes his power.

He prefaces his call on *our* lives with the same statement: *Do not be afraid.* He is not sending us out on our own to muddle through the best we can. He is inviting us to be the vessels through which he will work. He is inviting us to let him impregnate us with his desires, to gestate his vision in us, and then to bring it into the world through our lives. A big call, to be sure, but introduced with the words *Do not be afraid.*

Is there something in your life that you feel drawn to but are afraid to attempt? Does insecurity become a weapon wielded skillfully by your enemy to hold you back and paralyze you? Would you be willing to listen with a newly responsive heart to God's call when you hear his promise, "Do not be afraid or discouraged. For the LORD your God is with you wherever you go"?

Lord, your call comes to me with a promise. A promise of power. A promise of provision. A promise of your presence. I will not fear.

Jennifer

Fear is born of Satan, and if we would only take time to think a moment we would see that everything Satan says is founded upon a falsehood. He is the father of lies.

—A. B. SIMPSON (1843–1919), Canadian preacher, theologian, and author

REMEMBER

JOSHUA SAID TO THE ISRAELITES, "IN THE FUTURE YOUR CHILDREN WILL ASK, 'WHAT DO THESE STONES MEAN?' THEN YOU CAN TELL THEM, 'THIS IS WHERE THE ISRAELITES CROSSED THE JORDAN ON DRY GROUND.' FOR THE LORD YOUR GOD DRIED UP THE RIVER RIGHT BEFORE YOUR EYES, AND HE KEPT IT DRY UNTIL YOU WERE ALL ACROSS, JUST AS HE DID AT THE RED SEA. . . . HE DID THIS SO ALL THE NATIONS OF THE EARTH MIGHT KNOW THAT THE LORD'S HAND IS POWERFUL, AND SO YOU MIGHT FEAR THE LORD YOUR GOD FOREVER."

Joshua 4:21-24

THE BIBLE is full of reminders to God's people to remember his mighty deeds. He calls us to remember because looking at what God has done in the past builds our faith for the present and for the future. He is promising that the same power he has demonstrated in the past is available in the present.

In today's verses, Joshua is addressing the people after God had brought them across the Jordan River on dry land and into the Promised Land. Joshua tells them to build a memorial of this event, an altar they could see and touch and return to when they needed a reminder of who God is and what God had done in their lives.

When my sons were little, my husband told them this story, and then he established a new tradition. He bought a small fishbowl and a bag of quarter-sized rocks. It was summer, and school was out. Throughout the summer days, whenever we saw evidence of God's work in our lives, even in the little things, we would put a rock in the bowl. The days became like treasure hunts because we were always on the lookout for signs of God's hand.

I had forgotten about that experiment until today, as I was thinking about this passage. I now realize that what was intended to be a visual for our boys turned out also to be a reminder for my husband and me. Building an altar of memory stones created in us an alertness to God's hand in our lives.

Lord, let my life be an altar and a tangible expression of your power and provision.

Jennifer

Let us remember the loving-kindness of the Lord and rehearse His deeds of grace. Let us open the volume of recollection, which is so richly illuminated with memories of His mercy, and we will soon be happy.

—**ALISTAIR BEGG** (1952–), Scottish pastor, radio preacher, and author

12 EXPLOSIVE FAITH

THE LORD SAID TO JOSHUA, "I HAVE GIVEN YOU JERICHO, ITS KING, AND ALL ITS STRONG WARRIORS."

Joshua 6:2

AS GOD WAS SPEAKING these words, the Israelites were standing outside the fortified city of Jericho. It was surrounded by two parallel walls about fifteen feet apart.

Jericho was no illusion. There it stood—fortressed, barricaded, impenetrable. To the Israelites' physical sight, taking Jericho was difficult, if not hopeless. Cities such as Jericho had convinced ten of the twelve spies sent to scout out the land forty years earlier that Israel could not conquer it (see Numbers 13:27-28). Fear activated by the sight of such an intimidating obstacle had already stolen forty years as well as an entire generation of people. Now, everything their eyes could see told them that this was still a lost cause.

But when God spoke to Joshua and called him to battle, he said, "I *have given you* Jericho" (emphasis added). The verb tense indicated that it was already a done deal. Finished work. Just waiting for the people's obedience to bring that completed promise into their experience.

The writer of Hebrews tells the story in a few well-chosen words: "It was by faith that the people of Israel marched around Jericho for seven days, and the walls came crashing down" (Hebrews 11:30). When the people obeyed the Lord's command and marched around Jericho for seven days, the walls fell.

When the promise of God comes into contact with our faith-fueled obedience, an explosion of power results. Walls fall. Obstacles disappear. Enemies flee.

You may be looking at a Jericho today. Maybe something in your life looks too big for you. Your enemy might be pointing out all the reasons why your obstacle will win the day. If so, remember this: when God calls you to battle, he has already won the victory. The only way your Jericho will stand is if you believe your limited perceptions instead of God's Word and slink away, missing the opportunity to see God's power in action.

Father, teach me to walk by faith and not by sight. I believe you, not my own perceptions and interpretations. I receive your victory.

Jennifer

How shall I feel at the judgement, if multitudes of missed opportunities pass before me in full review, and all my excuses prove to be disguises of my cowardice and pride?

—WILLIAM EDWIN SANGSTER (1900–1960), English pastor

FOR THE LOVE OF GOD

IF YOU ARE FAITHFUL IN LITTLE THINGS, YOU WILL BE FAITHFUL IN LARGE ONES. BUT IF YOU ARE DISHONEST IN LITTLE THINGS, YOU WON'T BE HONEST WITH GREATER RESPONSIBILITIES.

Luke 16:10

TRAINING IN the small things is where the seeds of big things can be found.

Only when the Lord has taught you to do the small, behind-the-scenes, unnoticed work with integrity and joy can he entrust you with the bigger things. The key is to learn to do the work God calls you to for love of him only.

Very early in my ministry, when I was young and untried, I was invited to speak at an event and anticipated a good attendance. When I arrived, the attendance was very low. I was exhausted and discouraged. I went to a private room to prepare, thinking that I would just give the message I had outlined and get back home as soon as I could. But the Lord spoke so clearly to my heart in that moment: *You speak to these few women as if they were thousands. You give full measure, pressed down, shaken together, running over. The mark of a servant who serves me out of love is that she will be faithful in the small things as if they were large.* I heard that message so clearly. It changed my attitude forever. That night I gave all I had to those women God had brought, and I saw the power of God demonstrated. Years later I was still hearing from women who were there and saw God change lives. I saw what God could do when my pride was out of his way, and nothing else would ever satisfy me again. Large crowds? I don't care. Large power? I can't live without it.

Embrace this promise in your life: the small things matter. In God's eyes, small is big. Put your whole heart into whatever small opportunity for obedience meets you. It matters.

> Lord, let my obedience in this small thing loom large. I offer you my faithfulness in the obscure and unnoticed moments as pure worship. When no one else sees, there's nothing in it for me except your pleasure.
>
> *Jennifer*

I prefer the monotony of obscure sacrifice to all ecstasies. To pick up a pin for love can convert a soul.

—**THERESE DE LISIEUX** (1873–1897), French nun and writer

14 FAITH TO MOVE A MOUNTAIN

IF YOU HAD FAITH EVEN AS SMALL AS A MUSTARD SEED, YOU
COULD SAY TO THIS MULBERRY TREE, "MAY YOU BE UPROOTED
AND THROWN INTO THE SEA," AND IT WOULD OBEY YOU!

Luke 17:6

A BEDRIDDEN young girl lay in the dormitory of a Christian orphanage in Japan. After
World War II, she had been left to die by a society that placed no value on the lives of the
many half-Japanese/half-American children. One evening the girl heard a sermon on how
having faith—even as small as a mustard seed—can enable a person through prayer to
accomplish great things, like moving mountains or asking God to uproot a tree and cast it
into the sea. She was struck by this, because her greatest desire was to see Japan's Inland
Sea again. She was too ill to go to the beach herself, and a large mountain sat between the
orphanage building and the sea, blocking her view.

At bedtime she prayed that God would move that mountain. Irene, the missionary
director, said gently, "No, child. God wouldn't want to move a big mountain like that.
He meant we should pray about the big mountains of trials in our lives." But the little girl
continued to pray, and the other orphan girls gathered at her bedside, praying together for
God to move the mountain. Irene went on furlough in England for several months, and
when she returned, she saw the girls clustered in front of the window. Looking out, Irene
could hardly believe what she saw—the Inland Sea in full view!

"We saw many bulldozers going up and down the mountain moving dirt," they
explained. Irene checked with town officials and found that because the coastal waves
were eroding the land, the earth had to be moved from the mountain to backfill the coast-
line. Sure enough, the workers had moved the mountain and "cast it into the sea." A few
months later, the orphan who had prayed with mountain-moving faith died. And although
the old orphanage has been torn down, many years later the view of the Inland Sea is still
there, reminding us of that little girl's great lesson in faith.

*Lord, grant us the faith to believe all your promises and to pray with
perseverance, trusting you to move even things that look immovable
and impossible.*

Cheri

Faith comes from looking at God, not at the mountain.
—BILL HYBELS (1951–), American pastor

SPRINGS OF JOY

WHAT JOY FOR THOSE WHOSE STRENGTH COMES FROM
THE LORD
WHO HAVE SET THEIR MINDS ON A PILGRIMAGE TO JERUSALEM.
WHEN THEY WALK THROUGH THE VALLEY OF WEEPING,
IT WILL BECOME A PLACE OF REFRESHING SPRINGS.
THE AUTUMN RAINS WILL CLOTHE IT WITH BLESSINGS.

Psalm 84:5-6

WHEN THE PSALMIST penned these words, Jerusalem was where the presence of God dwelt. For us, however, the presence of God is not in one physical location but in us, with us, around us, and always available. He is always present to us, but we are not always present to him. For us, setting our minds on a pilgrimage to Jerusalem means learning to be mindful of the ever-presentness of God. It means to make it our determined purpose to be always aware of and open to his continual activity.

Having set our minds on this pilgrimage—to move from self-centered living to Godward living—we will be making this journey through the Valley of Weeping. Earth and time are not our home. We are strangers and aliens here. Our home is eternity. So don't be surprised that earth's landscape is often unfriendly. We were made for another biosphere, and we will never be fully assimilated into our earthly environment. The traversing of this terrain will always include tears and sorrow along the way.

God never promises that you will not walk in the Valley of Weeping, but he does promise that the Valley of Weeping will also have places of refreshing springs. The presence of God can makes gardens in the wasteland: "He also turns deserts into pools of water, the dry land into springs of water (Psalm 107:35).

Father, I am not at home here; I am passing through. Your presence is my only destination, and you have promised that my springs of joy will be found in you.

Jennifer

Transiency is stamped on all our possessions, occupations, and delights. We have the hunger for eternity in our souls, the thought of eternity in our hearts, the destination for eternity written on our inmost being, and the need to ally ourselves with eternity proclaimed by the most short-lived trifles of time. Either these things will be the blessing or the curse of our lives. Which do you mean that they shall be for you?

—**ALEXANDER MACLAREN** (1826–1910), British preacher and Bible expositor

16 TO WHOM SHOULD I GO?

ONE DAY JESUS TOLD HIS DISCIPLES A STORY TO SHOW THAT THEY
SHOULD ALWAYS PRAY AND NEVER GIVE UP.

Luke 18:1

LUKE RECORDS a parable that Jesus told with the express purpose of teaching this one lesson: pray and never give up. All wrapped up in that instruction is the promise that prayer works. All the time.

Why would Jesus tell a parable with such a specific focus and goal? Obviously he knew that his disciples would have experiences in prayer that would make them want to give up. He knew times would come when prayer felt like knocking on a door that no one was answering.

Look at the characters Jesus created: two people from the extreme opposite ends of society's order—a judge and a widow. The judge had absolute power. He answered to no one. He made decisions about people's lives. A widow was one of society's most defenseless beings. A widow in the Palestine of Jesus' day had no voice. She could cry out day and night, and no one had to pay any attention to her. She had no way to stand up for herself.

This widow had a need, and she knew that only the judge had the power to do what she needed to have done. So she kept knocking on his door. She was not dissuaded by the fact that he did not care about her. She did not give up, because *she had nowhere else to go*. She didn't keep trying to do battle with her adversaries. She didn't keep trying to manipulate the situation until she got what she wanted. She knew where her answer could be found.

The judge is the opposite of God. If this judge, loathsome as he was, gave the widow what she needed, surely the Father, who loves you, will give you what you need.

Sometimes in prayer, you will feel like the widow. You will feel as if you are being ignored. If, like the widow, you keep knocking in spite of how discouraged you feel, you will find that your Father has indeed heard and has been responding from the very first knock.

> *Lord, you are our hope and our salvation. We come to you because you have the words that give eternal life.*

Jennifer

Prayer is not overcoming God's reluctance, but laying hold of His willingness.
—**MARTIN LUTHER** (1483–1546), German theologian and reformer

A BLIND BEGGAR WAS SITTING BESIDE THE ROAD. WHEN HE HEARD THE NOISE OF A CROWD GOING PAST, HE ASKED WHAT WAS HAPPENING. THEY TOLD HIM THAT JESUS THE NAZARENE WAS GOING BY. SO HE BEGAN SHOUTING, "JESUS, SON OF DAVID, HAVE MERCY ON ME!"

Luke 18:35-38

"THAT'S A VERY nice story," a woman in my Bible study commented after our teacher had read the story of the blind beggar's healing. "But what relevance does it have for us today? My pastor always taught that this kind of miracle happened only in Bible times."

I knew from personal experience that God is still bringing healing and wholeness to his people, so I shared my story with her. Although it wasn't anywhere near as dire a need as the blind man's, when I was thirty-five, I had developed a severe inflammation in my ribs. I could barely move without pain (a problem when you have three active children to care for), and when I coughed, laughed, turned over in bed, or even took a deep breath, it felt like a knife sticking in my chest. The doctor said it would take weeks, perhaps months, to heal; in the meantime, there was nothing to do but take aspirin.

Nevertheless, my husband and I came to Jesus with this need, believing that prayer was inviting Jesus into our infirmities and concerns. So we asked the Lord to heal my painful ribs. A week or more went by. Then one Sunday our pastor stopped in the middle of his sermon and said he sensed the Lord wanted to heal someone. His description of inflamed ribs sounded just like what I'd been experiencing. When he offered to pray for that person, I quietly got out of my chair and went to the front. After his simple prayer of faith in Christ's name, I took a few deep breaths and realized every bit of pain was gone—completely gone—and it never returned. God's power had touched my point of need, and I praised him. So did my husband and all the others who attended that day.

Thank you, Lord our Healer, that you are willing and able to touch the smallest to the greatest of our physical, emotional, and spiritual needs.

Cheri

Will we give Jesus access to our needs? That is the one great fundamental question in connection with prayer.

—**OLE HALLESBY** (1879–1961), Norwegian pastor and writer

18

THE PROMISE OF NEW LIFE

JESUS [SAID], "SALVATION HAS COME TO THIS HOME TODAY, FOR THIS MAN HAS SHOWN HIMSELF TO BE A TRUE SON OF ABRAHAM. FOR THE SON OF MAN CAME TO SEEK AND SAVE THOSE WHO ARE LOST."

Luke 19:9-10

JESUS KNEW all about Zacchaeus, the little man who sat in a sycamore tree to see him better. Yet he offered him salvation and forgiveness. Although Zacchaeus was a son of Abraham by birth, his salvation didn't come from his standing as an Israelite but from his connection with Christ. After that encounter, many were outraged that Jesus would visit the home of a sinner, but he responded that his mission and purpose were "to seek and save those who are lost."

The man speaking to our leadership class as we were touring a prison wore gray clothes with "Department of Corrections" across the back of his shirt. He had been incarcerated most of his adult life, after first selling drugs early in life and a few years later being involved in a bar fight in which a man was killed. Although he was serving a life sentence, he had experienced the greatest miracle of all—salvation. In a Kairos spiritual retreat in the prison, the man had a life-changing encounter with Jesus, and he turned his life over to God. "I've never been happier in life because of the new beginning the Lord gave me. We're all really broken people in here. But though I'm behind bars, I have peace for the first time in my life," he said.

In discovering that God had purchased his freedom with Christ's blood and had forgiven all his sins, this prisoner was set free. Now he spends his time teaching Bible studies and helping young guys who are newly behind bars know Christ.

Lord, your love and salvation know no barriers. And just like this prisoner and Zacchaeus, I, too, am a sinner in need of your grace. Thank you with all my heart that you came to seek and save those who are lost.

Cheri

In new birth God does three impossible things: the first is to make a man's past as though it had never been; the second, to make a man all over again, and the third, to make a man as certain of God as God is of himself.

—**OSWALD CHAMBERS** (1874–1917), Scottish minister and teacher

A HOUSE OF PRAYER

JESUS ENTERED THE TEMPLE AND BEGAN TO DRIVE OUT THE
PEOPLE SELLING ANIMALS FOR SACRIFICES. HE SAID TO THEM,
"THE SCRIPTURES DECLARE, 'MY TEMPLE WILL BE A HOUSE OF
PRAYER,' BUT YOU HAVE TURNED IT INTO A DEN OF THIEVES."

Luke 19:45-46

OFTEN WHEN we read this passage and the corresponding passages in Matthew and Mark, we're struck by Jesus' forceful ousting of the merchants from the Temple. What struck me this time, however, wasn't the action Jesus took but the reason behind it: the Scriptures had declared that his Father's house was to be a house of prayer. Not a den of thieves, a bank where money is exchanged, or a local market—but a place of prayer. It wasn't the first or last time a religious group would seek to make God's house into something other than its intended purpose. Throughout history there have been (and are today) churches that resemble social clubs or social activist groups more than houses of prayer.

Yet the enduring promise in the words of Luke 19 is this: no matter what humanity tries to turn God's house into, his communities of people will ultimately come back to his intended purpose as people of prayer. In a sense, these verses are a call to continual, earnest prayer—prayer that includes praise and adoration, confession, intervention on behalf of those who are sick, intercession for our cities and nation and for missionaries to take the gospel to the ends of the earth, and thanksgiving for who God is and for the blessings he has given us through his Son's life, death, and resurrection. Would you pray that your church and all churches throughout this country and around the world will become what the Father has desired all along—houses of prayer?

> *Oh Lord, forgive us for all the ways we neglect prayer in our personal and community life. Restore us to spiritual awakening and grant us the Spirit of prayer. In Christ's name and for his glory, amen.*
>
> *Cheri*

Jesus Christ carries on intercession for us in heaven; the Holy Ghost carries on intercession in us on earth; and we the saints have to carry on intercession for all men.

—OSWALD CHAMBERS (1874–1917), Scottish minister and teacher

20 WHO CAN COMPARE WITH THE LORD?

ALL HEAVEN WILL PRAISE YOUR GREAT WONDERS, LORD;
MYRIADS OF ANGELS WILL PRAISE YOU FOR YOUR FAITHFULNESS.
FOR WHO IN ALL OF HEAVEN CAN COMPARE WITH THE LORD?
WHAT MIGHTIEST ANGEL IS ANYTHING LIKE THE LORD?

Psalm 89:5-6

IN OUR childhood years, wonder is a natural response to the miracles of nature—the green-striped caterpillar, the sparkling night sky, a butterfly's wings. Our sense of wonder and amazement often diminishes in adulthood as we become preoccupied with the reality of work and other responsibilities. But as the psalmist pens these praiseful verses, he is filled with wonder at God's miracles in creation and in his working in humanity. Wonder: an awe-filled response to God that leads to praise and worship. Wonder: a sense of surprise or state of amazed admiration. Wonder: experiencing something far beyond anything we've previously known.

Wonder must have been what the Israelites felt when Moses stretched out his staff over the Red Sea and the waters parted to cut a pathway for them to walk safely to the other side. It must have been what young David felt when he slung a stone at the giant Philistine warrior Goliath and watched him keel over. What the astonished onlookers must have felt when Lazarus walked out of the tomb at Jesus' command, or what the disciples experienced as Jesus fed the five thousand with only a few loaves of bread and a couple of fish.

Does God still do things that inspire us? God didn't create everything in the world gray or leave everything unscented. Instead, in his creative grace, he has given us rich blessings in the world around us.

Look around you and be amazed at his "little" miracles and the mystery of his grace. Ask for eyes and ears that are sensitive to his faithful working in your life and in the lives of those around you. For "who in all of heaven can compare with the LORD?"

Father God, you have created all things in the heavens and on earth, visible and invisible. You are worthy to receive glory, honor, and praise. Thank you for your wondrous miracles!

Cheri

Joy is to behold God in everything.
—JULIAN OF NORWICH (c. 1342–after 1413), English Christian mystic and writer

A GOD YOU CAN TRUST

Happy are those who hear the joyful call to worship,
    for they will walk in the light of your presence, Lord.
They rejoice all day long in your wonderful reputation.
    They exult in your righteousness.
You are their glorious strength.
    It pleases you to make us strong.

Psalm 89:15-17

ONE OF THE marvelous things about reading the Bible is that throughout its pages we are given hundreds of snapshots of who God is and what his character and nature are like. His Word declares that God is gracious and compassionate, holy and awesome. He is our shelter in the storm. He is the Lord who provides and forgives and the one who gives us inner peace regardless of our circumstances.

In today's verses, we learn that God is righteous, that he is our source of strength, and that any power or influence we have comes from his favor. How kind of God that he didn't hide his nature or didn't leave us alone to figure out what he is like or didn't intend for us to take the opinions of CNN or our culture about who he is. This is of crucial importance because *you will not trust a God you do not know.*

God reveals himself throughout his Word because he wants us to know *him*, not just about him and what others say he's like. Discovering God's reputation as revealed in his interaction with men and nations throughout history is important, but he wants us to hear his voice speaking to us through the Scriptures, lighting our paths through daily life. We will never fully know God's greatness until we see him face-to-face, but when we read his Word, we discover more of who he is and are drawn closer to him. Just think: the infinite, almighty God, maker of heaven and earth, wants us to live in intimate relationship with him. This news will cause us to hear the joyful call to worship and rejoice in the Lord daily.

Oh God, how gracious you are to reveal yourself to us through your Word, through Jesus, and through your Holy Spirit. Thank you for the gift of salvation, which allows us to walk with you and talk with you every day we live.

Cheri

Only God is permanently interesting. Other things we may fathom, but he out-tops our thought and can neither be demonstrated nor argued down.

—JOSEPH FORT NEWTON (1880–1950), American pastor and author

22 SMALL IS THE NEW BIG

"I TELL YOU THE TRUTH," JESUS SAID, "THIS POOR WIDOW HAS
GIVEN MORE THAN ALL THE REST OF THEM. FOR THEY HAVE GIVEN
A TINY PART OF THEIR SURPLUS, BUT SHE, POOR AS SHE IS, HAS
GIVEN EVERYTHING SHE HAS."

Luke 21:3-4

JESUS SAW numerous displays of wealth as the pillars and leaders of the community dropped their offerings—many of them with great fanfare—into the treasury chests that sat in the Temple's outer courtyard.

Jesus didn't dismiss the gifts of the wealthy, but he did call attention to the widow's gift. In a setting where many were hoping to be noticed and admired, the widow quietly gave her gift, assuming it to be so paltry that it would not make any difference. She was not giving out of a desire to be admired but out of love and obedience. That's what set her gift apart. That's what gave her gift its heft. The value of our monetary gifts to the Kingdom is that they are a measure of our hearts.

The most important gift given that day was the smallest gift of all, given extravagantly. The amount of money we give to support Kingdom causes really doesn't matter. God can multiply small gifts and use them to accomplish big results. If the wealthiest people on earth were to give all they have to the work of the Kingdom, it would be a small amount. God values a gargantuan sum no more than he does the widow's gift. What matters is what your financial gifts to the Kingdom say about your priorities.

God knows how easily we can come to love money and let it dictate our lives, influence our decisions, determine our emotional states. Money can become an idol faster than almost anything you can name. That's why God wants us to remember that it is all his.

Why do you think he chooses to finance his work and meet the needs of his children through the financial gifts of his people? I think he allows his people to give because their obedience releases his abundance.

Father, everything I have is yours. Use it as you will.

Jennifer

God doesn't need us to give Him our money. He owns everything. Tithing is God's way to grow Christians.

—ADRIAN ROGERS (1931–2005), American pastor and author

THE PROMISE OF PROTECTION

> HE WILL ORDER HIS ANGELS
>   TO PROTECT YOU WHEREVER YOU GO.
> THEY WILL HOLD YOU UP WITH THEIR HANDS
>   SO YOU WON'T EVEN HURT YOUR FOOT ON A STONE.
>
> *Psalm 91:11-12*

THESE VERSES are very good news when you are on a plane or have a son or daughter in active duty in the air force. When my friend Dorothy's son Richard was in training flying T-38s, he was excited about his dream job. He and the other pilot-in-training would fly in formation at extremely high speeds, thrilled at every assignment and challenge they were given. Not so his mom! She was panicked for her son. In Arizona, skies were blue every day, and that meant Richard would be up there streaking through the sky. Worry totally occupied her mind.

During this time, a friend visited for lunch. After Dorothy poured out her worries, her friend said, "Dorothy, I'm ashamed of you! Why are you worried about your son? Don't you know God loves him a lot more than you do?" The friend suggested Dorothy pray for the Lord to assign an angel to fly on Richard's wing.

From then on, Dorothy didn't worry about her son. She prayed every day for an angel to fly on the wing of his plane and trusted that God's angel would protect Richard wherever he went. Flying in the air force and later for a commercial airline, he has had close calls, flying in dense fog, storms, and even blizzards. But time after time, his mom saw that the angel on his wing brought him safely home.

Wherever we or our loved ones are, God is there. Psalm 139 assures us that even if we go up to the heavens, he is there. If we rise on the wings of the dawn or settle on the far side of the sea, even there God's hand will guide us and hold us fast.

All your promises prove true, and your children are held safe in the palm of your hand. Thank you for your ministering angels that watch over us and protect us wherever we go. In Christ's name, amen.

Cheri

It seems to be God's plan to allow all sorts of things to happen that would naturally cause fear, but to forestall them by the assurance of his presence.

—**AMY CARMICHAEL** (1867–1951), Irish missionary to India

24 GIVE THANKS

IT IS GOOD TO GIVE THANKS TO THE LORD,
  TO SING PRAISES TO THE MOST HIGH.
IT IS GOOD TO PROCLAIM YOUR UNFAILING LOVE
  IN THE MORNING,
  YOUR FAITHFULNESS IN THE EVENING.

Psalm 92:1-2

WHAT IF we started each day doing just what this psalm describes: giving thanks to the Lord in the morning and proclaiming his love and faithfulness at bedtime? As these verses say, "*It is good* to give thanks to the LORD" (emphasis added). Throughout the Bible we find encouragement to thank God. Psalm 79:13 encourages us to thank God forever and praise his greatness from generation to generation, and Philippians 4:6-9 promises that those who present their requests *with thanksgiving* will receive the peace of God.

Yet how often when we pray we forget to thank God for the ways he has blessed us! We're a bit like the nine lepers who didn't take time to go back and thank Jesus for their miraculous healing (see Luke 17:17). Just as a spirit of humility draws us to God, thanksgiving is a key to power in prayer; it is a powerful agent of transformation. Research shows thanksgiving can even change our brain chemistry for the better. Giving thanks helps our faith grow and draws us to the heart of God. Gratitude is the door to giving and receiving love and joy.

Most of all, thanking God gets our eyes off me-myself-and-I-and-my-problems and directs our focus to the King of kings and Lord of lords. Let me encourage you to give thanks to God, and as you do, you'll be reminded that he is present in your life in this moment and throughout your days.

Gracious Lord, so often in the muddle and busyness of life I forget to thank you.
But you are good, full of unfailing love and faithfulness. Thank you for these
blessings that fill my life. Grant me a thankful spirit, I pray, in Christ's name.

Cheri

It is only with gratitude that life becomes rich.

—DIETRICH BONHOEFFER (1906–1945), German pastor, theologian, and author

DESTINED 25

I CRIED OUT, "I AM SLIPPING!"
BUT YOUR UNFAILING LOVE, O LORD, SUPPORTED ME.
WHEN DOUBTS FILLED MY MIND,
YOUR COMFORT GAVE ME RENEWED HOPE AND CHEER.

Psalm 94:18-19

FEAR OF FAILURE can stop us in our tracks. It can keep us from taking the next step and keep us frozen in place. Can you fathom this promise? Anytime you slip, the Lord is there to catch you. You can't fall flat, because "the LORD directs the steps of the godly. He delights in every detail of their lives. Though they stumble, they will never fall, for the LORD holds them by the hand" (Psalm 37:23-24).

You exist because it is God's purpose and desire that you exist: "You created all things, and they exist because you created what you pleased" (Revelation 4:11).

You are not random. You are deliberately created and designed and placed on earth at the right time, in the right place, with the right gifts and talents: "We are God's masterpiece. He has created us anew in Christ Jesus, so we can do the good things he planned for us long ago" (Ephesians 2:10).

You were born for a purpose tailor made for you. You don't have to cram yourself into it or bear up under it: "You saw me before I was born. . . . Every moment was laid out before a single day had passed" (Psalm 139:16).

A sense of destiny comes from recognizing purpose. God fuses the hard times and confusing circumstances and seeming setbacks into an understanding of destiny. Only when you view each circumstance as a significant piece of a whole will you begin to see life as integrated and meaningful.

Lord, direct my steps. Hold my hand. I embrace your purpose for my life and step out fearlessly in response to your call.

Jennifer

The man who measures things by the circumstances of the hour is filled with fear; the man who sees Jehovah enthroned and governing has no panic.

—G. CAMPBELL MORGAN (1863–1945), English evangelist, preacher, and Bible scholar

26 THE STRENGTH YOU HAVE

The Lord turned to [Gideon] and said, "Go with the strength you have, and rescue Israel from the Midianites. I am sending you!"

Judges 6:14

IN JUDGES 6, God comes to a young Israelite named Gideon during a time when God's people were being harassed and overrun by the Midianites. Gideon is hiding when God interrupts his life and calls him: "Mighty hero, the Lord is with you!"(v.12). Gideon wants to make sure that God has not accidentally called the wrong person, so he replies, "How can I rescue Israel? My clan is the weakest in the whole tribe of Manasseh, and I am the least in my entire family!" (v. 15). Here's the sentence that got me. After Gideon carefully explains why he cannot possibly be the one for the job, God says to him, "Go with the strength you have, and rescue Israel from the Midianites. I am sending you!"

Whatever you have—surrendered for God's use—will do. In the end, Gideon wins a great victory. But the road to a big victory was paved with a whole lot of small.

The Spirit of the Lord fell on Gideon, and this essentially weak, frightened man began to behave as if he were a mighty hero, even as he sees God downsize his already small army: "You have too many warriors with you. If I let all of you fight the Midianites, the Israelites will boast to me that they saved themselves by their own strength" (7:2).

A silly riddle—the kind that comes on bubble gum wrappers—says, "What gets bigger the more you take away?" The answer is "a hole." But I think we might answer the question "faith." God wants the resources to be scarce so that no one will be confused about the source of the victory. When we learn how to answer a big call with small resources, we have a recipe for flourishing faith. The old, small Gideon had become the mighty hero. When our resources are diminishing, we must trust that the strength we have is the strength we need.

Lord, here I am. The strength I have is yours. Fill in the gaps with yourself.

Jennifer

The will of God will never take you to where the grace of God will not protect you. To gain that which is worth having, it may be necessary to lose everything else.

—**BERNADETTE DEVLIN** (1947–), Irish activist and former member of Parliament

VICTORY SHOUT

Sing a new song to the Lord,
for he has done wonderful deeds.
His right hand has won a mighty victory;
his holy arm has shown his saving power!

Psalm 98:1

HOW STUNNING a victory our God has won for us, overcoming sin and death in the person and work of Jesus. Born a helpless babe, he stormed the enemy's camp and then administered the coup de grâce, the deathblow to the enemy, delivered when his crucifixion gave way to resurrection.

Only he could have devised and then implemented such a plan. Only God could have found the way for heaven to invade earth, not through force or might but through a tiny baby. On that holy night in Bethlehem, the Babe cooed and cried and nursed at Mary's breast. His hands, which would one day feel the tear of nails, curled around her finger. His feet, which would be pierced for my transgressions, kicked the air in the awkwardness of infancy. His head, which would be gouged by thorns, lay peacefully in Mary's arms.

His birth was barely a ripple in the course of humankind's doings, yet he came and changed the balance of power for all eternity. With a battle shout that sounded to earthly ears like a newborn baby's cry, he set in motion our redemption. The sound heard in the heavens that first Christmas moment was one of victory that rattled the enemy's forces and ensured their defeat.

Without him, my thoughts were entangled by the dictates of my flesh. They poisoned and polluted my life. They were infused with the stench of death, corruption, and decay and marched steadily toward the grave.

Then Incarnate Word came to set my captive thoughts free and to captivate my restless mind and anchor it in him.

I was death's child, sin's slave. A mind managed by my flesh. No future but the grave. Until you, Jesus. Thank you for recasting my thoughts into the mold of yours. Teach me how to receive that gift in its fullness. Make me so pliable that my thoughts and intents are reflective of your life in me.

Jennifer

The Son of God has been poured into us, and we have received him, and appropriated him. What a heartful Jesus must be, for heaven itself cannot contain him!

—CHARLES HADDON SPURGEON (1834–1892), English preacher and writer

28 PRESENT TO THE PRESENCE

WHY ARE YOU LOOKING AMONG THE DEAD FOR SOMEONE WHO
IS ALIVE? HE ISN'T HERE! HE IS RISEN FROM THE DEAD!

Luke 24:5-6

WE SERVE a risen, living, present Lord. We don't have to try to find him among musty laws or stale ceremonies or stagnant rituals. We don't seek the Living among the dead.

The promise of a vibrant and attendant Savior, who offers his own power, wisdom, and peace in any given moment is the promise that gathers all other promises into one. He offers himself. When we have him, we have everything the Father has to give:

- God in all his fullness was pleased to live in Christ. (Colossians 1:19)
- In [Christ] lie hidden all the treasures of wisdom and knowledge. (Colossians 2:3)
- In Christ lives all the fullness of God in a human body. So you also are complete through your union with Christ, who is the head over every ruler and authority. (Colossians 2:9-10)

He is so present that he is in you, making himself available to you and through you. He is living in your world, your circumstances. Is there any situation for which Jesus is not adequate? Is there any dilemma for which Jesus does not have wisdom? Is it possible to experience any challenge for which Jesus is not equipped? If you have Jesus—the living-right-now Jesus—then you have all you need.

What concerns you right now? What frightens you? Hand it over to Jesus, who is closer to you and more available to you than any mere human being can ever be. Sit quietly, and let the reality of his presence settle on you. Take time to be aware. Be present to the Presence.

Christ in me, let me live with such keen attentiveness to your indwelling life that you are the focal point that defines how I see every circumstance.

Jennifer

On the first day of Pentecost He returned, not this time to be with them externally—clothed with that sinless humanity that God had prepared for Him, being conceived of the Spirit in the womb of Mary—but now to be in them imparting to them His own divine nature, clothing Himself with their humanity. . . . He spoke with their lips. He worked with their hands. This was the miracle of new birth and this remains the very heart of the gospel.

—**MAJOR W. IAN THOMAS** (1914–2007), English writer and theology teacher

OPEN MINDED 29

HE OPENED THEIR MINDS TO UNDERSTAND THE SCRIPTURES.

Luke 24:45

THE SCRIPTURES make this statement after Jesus' crucifixion and resurrection but before his ascension. It is referring to his disciples, who had been with him for three years, learning from him in a variety of settings. He had been expounding the Scriptures—what we call the Old Testament—day and night. Besides that, they—as Jewish men—knew the Scriptures very well. Probably better than you and I will ever know them. Yet until Jesus himself opened their minds, they did not understand its teachings.

Paul prays in Ephesians 1:17, "I keep asking that the God of our Lord Jesus Christ, the glorious Father, may give you the Spirit of wisdom and revelation, so that you may know him better" (NIV). The word *revelation* means "unveiling or uncovering." The Scriptures say that when you turn to Christ, the veil that lies over your mind is removed (see 2 Corinthians 3:16). The Spirit is continually lifting the veil that hides deep truth so that you see and comprehend more and more of his Word each day. Just as he did for the disciples. God is giving you "spiritual wisdom and insight" so that you will know him better (see Ephesians 1:17-19).

God unveils his truth to our minds in many ways. He has appointed and gifted members in the body through whom he unveils truth. He often uses those who have the gift of teaching or preaching or prophecy, but they are not the source of understanding. God is the only one who can bring understanding of spiritual truth to your mind. Truth comes *from* his Spirit *to* your mind.

God reveals the truth in his Word at progressively deeper levels. Only he can do that. No matter how wonderful you may think a speaker or writer is, he or she cannot give you understanding of the truth spoken. If someone's words have produced new insight in you, it is because Jesus himself has revealed it. Information comes from outside sources; revelation comes from Jesus within you. He promises to open your mind to understand the deep truths of his Word.

Jesus, speak deeply.

Jennifer

Love God, and he will dwell with you. Obey God, and he will reveal to you the truth of his deepest teachings.
—FREDERICK WILLIAM ROBERTSON (1816–1853), English clergyman

30 THE FULLNESS OF CHRIST

FROM HIS ABUNDANCE WE HAVE ALL RECEIVED ONE GRACIOUS
BLESSING AFTER ANOTHER.

John 1:16

JESUS IS the storehouse of all God's treasure. He is full of all the fullness of God. "God in all his fullness was pleased to live in Christ" (Colossians 1:19). *The Message* puts that verse this way: "So spacious is he, so roomy, that everything of God finds its proper place in him without crowding." Jesus is full and overflowing with all that heaven has available, and he fills us up from his own abundance.

This is the surprise that salvation holds. It is both what Christ did for you and who Christ is in you. He forgives our sins because of what he did for us, and he cleanses us of the unrighteousness that causes us to sin because of who he is in us. First John 1:9 says that "he is faithful and just to forgive us our sins and to cleanse us from all wickedness." He poured his life out for us so he could pour his life out in us.

Therefore, we "are complete through [our] union with Christ" (Colossians 2:10). Jesus describes this relationship as that of a vine and a branch. The life that flows in the vine is the life that flows through the branch. This description shows us that it is not a one-time filling, but a continuous flow. A living union. The living Jesus being the Jesus living in us and through us. From his dwelling place in us, he circulates through us, cleansing us and progressively flushing out unrighteousness and pouring out one blessing on top of another.

All we do to receive this promise is to rest in him and let him pour himself into whatever faces us.

> *Jesus, words fail me when I think of the fullness of my salvation. Open my eyes to behold how utterly immense your love is. May I experience your incomprehensible love more fully. Make me complete with all the fullness of life and power that comes from you.*
>
> *Jennifer*

As the cistern receives water from the fulness of the fountain, the branches sap from the fulness of the root, and the air light from the fulness of the sun, so we receive grace from the fulness of Christ.

—**MATTHEW HENRY** (1662–1714), English pastor and Bible commentator

MAY

A SPIRITUAL TRUST FUND

THE CHILDREN OF YOUR PEOPLE
   WILL LIVE IN SECURITY.
THEIR CHILDREN'S CHILDREN
   WILL THRIVE IN YOUR PRESENCE.

Psalm 102:28

WE CAN LEAVE behind a spiritual inheritance for our descendants. Salvation is not inherited, but we can infect future generations so that there is a bent in that direction.

The spiritual inheritance I will leave behind for future generations begins with my own walk with the Lord. "Lord, through all the generations you have been our home!" (Psalm 90:1). Part of my estate is my dwelling place. "The LORD is *my* fortress; my God is the mighty rock where *I* hide" (Psalm 94:22, emphasis added). I have a dwelling place that is also a fortress.

All that I invest in my personal relationship with the Lord will provide spiritual shelter for future generations. I still take refuge in the faith of my parents. When times are hard, their faith, tested and proved through the years, is a safe place for me to run to. Because I have taken shelter there time and again, I have developed my own faith.

As I continue personally to discover new depths of faith, I am building a home place for my own children and for generations to come. As I invest myself in knowing God, I am creating an increasingly secure fortress for my children. "Those who fear the LORD are secure; he will be a refuge for their children" (Proverbs 14:26).

Proverbs 24:3-4 says, "A house is built by wisdom and becomes strong through good sense. Through knowledge its rooms are filled with all sorts of precious riches and valuables." Wisdom is the material of which your dwelling place is built, understanding is its foundation, and knowledge makes it beautiful and pleasant: "There is treasure in the house of the godly" (Proverbs 15:6).

You are creating for your descendants a spiritual home place. As you come to know God for yourself through firsthand experience, your descendants will be the beneficiaries.

Lord, let me invest in eternal treasure and leave a spiritual trust fund for generations to follow.

Jennifer

Every prayer and every sigh which you have uttered for [your descendants] and their future welfare will, in God's time, descend upon them as a gentle rain of answers to prayers.

—**OLE HALLESBY** (1879–1961), Norwegian pastor and writer

2 RESILIENT BY DESIGN

THE LORD IS LIKE A FATHER TO HIS CHILDREN,
TENDER AND COMPASSIONATE TO THOSE WHO FEAR HIM.
FOR HE KNOWS HOW WEAK WE ARE;
HE REMEMBERS WE ARE ONLY DUST.

Psalm 103:13-14

THE OFT-REPEATED metaphor of God as our Father paints a portrait of God's love for us as protecting, providing, guiding, teaching. It's a love that is personal and intimate, tender and compassionate.

Your relationship to God as your Father can be the basis for restful living. Consider who your Father is. The fact that God is your Father is not just a lovely idea or a comforting thought. It has day-by-day, minute-by-minute practical effects in your life. He is your provider. He knows what you need and has already made arrangements to provide it. He's going to take care of you.

Jesus portrayed the Father-heart of God in showing us that God is attentive to us and watchful over us. He directed us to consider how the lilies grow. Effortlessly. Without strain or anxiety. They simply receive what they need. They soak up the sun and the rain that the Father sends. They weather the droughts and endure the harsh seasons and then thrive again. Droughts end. Seasons change. The lilies of the field grow. God created them and designed them to receive and then to flourish.

If he created them so carefully, with resilience built in, surely his blueprint for us includes the ability to flourish under any circumstances. With God as our Father, we can live at peace. He will not lead us into disaster. He will not leave us on our own to wander into danger for which he has not planned our rescue. He always takes into account our frailty and puts his strength in its place. He carries us like a father carries his child. We are safe in his arms.

Dearest Father, you do not leave me exposed to any danger or lack. Though you have a universe to rule and manage, you know and care about the details of my life. God Almighty, Creator, Ruler, Sustainer—my Abba Daddy.

Jennifer

God incarnate is the end of fear, and the heart that realizes that He is in the midst will be quiet in the middle of alarm.

—ALEXANDER MACLAREN (1826–1910), British preacher and Bible expositor

BLOWING WIND

HUMANS CAN REPRODUCE ONLY HUMAN LIFE, BUT THE HOLY SPIRIT GIVES BIRTH TO SPIRITUAL LIFE. SO DON'T BE SURPRISED WHEN I SAY, "YOU MUST BE BORN AGAIN." THE WIND BLOWS WHEREVER IT WANTS. JUST AS YOU CAN HEAR THE WIND BUT CAN'T TELL WHERE IT COMES FROM OR WHERE IT IS GOING, SO YOU CAN'T EXPLAIN HOW PEOPLE ARE BORN OF THE SPIRIT.

John 3:6-8

WIND AND SPIRIT are often paired in Scripture. Both English words are translated from the same Greek or Hebrew words. Those same words are also sometimes translated "breath." Spirit, wind, breath. I assume that Jesus was using a familiar earthly concept—wind—to explain an unfamiliar spiritual one.

Those who have been born again, or given new life by the Spirit, have the Spirit of God dwelling in them. They have the resources of the Spirit and can access the mind of the Spirit. They are born into a new way of looking at life.

Jesus compared the ways of the Spirit with the ways of wind. The wind has no material substance. You don't know where it comes from or where it's going. You can't grab hold of it and feel its texture. You only know wind because you can see its effects.

Suppose, then, that some people decide they do not believe in the wind. They will believe that trees lean over all by themselves or that leaves lying quietly on the ground sometimes suddenly jump up and twirl through the air. They will ascribe power where there is no power. They will not understand that the trees and the leaves are responding to a power that is acting on them.

If a person who does not believe in the wind and a person who does look at the same scene, they will see two startlingly different realities. The first will see trees bending over; the second will see the wind blowing. That person will not be limited to time-bound, earthbound perceptions and shortsighted vision. He or she will also recognize the work of the wind.

Jesus, I want to see the Wind blowing in my life. Sharpen the eyes of my heart so that I will recognize your work when I see it.

Jennifer

We can set our sails to catch the wind from heaven when God chooses to blow upon His people.

—G. CAMPBELL MORGAN (1863-1945), British evangelist and Bible scholar

4 WHAT'S MINE IS HIS

JOHN REPLIED, "NO ONE CAN RECEIVE ANYTHING UNLESS GOD GIVES IT FROM HEAVEN."

John 3:27

JOHN THE BAPTIST had cornered the market on the repentance message, and people were streaming to him to hear his blunt, pointed preaching. John's disciples had a personal investment in his ministry. They were identified with him and his message and had made personal sacrifices in order to follow him. Whatever affected his ministry affected them.

Now Jesus had come on the scene, and the crowds were drawing away from John the Baptist. Jesus' message and John's were the same: turn away from your sins and turn to God, for the Kingdom of Heaven is near. You can imagine the concern of John's disciples that a new upstart rabbi was appealing to the same crowds that had once followed their leader, so they aired their concerns to John: "Rabbi, the man you met on the other side of the Jordan River, the one you identified as the Messiah, is also baptizing people. And everybody is going to him instead of coming to us" (v. 26).

This is the setting in which John spoke the words in today's verse, defining a promise that John understood and lived by. When success comes into your life, it is because God has given it. When success comes to another, it is because God has given it. When John's audience began to shift to Jesus, that was the pinnacle of John's success. That was the reason for his ministry—to hand it all over to Jesus.

What might you feel competitive about? Or proud about? Or possessive about? Is there anyone whose success causes you feelings of bitterness instead of pleasure?

Listen to this promise: "No one can receive anything unless God gives it from heaven." Can you rest in the truth of these words and release any sense of slight or of ownership? If you do, you will find rest for your soul.

Lord, thank you for what you have designated and assigned. My greatest success is to hand everything over to you.

Jennifer

If someone is leaving you behind, and you are becoming jealous and embittered, keep praying that he may have success in the very matter where he is awakening your envy; and whether he is helped or not, one thing is sure, that your own soul will be cleansed and ennobled.

—**WILLIAM LAW** (1686–1761), British theologian and writer

NOURISHED BY OBEDIENCE

JESUS EXPLAINED, "MY NOURISHMENT COMES FROM DOING THE WILL OF GOD, WHO SENT ME, AND FROM FINISHING HIS WORK."

John 4:34

JESUS HAD BEEN TRAVELING and was tired and hungry when he came to a stopping place beside a well in Samaria. The disciples had gone into the village to buy food. When they returned, he was busy ministering to the people streaming from the village because of the testimony of a woman whose life he had transformed.

What had reenergized Jesus? Doing what God had sent him to do.

Following the will of God in your life is invigorating. Of course you need nourishment and rest for your physical body, but it is amazing how physical energy flows from a super-natural wellspring when we are doing what God has called us to do.

My first ministry event after my husband's death was only six weeks after he had died. I was a bona fide emotional mess. I couldn't focus, couldn't talk without crying, melted down at the slightest thing. I couldn't imagine how I would manage, but I felt strongly that the Lord had told me to be about my Father's business. Grieving didn't stop. I carried it with me wherever I went. Until the minute I stepped onto the stage to speak, I was a wreck in every way.

But when my foot hit the platform, peace descended on me. I felt the change physically in what I can describe only as power holding me up. I was me again. I spoke the message just as I always had. As soon as I walked down off the platform, I was a messy puddle of emotions. But I had learned that no matter what, God's anointing will meet me when I step into the call of God on my life.

That dramatic moment is burned into my innermost being. From that lesson, I know as never before that obedience is met with empowerment at the instant it is needed.

Thank you for the strength that comes with the command to obey.

Jennifer

There's some task which the God of all the universe, the great Creator, your redeemer in Jesus Christ has for you to do, and which will remain undone and incomplete until by faith and obedience you step into the will of God.

—**ALAN REDPATH** (1907–1989), English evangelist, pastor, and author

6 FROM CROWN OF THORNS TO CROWN OF GLORY

HE CALLED FOR A FAMINE ON THE LAND OF CANAAN,
   CUTTING OFF ITS FOOD SUPPLY.
THEN HE SENT SOMEONE TO EGYPT AHEAD OF THEM—
   JOSEPH, WHO WAS SOLD AS A SLAVE.

Psalm 105:16-17

THE NATION of Israel was in its infancy, only about seventy-five in number. They were living as strangers and nomads in the land of Canaan. They were "few in number, a tiny group of strangers in Canaan" (Psalm 105:12). But God intended to grow them into a mighty nation, great both in number and in character. He intended for them to possess the land where they now lived as wanderers. He had revealed his *will*, but his *ways* are beyond understanding (see Romans 11:33). Don't be discouraged about what he is doing because of how he is doing it.

What did God need to do in order to make his will for Israel a reality? He needed to give Israel a safe place to grow, prosper, learn skills, and multiply. He needed to put them under the protection of a larger, more advanced civilization for a time. He needed them in Egypt, so "he sent someone to Egypt ahead of them—Joseph, who was sold as a slave" (Psalm 105:17).

God had promised Joseph that he would be a great leader. Now it looked as if Joseph's evil brothers had sent him to Egypt and God's will was being thwarted. But Joseph explained it later to his brothers like this: "God has sent me ahead of you to keep you and your families alive and to preserve many survivors. So it was God who sent me here, not you!" (Genesis 45:7-8). God used seemingly adverse circumstances to position Joseph for receiving the promise.

How did God get Israel out of Canaan and into Egypt? "He called for a famine on the land of Canaan, cutting off its food supply" (Psalm 105:16). He brought famine on the land, but first he prepared their deliverance in Egypt. What appeared to be a disaster and a tragedy drove God's people to the place of God's provision.

Father, when it seems that everything is working against me, remind me that, in truth, everything is working for me.

Jennifer

The strong hands of God twisted the crown of thorns into a crown of glory; and in such hands we are safe.

—**CHARLES WILLIAMS** (1886–1945), English writer and lay theologian

LIKE FATHER, LIKE SON

JESUS EXPLAINED, "I TELL YOU THE TRUTH, THE SON CAN DO
NOTHING BY HIMSELF. HE DOES ONLY WHAT HE SEES THE FATHER
DOING. WHATEVER THE FATHER DOES, THE SON ALSO DOES. FOR
THE FATHER LOVES THE SON AND SHOWS HIM EVERYTHING HE
IS DOING."

John 5:19-20

JESUS, WHO WAS EQUAL with God in every way, was willing to so humble himself
for our sakes that he put himself in a subservient position to the Father while he walked
out his earthly ministry: "He took the humble position of a slave and was born as a human
being. When he appeared in human form, he humbled himself in obedience to God"
(Philippians 2:7-8).

Every step Jesus took, every breath he breathed, every word he spoke, was in obedience to the Father. He lived on alert, watching for what the Father was doing.

Jesus may not have seen with his physical eyes everything the Father was doing, but the
Father revealed those things to the eyes of Jesus' heart. His spiritual senses could discern the
Father at work.

In the incident that led up to Jesus' statement in today's verses, Jesus walked through
a location where many blind, lame, and paralyzed people waited, seeking a cure in the
waters of a pool. He went to one of the men and healed him. Everyone with him saw the
hurting people. Everyone with him saw the same man he saw. But only Jesus perceived
exactly what the Father was doing. He was so identified in heart with the Father that the
Father showed Jesus everything he was doing.

Jesus promises the same thing to his disciples. Just as Jesus can do nothing apart from
the Father, so we can do nothing apart from him (see John 15:5). Jesus promises that he
will show himself to those who obey him (see14:21) and that he will teach us everything
the Father makes known to him (see15:15).

*Jesus, I turn my gaze from earthly circumstances to you. Let me see the things of
earth through your eyes and align myself with your work around me.*

Jennifer

Faith demonstrates to the eye of the mind the reality of those things which cannot be
discerned by the eye of the body.

—**MATTHEW HENRY** (1662–1714), English pastor and Bible commentator

8

THE LISTENER

THE LORD CAME AND CALLED AS BEFORE, "SAMUEL! SAMUEL!"
AND SAMUEL REPLIED, "SPEAK, YOUR SERVANT IS LISTENING."

1 Samuel 3:10

SAMUEL HAD BEEN raised in the Temple by Eli the priest and was certainly knowledge-able about the outer trappings and rituals of his faith. On this night in young Samuel's life, those outer ceremonies of worship gave way to a personal encounter with the Lord to whom the forms and sacraments pointed. Throughout his life, Samuel would hear and know the Lord's voice over and over. But this was his entrance into the inner circle where the Lord calls his own by name.

In this encounter, God revealed to Samuel who he promises to be in our lives. He calls us by name and speaks clearly to our hearts. As he was with Samuel, whose name he called three times before Samuel recognized him, he is patient and persistent. He pursues us until we turn and say, "Speak, your servant is listening."

To know intimately the Lord who calls us by name changes everything about how we live. To be so cherished gives our lives new meaning and value. When the Lord says, "Do not be afraid, for I have ransomed you. I have called you by name; you are mine" (Isaiah 43:1), we receive assurance that we are safe and protected.

God knows you. He speaks to your heart. Jesus has pulled you into his inner circle, those to whom he will impart his secrets. Listen: "I no longer call you slaves, because a master doesn't confide in his slaves. Now you are my friends, since I have told you every-thing the Father told me" (John 15:15). A person who is following only a doctrine need not listen. There is nothing new to know. The one who is following Christ must be always listening. Listen to his living, present voice as he reveals his heart to you and reproduces his heart in you. Live your life alert to his whisper.

Speak, Lord. I, your servant, am listening.

Jennifer

God is whispering to us well-nigh incessantly. Whenever the sounds of the world die out in the soul, or sink low, then we hear these whisperings of God. He is always whispering to us, only we do not always hear, because of the noise, hurry, and distraction which life causes as it rushes on.

—FREDERICK WILLIAM FABER (1814–1863), English hymn writer and theologian

PRIVATE TUTORING

[THE DISCIPLES] HAD ROWED THREE OR FOUR MILES WHEN SUDDENLY THEY SAW JESUS WALKING ON THE WATER TOWARD THE BOAT. THEY WERE TERRIFIED, BUT HE CALLED OUT TO THEM, "DON'T BE AFRAID. I AM HERE!" THEN THEY WERE EAGER TO LET HIM IN THE BOAT, AND IMMEDIATELY THEY ARRIVED AT THEIR DESTINATION!

John 6:19-21

FOLLOWING THE AMAZING display of power when Jesus fed a crowd of five thousand with a few barley loaves and fish, the disciples got into their boat to cross the lake while Jesus went into the hills to pray. And it was then, after a series of very public incidents culminating with the breaking of bread for the crowd, that Jesus gave his disciples a private lesson.

They were making the short, six-mile trip across the lake, but the trip was harder than it should have been because the weather was against them. While they were straining at the oars and fighting the wind, Jesus was alone on the mountain praying, from where he had a view of his disciples' dilemma. Mark says, "He saw that they were in serious trouble, rowing hard and struggling against the wind and waves" (Mark 6:48).

Jesus' unexpected appearance and his unheard-of mode of travel—making the surface of the water his solid ground—elicited a reaction of strong fear, even terror, in the disciples.

Once they recognized him, they took him into the boat. At that very moment, the wind died down, and "immediately they arrived at their destination!" (John 6:21). What the disciples were learning is that the presence of Jesus is the destination. He is our safe haven. When we receive him into our experience, everything else is put in perspective.

Jesus, remind me that I don't have to row against the wind and strain at the oars. All I need to do is let you into the boat.

Jennifer

There is an experience of the love of God which, when it comes upon us, and enfolds us, and bathes us, and warms us, is so utterly new that we can hardly identify it with the old phrase, God is love. Can this be the love of God, this burning, tender, wooing, wounding pain of love that pierces the marrow of my bones and burns out old loves and ambitions—God experienced is a vast surprise.

—**THOMAS R. KELLY** (1893–1941), Quaker educator

JESUS REPLIED, "I AM THE BREAD OF LIFE. WHOEVER COMES TO ME WILL NEVER BE HUNGRY AGAIN."

John 6:35

I SAT ACROSS the long, elegant table from the wife of a high-ranking Thai official. She had invited me to talk for one hour to Thai women regarding their children. This powerful woman had called our missionary host the night before; the problem was that she would not say ahead of time what topic she wanted me to speak on. *Was it how to help their children be more successful in school?* I wondered. Did she have in mind something on encouraging their children or more along the lines of understanding children's learning styles and gifts? She would tell me when I arrived at noon.

Normally I know the topic ahead of time and bring notes with specific points to highlight in my message. However, Chiang-Mai, Thailand, was thousands of miles from my office in Oklahoma, so I couldn't run back and get a portfolio with a talk, and there was no time to prepare a new one.

The night before I was to speak, exhausted from more than ten days of ministry and suffering from a severe intestinal infection, I was beginning to be anxious and went to bed feeling inadequate and downhearted. Then I sensed the Lord's quiet whisper reminding me, *Offer the bread that you have. You may feel it is inadequate, but I am the Bread of Life, fully able to fill these women's hearts as you share the life experiences and words I've given you. Don't worry about anything. Just give yourself to me, and I will do my work through you.*

Those words of life shifted my focus from my inadequacy to Christ's sufficiency. The next day, as I opened my mouth to speak without an outline or notes, the words flowed for one hour. Afterward, the hostess hugged me and tearfully said, "I wish you were my mother. This was perfect, just what we needed to hear." My heart filled with gratitude for Jesus, the Bread of Life, our inexhaustible resource.

Jesus, Bread of Life, thank you that you can do great and unexpected things using our simple, flawed gifts when we surrender them to you.

Cheri

If you wish to be disappointed, look to others. If you wish to be downhearted, look to yourself. If you wish to be encouraged . . . look upon Jesus Christ.

—ERICH SAUER (1898–1959), German theologian and writer

SPIRIT AND LIFE

The Spirit alone gives eternal life. Human effort accomplishes nothing. And the very words I have spoken to you are spirit and life.

John 6:63

HAVE YOU ever heard the saying "God helps those who help themselves" and been told it's in the Bible? I have. But those words are not there. Instead, verses such as today's reading from John underscore the reality that our human efforts accomplish *nothing*—not obtaining eternal life or even understanding the Word of God. The truth is, apart from Christ and his Spirit we can do nothing (see also John 15:5). Surprisingly, this truth isn't cause for consternation but for *rejoicing*.

In the context of the story, the people and disciples were arguing about Christ's teachings that he would rise from the dead, that his flesh was the Bread of Life, and that anyone who eats this bread and drinks his blood would live forever. The crowds soundly rejected his teaching, but the disciples were frustrated that they couldn't understand it—even as Jesus was referring to the Holy Spirit who would be poured out in those who believe.

This passage reminds me once again that it is God the Father who has initiated the whole redemption process and sent Jesus to draw us to himself. As Jesus said in verse 44, "No one can come to me unless the Father who sent me draws them to me." Even after we've accepted the truth, our natural tendency is to move independently of God and lean on self-effort to deliver us or accomplish our work. In those times, the words in John 6 call us to greater dependence on Christ. How marvelous to stop and ponder the fact that it was the Father's initiative to provide a place of rest for us to dwell as well as the means for our eternal life. All praise and honor and glory be to the Father; to his Son, Jesus Christ; and to the Holy Spirit.

Father, forgive my self-efforts. Thank you for always encouraging me to come to you and receive your words, which are spirit and life. Draw me, oh, draw me to yourself, to live in deeper communion and dependence on you and your Spirit.

Cheri

If you live in God and die to your own will,
How simple it will be his precepts to fulfill.

—ANGELUS SILESIUS (1624–1677), German mystic and poet

GENTLE WORDS ARE A TREE OF LIFE;
A DECEITFUL TONGUE CRUSHES THE SPIRIT.

Proverbs 15:4

WHEN GENTLE WORDS are planted, hope, courage, and confidence grow. As the proverb for today declares, gentle words bring life. Such words dispel discouragement, banish the blues, and bring out the best in people. They release potential, light our paths, and spur us on to amazing accomplishments. The contrast in this verse is clear and gives us a real promise to count on: when we speak kind, loving words, they heal and help others; but deceitful words crush and wound the human spirit.

In this high-stress, broken world, I see children, spouses, grandparents, friends, and other people we meet every day who long for the blessing of encouraging words. In fact, they need this as much as plants need water. During the summer of 2011, our state of Oklahoma went through one of the hottest, most severe droughts in history. With more than fifty days of constant, over one-hundred-degree heat, trees died, hundreds of farmers' fields dried up and yielded no fruit or vegetables, and destructive fires raged, destroying homes and futures.

That's a picture of what our souls become without the life-giving effects of encouraging words. Think of the potential of gentle words, the life and encouragement that can come from them. I love what Max Lucado said: "Plant a word of love heart-deep in a person's life. Nurture it with a smile and a prayer, and watch what happens." To whom can you speak a gentle word of life today?

*Lord, I confess that not all my words are gentle and kind. When I've been impatient
or angry, my words have hurt and wounded others. Grant me the grace of your
Spirit to speak gently and lovingly so that life will grow in others' hearts.*

Cheri

If your words have cheered one failing heart
Kindled anew one fading altar fire,
Your work is not a failure;
Chords are touched that will re-echo from the angel choir.

—**CYNTHIA D. HARVEY THOMAS** (1841–?), American poet

THE GREAT SALVATION

On the last day, the climax of the festival, Jesus stood and shouted to the crowds, "Anyone who is thirsty may come to me! Anyone who believes in me may come and drink! For the Scriptures declare, 'Rivers of living water will flow from his heart.'"

John 7:37-38

THIS SCENE is set at a climactic moment—the seventh day of the weeklong Feast of Tabernacles, or Festival of Shelters. The whole week was a celebration of tremendous joy and pageantry. As many Jews as could make the trip were in Jerusalem joining the great celebration. The Holy City was packed with people.

The last day was known as Hoshana Rabbah, which means "Great Salvation."

On that day, the people were wakened at dawn by the priests blowing the shofar, or ram's horn. As the people headed for the Temple, they carried in their right hands a *lulabh*, a branch of myrtle, willow, and palm tied together. In their left hands they carried an *ethrog*, a kind of fruit. When they reached the Temple, the people divided into three groups. One group participated in the Water-Pouring Ceremony.

The Water-Pouring Ceremony was the high point, the most joyous ceremony of all, because it pictured Jehovah's promise to pour out his Spirit upon his people.

A white-robed priest carrying a golden pitcher led a procession of worshipers through one of the Temple gates to the Pool of Siloam, where he filled the pitcher. The procession followed him back to the Temple, singing, waving their branches, and dancing.

As they sang, the priests, waved branches and marched around the altar seven times. In the midst of this charged, holy moment, Jesus cried out in a loud voice. Jesus was watching the joy and exuberance the people were experiencing as they saw physical water poured out, and the words burst from him: "Are you thirsty? I have the water! Are you thirsty? Believe in me. Come to me. Rivers of water will be within you! You will never thirst again."

Jesus, keep filling me with living water now and forever.

Jennifer

If the life of Christ is flowing through us, the water from the Rock turning the wheel, as it flows into the heart, it will fill us with joy; and if so, we cannot contain it, it must flow out.

—**G. V. WIGRAM** (1805–1879), English Bible scholar

14 WALKING IN THE LIGHT

Jesus spoke to the people . . . and said, "I am the light of the world. If you follow me, you won't have to walk in darkness, because you will have the light that leads to life."

John 8:12

JESUS WAS WALKING through the Court of Women during the Feast of Tabernacles when he encountered an angry crowd about to stone a woman accused of adultery. He not only rescued her from certain death but also brought her out of darkness into the light of his truth. Then he called her not to walk in sin or the darkness of secret shame any longer but to walk in the light and freedom. With that instruction, he turned to the people and declared one of the most wonderful promises in the Bible: "I am the light of the world."

In the Psalms, David spoke of the Lord as his light (see Psalm 27:1). Isaiah 60:1 prophesied that the light would come; the glory of the Lord would shine. As John described it, the glory of the Lord did indeed come in Jesus: "The Life-Light blazed out of the darkness; the darkness couldn't put it out" (John 1:5, *The Message*).

How wonderful that the promise of God's light isn't reserved for just a few people. Everyone is invited to receive his light! In Jesus, the Bright and Morning Star, is life, and that life is the light of men and women all over the world. Wherever he went, Christ's light banished the darkness. Just as Jesus transformed the dire situation of the woman accused of adultery, his light can transform the things that need changing in our lives and families. We are invited to be Christ bearers, to share his light with others, taking hope and peace into a dark world.

> *Father, thank you for sending your light in Jesus, for lighting up our own dark places and every difficult situation we face. Grant that we would be bearers of your light and so bring encouragement and hope today to someone who needs you.*

Cheri

God hath not promised sun without rain,
Joy without sorrow, peace without pain.
But God hath promised strength for the day,
Rest for the labor, light for the way.

—"WHAT GOD HATH PROMISED" BY ANNIE JOHNSON FLINT (1866–1932),
American poet and hymn writer

GIANT BUSTER

[DAVID SAID,] "THE LORD WHO RESCUED ME FROM THE CLAWS OF THE LION AND THE BEAR WILL RESCUE ME FROM THIS PHILISTINE!"

1 Samuel 17:37

THE GIANT GOLIATH was intimidating. He was big, he wore big armor, and he carried a big weapon. Big any way you cut it.

For forty days, morning and night, Goliath mocked God's people. Eighty times he shouted out his defiance and was met with fear and flight on the part of the Israelites. But the eighty-first time, he got the surprise of his life.

Israel's army was focused on Goliath's size. That's what did them in. He was big and loud. When David first heard Goliath's taunts, his reaction was, "Who is this pagan Philistine anyway, that he is allowed to defy the armies of the living God?" (1 Samuel 17:26). David didn't even mention Goliath's size. David was comparing Goliath to God, and Goliath was not coming out the winner. In David's eyes, Goliath was puny.

Young David decided to take on the giant. This monumental event had some precedents in David's life, as we read in today's verse. David had not been trained in battle, but he had been trained in the power of God.

When David stepped out to meet Goliath, the giant couldn't believe his eyes. He looked David over and saw that he was only a boy, and he despised him.

But David was undaunted. He ran right at Goliath, took a stone out of his shepherd's bag, slung it, and Goliath fell. "So David triumphed over the Philistine with only a sling and a stone, for he had no sword. Then David ran over and pulled Goliath's sword from its sheath. David used it to kill him" (1 Samuel 17:50-51).

Goliath was big and loud and intimidating, but his size also made him a big target. His armor kept him from being light on his feet.

David, on the other hand, was small and nimble and unencumbered. What looked like strength was really weakness; what looked like weakness was really strength.

Father, with my eyes fixed on you, there is no reason to fear a giant.

Jennifer

For David, the size of the giant was irrelevant.

—DAVE HUNT (1926–), American Christian apologist, speaker, and author

16 WHEN LIGHT CAME BURSTING IN

LIGHT SHINES IN THE DARKNESS FOR THE GODLY.

Psalm 112:4

BEFORE HUDSON TAYLOR was born, his parents dedicated him to God for mission work in China. But although he was raised in a godly home, he went through troubled times as a teenager. He resisted the authority of his father, wanted nothing to do with the church, and experienced many struggles and spiritual doubts. He moved away from the Christian beliefs of his parents, which led his mother and sister to pray for him constantly.

When Hudson was seventeen and in great turmoil and rebellion, his mother was so concerned for the darkness overtaking his soul she locked herself in a room at her sister's house fifty miles away from their home. She resolved to stay there in prayer until she had clear assurance from God for her son's conversion.

Hudson Taylor later reported that the very afternoon his mother was interceding so earnestly for him he came upon a gospel tract about the finished work of Christ. He read it and accepted the Savior and his salvation. This young man's whole life underwent sweeping transformation as light came bursting into his soul. Several months later, during intense prayer for guidance, Taylor heard God call him to ministry in China, and he immediately began studying and preparing to go. From that point on, he lived by faith, devoting himself to the poor and preaching to the needy. He pursued medical studies so he would be more useful on the mission field and arrived in Shanghai, China, in 1854.

In his fifty-one years in China, Taylor took more than eight hundred missionaries to serve throughout the provinces of China, in three hundred mission stations. Historians record that no other missionary since the apostle Paul has had a greater vision, plan, and reach for a vast nation than did Hudson Taylor. As a result of his life's work, millions of Chinese heard the gospel of Christ, and generations of people after him were inspired to full-time missionary service.

I praise you, God, that your light pierces the darkness and that there is no place so dark that your light and love cannot penetrate it.

Cheri

Darkness is my point of view, my right to myself; light is God's point of view.

—**OSWALD CHAMBERS** (1874–1917), Scottish minister and teacher

THE PROMISE OF A HAPPY HEART

FOR THE HAPPY HEART, LIFE IS A CONTINUAL FEAST.

Proverbs 15:15

WE ALL FACE circumstances in life that make our hearts anything but happy. Even our own thoughts can make us miserable: *I can't be happy until I lose forty pounds*, or *My teenagers are driving me crazy*. Difficult situations and people who hurt us can make our hearts unhappy, cars break down, illness and trials can steal our joy. But although there is always something that might sabotage our happiness, it is possible to live with a happy heart. And the promise in this verse is that, regardless of the circumstances, with a happy heart we can enjoy life as a continual feast, appreciating and enjoying God's abundant blessings.

Living with joy glorifies God; it's at the heart of abundant living and is a powerful testimony and witness to the reality of his presence. A happy heart is a source of strength and energy, even in the toughest of times. There is an old saying that if Satan can steal our joy, he can get everything else—our strength, our hope, and even our faith. Let's not give him the opportunity!

Despite the sadness of life in a world that's deeply broken, Jesus still invites us to experience joy, and his Word reveals practices that lead to a happy heart: fixing our eyes on Jesus instead of on ourselves and our problems, casting our burdens on him instead of carrying them ourselves, investing in friendships, serving others, and choosing to give thanks in all circumstances, just to name a few. Even that one choice—giving thanks—is a prescription for a cheerful heart. Researchers report that gratitude is the healthiest emotion a person can have and produces more positive emotional energy, leading to happiness and joy, than any other attitude.

> *Lord, I confess I've had my eyes on my circumstances instead of on you. Would you be the lifter of my heart and mind and restore my joy so I can live life as a continual feast of your blessings?*

Cheri

At every moment of our life we have an opportunity to choose joy. . . . It is in this choice that our true freedom is, and that freedom is the freedom to love.

—**HENRI NOUWEN** (1932–1996), Dutch writer and priest

18
THE GOOD SHEPHERD

> [JESUS SAID,] "I AM THE GOOD SHEPHERD; I KNOW MY OWN
> SHEEP, AND THEY KNOW ME, JUST AS MY FATHER KNOWS ME AND
> I KNOW THE FATHER."
>
> *John 10:14-15*

JESUS GIVES an extended discourse on his role as a good shepherd. He protects, provides, leads, loves. He lays down his life for his sheep.

He promises that he knows his own, and that his own know him. He expounds on that promise, comparing it to the way he and his Father know each other. In the same way that he knows and fully trusts the Father, so we can know and fully trust him. And in the same way the Father shows himself through the life of the Son, Jesus shows himself through our lives.

Jesus lived his earthly life in utter obedience to the Father because he knew he could count on the Father. If we know Jesus—really know him—then we will be as obedient and as trusting of him as he is of the Father.

We've mentioned earlier that a promise is only as good as the person who makes it. We can't trust the word of a stranger whose character and nature we do not know. The promise might be trustworthy, but we can't know that. Jesus has made it possible for us to trust his promises because we can know him as intimately as he knows the Father.

We can trust his work in our lives because we know him. And because we know him, we don't have to understand what is happening while it is happening. If we have faith, we know that God sees what we cannot. All we really need to know is him, and with that we can live at peace. The only work required of us is to believe in Jesus. "This is the only work God wants from you: Believe in the one he has sent" (John 6:29). Everything else flows from that.

Jesus, I believe your promises because I believe in you. I believe in your love for
me and in your wisdom that works only for good in my life.

Jennifer

If God would concede me His omnipotence for 24 hours, you would see how many changes I would make in the world. But if He gave me His wisdom too, I would leave things as they are.

—JACQUES-MARIE-LOUIS MONSABRÉ (1827–1907), French preacher

A TWO-HANDED GRASP

> [JESUS SAID,] "MY SHEEP LISTEN TO MY VOICE; I KNOW THEM, AND THEY FOLLOW ME. I GIVE THEM ETERNAL LIFE, AND THEY WILL NEVER PERISH. NO ONE CAN SNATCH THEM AWAY FROM ME, FOR MY FATHER HAS GIVEN THEM TO ME, AND HE IS MORE POWERFUL THAN ANYONE ELSE. NO ONE CAN SNATCH THEM FROM THE FATHER'S HAND. THE FATHER AND I ARE ONE."
>
> *John 10:27-30*

I LOVE THE WAY Jesus describes our position in these verses. If we are in Jesus' hand, then we are in the Father's hand. Let the eyes of your heart see this: you and those you love are held in the palm of Jesus' hand. Jesus' hand is held in the Father's hand. You are held in a two-handed grasp.

When Jesus uses the metaphor of sheep to describe his people, he is creating a picture of defenselessness and dependence. That doesn't sit well with our I'm-in-charge human nature. Yet it is our reality. No matter how smart or strong or brave we might be, we are at the mercy of circumstances we can't control. No matter how determined and disciplined we might be, we are at the mercy of impulses and ingrained behaviors that defy our best efforts to control them. When we come to grips with our own weakness, then we can begin to live in God's strength.

The realization of our weakness is swallowed up in the certainty of his strength. Until we come to terms with our own vulnerability and dependence, we miss out on the stunning promise that we are never, ever, ever outside his protection and care. When we do, we can live with courage and power and strength, never at the mercy of circumstances or impulses. We find freedom knowing we are in God's two-handed grasp.

Jesus, I rest in the palm of your hand.

Jennifer

In Jesus the weak are strong, and the defenseless safe; they could not be more strong if they were giants, or more safe if they were in heaven. Faith gives to men on earth the protection of the God of heaven. More they cannot need, and need not wish.

—CHARLES HADDON SPURGEON (1834–1892), English preacher and writer

20 LESS IS MORE

[MARY AND MARTHA] SENT A MESSAGE TO JESUS TELLING HIM, "LORD, YOUR DEAR FRIEND IS VERY SICK."

John 11:3

LAZARUS WAS the only brother of two sisters, Mary and Martha. Jesus and his disciples were often guests in their home, and the three siblings knew Jesus as well as anyone knew him. They knew what they could expect from him because they knew his heart and his compassion and his power.

When the crisis hit and Lazarus fell fatally ill, the sisters knew from experience that all they had to do was take their need to Jesus. Do you see how very simple and unadorned their prayer is? "Your dear friend is very sick." No flowery language, no cajoling or pleading, no instructions. They didn't feel compelled to offer suggestions or remind Jesus of the answer to their problem. They knew it was enough to present their need to him.

I imagine they had learned by experience that any need—great or small—spoke for itself because of Jesus' great compassion. They had learned that he was a living, breathing promise and that in him was the supply for every need. So when the emergency came out of nowhere and took them by surprise, they did what they were used to doing. They took their need to Jesus.

But Jesus did not act in accordance with their expectations of him. He did not hurry to Bethany to heal Lazarus before he died, as Mary and Martha had anticipated he would. He planned to do *more* than they could think or imagine. He was not content to leave Mary and Martha with what they knew of him so far. He was not interested in meeting their expectations, because he intended to *exceed* them. He did not act in a way that confirmed their faith but rather stretched their faith, and because he did, they saw his miraculous power over death.

All it took to experience the fullness of Jesus was to take their need to him.

Jesus, do in my life as you will, when you will, how you will.

Jennifer

It makes no matter where He places me, or how. That is rather for Him to consider than for me; for in the easiest positions He must give me His grace, and in the most difficult, His grace is sufficient.

—**(JAMES) HUDSON TAYLOR** (1832–1905), English missionary to China

BROKEN AND POURED OUT

THE HOUSE WAS FILLED WITH THE FRAGRANCE.

John 12:3

IN THE DAYS leading up to the Crucifixion, we find Mary, sister of Martha and Lazarus, pouring out a costly anointing on the body of Jesus. She poured out perfumed ointment on his feet as an act of worship and gratitude and adoration. The perfume she poured out was the outward expression of her pouring out her heart at his feet.

This perfume had been meant for her. It was to beautify her, to call attention to her. It was extravagant, and a woman who owned such a perfume would consider carefully how she used it. Mary chose to use all of it as an offering to Jesus.

Many years ago, something very unfair happened to me in the course of ministry. Someone I trusted reneged on a promise and left me in a difficult position. I was furious and offended and indignant. I was ready to walk away to preserve my dignity and guard my pride. As I fumed and readied my exit, the Lord insistently pulled me aside and impressed my heart with this question: *Jennifer, what's the problem?*

"Well, Lord, I've been treated as if I were nothing."

Jennifer, how often do you say to me, "Lord, I'm nothing, and you're everything"? Would you be willing to be nothing for my sake? If you will minister right now in the midst of your hurt, it will be a costly anointing poured out on the body of Christ. It will cost you something you had held in reserve for yourself. But the aroma of your act of worship will fill this place.

I still cherish that moment when the Lord allowed me to be nothing for him.

Is the Lord calling you to offer a costly anointing? Is there someone who doesn't give you the proper respect? Is there a situation in which you don't get the credit you feel you deserve? Would you pour out a blessing on the body of Christ because you love the one who poured out everything—even his blood—for you?

Lord, take me at my word. I am nothing, and you are everything.

Jennifer

When Christ calls a man, he bids him come and die.

—DIETRICH BONHOEFFER (1906–1945), German pastor, theologian, and author

22 THIS IS THE DAY

THIS IS THE DAY THE LORD HAS MADE.
WE WILL REJOICE AND BE GLAD IN IT.

Psalm 118:24

DO YOU HEAR the promise in these words? This day, the day you are living right now—this is the day the Lord has made. This is the day the Lord has designed, arranged, scheduled. Take joy in this day.

It's easy to get stuck living in the past. Past hurts can infect present relationships. Past disappointments can diminish present joy. Past failures can cripple present opportunities. If we let it, the past can hold us in a viselike grip and hold our emotions hostage. The Creator, who knows our propensity for backward living, warns us to let the past go. Let him redeem it: "Forget the former things; do not dwell on the past. See, I am doing a new thing! Now it springs up; do you not perceive it?" (Isaiah 43:18-19, NIV).

On the other hand, we can use up today worrying about tomorrow. We can get so caught up in what-ifs and imagined scenarios that will likely never happen that the joy of today gets lost in the anxiety of tomorrow. If you were to graph what you have worried about compared to what actually happened, would you find that too much of your life is taken up uselessly by worry? Even if something you worried about did occur, did your worrying stop it or change it? How many of the Lord's "todays" have you missed out on because you were projecting worry into tomorrow?

God has arranged today. It is full of promise, so get everything out of this day that you can. Yes, it will hold challenges, but God holds the power to face those challenges. It will hold numerous delights, but you may have to train your eye to see them. Recognize the promise that today is the day God has for you; he has packed it with evidences of himself and the potential for taking delight in his arrangements. This is the day the Lord has made. Enjoy it to the full.

Lord, I embrace this day and receive its promise. Keep me alert and present to its delights.

Jennifer

The remarkable thing is, we have a choice every day regarding the attitude we will embrace for that day.

—**CHUCK SWINDOLL** (1934–), American pastor and writer

THE JOY OF OBEDIENCE

JOYFUL ARE PEOPLE OF INTEGRITY,
WHO FOLLOW THE INSTRUCTIONS OF THE LORD.
JOYFUL ARE THOSE WHO OBEY HIS LAWS
AND SEARCH FOR HIM WITH ALL THEIR HEARTS.

Psalm 119:1-2

JOY IS THE HALLMARK of those who walk with integrity and in step with God's instruction. God's law doesn't weigh us down or hold us back; instead it sets us free. Outside his law, we are making decisions about our behavior based on our own best ideas. But we don't have the ability to look at situations from every perspective or the power to know what we will encounter next or the wisdom to know the inner workings of the human mind. God created all the complexities of human nature, and he knows how to protect us from self-destruction.

Sociologists and biologists have come to understand that guilt, bitterness, anger, stress—any negative emotions—have a direct effect on the body and the psyche. Those negative emotions actually create chemical and hormonal responses in our bodies that damage our organs and wear out our muscles and compromise our immune systems. Stealth anger ravages our physical systems and spills over into our relationships, poisoning them.

Trying to be our own bosses results in misery at every level. But the by-product of obedience to God is joy. That defies human logic. Shouldn't it work the other way around? No, thousands of generations of humanity have proved it out.

We are all in a pursuit of joy from the moment we are born. It drives us. We build our lives around what we believe will bring us joy. But anything outside of Jesus is a guaranteed letdown. Walking out our days apart from him and his loving law is a recipe for unhappiness. Spending yourself in pursuit of the joy that eludes you, only to find that it is a dead end, is life's tragedy. That is what God is protecting you from when he promises that joy is found in walking out his law.

Father, teach me to obey gladly, knowing that the promise of joy flows from walking in your ways.

Jennifer

The loneliest moment in life is when you have just experienced that which you thought would deliver the ultimate, and it has just let you down.
—RAVI ZACHARIAS (1946–), Christian apologist and writer

24 OPEN MY EYES

OPEN MY EYES TO SEE
THE WONDERFUL TRUTHS IN YOUR INSTRUCTIONS.

Psalm 119:18

WE MIGHT think of the Word of God as encrypted. That is, we require the proper equipment to really understand it. Although we may understand the words on the pages, without the Holy Spirit revealing its secrets, the spiritual truths of God's Word remain unavailable to us.

These riches are not sitting on the surface to be skimmed off by the casual observer. They have to be mined, like gold or silver. God has set it up this way on purpose, because his Word is not something that stands alone, separate from his person. His living Spirit, speaking his Word in present tense, takes the Scriptures from the realm of mere words on pages in his Book to a living, active, powerful expression of himself.

I'm always amazed at the way a passage or verse of Scripture that I have known for years suddenly says something new to me or the way I learn old truths at deeper levels. I simply can't come to the end of what the Word of God has to say to me, because the Word is a universe of truth that seems to keep expanding. Out there, beyond what I have discovered, are galaxies yet unexplored.

Paul says that to a person without the Spirit of God, the things of God are foolishness. That person is unable to understand spiritual things, not because he is unintelligent but because it is the Spirit who explains the Scriptures so that we can understand them. As believers, we have that Spirit, so we can understand: "People who aren't spiritual can't receive these truths from God's Spirit. It all sounds foolish to them and they can't understand it, for only those who are spiritual can understand what the Spirit means" (1 Corinthians 2:14).

God promises that he will open our "eyes," that is, our understanding, and call our attention to new spiritual truths that will work in our lives, bringing us into the depths of his Kingdom and the "treasures hidden in the darkness—secret riches" (Isaiah 45:3).

Lord, show me wonderful things stored in your Word. Show me the deep and hidden things that only your Spirit can reveal. Wrap those things around my heart and anchor them in my life.

Jennifer

There is no worse screen to block out the Spirit than confidence in our own intelligence.

—JOHN CALVIN (1509–1564), French theologian and pastor

POWERED BY JESUS

[JESUS SAID,] "WHEN THE FATHER SENDS THE ADVOCATE AS MY REPRESENTATIVE—THAT IS, THE HOLY SPIRIT—HE WILL TEACH YOU EVERYTHING AND WILL REMIND YOU OF EVERYTHING I HAVE TOLD YOU."

John 14:26

JESUS SAID that it is through the Holy Spirit that the life of Christ is operative in you. He is Christ's life transfused into you and flowing through you, and he makes the thoughts of God known to you.

Jesus lived his earthly life in the Spirit's power. He was full of the Holy Spirit after his baptism and was led by the Spirit into the wilderness, where he was tempted by the devil (see Luke 4:1-2). After his time of testing, he returned to Galilee in the power of the Spirit (see Luke 4:14). He opened his ministry by declaring, "The Spirit of the LORD is upon me" (Luke 4:18). He offered himself to God as our sacrifice through the power of the eternal Spirit (see Hebrews 9:14).

The same Spirit in whose power Jesus lived on earth is the Spirit he has poured out in us. When the Spirit of Christ, the life of Christ, begins to flow through us as a vine's life flows through a branch, a progressive transformation is in process. We begin to recognize and cooperate with the indwelling Christ in the form of his Holy Spirit, and we learn that we can draw on him for every need. He will reveal to us the mind of Christ in every situation and will also reveal it in us and through us. The Spirit changes us from the inside out and empowers us to live out the call of God.

Jesus, let your Spirit flow into every corner of my personality, transforming me until you are exactly reflected in my life.

Jennifer

When God redeemed you through the precious blood of His dear Son, He placed . . . a powerful engine under the hood—nothing less than the resurrection life of God the Son, made over to you in the person of God the Holy Spirit.

—MAJOR W. IAN THOMAS (1914–2007), English writer and theology teacher

26 THE BRIGHTNESS OF GOD'S PROMISES

REMEMBER YOUR PROMISE TO ME;
   IT IS MY ONLY HOPE.
YOUR PROMISE REVIVES ME;
   IT COMFORTS ME IN ALL MY TROUBLES.

Psalm 119:49-50

ONE DAY in the darkness of Ravensbrück concentration camp, Corrie ten Boom heard that a large group of Dutch young people at the camp were being put on a train and sent away that night. People whispered about where they were being sent: was it to a factory, a different concentration camp, or even to their deaths? As Corrie prayed for the young people, God showed her how to help.

That night she crawled out the window of the bathroom and hid in the shadows where the prisoners might pass. All was silent except for the sounds of an approaching guard's boot crunching on gravel and low moans from the barracks. Knowing she'd be brutally killed if she was discovered, she knelt in the dark and asked God to give her a personal word that would comfort each person being transported.

As they passed by her, Corrie whispered one of God's promises to every one of the 250 young people: "*Jesus is Victor.*" "*Fear not; only believe.*" "*Underneath are the everlasting arms.*" The promises were personal and distinct, and as she spoke them, she prayed God would encourage and revive the hearts of those who heard them. Just as she and her sister Betsie had experienced, they could count on God's promises. Even in the darkest of places, his promises would shine brightly and give hope, because in the Bible there are no broken promises from God.

After the war, Corrie met one of those young people, who told her that all but one of the 250 prisoners transported that night survived. He described how God had powerfully used the promises she spoke to bring them peace in the trials, bombing, and danger they later faced. They discovered, as you and I can each day, that God's Word will be our light in the darkness and that through his promises we can experience the miracle of his presence.

Lord, write your promises on my heart, not only to encourage me but also so that I might share them with others.

Cheri

God's promises are like the stars; the darker the night, the brighter they shine.
—**DAVID NICHOLAS** (1934–2011), American pastor

[JESUS SAID,] "HERE ON EARTH YOU WILL HAVE MANY TRIALS AND SORROWS. BUT TAKE HEART, BECAUSE I HAVE OVERCOME THE WORLD."

John 16:33

JESUS NEVER sugarcoated the truth. We can expect real difficulties in this life. He did not promise to take away our problems, but he did promise to take the poison out of their sting.

His life in us does not make us immune to pain or disappointment, but Jesus does make us indestructible. When we encounter the difficulties of this life, big or small, we have a new prism through which to view them. We have a new confidence in which to face them. And we have a new power with which to tackle them, because Jesus has overcome every problem we face. Before it gets to us, he has already declawed and defanged it.

That problem, challenge, sorrow, or disappointment has been weighed in his balance. When the glory it will bring outweighs the pain it will cause, only then does it reach your experience. Even those difficulties have been filtered through his sieve so that anything that would destroy you has been strained out. The enemy's plan to weaken and discourage you blows up in his face when Jesus steps in with his overcoming might. He strips sorrow of its gale-force winds and turns a hurricane of heartache into a common windstorm. Fierce, perhaps, until we compare it to what was forecast. In every storm we are anchored, safe and immovable, in Jesus.

Has a storm hit? Take heart. He has overcome, and your moorings will hold. That's a promise. With Paul, you can testify, "We are pressed on every side by troubles, but we are not crushed. We are perplexed, but not driven to despair. We are hunted down, but never abandoned by God. We get knocked down, but we are not destroyed" (2 Corinthians 4:8-9).

Anchor me in you. Life's storms will not sweep me away, because in you I am unshakable and immovable.

Jennifer

Every tear of sorrow sown by the righteous springs up a pearl.

—**MATTHEW HENRY** (1662–1714), English pastor and Bible commentator

28 IN THE WORLD

[JESUS SAID,] "I'M NOT ASKING YOU TO TAKE THEM OUT OF THE
WORLD, BUT TO KEEP THEM SAFE FROM THE EVIL ONE. THEY
DO NOT BELONG TO THIS WORLD ANY MORE THAN I DO. MAKE
THEM HOLY BY YOUR TRUTH; TEACH THEM YOUR WORD, WHICH
IS TRUTH. JUST AS YOU SENT ME INTO THE WORLD, I AM SENDING
THEM INTO THE WORLD."

John 17:15-18

JESUS HAS SENT us into the world. That is our assignment. While we are in the world, he has made provision for us to live in the world and still be protected from its warping influence. What is that provision? His Word.

The Word of God acts in our lives like the pitch that covered Noah's ark, sealing it and keeping the water from penetrating. God's Word fills in the gaps, covers us, and protects us from worldly influences.

We must not be so afraid of being contaminated by the world that we run away and hide. This is not what Jesus called us to. He called us to be his agents in the world. Philippians 2:15 tells us to "live clean, innocent lives as children of God, shining like bright lights in a world full of crooked and perverse people." We can't do that in hiding.

God has placed us in the world strategically. Our life's vocation is to become like Christ right in the middle of the mess. We don't tuck ourselves away so that we can become like Christ without opposition. We don't hide our light under a bushel so nothing will threaten it. Growth in Christlikeness is cultivated right here in the middle of the muck. And like a tree that grows stronger as it is blown by the wind, our own growth is enhanced when the opposing forces of this world bump up against us.

Jesus promised that he has made provision to protect you in the world. You can trust him. Take advantage of his provision by marinating your life in his Word. Let it soak in and flavor every aspect of your life.

Here I am. Send me. I will be salt and light to the world for which you sent your Son.

Jennifer

We should not ask, "What is wrong with the world?" for that diagnosis has already been given. Rather, we should ask, "What has happened to the salt and light?"

—JOHN R. W. STOTT (1921–2011), English minister and writer

HOW SWEET YOUR WORDS TASTE TO ME;
THEY ARE SWEETER THAN HONEY.

Psalm 119:103

SUPPOSE YOU were to look at an apple sitting on your kitchen counter. You might admire its shape and color. You might think about the nutrients in it and consider the effect it would have on your body. But until you eat it, all its potential is lifeless for you. Once you eat it, all its nutrients come to life in you and are applied to your cells to impart their power.

When you eat, your digestive system knows how to use the food to nourish your body. The nutrients from your food are absorbed into your bloodstream and then deposited in the right cells. This process works without your conscious effort. All you have to do to fuel your body is ingest the proper foods.

The Scripture often uses the idea of eating to describe the taking in of God's Word: "When I discovered your words, I devoured them. They are my joy and my heart's delight" (Jeremiah 15:16). What does that analogy communicate? Just this: the Word of God nourishes your spirit just as food nourishes your body.

The Word of God is not something that is applied to the surface of your life for cosmetic purposes. It is to be taken into your life, where it can nourish you from the inside out. God's words shape your thoughts and renew your mind. They become the mold in which your life is formed. In the same way, when your spirit knows how to digest and apply the Word of God, it will taste sweet and delight your heart.

Let your Word be my nourishment. Feed me from its delicacies.

Jennifer

It is not hasty reading, but seriously meditating upon holy and heavenly truths that makes them prove sweet and profitable to the soul. It is not the bee's touching on the flowers that gathers the honey, but her abiding for a time upon them, and drawing out the sweet. It is not he that reads most, but he that meditates most on divine truth, that will prove the choicest, wisest, strongest Christian.

—**JOSEPH HALL** (1574–1656), English bishop and satirist

30 WATCHFUL WAITING

MY EYES STRAIN TO SEE YOUR RESCUE,
TO SEE THE TRUTH OF YOUR PROMISE FULFILLED.

Psalm 119:123

WATCH AND PRAY. Be alert to the Spirit. Pray expectantly, vigilantly attuned to what the Spirit is showing you. Have you heard these exhortations before? In today's verse, the psalmist uses the language of physical sight to describe his attentiveness in looking for the fulfillment of the Lord's promise: "My eyes strain."

The Scriptures often use the language of seeing as a metaphor for spiritual understanding. Paul wrote, "I pray also that the eyes of your heart may be enlightened in order that you may know the hope to which [Christ] has called you, the riches of his glorious inheritance in the saints, and his incomparably great power for us who believe" (Ephesians 1:18-19, NIV 1984).

Jesus used the language of "seeing" when he explained how he knew God's will while in his earthly body: "I tell you the truth, the Son can do nothing by himself. He does only what he sees the Father doing. Whatever the Father does, the Son also does. For the Father loves the Son and shows him everything he is doing" (John 5:19-20). Jesus later said that he would show us everything that he is doing. All these references to seeing are describing the ability to see with spiritual eyes, to look at the earth and see the activity of God by spiritual perception.

When I was a child, every summer my whole family would pile into the car and set out on a cross-country adventure. My dad would tell us what we should be watching for. "Not long now and we'll see mountains," he might say. Then he would always say, "Keep your eyes peeled," which meant, "Keep watch until what you are looking for comes into view. Don't get distracted. Don't lose focus."

In the same way, God invites us to take hold of his promises, believe them, and tenaciously look for their fulfillment.

God's promises are sure. If we keep our eyes peeled, we will see that he is always at work, always moving, always bringing his promises into our experience. When we live on the lookout for God's activity, expecting him to fulfill his promises, our praying becomes keeping watch.

Father, teach me how to keep my eyes peeled so that I see you at work.

Jennifer

Hope is patiently waiting expectantly for the intangible to become reality.
—AVERY D. MILLER

Your promises have been thoroughly tested;
that is why I love them so much.

Psalm 119:140

HAVE YOU ever spent time in God's waiting room? God brings waiting periods into our lives for a very good reason: so that we can test-drive our faith.

If we were planning to buy a car, we could research our purchase and decide what car we wanted—what make and model, what color, what add-on features. We could know everything about the car we wanted *except* how it handles in our hands. Not until we get behind the wheel and drive it for ourselves will we know the feel of the car. We have to drive it before we can know exactly how to adjust the seat and the mirrors, how much pressure to put on the brake pedal to come to a smooth stop, or how responsive the steering wheel is. We won't make our purchase until we've handled the car ourselves— until we've given it a test-drive.

It's the same way with our faith. We can study faith. We can memorize verses about faith. We can learn slick, pithy definitions of faith. But until we have the opportunity to test-drive our faith, we will never know how well it responds. That's where God's tested promises come in.

How are the promises tested? Believing God's promises activates our faith and puts it to work. Accessing the promises entails waiting to see them fulfilled. The Scripture instructs us to "imitate those who through faith and patience inherit what has been promised" (Hebrews 6:12, NIV 1984). Testing and proving the promises calls for faith and patience—in other words, waiting.

When God allows you to test-drive your faith over and over again, you learn how to operate with confidence. You become a mature and seasoned faith walker. You know you can trust the promises because you have seen them thoroughly tested in the laboratory of real life.

Father, thank you for waiting periods in my life. Thank you for letting me see
your promises at work. Pedal to the metal. Full speed ahead.

Jennifer

Biblically, waiting is not just something we have to do until we get what we want. Waiting is part of the process of becoming what God wants us to be.
—**JOHN ORTBERG** (1957–), American pastor, writer, and speaker

JUNE

HIDDEN TREASURE

I REJOICE IN YOUR WORD
LIKE ONE WHO DISCOVERS A GREAT TREASURE.

Psalm 119:162

THE PROMISES of God often come as delightful surprises. Imagine stumbling upon a treasure trove of every kind of abundance. Before, you were making do, and now, suddenly, you have discovered unimaginable wealth.

When we uncover the power in the promises of God, we are like a person who happens upon great spoil. Until we encounter the promises, we have no idea what God has available for us. The promises usher us into lives rich in expectant hope and overflowing with confidence in God. No more meager living. No more merely existing. Now we can live the abundant life.

How will you come upon God's promises? How will you discover the great treasure waiting to be found? By mining the Word of God. God's promises are found nowhere else. It's no mystery where you have to be to come across the rich and powerful promises.

Stinson, the youngest of my three sons, was always a great little treasure hunter: bugs, rocks, sticks that looked like swords. Our neighborhood was a daily discovery project for him. He would burst exuberantly into the house at the end of the day and lay out all his finds for us to inspect and admire and *ooh* and *ahh* over. Having to contend with two older brothers, he soon learned that if he meant to keep his treasures safe, he had to hide them so they wouldn't be taken away from him and so he knew right where they were when he needed them. When I cleaned the house, I often came across Stinson's hiding places. The things he valued, he hid.

The psalmist gives us that same suggestion for the great treasure we find in God's Word: "I have hidden your word in my heart, that I might not sin against you" (Psalm 119:11). As you come upon God's promises, hide them in your heart so they won't be snatched away by the enemy and so that you know right where they are when you need them.

Lord, lead me into the great depository of your promises. Your Word is my most valued possession. I treasure it. I rejoice in it. I hide it in my heart.

Jennifer

Nobody ever outgrows Scripture; the book widens and deepens with our years.
—**CHARLES HADDON SPURGEON** (1834–1892), English preacher and writer

2 THE GOD WHO ANSWERS PRAYER

I TOOK MY TROUBLES TO THE LORD;
I CRIED OUT TO HIM, AND HE ANSWERED MY PRAYER.

Psalm 120:1

PSALM 120 contains a wonderful promise: when we take our troubles to the Lord and turn to him, he will answer our prayer. A wonderful illustration of this promise was a mother named Dorothy, whose three sons served in World War II. She was most concerned about her youngest, Jack. Though he grew up in a strong Christian family, in high school he drank and partied with a wild group of guys.

Jack got his orders to ship out for service in Germany, and when Dorothy heard him telling his brothers he couldn't wait to taste all the German beers, she began to cry out to God. Every day she prayed for protection for her sons in combat. But she prayed especially for her youngest son: "Oh, Lord, may every glass of beer he tries taste like bitter gall!" Though she received only a few letters from Jack in four years, she kept praying.

Soon after the war was over, Jack came home, gave his mom a huge hug, and sat down to a home-cooked lunch. Throughout the meal, Jack talked about his experiences and then suddenly said, "The strangest thing that happened, Mom, was that every time I drank a different type of German beer, they all tasted like bitter gall, so disgusting I couldn't drink them."

Dorothy got out her prayer journal and showed her son what she had asked God, keeping Jack safe but also guarding him from the destructive influence of alcohol. As he looked at the four years of entries, he realized he'd felt the influence of his mother's prayer thousands of miles away. He was so amazed at God's power that on that very day Jack committed himself to Christ and eventually became a pastor who served God the rest of his life.

Lord, grant me grace to cry out to you when I face troubles. Thank you that when we cry out to you, you hear and answer our prayers in your timing and for your purpose. In Christ's name, amen.

Cheri

If [the children of God] desire anything for God's glory, they should pray until they get it. Oh how good, kind, gracious, and condescending is the One with Whom we have to do!

—**GEORGE MÜLLER** (1805–1898), German evangelist and orphanage director

PRAYER CHORUS

THEY ALL MET TOGETHER AND WERE CONSTANTLY UNITED IN PRAYER, ALONG WITH MARY THE MOTHER OF JESUS, SEVERAL OTHER WOMEN, AND THE BROTHERS OF JESUS.

Acts 1:14

THIS PASSAGE from Acts describes the early Christians, who continually met together, praying and waiting for the promised Holy Spirit. And they were not disappointed! Cumulative intercession—whether people are praying in the same room or across a community or nation—has a mighty impact.

A good illustration of this principle appears in the opening scene of the classic Christmas movie *It's a Wonderful Life*. Snow is falling on the streets and buildings of Bedford Falls, while inside homes and offices, many people are praying: "I owe everything to George Bailey. Help him, dear Father." "George is a good guy. Give him a break, God." "He never thinks about himself, God. That's why he's in trouble."

Finally a little girl pleads, "Please, God, something's the matter with Daddy. Please bring Daddy back!"

Although each person prays alone, the voices join together from all over the community, asking God to aid a man named George Bailey. In the movie, God hears those prayers and sends an angel to help George.

That movie is just a story, but it does express a real truth. Maybe the babble of prayer in the movie is what it sounds like when God hears people all over a city or even the world praying for a person or situation. Each voice may start out alone, but by the time it reaches God's throne of grace, it's part of a huge chorus, each voice asking for the same thing.

Even if you're praying alone, you never know how your prayers contribute to God's greater plan. If you feel lonely when praying for something big, ask God to bring you a prayer partner and to raise up more pray-ers to join in your petitions.

Father God, when we think our voices are small and don't count, help us to remember that we are not alone. Use our prayers, rising from all over the world, and join them together to fulfill your purposes. Thank you for letting our prayers be a part of your big plans.

Cheri

Units of prayer combined, like drops of water, make an ocean which defies resistance.

—E. M. BOUNDS (1835–1913), American minister and writer

4 AT GOD'S RIGHT HAND

DAVID WAS LOOKING INTO THE FUTURE AND SPEAKING OF THE MESSIAH'S RESURRECTION. HE WAS SAYING THAT GOD WOULD NOT LEAVE HIM AMONG THE DEAD OR ALLOW HIS BODY TO ROT IN THE GRAVE.

GOD RAISED JESUS FROM THE DEAD, AND WE ARE ALL WITNESSES OF THIS. NOW HE IS EXALTED TO THE PLACE OF HIGHEST HONOR IN HEAVEN, AT GOD'S RIGHT HAND.

Acts 2:31-33

WHEN PETER TAUGHT masses of people gathered in Jerusalem on the Day of Pentecost, he gave them assurance that what had been prophesied centuries before had come to pass in Christ's resurrection and ascension to heaven. Ever since Jesus sat down on the throne of highest honor in heaven, he has been interceding for us. In fact, Hebrews tells us that he lives to pray for those who belong to God.

I've found this one of the most remarkable aspects of prayer: that when we pray for others, we are joining our Savior in his full-time, eternal vocation—making intercession for the saints. When you and another person run a marathon, serve together, or pray together, you grow closer to each other. That's what happens in our relationship with God: this partnership in prayer can bring a deeper friendship and intimacy between us and Christ than we ever imagined possible. Moreover, it is a profound mystery that when we pray, we are joining the Son who sits on the throne next to the Father in highest heaven. It is his life, his Spirit, within us that is praying as we live and move and have our being in him.

Through the gift and vehicle of prayer, we are privileged to draw into ever closer union with Jesus as we experience his heart of compassion and love for others.

> *Open my eyes to the great gift of joining Jesus Christ as he intercedes for all believers. Forgive me for taking for granted the access I have to the throne of grace. Grant me a fresh vision of the Savior, that I might more often and more earnestly enter into this gift of prayer.*

Cheri

Around us is a world lost in sin, above us is a God willing and able to save; it is ours to build the bridge that links heaven and earth, and prayer is the mighty instrument that does the work. If we do our part, God will do His.

—E. M. BOUNDS (1835–1913), American minister and writer

TURNING TO GOD

REPENT OF YOUR SINS AND TURN TO GOD, SO THAT YOUR SINS
MAY BE WIPED AWAY. THEN TIMES OF REFRESHMENT WILL COME
FROM THE PRESENCE OF THE LORD, AND HE WILL AGAIN SEND
YOU JESUS, YOUR APPOINTED MESSIAH.

Acts 3:19-20

THIS PROMISE that Peter spoke to the Jews in the Temple centuries ago is equally alive and relevant today. As everyone in the city rushed to Solomon's Colonnade to see the once-lame beggar who was now walking, leaping, and praising God, Peter explained that the beggar had been healed not by human power or godliness but by *faith in the name of Jesus*: "This is the same Jesus whom you handed over and rejected before Pilate. . . . You killed the author of life, but God raised him from the dead" (Acts 3:13, 15). Peter acknowledged that what they and their leaders did to Jesus was done in ignorance, but now they had the opportunity of a lifetime—if they would turn from their sins and turn to God.

This is the same offer the Father graciously makes to each person on earth today. Because of the life, death, and resurrection of his Son, Jesus, we can humble ourselves before God and confess our sins; then the gates of heaven open wide. If we refuse God's invitation, the lines of communication get clogged to the point where we can't sense the Lord's presence. In addition, Psalm 66:18 says that the Lord does not listen to the prayers of those who harbor sin in their hearts and reject repentance.

When we confess our wrongs, we enter into a relationship with the living Lord, and he gives his Spirit to live in us. He creates a new heart within us. Times of refreshment come, just as he promised: his living water and life flow through us and overflow to others. What a great promise and invitation to turn from a life of sin to experience the freeing power of forgiveness!

> *God of mercy, what a great promise and invitation to turn from our sins and experience the freeing power of forgiveness. Create a clean heart in me, and let the times of refreshment come!*

Cheri

The most marvelous ingredient in the forgiveness of God is that he also forgets, the one thing a human being can never do. Forgetting with God is a divine attribute; God's forgiveness forgets.

—OSWALD CHAMBERS (1874–1917), Scottish minister and teacher

6

WORDS THAT BRING LIFE

Kind words are like honey—
sweet to the soul and healthy for the body.

Proverbs 16:24

STUDIES SHOW that with the best of intentions, mothers tend to criticize their children *ten times more* than they say a positive remark, and dads do their fair share as well. There may be practical reasons, such as getting children to brush their teeth or do their homework, but critical words only discourage children and derail the loving relationship we hope to build. Why? Because children and teenagers tend to move *toward* those who encourage them and *away from* those who discourage them.

A negative approach focuses on what I call the "hole"—what young people are *not* doing well or how they're falling short. Negative words, however unintentional, begin to demotivate and deflate those who hear them.

Today's reading offers a better approach: speaking kind words that bless your children and are sweet to their souls and healthy for their bodies. You encourage and build up your daughter when you focus on how much she *tried* in the soccer game rather than on whether her team won or lost, or on a young boy's *progress* (seventy-eight this week on the math test—five more right than last week!). Giving children "snapshots" of how they're growing or progressing helps motivate their efforts: "You kept trying even though writing the essay was difficult; that's what I call perseverance." These words may seem small, but they are seeds of promise and blessing.

Don't wait to offer kind words to the children around you until they are older, become more successful, make top grades, or behave better. Focus on what you can be thankful for, the hidden gifts God has put within, and encourage children right where they are.

Father, you who are the essence of love, forgive my negativity and perfectionism, my critical words to those I love. Transform my heart to see those children around me with your eyes and to speak words of life to them. Help me to believe in them, even before I see the finished product, and to be patient even as you are infinitely patient with me.

Cheri

Everyone has inside of him a piece of good news. The good news is that you don't know how great you can be! How much you can love! What you can accomplish!

—ANNE FRANK (1929–1945), Jewish author and victim of the Nazi Holocaust

IN THE PLACE OF HONOR

PETER AND THE APOSTLES REPLIED, "WE MUST OBEY GOD RATHER
THAN ANY HUMAN AUTHORITY. THE GOD OF OUR ANCESTORS
RAISED JESUS FROM THE DEAD AFTER YOU KILLED HIM BY HANGING
HIM ON A CROSS. THEN GOD PUT HIM IN THE PLACE OF HONOR AT
HIS RIGHT HAND AS PRINCE AND SAVIOR."

Acts 5:29-31

IF WE ARE reading our daily passages in the Bible and are pressed for time, it's easy to
skip over significant gems of truth—like the shining promise in the fifth chapter of Acts.
Peter and the apostles are speaking to the Temple council. But just the night before, Peter
and the apostles were in prison. An angel came to their jail cell, opened the gates, and
brought them out to freedom. As soon as the next day began, they went about the business of obeying the angel's command to go to the Temple and share the message of life.

Within their words to the authorities in Acts 5 appears a great truth: *The Father put Jesus
as Prince and Savior in the place of honor right beside him at the throne of grace.* As I pondered that
verse, I was filled with awe that Jesus, who was crucified for your sins and mine when we
were still sinners, is seated at the Father's right hand. And what is he doing? He is preparing
a place for us in heaven, John tells us in John 14:2, and "sustain[ing] everything by the mighty
power of his command" (Hebrews 1:3). He was rejected and crucified that we might be
accepted. And someday he will present us to the Father with great joy because there—at that
place of honor—Christ is interceding for us day and night.

*I praise you, Jesus, as Prince and Savior! Thank you, Father, for raising your
Son from the dead and seating him at your right hand in the place of honor.
I worship you and give you all praise and love because you are worthy!*

Cheri

The Lord appeared in the flesh, that he might arouse us by his teaching, kindle us by his
example, redeem us by his death, and renew us by his resurrection.

—**GREGORY THE GREAT** (540–604), Roman pope

8

THE LORD RESTORES

When the LORD brought back his exiles to Jerusalem,
  it was like a dream!
We were filled with laughter,
  and we sang for joy.
And the other nations said,
  "What amazing things the LORD has done for them."
Yes, the LORD has done amazing things for us!
  What joy!

Psalm 126:1-3

ONE OF THE THINGS I love about the Lord is that he is a God of second chances, who delights in forgiving and restoring his people. How many of us need a second chance when we have made poor choices? At other times our hearts break over someone who betrays us, over a self-destructive child, or over a broken relationship. Can you identify with the song the exiles were singing on the way to Jerusalem following their long exile?

Restoration is one of the great themes of the Bible, and it reflects God's unfailing mercy and grace. God gave a second chance to Moses after he had committed murder, to David after his sin with Bathsheba, to Hezekiah when he became deathly ill, to Jonah when he ran from God, to Peter after his denial of Christ. Throughout history, countless people, once running from God or having made a mess of their lives, have received a fresh chance to fulfill God's purpose.

Just as God restored these people, he offers restoration to you. The key is to run away from your own way and run to God. There is no pit so deep or dark that he can't reach you! When you come with a heart sorry for your sins, the Lord will give you a second chance at life. Then, like God's people returning from exile, you will be filled with so much joy that it overflows into laughter and singing. And those around you will see what amazing things the Lord has done for you!

Father, thank you for not giving up on me. How I praise you for your grace that brings restoration. My heart is filled with the joy of knowing that you hold out a loving hand and say, "Trust me! Try again and know that I am with you!"

Cheri

If it weren't for second chances, no one would get into heaven. It would just be God and Jesus and that is not God's plan.
—UNKNOWN

THE PROMISE OF CHILDREN

CHILDREN ARE A GIFT FROM THE LORD;
    THEY ARE A REWARD FROM HIM.
CHILDREN BORN TO A YOUNG MAN
    ARE LIKE ARROWS IN A WARRIOR'S HANDS.
HOW JOYFUL IS THE MAN WHOSE QUIVER IS FULL OF THEM!

Psalm 127:3-5

ONE OF GOD'S most gracious gifts is children. The Giver of every good and perfect gift delights to reward parents and families with new life. Throughout the Old and New Testaments (for example, Genesis 48:9; Joshua 24:3; Ruth 4:13; Isaiah 8:18; Luke 18:15-17), we see that when God wanted to do something good for his people, he gave them children. Babies are not accidents; they come through the blessing of God.

In these verses the psalmist compares children with arrows that go forward, penetrating the future and bringing hope. They are the legacy of their families and will be directed into the future, fulfilling their destiny and purpose.

Although some in our society may find babies to be inconveniences or burdens, the Lord intends them to bring great joy and blessing. I can also attest that children are the crowning glory of their grandparents—our six grandchildren light up our world and bring us more joy than I could have imagined. God formed each of them, making them marvelous creations. He watched them grow from conception to birth and designed them for unique purposes. And as Matthew 18:5 says, when we receive a little child, we are receiving Christ. Whether we are aunts or uncles, mothers or fathers, we should receive such marvelous gifts as children with great rejoicing and thankfulness, with open hearts that will embrace, love, nurture, and pray for them all our days.

> *Thanks be to God for his indescribable gift of salvation that came into the world as a baby! Thank you, Father, for the gift of children, your gracious blessing wrapped up in love. Give us hearts to receive and cherish your gifts and to bless each child who comes across our paths.*

Cheri

Children are not casual guests in our home. They have been loaned to us temporarily for the purpose of loving them and instilling a foundation of values on which their future lives will be built.

—JAMES C. DOBSON (1936–), American author and radio host

10 GOD IS IN THE DETAILS

WE MAY THROW THE DICE,
BUT THE LORD DETERMINES HOW THEY FALL.

Proverbs 16:33

ONE OF THE most important truths God has woven into his Word is that he is engineering even the smallest details in order to accomplish his divine purpose in every situation. Happenings that seem random, choices and decisions that seem spontaneous and uncalculated, paths that cross in seemingly serendipitous ways—all are being ordered by the Lord: "The LORD directs the steps of the godly. He delights in every detail of their lives" (Psalm 37:23).

Does anything seem more random than the tossing of dice? Yet the Scripture teaches us that the Lord orders even those things that seem unplanned or uncontrolled.

Nothing—not one detail—is random. God's Word points us to his ways: one of the psalmists says, "I will study your commandments and reflect on your ways" (Psalm 119:15). God tells us to observe his ways, to consider them and learn his ways and his well-worn paths. He tells us to become familiar with his consistent methods of dealing with situations and people. When we know his ways and recognize the underlying consistency in all his doings, we will see the divine will in the center of everything. It is his way to manage the details, to act according to an eternal plan. "O LORD, I will honor and praise your name, for you are my God. You do such wonderful things! You planned them long ago" (Isaiah 25:1). Whatever is happening in your life right now, even though it may seem as if circumstances are taking on a momentum of their own, God is acting according to a plan that has been in place since the beginning of time. It may look as if the dice have been randomly cast, but remember—the Lord determines how they fall. Through every page of Scripture, God shows us his ways. He uses everything to work out his purposes.

Father, I thank you that you are always carefully managing the details of my life. Your purpose for me always prevails, even though I am prone to forget that and make my own plans.

Jennifer

How often we look upon God as our last and feeblest resource! We go to him because we have nowhere else to go. And then we learn that the storms of life have driven us, not upon the rocks, but into the desired haven.

—GEORGE MACDONALD (1824–1905), Scottish author and minister

GLORY TO GOD

THE GLORIOUS PRESENCE OF THE LORD FILLED THE TEMPLE.

1 Kings 8:11

SOLOMON, THE SON of David, had built the Temple his father had envisioned but was not allowed to build. The Temple was a permanent form of the Tabernacle, the portable place of worship that the Israelites took with them wherever they went. When the Tabernacle was first erected, according to detailed instructions given Moses, the glory of the Lord filled it. "The cloud covered the Tabernacle, and the glory of the LORD filled the Tabernacle" (Exodus 40:34). And when the Temple was completed, "the glorious presence of the LORD filled the Temple."

In both instances, the glory of God appeared in the form of a cloud so concentrated that it interrupted normal activities: "Moses could no longer enter the Tabernacle because the cloud had settled down over it" (Exodus 40:35). "The priests could not continue their service because of the cloud" (1 Kings 8:11).

In the Old Testament, God often made his presence evident in a cloud. As we move into the New Testament era, the temple—God's dwelling place on earth—is God's people, each one of us: "We are the temple of the living God. As God said: 'I will live in them and walk among them'" (2 Corinthians 6:16). Now God's presence is made visible through us. It will interrupt the normal course of activity in our lives, and we will learn to live "abnormally."

Here is what the Lord promises concerning his house, his temple: "The future glory of this Temple will be greater than its past glory, says the LORD of Heaven's Armies. And in this place I will bring peace. I, the LORD of Heaven's Armies have spoken!" (Haggai 2:9). Now we are his dwelling places, and he will fill us with his glory and grant us peace.

Father, dwell richly in me.

Jennifer

There must be an emptying before there can be a filling; and when the heart is turned upside down, and everything is turned out that is contrary to God, then the Spirit will come, just as he did in the tabernacle, and fill us with his Glory.

—**DWIGHT L. MOODY** (1837–1899), American evangelist and publisher

12 PURIFIED

> FIRE TESTS THE PURITY OF SILVER AND GOLD,
> BUT THE LORD TESTS THE HEART.
>
> *Proverbs 17:3*

WHAT A CRUCIBLE does for silver and a furnace does for gold, God does for the heart. The refining process for these precious metals requires intense heat. When the temperature is hot enough, the pure metal and the impurities separate. The pure metal settles to the bottom, and the impurities rise to the top, where they can be skimmed off. Heat brings impurities to the surface so they can be removed.

God chooses the picture of silver and gold to describe a purified heart.

Silver and gold are malleable metals. They can easily be molded into new shapes. A pure heart is soft, moldable, and pliable in the hands of the Master Artist. He wants to make you into someone beautiful and whole. He wants to make you a masterpiece of his work. As you respond to him in obedience, your heart becomes pure, able to be hammered into any shape he desires, and you become an expression of his genius.

Silver and gold are the best conductors of heat and electricity. A conductive substance is one through which power moves freely. A conductor transfers power from one object to another. A pure heart—a heart from which impurities have been removed—is a conductor of God's power into lives and situations on earth. Your life will be the conductor of Christ's life.

Silver and gold reflect light. Purified silver or gold reflects without distortion. The desires of a pure heart clearly reflect the desires of the Father. A pure heart is an undistorted reflection of his heart. Impurity will distort the reflection and will cause it not to be exact. This is why the Father wants to make you pure so that you desire what God desires.

God promises that anytime he turns up the heat, he does it to purify you so that his power can flow through you. Seek purity and you will find power.

> Lord, I surrender to whatever it takes to clean out my life and make me like pure silver and pure gold.
>
> *Jennifer*

Man willingly becomes the channel for the yearnings of God's heart.
—R. ARTHUR MATHEWS (1912–1978), missionary to China and author

LOST CAUSES **13**

IMMEDIATELY [SAUL] BEGAN PREACHING ABOUT JESUS IN THE
SYNAGOGUES, SAYING, "HE IS INDEED THE SON OF GOD!"
 ALL WHO HEARD HIM WERE AMAZED. "ISN'T THIS THE SAME
MAN WHO CAUSED SUCH DEVASTATION AMONG JESUS' FOLLOWERS
IN JERUSALEM?" THEY ASKED. "AND DIDN'T HE COME HERE
TO ARREST THEM AND TAKE THEM IN CHAINS TO THE LEADING
PRIESTS?"

Acts 9:20-21

AS A POTENTIAL convert to Christianity, Saul—later Paul—was about as lost a cause as
you could imagine. He was a zealous persecutor of believers in Jesus as Christ, even going
door to door to root them out. His religious zeal made him merciless in carrying out his
mission. He believed with all his heart that what he was doing was righteous and that he
was following God's commands.

 If you had said to a believer of that day, "Who is the least likely person on the planet
to believe in Jesus as Messiah?" the resounding answer would have been "Saul of Tarsus!"

 Saul's testimony stands as a promise that with God there are no lost causes. God can
so radically transform a life that the new person is almost unrecognizable.

 Sam seemed to be a lost cause. Everybody knew it. When I suggested to his wife that
we begin to pray for Sam's salvation, she agreed just to appease me. "We can try," she said,
and then explained why it would never work. Sam was of Asian descent and came from
generations of Buddhists. He was highly intelligent and successful. He lived a life of integrity and goodness. He was completely at peace with his life and felt no lack or need.

 Sam was very advanced in the martial arts, and unknown to his wife, his marital-arts
instructor was a devoted Christian who encouraged the men to stay after class for Bible
study. To compress a long story, Sam's life was radically changed when he accepted Jesus
as his Savior.

 Do you know a lost cause? Let the conversion account of Saul give you hope.

 *Father, I bring my lost cause to you. Pursue this one I love as only you know
 how to do.*

Jennifer

Once I knew only darkness and stillness—my life was without past or future—but a little
word from the fingers of another fell into my hand that clutched at emptiness, and my heart
leaped to the rapture of living.

—**HELEN KELLER** (1880–1968), American author

14 ALL DRESSED UP

MAY YOUR PRIESTS BE CLOTHED IN GODLINESS.

Psalm 132:9

THE SCRIPTURE says that once we accept by faith everything that Christ has provided for us, we are his priests and are clothed in him: "All who have been united with Christ in baptism have put on Christ, like putting on new clothes" (Galatians 3:27). We wear Christ's righteousness in the world because we are clothed in his life.

The Scripture beautifully pictures this in the parable of the Prodigal Son. The proud young man who had left so flippantly was coming back home a failure. Those who knew him would see his dirty face and hands and his tattered rags.

He could imagine the expressions on their faces as he made his way shamefaced to his father's house.

Then comes the most beautiful part of the story: "While he was still a long way off, his father saw him coming. Filled with love and compassion, he ran to his son, embraced him, and kissed him" (Luke 15:20).

While the son was still a long way off, his father *ran* to meet him.

Proud men did not run in public. But the father ran. He endured the shame that belonged to his son to welcome his son home.

When the father met his son, he called for the best robe. Who owned the best robe? The father. He called for his own robe to cover the son's shame and failure and shield his son from the scorn he deserved. By his actions, the father announced to all that his son was to be accepted.

Then the father prepared a banquet in the presence of his son's enemies (see Psalm 23:5) and invited all those who would have treated his son as dead to celebrate his resurrection: "This son of mine was dead and has now returned to life. He was lost, but now he is found" (Luke 15:24).

Father, thank you for your precious promise that I am clothed in Christ. You have covered my shame, and I am fully accepted.

Jennifer

Because we are united by faith to [Jesus Christ] who is perfectly righteous, God accepts us as perfectly righteous.

—JERRY BRIDGES (1929–), American author and conference speaker

GET IT TOGETHER

How wonderful and pleasant it is
when brothers live together in harmony!

Psalm 133:1

UNITY IS NOT just nice if you can get it; it is essential to God's work on the earth. It is central to his redemptive wooing of the lost world: "Your love for one another will prove to the world that you are my disciples" (John 13:35).

Unity is so rare that it stands as proof of the power of God at work: "May God . . . help you live in complete harmony with each other, as is fitting for followers of Christ Jesus. Then all of you can join together with one voice, giving praise and glory to God, the Father of our Lord Jesus Christ" (Romans 15:5-6).

Since God values unity so highly and it is so necessary to show the world proof of his presence in our lives, then clearly unity becomes a target for the enemy. His schemes will be directed at relationships, through which he seeks to destroy unity.

How well are his schemes working in your life? Are you holding a grudge? Is there someone who can always offend you? What has created a split between you and another person? Do you insist that everyone in your sphere of influence share your opinion or risk being ostracized?

I think the enemy succeeds at diluting our unity because, most of the time, maintaining or restoring unity requires humility. We are called on to lay aside our pet peeves and to allow someone else to have the last word.

Preserving unity in the bond of peace means we have to die to our fleshly pride. But that death will produce life. When we lay aside the pride that infects our relationships with one another, the kind of unity only God can produce accomplishes what he has in mind.

*Father, show me where my pride is cooperating with the enemy's schemes, and
instead, help me be a peacemaker.*

Jennifer

God cares nothing about our man-made divisions and groups and is not interested in our self-righteous, hair-splitting, and religious, man-made formulas and organizations. He wants you to recognize the *unity* of the body of Christ.

—**M. R. DEHAAN** (1891–1965), American Bible teacher

16 GIVE GOD YOUR EMPTINESS

AFTER A WHILE THE BROOK DRIED UP, FOR THERE WAS NO RAINFALL ANYWHERE IN THE LAND.

THEN THE LORD SAID TO ELIJAH, "GO AND LIVE IN THE VILLAGE OF ZAREPHATH, NEAR THE CITY OF SIDON. I HAVE INSTRUCTED A WIDOW THERE TO FEED YOU."

1 Kings 17:7-9

THROUGH HIS ACTIONS in the life of Elijah, God demonstrates what we can expect from him. He promises that he will always meet our needs wherever he calls us to go.

In the midst of a severe drought, God had sent Elijah to stay beside a brook in the wilderness. Elijah would drink from the brook, and ravens would feed him. God miraculously sustained Elijah in the first three years of the drought, sending provision by the most unexpected means.

But eventually the brook dried up, and God sent Elijah to Zarephath, where he had directed a widow to provide for Elijah. God had many ways in which he could have fed and nourished Elijah. The ravens could still have fed him. Or this same God who had made water gush from a rock and caused manna to appear every morning for the Israelites in the wilderness could have done that again. But he wanted the widow to provide for Elijah.

As the story unfolds, Elijah has an encounter with the very widow God had appointed to supply Elijah with food. When Elijah asks for bread, she reveals that she doesn't have any bread. She is at the end of her provision. There is no more, and she sees no possible way to get more.

This widow, fresh out of bread, is the one God has commanded to feed Elijah. So Elijah tells her to ignore her lack of provision and act as if she has plenty. As soon as she obeys, the provision is there. And every time she needs more flour and oil, flour and oil are there.

God appointed this destitute widow to give out of the little she had so that she could obtain the blessing that giving brings and could receive in the measure she gave. When she did, she set in motion the Kingdom law that releases the Lord's abundant and perfect provision in response to his people's obedience.

Father, teach me to live in the abundance of your promises instead of in my evaluation of my circumstances.

Jennifer

There can be no faith so feeble that Christ does not respond to it.
—**ALEXANDER MACLAREN** (1826–1910), British preacher and Bible expositor

PRAY UNTIL...

> AHAB WENT TO EAT AND DRINK. BUT ELIJAH CLIMBED TO THE
> TOP OF MOUNT CARMEL AND BOWED LOW TO THE GROUND
> AND PRAYED WITH HIS FACE BETWEEN HIS KNEES.
>
> *1 Kings 18:42*

JAMES 5:16-18 uses this incident in Elijah's life to illustrate the promise that prayer holds: "The earnest prayer of a righteous person has great power and produces wonderful results. Elijah was as human as we are, and yet when he prayed earnestly that no rain would fall, none fell for three and a half years! Then, when he prayed again, the sky sent down rain and the earth began to yield its crops."

To get the full impact of what James is teaching, we have to put the Old and New Testaments together. The story to which James refers is found in 1 Kings 17. James says Elijah prayed that it would not rain, and it did not rain. But the drought was God's idea, so when Elijah announced the drought, he was acting as God's spokesman.

God had sent the drought. What had Elijah done? He had prayed for the drought. So, (1) God says it, (2) Elijah prays it, and (3) God performs it. Elijah's prayers released the will of God on earth. God calls us into a cooperative venture with him, releasing his power and provision in response to our prayers.

Next, Elijah heard from God. He knew that God was ready to end the drought. He was so certain of this that he declared it publicly, and then, while Ahab went off to eat and drink, Elijah went to the top of Mount Carmel to pray.

Elijah knew that prayer was the conduit through which the will of God comes from heaven to earth, causing the will of God to be done on earth as it is in heaven.

> *Father, fill my heart with your desires so that when I pray out of the overflow of my heart, I am praying your will and your heart's desires.*
>
> *Jennifer*

There is such a thing as coming into such a sweet relation to the will of God that we are fused into oneness with it. His will becomes ours, and He gladly sets us free to carry our own wishes—they being His first and then ours.

—**G. GRANGER FLEMING** (ca. 1866–1922), South African architect and author

18 STILL SMALL VOICE

A MIGHTY WINDSTORM HIT THE MOUNTAIN. IT WAS SUCH A TERRIBLE BLAST THAT THE ROCKS WERE TORN LOOSE, BUT THE LORD WAS NOT IN THE WIND. AFTER THE WIND THERE WAS AN EARTHQUAKE, BUT THE LORD WAS NOT IN THE EARTHQUAKE. AND AFTER THE EARTHQUAKE THERE WAS A FIRE, BUT THE LORD WAS NOT IN THE FIRE. AND AFTER THE FIRE THERE WAS THE SOUND OF A GENTLE WHISPER.

1 Kings 19:11-12

GOD PROMISES that he will speak and that we can hear, but often he calls us away from noise and chaos to listen intently for what he will say to us. Sometimes his secrets come wrapped in silence.

Because we live in an age of "portable noise," stepping away and disconnecting from the constant bombardment of information must be an intentional act. Making silence part of our daily discipline opens our lives to the whispered wisdom of the Lord.

Approach your times of silence by listening for whatever he would say, not for what you want him to say. Let Habakkuk be your model: "I will climb up to my watchtower and stand at my guardpost. There I will wait to see what the LORD says and how he will answer my complaint" (Habakkuk 2:1).

When Habakkuk needed to hear from God, he stationed himself on a high tower. He got up high—got perspective. And then the first thing Habakkuk did was watch to see what God would say.

Too often we come to God expecting him to validate our decisions and so miss him altogether. Many times what he says will redefine our problem—help us see it as his opportunity to show his power. But when we are listening for what we want to hear instead of for what he wants to say, we will surely miss him. Ask him to open your ears "to listen like one being instructed" (Isaiah 50:4, NIV).

Lord, I want to hear your whispers. Woo me into the silence where I can hear your voice without distortion.

Jennifer

Christ is not a reservoir but a spring. His life is continual, active and ever passing on with an outflow as necessary as its inflow. If we do not perpetually draw the fresh supply from the living Fountain, we shall either grow stagnant or empty. It is, therefore, not so much a perpetual fullness as a perpetual filling.

—**A. B. SIMPSON** (1843–1919), Canadian preacher, theologian, and author

FAST AND PRAY

ONE DAY AS THESE MEN WERE WORSHIPING THE LORD AND FASTING, THE HOLY SPIRIT SAID, "DEDICATE BARNABAS AND SAUL FOR THE SPECIAL WORK TO WHICH I HAVE CALLED THEM."

Acts 13:2

TO HEAR God's present voice, we have to clear the clutter from our hearts and get the acoustics right. We want to hear his voice without distortion.

Keeping our lives clear of clutter is an ongoing task. Like keeping a house clean, it requires daily diligence. Fasting is one of the elements of a praying life that helps keep our hearts uncluttered. Notice that worship and fasting go together. One enhances and empowers the other.

Fasting is not a way to influence, impress, or manipulate God. Fasting does not prove anything to God. He knows your heart better than you do (see John 2:25; Hebrews 4:13; Psalm 33:15). Nor is fasting or a hunger strike designed to persuade God to release what he has, up to now, withheld. Instead, fasting is a way to let go of what binds you to this physical world—food—in order to receive your sustenance from the spiritual world.

When you fast, you determine that for a period of time you will deny your physical cravings to focus on your spiritual cravings. You allow your spiritual hunger to become stronger and more focused, and you feed your spirit with the same enthusiasm with which you would feed your physical body. Spiritual hunger takes priority over physical hunger. Ole Hallesby says, "Fasting loosens the ties which bind us to this world of material things and our surroundings that we may concentrate all our spiritual powers upon the unseen and eternal."

Fasting is not a last-ditch effort to get through to God. Instead, it sharpens your spiritual senses so that God can get through to you. It will sensitize you to the things of the spiritual realm so that you will be more aware of God's presence and his present-tense voice.

Father, cause me to desire you and seek after your voice above all else. I treasure your words more than daily food.

Jennifer

Faith needs a life of prayer in which to grow and keep strong. Prayer needs fasting for its full and perfect development.

—ANDREW MURRAY (1828–1917), South African pastor and author

20 OUR FATHER

THOUGH THE LORD IS GREAT, HE CARES FOR THE HUMBLE.

Psalm 138:6

THE GOD WHO PROMISES us his protection and his provision is exalted and lofty, yet he loves and cares for us.

He is our Father, yet he is clothed with splendor and majesty and hidden in light. He commands the morning and causes the dawn to know its place. He is great in wisdom and mighty in deed. For him, all the morning stars sang together and all the sons of God shouted for joy. The idols tremble at his presence and the hearts of his enemies melt within them. He is worthy of all praise. And he is our Father, who watches over us unceasingly and lavishes his love on us.

My earthly father retired from a career that included being an attorney, a legislator, a circuit judge, and finally a judge on the Missouri Court of Appeals. During his retirement festivities, people who had known him in various roles praised him. Some praised him for being a defender and protector, some praised him as a worthy adversary, others said that he was a fair and balanced creator of law, and still others had known him as a wise dispenser of justice and interpreter of law. All the praise was true and justified. But it fell short of the full picture of who my father is. His admirers missed the big picture because he was not their daddy.

Because I know him as "Daddy," I know someone entirely different. Of course I've known him as protector and defender. I've known him as a dispenser of justice and a creator of law. But do you see the difference it makes to know him in these roles as my daddy? When these roles are being enacted with personal, directed love as their motivating force, they have a different effect altogether.

Consider who God is. Consider his power, strength, and wisdom. Then realize that all he is and all he does flow out to you from a core of personal, intimate love. He is your Father, but he is also your Daddy.

Father, it is impossible not to trust you when I consider that you are my Daddy.

Jennifer

My Father, supremely good, beauty of all things beautiful.
 —**ST. AUGUSTINE** (354–430), Latin North African theologian and philosopher

WHAT GOD THINKS OF YOU

YOU GO BEFORE ME AND FOLLOW ME.
  YOU PLACE YOUR HAND OF BLESSING ON MY HEAD. . . .
YOU MADE ALL THE DELICATE, INNER PARTS OF MY BODY
  AND KNIT ME TOGETHER IN MY MOTHER'S WOMB.
THANK YOU FOR MAKING ME SO WONDERFULLY COMPLEX!
  YOUR WORKMANSHIP IS MARVELOUS—HOW WELL I KNOW IT.
YOU WATCHED ME AS I WAS BEING FORMED IN UTTER SECLUSION,
  AS I WAS WOVEN TOGETHER IN THE DARK OF THE WOMB.
YOU SAW ME BEFORE I WAS BORN.

Psalm 139:5, 13-16

MOST OF US have heard a barrage of criticism throughout our growing-up years and into adulthood—at school, at home, at our workplace. People may tell us we fall short in some area, or the voices within our own minds remind us of mistakes we've made. That's when we need to take to heart what God says about us.

Today's psalm says the Lord shaped us inside and out and loved us even before we were aware of him. He made us for a purpose and equipped us with the gifts and talents to accomplish what he's prepared for us to do (see Ephesians 2:10).

When you don't feel accepted by others, soak in the fact that God's Word says you are accepted in Jesus, the beloved (see Romans 15:7). Turn your ears and eyes to God's promises instead of to what the world and the people in it think about you—and you'll begin to experience the peace that comes with knowing you are loved deeply and unconditionally.

> *Master Creator, thank you for making me just the way I am. Through my weaknesses, demonstrate your power and strength. Use the gifts you put within me for your purposes. I come to you for the acceptance and encouragement I need to face the challenges of this day.*

Cheri

As we come to know ourselves through and through, we come to see ourselves more as God sees us, and then we catch some little glimpse of his designs with us. . . . Until we come to this knowledge, we must take all in faith, believing, though we know not, the goodness of God toward us.

—**EDWARD BOUBERIE PUSEY** (1800–1882), English theologian and preacher

22 KEEP THE OIL FLOWING

"WHAT CAN I DO TO HELP YOU?" ELISHA ASKED. "TELL ME,
WHAT DO YOU HAVE IN THE HOUSE?"
"NOTHING AT ALL, EXCEPT A FLASK OF OLIVE OIL," SHE REPLIED.

2 Kings 4:2

THE WIDOW in this story found herself in dire straits. She was almost out of provision. When she came to Elisha for help, he gave her instructions that, from a human perspective, were almost nonsensical. You would expect him to tell her to gather up jars full of oil, but he told her to gather up all the *empty* jars she could find and fill them from the single small flask she had. This miracle—happening to a real person at a real time—also acts as a parable of how God provides.

In the picture language of Scripture, clay or clay jars are often representative of human beings, and oil represents the Holy Spirit.

In order to increase the measure of oil the woman already possessed, Elisha told her to bring all the emptiness she could find. Emptiness was an asset because it provided the necessary condition for fullness.

Notice how this story ends: "Her sons kept bringing jars to her, and she filled one after another. Soon every container was full to the brim! 'Bring me another jar,' she said to one of her sons. 'There aren't any more!' he told her. And then the olive oil stopped flowing" (2 Kings 4:5-6). When there was no more emptiness, the oil stopped flowing.

As your emptiness is replaced with God's fullness, you have a never-ending supply to give to those around you. Trying to live and work in your own power will drain you dry. But living and working in God's provision open you to a further filling of power.

How can we keep our lives open to the continuing outpouring of the Spirit? By pouring out to others what he has poured into us.

Are you trying to fill your emptiness with things that are not eternal? Are you attempting to find fullness in your own resources? Bring your emptiness to God. Let the Spirit speak to you about your empty places and about the fullness you need to be pouring out to others.

Father, I bring all my emptiness to you so you can fill me. Show me where to pour out what you have poured in.

Jennifer

Thou must be emptied of that wherewith thou art full, that thou mayest be filled with that whereof thou art empty.

—**ST. AUGUSTINE** (354–430), Latin North African theologian and philosopher

YIELDING

Naaman went down to the Jordan River and dipped himself seven times, as the man of God had instructed him. And his skin became as healthy as the skin of a young child's, and he was healed!

2 Kings 5:14

WE ARE WIRED to try harder. Why do you think that is? I think it's because we need to feel in control. We see this in the story of Naaman in 2 Kings 5:1-14.

Naaman was a national hero, a valiant warrior. He had it all—except that he was a leper. He was living under a sentence of death.

He heard about a prophet in Samaria, a man named Elisha. Could this obscure, uncelebrated man of God possibly hold the key that would bring life out of Naaman's death?

Naaman set off to find Elisha. But it was not the prophet who answered the door. It was the prophet's servant who gave Naaman the prescription for his ailment: "Go dip yourself in the Jordan River seven times."

Outraged, insulted, and incredulous, Naaman refused to do such a degrading thing. There were better rivers back home! Where was the hand waving and the shouting and the drama—something to validate what an important man Naaman was!

Naaman had risked his life on the battlefield time and time again. His feats in battle had cemented his reputation for mettle and prowess. If the God of Israel had required something daring, something only the mighty Naaman could do, that would have been easy. The prophet's instructions were the death sentence for Naaman's pride, but following them was the only way for Naaman to have life. The choice—life or death—was his. The hardest thing Naaman ever did was dip himself in the Jordan River seven times.

And yet, when Naaman emerged from the river the seventh time, he had the skin of a little child. You might say he'd been born again. He had passed from death to life. You might say his death to himself had yielded a resurrection.

Lord, I want my life to prove your power, not my prowess. I will obey when you call me to the most humbling actions so that you can be glorified.

Jennifer

Just as water ever seeks and fills the lowest place, so the moment God finds you abased and empty, His glory and power flow in.
—**ANDREW MURRAY** (1828–1917), South African pastor and author

24 FARSIGHTED LIVING

"Don't be afraid!" Elisha told him. "For there are more on our side than on theirs!" Then Elisha prayed, "O Lord, open his eyes and let him see!" The Lord opened the young man's eyes, and when he looked up, he saw that the hillside around Elisha was filled with horses and chariots of fire.

2 Kings 6:16-17

THERE IS always more to a situation than meets the eye.

On this morning, when Elisha and his servant—unarmed and unprotected—woke up to find themselves surrounded by a well-armed and determined enemy, what met the eye was overwhelming. Elisha's servant was in a panic. But Elisha could already see what his servant could not. He could see the spiritual reinforcements that were already in place. His servant was blind to the spiritual realities. So Elisha prayed that God would open his servant's eyes to see what Elisha could see, and the Lord did just that.

The enemy army headed right toward Elisha and his servant. And Elisha—who had just prayed that his servant's eyes would be opened—now prayed that his enemy's eyes would be blinded. The enemy became deluded, and Elisha was able to lead them directly into the hands of the king of Israel. Instead of killing or even capturing them, Elisha counseled the king to feed the captives and send them home. This accomplished what all the defeats on the battlefield could not: "After that, the Aramean raiders stayed away from the land of Israel" (2 Kings 6:23).

The Lord promises that he will show us the reality that is hidden to our physical senses. We will be able to make decisions based on faith, not on fear. We will be able to act on reality, not on illusion. When we see past the visible, we will make unusual choices. We will take actions, or refrain from actions, that circumstances seem to dictate, and we will win battles that otherwise are not winnable.

Open my eyes, Lord, and let me see the abundance of your provision on my behalf.

Jennifer

We can walk without fear, full of hope and courage and strength to do His will, waiting for the endless good which He is always giving as fast as He can get us able to take it in.
—**GEORGE MACDONALD** (1824–1905), Scottish author and minister

GOD PROVIDES

As [THE WOMAN] CAME IN, THE KING WAS TALKING WITH
GEHAZI, THE SERVANT OF THE MAN OF GOD. . . . AND GEHAZI
WAS TELLING THE KING ABOUT THE TIME ELISHA HAD BROUGHT A
BOY BACK TO LIFE. AT THAT VERY MOMENT, THE MOTHER OF THE
BOY WALKED IN TO MAKE HER APPEAL TO THE KING.

2 Kings 8:4-5

THE WOMAN in 2 Kings 8 had gone to the land of the Philistines for seven years, as Elisha had instructed her. There God had provided for her and her son's needs. After the famine, she desired to have her land and home restored. In the Lord's timing, she entered the king's presence at the exact moment Gehazi was recounting God's miracle that had brought the woman's son back to life years before. The king decreed that everything taken from her be returned to her.

In a similar way, God provides what his people—especially widows or women who are alone—need. My friend Jane's husband had left, her company had downsized, and she had lost her job. When she had to move out of her house, all seemed lost.

Yet the more uncertain her circumstances became, the more aware she was that God was with her. Quietly but distinctly, little holes were punched in the dark clouds, and streams of light flowed through as God seemed to whisper, *You're not alone. You can trust me.* As Jane's bank account shrank, she turned to God and found security in his presence.

After a few months, an old college friend asked Jane to decorate her large, historic home. Jane's aunt opened her home to Jane, a part-time job became available, and her brother moved halfway across the country to be near and offer his love and support. She later married a wonderful man and was blessed with children, and Jane had hope and a future she had never dreamed of.

Lord, your Word says that you do good to those whose hearts are in tune with you and trust you. Grant me grace to turn to you in every adversity, to trust you and love you more each day—even when my present is dark or the future looks uncertain.

Cheri

Trust God where you cannot trace him. Do not try to penetrate the cloud he brings over you; rather look to the [rain]bow that is on it. The mystery is God's; the promise is yours.

—**JOHN R. MACDUFF** (1818–1895), Scottish minister and hymn writer

26 SPIRITUAL ASSIGNMENTS

[GOD] DECIDED BEFOREHAND WHEN [NATIONS] SHOULD RISE
AND FALL, AND HE DETERMINED THEIR BOUNDARIES. HIS PURPOSE
WAS FOR THE NATIONS TO SEEK AFTER GOD AND PERHAPS FEEL
THEIR WAY TOWARD HIM AND FIND HIM—THOUGH HE IS NOT
FAR FROM ANY ONE OF US. FOR IN HIM WE LIVE AND MOVE
AND EXIST.

Acts 17:26-28

ANGELA AND HER HUSBAND, Miles, have a strong sense of purpose. Convenience store owners in Blackfoot, Idaho, they get up at five each morning and ask God to open their eyes and ears to any assignment God has for them. In Angela's long, hectic workdays, she can be so busy that she misses the divine appointment. But this passage from Acts has been a daily reminder that God has placed nations, cities, and even people in small towns like Blackfoot just where they are. In his sovereign plan are opportunities Angela doesn't want to miss.

"Ministry encompasses so many avenues," Angela told me, "and my concept of spiritual assignments is an everyday thing, not just some big thing. I don't want to ever be so busy working that I miss whom God has put in my path."

One day an older woman came in. As she paid for her items, Angela could sense a heaviness. "I haven't seen you for a while. How are you and your husband?"

"He passed away recently," the woman replied. Angela put down the cups she was carrying, wrapped the lady in her arms, and prayed for her briefly. "Thank you so much; I really needed that. I've been having a very hard day," the woman said, wiping away a tear.

Whether she's writing a verse of encouragement on the newsletter that goes out with their employees' checks or encouraging a child after school, Angela aims to be sensitive to people and to God's assignments.

What is your spiritual assignment today? If you listen and respond to it, life can be a great adventure, even in the stresses of work.

*Lord, help me slow down enough to see the opportunities you've arranged. May
I be sensitive and willing to be your hands and feet and fulfill the spiritual
assignment you have for me today.*

Cheri

Blessed are those who see the hand of God in the haphazard,
inexplicable, and seemingly senseless circumstances of life.
—**ERWIN W. LUTZER** (1941–), North American pastor and author

GOD HEARS

THE LORD IS CLOSE TO ALL WHO CALL ON HIM,
    YES, TO ALL WHO CALL ON HIM IN TRUTH.
HE GRANTS THE DESIRES OF THOSE WHO FEAR HIM;
    HE HEARS THEIR CRIES FOR HELP AND RESCUES THEM.

Psalm 145:18-19

IRINA, A LITTLE GIRL growing up in the former Soviet Union, heard daily that God was only a fairy tale made up by ignorant people. She questioned why the teachers talked so much about this fake God and began to wonder if God might be real. One day she uttered her first prayer and saw God answer in a way that caused her to talk to him secretly each night when she was alone in bed.

She had no Bible and heard only atheistic teaching, but she kept asking God questions and seeking to know him. One night she wrote a heartfelt poem expressing her desire to find God, and she felt a warm, loving presence envelop her. Though Irina saw no evidence of the Lord in her society, her school, or her family, her heart cried out to him.

When Irina was twenty-three, someone gave her a Bible. As she read God's words for herself, she knew the Lord truly loved her and had been leading her all her life. At twenty-eight, because of her Christian faith, she was sentenced to seven years' hard labor and seven more years of internal exile. Despite all the persecution, Irina survived and was eventually released. She shared with others through speaking and writing how she had experienced God's love and faithfulness over and over as she sought him. His presence made her feel much as she had as a child: a loving eye watching over her, a sense of incredible warmth in a freezing prison cell.

Throughout Irina's horrible ordeal, God heard her prayers and continually assured Irina of his love. How beautifully her story shows that God hears us and loves us even when we don't know much about him. What does this tell you about how the Lord desires a relationship with you?

> *Thank you, Father, Son, and Holy Spirit, that you hear us no matter where we are and that no prison bars or other bleak circumstances can keep out your love. Thank you that when we seek you, we find you.*

Cheri

Be assured, if you walk with him and look to him and expect help from him, he will never fail you.

—GEORGE MÜLLER (1805–1898), German evangelist and orphanage director

28 THE PROMISE KEEPER

HE KEEPS EVERY PROMISE FOREVER.

Psalm 146:6

I PLACE NO VALUE on anything I have or may possess, except in relation to the kingdom of Christ," said David Livingstone, explorer and medical missionary to Africa during the 1800s. Livingstone rose from a job as a humble spinner in a cotton mill, where he had worked from ages ten through twenty-six, to attending a university in Glasgow, Scotland, solely on money he had labored for and saved.

Following medical and missionary training in London, he sailed for Africa in 1840. Throughout his many years there, going where no white man ever had gone, Livingstone faced constant dangers and was robbed multiple times. He often lacked food and suffered from severe illness and the loss of loved ones, including his wife.

Yet he was able to continue his mission because he believed and staked his life upon Jesus' words: "I have been given all authority in heaven and on earth. Therefore, go and make disciples of all the nations. . . . And be sure of this: *I am with you always, even to the end of the age*" (Matthew 28:18-20, emphasis added).

On a night of gravest peril, when a hostile chief and his people were coming to kill him, Livingstone wrote, "It's the word of a Gentleman of the most sacred and strictest honour, so there's an end on it!" In this as in all the pivotal moments of his life, he claimed the promise of Christ's presence and moved forward until his last breath in the mission God had appointed for him.

We may not be called to the darkest, most dangerous parts of a continent across the ocean as Livingstone was, but we can trust in God's promise of his constant presence protecting us and his Spirit living within us, for he is the one who keeps his promises forever.

Father, I thank you that your promises are eternally rock solid and that your very nature and character stand behind them. Grant me deeper faith, to not merely believe your word but to act on it. In Christ's name, amen.

Cheri

If anything will advance the interests of the kingdom, it shall be given away or kept, only as by giving or keeping it I shall promote the glory of Him to whom I owe all my hopes in time and eternity.

—DAVID LIVINGSTONE (1813–1873), Scottish explorer and missionary

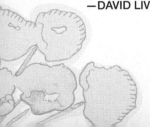

GOD'S BUSINESS

HOW GOOD TO SING PRAISES TO OUR GOD!
How DELIGHTFUL AND HOW FITTING!
THE LORD IS REBUILDING JERUSALEM
AND BRINGING THE EXILES BACK TO ISRAEL.
HE HEALS THE BROKENHEARTED
AND BANDAGES THEIR WOUNDS. . . .
HOW GREAT IS OUR LORD! HIS POWER IS ABSOLUTE!

Psalm 147:1-3, 5

THIS IS ONE of the great promises of Scripture, assuring us that God specializes in the business of healing the brokenhearted. He has compassion on those who are oppressed by suffering or are crushed in spirit and binds up their emotional wounds. When Joseph was betrayed by his own brothers, separated from his father, and sold into slavery in a strange land, the Lord healed his broken heart. When Naomi was brokenhearted over the deaths of her husband and sons, God healed her grief-stricken soul and gave her grandchildren who brought boundless joy.

Jesus hasn't changed in his desire to heal the hearts and minds of his people. The name *Jehovah-Rapha*, the Lord our Healer (see Exodus 15:25-26), doesn't refer only to the healing of bodies but also to the healing of the inevitable heartaches that afflict us in this broken world. He has compassion on those who experience the pain of divorce, the anguish of losing a child, or the tragedy of having a home torn to shreds in a hurricane.

Do you have a wound that others can't see, one that time has not healed? The Lord is standing ready to heal your broken heart, your troubled soul. Will you give yourself over to his healing love? The Lord's power to heal is absolute and continuous. As you humble yourself and ask, the very life of Jesus through the Holy Spirit will flow into your heart and make it new.

All praise to you, Lord Jesus Christ, who carried our sorrow in your own body on the cross. I give you my broken heart and ask you to flood me with your healing power and life. In your name and for your glory, amen.

Cheri

Come, Thou long-expected Jesus,
born to set Thy people free;
from our fears and sins release us,
let us find our rest in Thee.

—"COME, THOU LONG-EXPECTED JESUS" BY CHARLES WESLEY
(1707–1788), English minister and hymn writer

30 EVERY CREATED THING

PRAISE THE LORD FROM THE HEAVENS!
   PRAISE HIM FROM THE SKIES!
PRAISE HIM, ALL HIS ANGELS! . . .
PRAISE HIM, SKIES ABOVE!
   PRAISE HIM, VAPORS HIGH ABOVE THE CLOUDS!
LET EVERY CREATED THING GIVE PRAISE TO THE LORD,
   FOR HE ISSUED HIS COMMAND, AND THEY CAME INTO BEING.

Psalm 148:1-2, 4-5

AS I WATCHED from the balcony of our cabin on the MM *Westerdam* one summer morning, the snowcapped mountains of Alaska were so high that they reached the clouds in the crystal-blue sky. In contrast to the strong winds and waves that had sent the ship rolling and passengers searching for antinausea pills the night before, the coastal waters were calm. Brilliant sunlight broke through the layers of clouds as my heart lifted in worship: "Praise the LORD from the heavens. . . . Praise the LORD from the earth!"

That afternoon we saw the Hubbard Glacier, the largest tidewater glacier in North America, a mass of ice over seventy-five miles long and up to fourteen hundred feet thick. I stood in awe of the 350-foot ice wall that rises around the glacier—the same height as a thirty-five-story building!

Do you ever ponder about the one who made such wonders of nature? Scripture says they did not come about by chance. Psalm 148 reveals the loving Creator behind it all— birds and flowers, mountains and vast oceans, creatures of the ocean depths, twinkling stars, sun and moon, vapors high above the clouds. Our earth didn't result from a random process. It was spoken into existence by almighty God. And today's verses call us to lift our voices and hearts in praise to the Lord for his marvelous, incredible creation.

Lord, through you all things were made in heaven and on earth, and you sustain all life by the word of your power. I worship you, infinite Creator. Let me never take for granted your glory, which towers over both earth and heaven!

Cheri

[God says,] "I created beauty to declare the existence of My holy Being. A magnificent rose, a hauntingly glorious sunset, oceanic splendor—all these things were meant to proclaim My presence in the world. . . . This is a gift, and it carries responsibility with it. Declare My glorious Being to the world. The whole earth is full of My radiant beauty—My Glory!"

—**SARAH YOUNG,** contemporary American author and missionary

JULY

HE CROWNS THE HUMBLE

THE LORD DELIGHTS IN HIS PEOPLE;
HE CROWNS THE HUMBLE WITH VICTORY.

Psalm 149:4

THOUGH HANNAH HURNARD grew up in a strict Puritan home, she found church services depressing and felt she was the most miserable, unworthy of creatures. Because of a profound stuttering problem, she was tormented by fears. She was friendless and ridiculed every day at school. Worst of all, she began to perceive God as unreachable and unloving.

With every passing year Hannah sank deeper into despair—until one day in her cabin at a conference, she fell on her knees and asked God to make himself real to her. As Christ's love penetrated her heart, she realized she must yield her entire being *and* her stuttering to the Lord. She grew spiritually and eventually served as a preacher of the gospel. Her listeners thought God had given her a speaking gift.

After years of service in Palestine, Hannah and other missionaries were sent back to England because the war for Israel's independence was looming. Yet as the weeks grew into months, she longed to get back to her ministry to Arabs and Jews. Finally she was offered a position as a housekeeper in a Palestine hospital. At first she thought, *No, Lord! I'm called as an evangelist, not a housekeeper!* But she humbled herself and told the Lord she'd do whatever he asked of her, even housekeeping or janitorial work. Though she confessed her utter lack of experience to the administrator, the door opened.

Three weeks later Hannah flew back to the Holy Land and became housekeeping director for the hospital. Through this unlikely position, she had countless opportunities to minister to Jews and Arabs, even during wartime, while all the other Christians were cast out of the country. In the years ahead, she had a vibrant literary career and a great impact in the Middle East and England.

God, thank you that you delight in your people, and when we humble ourselves,
you crown us with salvation.

Cheri

We can be humble only when we know that we are God's children, of infinite value and eternally loved.

—**MADELEINE L'ENGLE**, (1918–2007), American author

2 A STRONG FORTRESS

THE NAME OF THE LORD IS A STRONG FORTRESS;
THE GODLY RUN TO HIM AND ARE SAFE.

Proverbs 18:10

WHERE DO YOU run when you need shelter? Where do you run when you're filled with pain? The word *fortress* in this verse refers to a place of security, a place you run to for safety. God has always been that refuge for his people, first in the Garden of Eden, then in the ark, and later in the cities of refuge God commanded his people to build so that if one person killed another unintentionally, the offender could seek protection in one of them (see Numbers 35; Deuteronomy 19; and Joshua 20.) No other civilization had ever designated cities of refuge where the gates were perpetually open, available, and accessible to all.

But perhaps the second part of the verse makes some of you wonder whether you are good or godly enough to run to the Lord and feel confident the gates are open to you. If so, remember, it's not those who have their act perfectly together, but those who are in right standing with God *through Christ* and who turn to him for help who are invited into the protection of his name and character.

Each of us needs a place where we'll be safe from our enemies. The only true refuge is Jesus—not only in this life but also in the one to come. What a deep, abiding comfort it is to realize the magnitude of that truth: in strife, in doubt and turmoil, in the best of times and the worst of times, Christ himself is our refuge, not due to anything we do but all because of his mercy and grace.

> *Father, grant me the long-range, panoramic perspective of how you are my fortress and refuge throughout all my days on earth and forever. What freedom there is to know that you protect me and I can always turn to you for help.*

Cheri

Rock of Ages, cleft for me,
Let me hide myself in thee;
Let the water and the blood,
From thy wounded side which flowed,
Be of sin the double cure;
Save from wrath and make me pure.

—**"ROCK OF AGES" BY AUGUSTUS TOPLADY** (1740–1778), English cleric and hymn writer

MORE OF YOU

THE WEALTH OF THE RICH IS THEIR FORTIFIED CITY;
THEY IMAGINE IT A WALL TOO HIGH TO SCALE.

Proverbs 18:11 (NIV)

MAYBE YOU read this verse and others that warn us of the dangers that come with riches, and you skip over it because you are not rich. But it is our natural tendency to think that wealth would solve our problems or make us happy or give us security. Those who pine for wealth as if it would guarantee safety are in the same position as people who trust in the wealth they already have.

Whatever we think we need to make us feel safe and secure stands in the way of what God wants to do in our lives. Any possession or relationship —whether we have it or think we need it—anything we look to as the source for what only God can provide becomes an idol.

The problem slips in when we're not paying attention. We begin to idolize something or someone, or the dream of that something or someone. We serve it. We meditate on it. We work for it. And if we get it, we find that it was not at all what we thought it promised to be.

Regardless of what you are clinging to or longing for, your desire is really for God himself. Nothing else satisfies. Everything else leaves you disillusioned and disappointed. Anything else empties you instead of filling you and cannot give you security.

When we think that the reason we pray is so that we can place our orders with the divine warehouse and expect timely delivery, then we are missing out on what God wants to give. This attitude is an extension of the idolizing that turns our hearts to the things we think God should give us and away from God himself. Contentment comes when we know that nothing but God will satisfy and that he will satisfy fully.

More of you. More of you.

Jennifer

At our first entrance into the school of waiting upon God, the heart is chiefly set upon the blessings which we wait for. God graciously uses our need and desire for help to educate us for something higher than we were thinking of. We were seeking gifts; He, the Giver, longs to give Himself and to satisfy the soul with His goodness.

—ANDREW MURRAY (1828–1917), South African pastor and author

4

WISE GUY

THOSE WHO WERE ABOUT TO INTERROGATE [PAUL] WITHDREW
IMMEDIATELY. THE COMMANDER HIMSELF WAS ALARMED WHEN
HE REALIZED THAT HE HAD PUT PAUL, A ROMAN CITIZEN,
IN CHAINS.

Acts 22:29 (NIV)

IN THIS INCIDENT from Paul's life we see how we can expect God to act in our lives: we can expect him to give us wisdom in the moment we need it. Paul's preaching had stirred up the crowd, and the uproar brought the Roman authorities, who arrested Paul on the spot and prepared to flog him. When Paul declared his Roman citizenship, they quickly changed course and backed off from whipping him.

The commander brought Paul before the Sanhedrin, the Jewish ruling body. They were all set to condemn him, but then he stirred up their favorite theological debate by proclaiming his belief in a physical resurrection: "This divided the council—the Pharisees against the Sadducees—for the Sadducees say that there is no resurrection or angels or spirits, but the Pharisees believe in all of these" (Acts 23:7-8).

At any given moment, the Lord knows all the dynamics, all the personalities, all the implications of a given situation. He can make a direct deposit of his wisdom into your mind. He can let you know exactly what to do or say. He will lead you so that his goals are accomplished.

Paul's dilemmas did not always work out so that he was spared. Often he found himself bound, beaten, and imprisoned. When that is how the situation unfolded, it was because God had a mission for Paul, and prison was where Paul would find it. In those instances, God gave immediate wisdom to Paul for what God wanted to accomplish then and there.

We are in relationship with the same God, who promises to be the same in our lives. In whatever situations we find ourselves, God knows their details inside and out. He knows how to spark an idea or awaken a thought or give an insight. "Trust in the LORD with all your heart; do not depend on your own understanding" (Proverbs 3:5).

> *Lord, teach me to so trust your constant presence with me and in me that I know how to lean on your wisdom for every situation.*

Jennifer

The danger may exceed thy resistance, but not God's assistance; the enemies' power may surpass thy strength, their subtlety outwit thy prudence, but neither can excel the wisdom and might of God that is with thee.

—ABRAHAM WRIGHT (1611–1690), English pastor and writer

FROM HUMILIATION TO EXALTATION

5

YOU, LORD, ARE A SHIELD AROUND ME,
MY GLORY, THE ONE WHO LIFTS MY HEAD HIGH.

Psalm 3:3 (NIV)

AS DAVID WROTE this psalm, his enemies, determined to destroy him and mocking him and his faith, were led by his son Absalom. This added insult to injury and rubbed salt in David's wounds. The pain of betrayal by a beloved son was played out on the battlefield. No wonder David's head was bowed—in grief, in defeat, in depression, in humiliation.

But throughout David's life he had thoroughly tested God's promises and proved them true. He knew that God was a shield around him, that God was present in all his power, repelling the enemy's death blows. God himself absorbed the shame and the hurt so that David could hold his head high again.

My friend Judith's husband was a successful pharmaceutical salesman, an upstanding member of the community, and a pillar of the church. Judith was proud to be his wife and actually found her identity in those terms—until her husband was convicted of selling diluted and out-of-date drugs and was sentenced to several years in the penitentiary.

Everything Judith had believed about her life was a lie. Her husband was not who she thought he was. Her lifestyle had come at the cost of the lives and health of others. Through no fault of her own, Judith saw her world crumble. She was betrayed, humiliated, grieved, defeated. Like David.

The hardest thing for her to do was to step out into her world again. But she clung to Psalm 3:3 as her lifeline, and God proved faithful. Judith began to redefine herself in light of God's Word instead of her husband's "success" and her possessions. She walked a painful path from humiliation to exaltation as the Lord lifted up her head, just as he had done for David. Judith now holds her head high because of whose she is.

Lord, in my devastation, I look to you as the one who lifts my head.

Jennifer

Rows of beautiful trees were laid low in a storm. Reason? The water was too near the surface; so the trees did not have to put their roots deep down to find water. . . . God may deny us a surface answer in order to get us to put our roots deeper into eternal reality, so that in some future storm we shall be unmoved.

—**E. STANLEY JONES** (1884–1973), American missionary and theologian

6

THE UNSEEN HAND

ANANIAS, THE HIGH PRIEST, ARRIVED WITH SOME OF THE JEWISH ELDERS AND THE LAWYER TERTULLUS, TO PRESENT THEIR CASE AGAINST PAUL TO THE GOVERNOR.

Acts 24:1

AS THE KEEPERS of the status quo put all their might into derailing Paul and his mission, God was always the on-site stage manager. As his enemies brought public charges against Paul, they didn't assign this matter to an underling. The high priest himself was on hand to oversee the proceedings. The authorities also brought in a local lawyer, who was trained in the oratory of the court and experienced in bringing cases before the governor. In other words they "lawyered up."

Paul stood alone—but he was not alone. His advocate was the Lord himself. We can see how the Holy Spirit gave Paul wisdom to know how to refute the charges and how to appeal to the governor. Paul had courage to speak and wisdom about what to say and how to say it. God was working out his own agenda to bring the message of the Messiah before Gentiles.

God promises us that he is always in control. No one else has power to manipulate our circumstances because God is in every scene, his unseen hand moving every actor.

Do you feel confronted right now? Do you find yourself in a seemingly helpless position while someone else calls the shots that impact your life? You can be sure that the Unseen Hand is moving. You do have an Advocate who is defending you and speaking on your behalf—not only in the courts of humanity and circumstance but in the heavenly courts. Your very situation is working toward an outcome that will have placed you where you need to be when you need to be there.

> Lord, I entrust my cause to you. I know that you are advocating on my behalf and that you are faithful and true.
>
> *Jennifer*

Because of the empty tomb, we have peace. Because of [Jesus'] resurrection, we can have peace during even the most troubling of times because we know He is in control of all that happens in the world.

—PAUL CHAPPELL, contemporary American pastor

CENTER STAGE

AGRIPPA AND BERNICE ARRIVED AT THE AUDITORIUM WITH
GREAT POMP, ACCOMPANIED BY MILITARY OFFICERS AND
PROMINENT MEN OF THE CITY. FESTUS ORDERED THAT PAUL
BE BROUGHT IN.

Acts 25:23

IN THE HISTORY of the church, Paul is one of the central figures. But in his time he wasn't well known. Most historians think he was probably physically unimpressive. There was no social media, so he had little name recognition. Certainly there was no earthly reason he should have been standing before King Agrippa and his sister Bernice.

Except that the plans of his enemy backfired, and Rabbi Paul, whose case was described dismissively by Governor Festus, had the floor and the undivided attention of King Agrippa. "It was something about their religion and a dead man named Jesus, who Paul insists is alive" (Acts 25:19), Festus had explained. Paul also had the attention of the king's sister, military officers, and prominent men of the city. God was setting the stage and directing every move. Had Paul's accusers not been so insistent and intent on his execution, Paul would never have had the ear of this company of people.

Do you see the promise on display in this scene? God is always in charge. *Always.* When evil seems to be winning the day, it never is. When you feel that you have been defeated, you never are. God is managing and arranging everything.

You have his promise that he is moving every circumstance toward his desired outcome. Be patient. Let them unfold. As you confront a situation that has a disappointing outcome, watch to see how that outcome sets the stage for the next situation, which opens the door to the next opportunity, which lays the groundwork for the next circumstance, and on and on. Finally, one day, you can look back and say, "I couldn't be where I am if I'd never been where I was."

You will see that God is using every seemingly negative event to bring together all the pieces for a stunning display of his power.

My life is yours, Lord. Do as you will, when you will, how you will.

Jennifer

So, your path with its unexplained sorrow or turmoil, and mine with its sharp flints and briers—and both our paths, with their unexplained perplexity, their sheer mystery—they are His paths, on which he will show himself loving and faithful. Nothing else; nothing less.

—**AMY CARMICHAEL** (1867–1951), Irish missionary to India

8

WISE WORDS

WISE WORDS SATISFY LIKE A GOOD MEAL;
THE RIGHT WORDS BRING SATISFACTION.
THE TONGUE CAN BRING DEATH OR LIFE;
THOSE WHO LOVE TO TALK WILL REAP THE CONSEQUENCES.

Proverbs 18:20-21

WORDS HAVE POWER. They can lift up, or they can tear down. Knowing what power our words have, aren't you glad to know that God has promised to instruct our words and train our tongues? "The Sovereign LORD has given me his words of wisdom, so that I know how to comfort the weary. Morning by morning he wakens me and opens my understanding to his will. The Sovereign LORD has spoken to me, and I have listened. I have not rebelled or turned away" (Isaiah 50:4-5).

The NIV translates the beginning of the passage this way: "The Sovereign LORD has given me a well-instructed tongue." Why does he instruct our tongues and give us his words of wisdom? So that we will know exactly what to say to comfort the weary. There is no formulaic language that will transfer from one situation to the next. Each person's heart will be lifted by specific words that only the Holy Spirit knows. He can instruct your tongue on the spot.

How often does he train us? Morning by morning. The Lord asks for the firstfruits of our days—the first morning hours—for giving us instruction, like a rabbi instructing his eager students. He awakens us in the morning to teach us and to pour himself into us. It's easy to choose more sleep time over time with him, but often it is the slacker's way and leads to an unkempt life instead of to a cultivated, rich life.

What is our response once he has spoken to us? To hear and respond. To listen every moment and hear well in our solitary time with him. Then we have his words to speak to those around us. God's words are never empty. They do just what he sent them out to do. They bring life to those around us.

Lord, let my words be the echo of yours.

Jennifer

There will come a time when three words, uttered with charity and meekness, shall receive a far more blessed reward than three thousand volumes written with disdainful sharpness of wit.

—RICHARD HOOKER (1554–1600), English theologian

SIN BACKFIRES

[THE WICKED] DIG A DEEP PIT TO TRAP OTHERS,
   THEN FALL INTO IT THEMSELVES.
THE TROUBLE THEY MAKE FOR OTHERS
   BACKFIRES ON THEM.
THE VIOLENCE THEY PLAN FALLS ON THEIR OWN HEADS.

Psalm 7:15-16

WE WERE not created for evil. Sin doesn't suit us. When God created human beings, he included instruction about the behaviors and attitudes that would diminish us and eventually destroy us, and he called those destructive behaviors sin.

Sin's punishment is built in. Going our own way, following our instincts without the restraining and protective wisdom of God's law, leads us to destruction. His law is a gift of love to us. It creates a hedge of protection around our lives. His promise to us is that obedience to him will shield us from the heartache sin brings into our lives.

Do I really believe and embrace that promise? I can easily see how certain blatant and obvious sins backfire on the sinner. The evidence is indisputable. We have all seen the destructive effects of substance abuse or infidelity or pornography or other sins that are out front and rampant in our world. It would be easy to point to those and let those sins illustrate the deep pit that sinners fall into. And it would be true and accurate.

But when I look at my own life, do I let anger settle in? Do I allow myself to be easily offended? Do I repay a wrong with a wrong? Do I manipulate others? The list could go on and on. We may dress these up in excuses or call them something else, but they are still sins.

God has classified these attitudes as sins because, just like the blatant sins, they have destructive effects on our lives. In the moment, it might seem, for example, as if lashing out in anger will relieve our anger. But any momentary relief we experience soon changes to regret. Wounding words can't be taken back. A relationship is tarnished, if not ruined. Our sin backfires on us, and we fall into the pit we have dug. Believe God's promise that his law is our protection.

Lord, lead me in your ways.

Jennifer

Every Christian will readily allow that sin is insidious, but it is one thing to recognize this in theory and quite another to be regulated by it in practice.

—A. W. PINK (1886–1952), English evangelist and Bible scholar

10 THE KNOWABLE GOD

THE HEAVENS PROCLAIM THE GLORY OF GOD.
 THE SKIES DISPLAY HIS CRAFTSMANSHIP.
DAY AFTER DAY THEY CONTINUE TO SPEAK;
 NIGHT AFTER NIGHT THEY MAKE HIM KNOWN.
THEY SPEAK WITHOUT A SOUND OR WORD;
 THEIR VOICE IS NEVER HEARD.
YET THEIR MESSAGE HAS GONE THROUGHOUT THE EARTH,
 AND THEIR WORDS TO ALL THE WORLD.

Psalm 19:1-4

GOD HAS not made himself hard to find. He is not playing a game of hide-and-seek with us. He has built his message into the DNA of the universe he created. Every time we look at his creation, we see evidence of him.

He promises that he is present and knowable. That there is no nook or cranny in the universe where we are hidden from him. That there is no location where he is hidden from us. The Creator of the vast universe wants to be in a personal relationship with each one of us. The psalmist wrote, "I can never escape from your Spirit! I can never get away from your presence! . . . I could ask the darkness to hide me and the light around me to become night—but even in darkness I cannot hide from you" (Psalm 139:7, 11-12).

Think of the heavens. Stars are clustered in galaxies, which average between one hundred billion and one trillion stars each. How many galaxies are there? Astronomers estimate that there are approximately one hundred billion to one trillion galaxies in the universe. If you multiply those two numbers together, there are between ten sextillion and one septillion stars. And God *calls each one by name*: "Because of [God's] great power and incomparable strength, not a single one is missing" (Isaiah 40:26).

Aren't you more precious to God than any star? Look at the work of his hands, and see his promise that he loves you and makes himself knowable.

I am awed to think that you set so high a value on me. I am never hidden from you, and you are never hidden from me.

Jennifer

God dwells in His creation and is everywhere indivisibly present in all His works. He is transcendent above all His works even while He is immanent within them.

—**A. W. TOZER** (1897–1963), American preacher and author

STRENGTHENED BY MY WEAKNESS

For two whole years Paul stayed there in his own rented house and welcomed all who came to see him. He proclaimed the kingdom of God and taught about the Lord Jesus Christ—with all boldness and without hindrance!

Acts 28:30-31 (NIV)

THE FINAL CHAPTERS of Acts tell a story of complicated intrigue and danger. Paul had concluded a third missionary journey, ending in Jerusalem. There he was attacked by an angry Jewish mob. He was rescued and then held in prison by a Roman governor, until he exercised his right as a Roman citizen to be judged in the emperor's court. After a treacherous journey Paul arrived in Rome, where for two years he awaited trial, under house arrest in his own rented residence.

Viewed from one perspective, Paul was the victim of one unfair occurrence after another. It seemed that people in opposition to God's message were able to thwart Paul's ministry and keep him down.

Viewed from heaven's perspective, God used the godless plans and intentions of people opposed to his gospel to spread his gospel. His plans cannot be thwarted: Job declared, "I know that you can do anything, and no one can stop you" (Job 42:2).

Through every page of Scripture, God shows us his ways. He uses everything to work out his own plan, and his purposes will prevail, no matter what the minds of men or women plan. Every one of God's enemies, though they plot and fight against his people, become the means to God's end. We are never at the mercy of any person or any circumstance. God is never surprised by any person's decisions or actions. He has already factored them into his purpose and plan for us.

Father, thank you for your careful attention to the details of my life. Thank you that you are always running the show. Teach me to be so confident in you that my difficult and challenging circumstances are not even a ripple on the still waters.

Jennifer

I am mended by my sickness, enriched by my poverty, and strengthened by my weakness.

—**ABRAHAM WRIGHT** (1611–1690), English pastor and writer

12 DOUBLE-DIPPING

I AM NOT ASHAMED OF THE GOSPEL, BECAUSE IT IS THE POWER OF GOD THAT BRINGS SALVATION TO EVERYONE WHO BELIEVES: FIRST TO THE JEW, THEN TO THE GENTILE. FOR IN THE GOSPEL THE RIGHTEOUSNESS OF GOD IS REVEALED—A RIGHTEOUSNESS THAT IS BY FAITH FROM FIRST TO LAST, JUST AS IT IS WRITTEN: "THE RIGHTEOUS WILL LIVE BY FAITH."

Romans 1:16-17 (NIV)

THE GOSPEL has never been popular. Paul, the church's first missionary and traveling evangelist, proclaimed a message that enraged the Jews and was ridiculed by the Gentiles. Paul knew well how unbelievable and how heretical the message sounded, because that is exactly how it had sounded to him when he first heard it.

Paul, though, had seen the gospel's effect. He had been radically changed by the power of God through the gospel message. That arrogant, legalistic, angry Saul, who had encountered the living Jesus, no longer lived. He was no more. In his body, there lived a brand-new creation. His life was a living authentication of the truth of the gospel.

Far from feeling ashamed of the gospel, Paul was so proud of it that he could not hold back. He had seen its effect over and over: the power of God brings salvation to everyone who believes on Jesus Christ. In the message, real righteousness is revealed—righteousness that God imparts, not the righteousness that the old Saul and many of his peers were trying to achieve by their own best efforts. This was a righteousness received by faith in who Jesus is and what he has done.

The gospel promises that the power of God will produce in you and do for you what you can't possibly accomplish for yourself: what Christ has done *for you* means that your sins are forgiven and you are in right standing with God. Who Christ is *in you* means that the power of God is at work to produce the righteous life he desires you to have.

What Christ did for you and who Christ is in you—this is real righteousness revealed.

Lord, thank you for such a full salvation purchased at such cost.

Jennifer

To be in Christ—that makes you fit for heaven; but for Christ to be in you—that makes you fit for earth! . . . The one makes heaven your home—the other makes this world His workshop.

—**MAJOR W. IAN THOMAS** (1914–2007), English writer and theology teacher

BELIEVING IS SEEING

YOU, GOD, SEE THE TROUBLE OF THE AFFLICTED;
  YOU CONSIDER THEIR GRIEF AND TAKE IT IN HAND.
THE VICTIMS COMMIT THEMSELVES TO YOU;
  YOU ARE THE HELPER OF THE FATHERLESS.

Psalm 10:14 (NIV)

EL-ROI, THE GOD Who Sees (see Genesis 16:13). God first revealed this name to a most unlikely prospect: Hagar, Sarah's Egyptian slave. One of the defining characteristics of God's work in the world is the preposterous way he insists on showing the worth of things we consider lowly.

At Sarah's command, Hagar bore Abraham a son named Ishmael. During her pregnancy, she had been driven into the desert by Sarah's harshness and jealousy. But when she was alone and forsaken, God sought her out. God chose the wilderness and the slave woman and the outcast son as the setting in which he revealed an astonishing aspect of his character.

Hagar called him El-roi, the God Who Sees. She didn't mean a god who glances or notices in passing. She meant the God who saw her when she thought no one knew she even existed, when everyone else had turned their backs on her, when everyone else had averted their eyes. Surely that enabled her to return to Sarah as El-roi commanded.

Fourteen years passed, during which Sarah remained childless, and Hagar's son Ishmael lived as the favored and adored son.

Let's fast-forward to the incident recorded in Genesis 21, the weaning of Isaac. Two events play out at the same time: a joyful party is being held to celebrate Isaac. Concurrently, Hagar and her son, Ishmael, are sent away and wander in the wilderness.

The celebration of Isaac gets scarce mention before our attention is drawn to the lowly and despised. While we celebrate the winners, El-roi comes to Hagar again and tends to her. The God Who Sees opens her eyes to reveal his provision: "God opened Hagar's eyes, and she saw a well full of water" (Genesis 21:19), and "God was with [Ishmael] as he grew up" (Genesis 21:20). El-roi has provision and promise for the discarded and forsaken. He not only sees, he seeks out, pursues, and protects.

My protector and defender, I look to you because you are watching over me.

Jennifer

A spiritual kingdom lies all about us, enclosing us, embracing us, altogether within reach of our inner selves, waiting for us to recognize it. God Himself is waiting our response to His presence.

—A. W. TOZER (1897–1963), American preacher and author

SONGS OF JOY AND VICTORY ARE SUNG IN THE CAMP OF
 THE GODLY.
 THE STRONG RIGHT ARM OF THE LORD HAS DONE
  GLORIOUS THINGS!
THE STRONG RIGHT ARM OF THE LORD IS RAISED IN TRIUMPH.
 THE STRONG RIGHT ARM OF THE LORD HAS DONE
  GLORIOUS THINGS!

Psalm 118:15-16

GOD ALWAYS comes out the winner. And he promises to give us victory when we are following him and doing the work he has called and empowered us to do.

Try to imagine a scenario that leaves God the loser. Is there any situation in which he would be unprepared for that turn of events? Might he ever be unable to set his plans in motion or position his people strategically? Every failing or sin has already been factored into his purpose. Victory belongs to the Lord. And we are on the winning side.

We prepare for what God calls on us to do, but the victory comes from him. "The horse is prepared for the day of battle, but the victory belongs to the LORD" (Proverbs 21:31).

How does God define victory? That is the question. His victory is in winning hearts to him and in forging character in us. Are our hearts aligned with the victory he has in mind? The circumstances in which he is winning this victory may sometimes look like failure from earth's point of view. But we aren't to live our lives governed by earth's point of view. The very thing that might seem like failure in the moment turns out to be the victory in the end.

Lord, I know that the victory is yours, and I stand by faith in what you are working in my life.

Jennifer

The eternal world will come alive to us the moment we reckon upon its reality. O God, quicken to life every power within me, that I may lay hold on eternal things. Open my eyes that I may see; give me acute spiritual perception; enable me to taste Thee and know that Thou art good. Make heaven more real to me than any earthly thing has ever been.

—A. W. TOZER (1897–1963), American preacher and author

THE WISDOM OF FORGIVING

A PERSON'S WISDOM YIELDS PATIENCE;
IT IS TO ONE'S GLORY TO OVERLOOK AN OFFENSE.

Proverbs 19:11 (NIV)

WISDOM IS the product of spending time and gaining experience with the Lord. It grows and deepens with the years. I know young adults who are wise beyond their years, but I also know that their wisdom is not in full bloom and that time and experience will season them and cause their wisdom to flower.

One of wisdom's most telling characteristics as it blossoms is patience with others' faults, especially when those faults offend you. This is not to say that we should never correct others or encourage them to grow out of a weakness. But we should be patient when the problem is that *you* are offended. We are quick to come to our own defense, and it takes maturity and grace to let offenses go unanswered.

God promises that it is to our own benefit and for the polishing of our characters when we can let an offense go by. Many times what offends us is not really something someone did wrong but rather something we took the wrong way. I find that discovering what offends me personally is often a window into my own personality. I try to ask myself, *What did I find offensive in that?* And usually I find that some lurking quirk or unhealed wound in my soul has been poked and that the other person had not set out to offend me.

What if someone intends to offend you—really means it? Well, what if that person could not offend you because you refuse to take offense? What if you say to yourself, *I have my own weaknesses and struggles. I can certainly overlook hers*. Or his. Or theirs. You could live in such freedom! You would be the one who benefits from overlooking an offense, just as God promised.

Father, I can be so sensitive to offenses and slights. Rescue me from being alert to offenses in order that I can be alert to opportunities to pour out your love.

Jennifer

The person who is living by grace sees this vast contrast between his own sins against God and the offenses of others against him. He forgives others because he himself has been so graciously forgiven. He realizes that, by receiving God's forgiveness through Christ, he has forfeited the right to be offended when others hurt him.

—**JERRY BRIDGES** (1929–), American author and conference speaker

HIS LIVING, ACTIVE WORD

THE WORDS OF THE LORD ARE FLAWLESS,
LIKE SILVER PURIFIED IN A CRUCIBLE,
LIKE GOLD REFINED SEVEN TIMES.

Psalm 12:6 (NIV)

GOD'S WORD is flawless and timeless. We can put full confidence in it: "The grass withers and the flowers fade, but the word of our God stands forever" (Isaiah 40:8), and "Your eternal word, O LORD, stands firm in heaven" (Psalm 119:89).

The value of a person's word lies in the nature and character of the person who has spoken it. God's word is eternal because he is eternal. His word is trustworthy because he is trustworthy. When he invites us to trust in his word, he is calling us to trust in him.

God's words are different from your words or my words. In the material realm, words have no substance. They do not have mass and take up space. They are puffs of air. Earthly words communicate, but they do not accomplish work. I can't say to an object, "Move from here to there," and expect the object to move. I have to use physical force to move an object from one place to another. My words do not do my work.

In contrast, God does his work by his word: "The LORD merely spoke, and the heavens were created. He breathed the word, and all the stars were born" (Psalm 33:6).

In the spiritual realm, God's words have substance. They are not puffs of air; they are the instruments of his action. "God said, 'Let there be light,' and there was light" (Genesis 1:3). He created the earth by his word. And he saw his word carried out.

God still does his work by his word. He is still speaking his creating, sustaining, and ruling word. And he speaks his timeless, unchanging, eternal truth in real time.

Lord, I put my full trust in your powerful word.

Jennifer

The best evidence of the Bible's being the word of God is to be found between its covers. It proves itself.

—CHARLES HODGE (1797–1878), American theologian

BELIEVE THE PROMISER 17

WHAT DOES SCRIPTURE SAY? "ABRAHAM BELIEVED GOD, AND IT WAS CREDITED TO HIM AS RIGHTEOUSNESS."

Romans 4:3 (NIV)

THIS STATEMENT about Abraham is foundational to our understanding of our salvation. Paul, writing here to the church in Rome, is going against the tide of doctrine taught and believed for generations. Even the great Abraham had not earned his standing before God but had received it as a gift when he believed God. Let's look at Genesis 15:3, the context in which the statement first occurred.

God has made a promise to Abraham and that promise is a son—an heir through whom will come a great nation. The great nation will have a land all its own. But the promise rests on the foundation of a son for Abraham.

Abraham at this point is about seventy-five years old. He has no child. Abraham says, essentially, "How can you give me what you promised? How can you give me a land for my descendants or guarantee that they will become a great nation? You haven't even given me a son!" He evaluates the empirical evidence and concludes it's too late. The opportunity is past. He'll have to make do with what he has.

"Then the LORD took Abram [later renamed "Abraham"] outside and said to him, 'Look up into the sky and count the stars if you can. That's how many descendants you will have!' And Abram believed the LORD, and the LORD counted him as righteous because of his faith" (Genesis 15:5-6).

Before, Abraham had believed the promise because what God promised was believable. He and Sarah were still in their childbearing years. *Sure,* he must have said to himself, *that could happen.* So Abraham believed the promise.

But now the promise was no longer "believable." Sarah was past the age of childbearing. This time Abraham did something different. Abraham believed God, and he received the reward due the righteous. His faith rested in who God is. And God looked on Abraham's faith and saw it as righteousness.

The same way we enter into faith, we walk in faith—by believing God. When circumstances belie the promise, we choose to believe God.

Father, I believe. Help my unbelief.

Jennifer

High degrees of true assurance cannot be enjoyed by those who persist in low levels of obedience.
—**SINCLAIR B. FERGUSON** (1948–), Scottish preacher and theologian

18 BELIEVING GOD

BECAUSE OF OUR FAITH, CHRIST HAS BROUGHT US INTO THIS
PLACE OF UNDESERVED PRIVILEGE WHERE WE NOW STAND, AND
WE CONFIDENTLY AND JOYFULLY LOOK FORWARD TO SHARING
GOD'S GLORY.

Romans 5:2

IT'S ALWAYS important to look at what comes before the word *therefore* in the Bible. The chapter before *therefore* in Romans 5:1 describes God's interaction with Abraham and gives us a clear picture of what is *our part* and what is *God's part* in the whole scheme of things. It tells us that Abraham received the promise not because he was "good enough" in God's sight, not because he kept all the commandments—but *because he believed in God,* who raises the dead and makes something out of nothing (see Romans 4:17). That's faith.

If we want to enter into "this place of undeserved privilege" and have peace with God because of what Jesus has done for us, our part is to believe. To believe God is able to accomplish his will instead of doubting whether he could work on our behalf. To believe that God is the initiator and that nothing is too hard for him. To believe that he will speak to us and guide us. And to believe this amazing promise in Romans 5: that we've been put in right standing with almighty God *by faith*, that by faith Christ has brought us into an intimate relationship with an infinite God so we can live with great hope that someday we will share in his glory.

We need to give up our own efforts to be "good enough" to receive God's promise. We'll probably need to let go of all the what-ifs: *What if I miss the Lord? What if he speaks and I don't hear him? What if I take the wrong turn and mess everything up?* But we can remember that the same God who has made a way for us to be accepted, embraced, and invited into the place of grace shall in his timing direct us back onto the right path.

*I praise you, Father, that through the Cross you made a way to forgive my sins
and bring me into right relationship with you. Lord, increase my faith!*

Cheri

Faith isn't the ability to believe long and far into the misty future. It's simply taking God at his Word and taking the next step.

—JONI ERICKSON TADA (1949–), American author, artist, and advocate for the disabled

THE MIRACLE OF FRIENDSHIP

WE CAN REJOICE IN OUR WONDERFUL NEW RELATIONSHIP WITH GOD BECAUSE OUR LORD JESUS CHRIST HAS MADE US FRIENDS OF GOD.

Romans 5:11

FRIENDSHIP WITH other women has truly been a wonderful gift in my life. I've found that friends can be a source of comfort in times of need. Friends lift us up, pray for us, encourage us, laugh with us, and cry with us when we're sad. Yet as precious as these earthly relationships are, the truth is that in and of itself human friendship can't fill the God-shaped space in our hearts. That space was created for relationship with our Creator. Fame can't fill it; no amount of wealth, stardom, or success can meet that longing for connection.

At age twenty-nine I had a life-changing encounter with Jesus and began to discover that I was invited into friendship with the Father, all because of Christ's life, death, and resurrection. No longer was I an outsider, a stranger, or merely a servant. What a miracle—I was a friend of God!

How amazing it is that we are offered friendship with the King of the universe. He is our greatest and best encourager, especially in difficult times—2 Corinthians 7:6 says that God encourages those who are discouraged. Sometimes when we are overwhelmed by fear or sorrow, our friends are fast asleep. But Christ is the friend who never slumbers nor sleeps. Favorite friends may move away, but he is always with us, even until the end of the world. Jesus listens to us and prays for us constantly. He invites us to walk with him and talk with him, to roll our burdens and cares upon his shoulders, and to experience his peace. What a friend we have in Jesus!

Thank you for your unconditional love and friendship, Lord. Thank you for calling me your friend and laying down your life that I might know you and spend eternity with you.

Cheri

What a friend we have in Jesus,
All our sins and griefs to bear!
What a privilege to carry
Everything to God in prayer!

—"WHAT A FRIEND WE HAVE IN JESUS" BY JOSEPH SCRIVEN (1820–1886), Irish-Canadian hymn writer

20 FINDING GOD'S PURPOSE

YOU CAN MAKE MANY PLANS,
BUT THE LORD'S PURPOSE WILL PREVAIL.

Proverbs 19:21

IT IS COMFORTING to know that God doesn't expect us to accomplish his will on our own. Yes, he gives us brains with which to plan and tools, pro-and-con lists, and organizational systems. We humans brainstorm the best options and try to plan so that our lives will turn out well—how to be successful and make a living, how to have a great marriage or relationships. But we don't have the whole blueprint of the purpose for our lives on earth and how to "get there."

However, as we give ourselves to God with abandon, discover how he has gifted us, what we're passionate about and called to, he leads us one step at a time. So how do we find those things?

Just as a miner's hat in a dark cave casts a beam six feet ahead to give enough light to illuminate the miner's next steps, the Lord will show us the steps we need to take. He promises that his written Word, the Bible, will light our paths. Yet until we walk those steps, or "six feet," we won't be able to see more of the paths. Taking those steps often involves faith, risk, and launching out into unfamiliar territory. Things may seem to fall apart even when we have good intentions and good plans. A situation or person may derail us temporarily. We may get off the right paths and think that all is lost.

But today's verse assures us of a wonderful and freeing truth: the Lord's purpose will prevail. His plans for us will stand against our failures and limitations, against the curveballs life throws at us, even in the midst of the broken, fallen world we live in. Nothing will thwart the Lord's plans!

I praise you, God, that you have a plan even when I don't know what it is. Thank you that your plan will prevail! May I rest in your eternal, sovereign purpose and walk in obedience to you, step by step.

Cheri

In spite of all appearances to the contrary, God has a plan for this bankrupt world. He still has something in store for it. This dark, satanic earth, drowned in blood and tears, this earth of ours he still wants as a theatre for his grace and glorious direction.

—HELMUT THIELICKE (1908–1963), German theologian

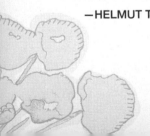

SAFE AND SECURE FROM ALL ALARMS

FEAR OF THE LORD LEADS TO LIFE,
BRINGING SECURITY AND PROTECTION FROM HARM.

Proverbs 19:23

TO FEAR THE LORD means to be in awe of him. It means to reverence him, to respect him. When we have this right view of God, we live life as we are meant to. With the majesty and power of God as our reference point, we have a proper perspective. When we measure life's circumstances against the sovereignty of God, things don't get blown out of proportion.

When we do not revere God, life becomes a burden. One worry piles on another, problem on problem, disappointment following disappointment. Of course, no one gets to live problem free. No one escapes heartache. But if we live with ourselves as the reference point, life's difficulties will be overwhelming. We might put up a good front, but we'll be worn down inch by inch. If we try to shoulder life's problems, they will outweigh the good things we experience because difficulties simply keep coming.

Living with a right view of God is the only way to live a life that is more than just existing. A life bigger than just making it through. God means for life to be abundant, joyful, overflowing. He means for life to be a celebration and a gift. He promises that fear of the Lord will lead to that kind of life. He doesn't promise that harm or difficulties will never come but that when they come, they will be stepping stones, not stumbling blocks. Troubling though they may be, they will not cause us real harm.

What is your view of God? Do you meditate daily on his majesty and power? Is he your first thought when you awake and your last thought before you sleep? Do you let every problem and challenge be swallowed up in the reality of his presence? If you learn to live with him as your reference point, you will find peace in any circumstance. If you do not, nothing can ever bring lasting peace and security.

Father, I fix my eyes on you. When my vision wanders, call me back.

Jennifer

If we have not quiet in our minds, outward comfort will do no more for us than a golden slipper on a gouty foot.

—**JOHN BUNYAN** (1628–1688), English writer and preacher

22 GOD SHOWS UP WHEN HIS PEOPLE PRAY

IN MY DISTRESS I CRIED OUT TO THE LORD;
YES, I PRAYED TO MY GOD FOR HELP.
HE HEARD ME FROM HIS SANCTUARY;
MY CRY TO HIM REACHED HIS EARS.

Psalm 18:6

IN PSALM 18, David pours out his thanksgiving to the Lord for rescuing him from Saul's troops. Inherent in his praise is his acknowledgment of how God responded to his fervent prayers for help. The Lord didn't just hear David in his great distress—he acted! Verses 7-17 tell us God shook the earth and the mountains, opened the heavens, and came down and defeated David's enemies.

This psalm has an important application for our lives: God shows up when his people pray! It doesn't matter how old or young you are or whether you are a king or a theologian, a brand-new believer or even a little child. The simple truth is that God works powerfully when people pray.

A family I know once gathered around their father and grandfather's bed for what doctors believed would be their loved one's last moments. In a coma for days, he showed no signs of recovering. With the family stood a five-year-old grandson. "Grandma, what's wrong with Grandpa?" the boy asked.

"Honey, he's very, very sick," she answered.

Very loudly the boy cried out, "Oh God, send down your big hand and heal my grandpa, right now!" and the few remaining family members said, "Amen."

To their surprise, within the hour the elderly man came out of the coma. His vital signs returned to normal, and in a few days he was released from the hospital. He lived for three more months, during which time he committed his life to Christ for the first time. His eternal destiny was changed by the prayers of the youngest member of the family and the wonder-working God who heard his cries and answered.

Father, you are a God that hears and answers prayer. How gracious that you act on behalf of those who seek you.

Cheri

The prayer of the feeblest saint on earth who lives in the Spirit and keeps right with God is a terror to Satan. The very powers of darkness are paralyzed by prayer. . . . No wonder Satan tries to keep our minds fussy in active work till we cannot think in prayer.

—**OSWALD CHAMBERS** (1874–1917), Scottish minister and teacher

EVERYTHING OLD IS NEW AGAIN **23**

CHRIST LIVES WITHIN YOU, SO EVEN THOUGH YOUR BODY WILL
DIE BECAUSE OF SIN, THE SPIRIT GIVES YOU LIFE BECAUSE YOU
HAVE BEEN MADE RIGHT WITH GOD. THE SPIRIT OF GOD,
WHO RAISED JESUS FROM THE DEAD, LIVES IN YOU.

Romans 8:10-11

CHRIST LIVES in you by his Spirit. That is the consummation of the gospel. He has moved in and taken up residence in you, expressing himself through your personality and transforming your mind to contain his thoughts.

Even though your physical body is winding down, growing older day by day, it is only the tent in which you live as you move through this world. Inside, where the Spirit of Christ resides, you are new and getting newer every day.

Paul says that the very Spirit who raised Jesus from the dead lives in you right this minute. Jesus' body was dead. His heart didn't beat. His lungs didn't draw air. His brain didn't produce brain waves. He was dead by every measure. Then, on the third day, the Spirit of God—the Spirit of Christ—entered his dead body and made him alive. The same body that was laid in the tomb walked out of it. From that instant, he lived in the power of resurrection, though present on earth in a form that could be seen and touched and recognized for forty more days.

We don't have resurrection bodies yet. We are still living in our old, dying bodies. But everything else about us has access to the power of Christ's resurrection. We have been brought from death to life by his indwelling. And no problem we ever encounter will be too difficult for the Spirit, who has already performed the universe's grandest power display.

Resurrection power, flow freely in me and through me.

Jennifer

On the first day of Pentecost [Christ] returned, not this time to be with them externally . . . but now to be in them, imparting to them His own divine nature, clothing Himself with their humanity. . . . He spoke with their lips, He worked with their hands. This was the miracle of the new birth, and this remains the very heart of the gospel!

—**MAJOR W. IAN THOMAS** (1914–2007), English writer and theology teacher

24 NOTHING CAN SEPARATE US FROM HIS LOVE

I AM CONVINCED THAT NOTHING CAN EVER SEPARATE US FROM GOD'S LOVE. NEITHER DEATH NOR LIFE, NEITHER ANGELS NOR DEMONS, NEITHER OUR FEARS FOR TODAY NOR OUR WORRIES ABOUT TOMORROW—NOT EVEN THE POWERS OF HELL CAN SEPARATE US FROM GOD'S LOVE. NO POWER IN THE SKY ABOVE OR IN THE EARTH BELOW—INDEED, NOTHING IN ALL CREATION WILL EVER BE ABLE TO SEPARATE US FROM THE LOVE OF GOD THAT IS REVEALED IN CHRIST JESUS OUR LORD.

Romans 8:38-39

HANNAH WHITALL SMITH, author of *The Christian's Secret to a Happy Life*, a book that has touched millions of people even into the twenty-first century, had many reasons to be extremely *unhappy*, even despairing. Four of her children died. Her husband was unfaithful and fell into a scandal that brought national humiliation and destroyed his ministry. Hannah's three grown children rejected Christ, and Hannah suffered financial hardship and rejection, even from her own Quaker family.

Yet she was sustained by a vision of the extravagant love of Christ, which enabled her to not allow these trials to sink her faith but rather to see them as gateways to deeper dependence on God. And she chose to believe the truth of Romans 8, that nothing, absolutely nothing, could separate her from God's love in Christ Jesus—even when her husband failed her and her grown children pursued destructive lifestyles.

She no doubt pondered the verses that come before Romans 8:38-39: *Does it mean he no longer loves us if we have trouble or calamity, or are persecuted, or are hungry or cold or in danger or threatened with death?* But despite all her difficulties, Hannah Whitall Smith stood on the truth that God's love is enough. Until Hannah's dying day, God's love gave her the strength to serve him and teach his Word to others.

> Help us, Lord of all comfort, to discover over and over again that you are enough. Empower us to choose to believe and receive your unfailing love, no matter how we are feeling or how fierce the trials we face.

Cheri

I said, "Lord, thou art enough for me." . . . I am not very well and feel what I expect thou would call "low." But it makes no difference how I feel. He is just the same, and He is with me, and I am His, and I am satisfied.

—**HANNAH WHITALL SMITH** (1832–1911), American lay speaker and author

COMMITTED TO HIM

THE EYES OF THE LORD SEARCH THE WHOLE EARTH IN ORDER
TO STRENGTHEN THOSE WHOSE HEARTS ARE FULLY COMMITTED
TO HIM.

2 Chronicles 16:9

I DON'T BELIEVE the Lord saves us and brings us out of darkness into his marvelous light for us to stay in our comfort zones. Instead, I've found that he wants to transform our inner being so we will passionately follow Christ and his purpose for our lives. Following Jesus won't always be easy; changes can be scary and uncertain, and difficulties and trials may face us on the journey. But we were created for the journey, not just for the destination. We were created for the adventure of doing the work God called us to. We are pilgrims who are to travel light along life's journey as we seek his will and presence.

That's precisely why today's promise in 2 Chronicles 16:9 is a boost of encouragement and hope. If we follow Christ's call, difficult situations may be daunting. But if we think of life as the great adventure God means it to be, then every difficulty, every obstacle, can be the door to purpose and growth. One way to have this perspective is to show up for service. For when we offer our lives to God, fully committed to him and his purposes, the adventure will accelerate, *because God is looking for willing vessels, and he pledges to strengthen those whose hearts are fully committed to him.*

As you give yourself to the Lord with what Oswald Chambers called a reckless abandon, you'll begin to discover the purpose or mission you were created for in this particular season of your life. You may need some more training or preparation, but your Creator has gifted you and will equip you. Not only that, he will strengthen you to fulfill the very purpose he made you for.

Oh Lord, my God, how I praise you for your precious promises. I stand on your promise to strengthen those who are fully committed to you and commit myself to you for whatever purpose you have for me.

Cheri

The weaker we feel, the harder we lean on God. And the harder we lean, the stronger we grow.

—JONI EARECKSON TADA (1949–), American author, artist, and advocate for the disabled

26 THE PROBLEM WITH CHARIOTS

SOME NATIONS BOAST OF THEIR CHARIOTS AND HORSES,
BUT WE BOAST IN THE NAME OF THE LORD OUR GOD.

Psalm 20:7

EVERY WEEK, it seems, the news reports on a new poll that takes the temperature of the public and provides a snapshot of how people feel on a given day. One poll might ask, How confident do you feel about the future? Another questions, Do you think the country is on the right track? These polls change weekly, and so do the results. I remember when most people felt pretty confident about our future and were optimistic about what lay ahead. It was unusual for a large percentage of those polled to think we were on the wrong track.

Lately, not so. For several years now the polls have shown a decline in our expectations for the future. Even young adults graduating from college and starting their adult lives tend to feel despondent about their prospects.

We live in turbulent times: wars, severe weather, a declining economy, debt, unemployment, foreclosures, layoffs, a weak stock market. Everything we once built our confidence on seems to have proved unstable. Everything we put our trust in has proved untrustworthy.

That, I think, is the problem with chariots and horses. They are not unshakable. Remember Pharaoh's army (see Exodus 14:21-28)?

Are you feeling shaken right now? Are you feeling unsettled because of the times in which we live? Can you remember different times? Times when the world's economy seemed unstoppable, and it seemed the good times would never end? Did you feel more secure then?

Is it time for us to stop and take inventory of what we lean on? I am surprised to discover what my confidence rests in, and often I don't see it until it has been stripped away. It wasn't until the state of the world came crashing down that I realized how much of my optimism hung on the state of the world.

Let these days of uncertainty be an opportunity for us to reassess where our sense of assurance lies and get it anchored in the right place. Let's boast in the name of the Lord our God.

Lord, I rest in you.

Jennifer

Real true faith is man's weakness leaning on God's strength.
—DWIGHT L. MOODY (1837–1899), American evangelist and publisher

LOOK UP 27

WE ARE POWERLESS AGAINST THIS MIGHTY ARMY THAT IS ABOUT TO ATTACK US. WE DO NOT KNOW WHAT TO DO, BUT WE ARE LOOKING TO YOU FOR HELP.

2 Chronicles 20:12

BECAUSE GOD is faithful to his promises, all we need to do in times of trouble or confusion is turn to him.

He helps us understand our circumstances from his perspective.

Earth's view gives only a vague outline and offers only a linear perspective. The earthbound point of view is like an artist's *ébauche*. An ébauche is the initial underpainting that establishes the broad lines of emphasis in a projected painting. It is unfinished. It is a rough outline, meant only to establish the painting's basic components. If you did not wait to see the finished work and walked away having seen only the ébauche, you would never truly see the painting. The finished work exists only in the mind of the artist.

In the reading for today, Jehoshaphat was not anticipating the attack that was looming on his horizon. Yet God had allowed the event in order to put his power on display and to cause faith to grow in his people.

Scripture first defines the earthbound view—the ébauche—of Judah's situation: "A vast army . . . is marching against you" (20:2). Jehoshaphat understood that this dire description of the facts did not constitute the whole of reality. He was alarmed, but that alarm pushed him to seek God. He inquired of the Lord rather than take facts at face value. He knew God had something to impart to him that would give him direction.

The painting of your life story is already completed in God's mind. The circumstances on earth are only an outline, alerting you to areas where God is going to complete the picture with his power. Don't mistake an ébauche for a finished work of art.

Lord, I do not know what to do, but I am looking to you for help.

Jennifer

God has wisely kept us in the dark concerning future events and reserved for himself the knowledge of them, that he may train us up in a dependence upon himself and a continued readiness for every event.

—**MATTHEW HENRY** (1662–1714), English pastor and Bible commentator

28 FROM THEOLOGY TO DOXOLOGY

EVERYTHING COMES FROM HIM AND EXISTS BY HIS POWER AND IS
INTENDED FOR HIS GLORY.

Romans 11:36

GOD PROMISES that he is always and everywhere in charge. He is not haphazard in his work. He is strategic. Things are unfolding according to a carefully orchestrated plan, and each person and circumstance has an assigned place in his purpose.

We are not automatons or robots. We are invited to cooperate with him in accomplishing his purposes. Only God could have put together such a perfect arrangement of details. In contemplating all the complexities, Paul reaches the end of his prodigious intellect's ability to comprehend it all, and breaks out in praise for the God who is so amazing that the only thing we can do is adore him.

OH, HOW GREAT ARE GOD'S RICHES AND WISDOM AND
KNOWLEDGE! HOW IMPOSSIBLE IT IS FOR US TO UNDERSTAND
HIS DECISIONS AND HIS WAYS!

Romans 11:33

How do your own circumstances look to you when you recognize that everything that happens is somehow serving God's purpose? Does today's verse force you to come to grips with things going on in your life in light of his plan? That's all right. You can do that. It might bring you to a moment of deeper devotion than ever before as you realize that God is working something out for your good and for his glory, even though that is not evident to you right now. Choose to believe his promise. When I'm struggling, as I often do, I finally come to the point where I say, "I will not *not* believe."

You are not abandoned. God is carefully working things out.

I surrender all. All to you, Jesus, I surrender. I surrender all.

Jennifer

Frequently we hold on so tightly to the good that we do know that we cannot receive the greater good that we do not know. God has to help us let go of our tiny vision in order to release the greater good he has in store for us. . . . A settled peace is the most frequent experience of those who have trod the path of relinquishment.

—**RICHARD FOSTER** (1942–), American minister and author

WHAT GOD WANTS US TO DO 29

DEAR BROTHERS AND SISTERS, I PLEAD WITH YOU TO GIVE YOUR BODIES TO GOD BECAUSE OF ALL HE HAS DONE FOR YOU. LET THEM BE A LIVING AND HOLY SACRIFICE—THE KIND HE WILL FIND ACCEPTABLE. THIS IS TRULY THE WAY TO WORSHIP HIM. . . . LET GOD TRANSFORM YOU INTO A NEW PERSON BY CHANGING THE WAY YOU THINK. THEN YOU WILL LEARN TO KNOW GOD'S WILL FOR YOU, WHICH IS GOOD AND PLEASING AND PERFECT.

Romans 12:1-2

I HAD NO IDEA when I had a quiet, yet life-changing, encounter with Christ as a young woman where that would take me. But when I read Romans 12:1-2, I began to offer myself to him as a living sacrifice.

Day by day, I would pray this verse and believe the promise that as I surrendered to God and let his Word transform me, he would show me his plan for my life. Eventually that led me to leave what I thought was my calling as a high school teacher and start writing my first book. That book led to my being asked to speak to various groups. I didn't know it would lead me years later to the shores of the Zambezi River in Africa and to South America and to Singapore. The first time I was invited to speak, I didn't really want to accept. Public speaking was terrifying to me.

But God's Spirit reminded me of the promise of Romans 12. So I agreed. When I got up to speak to a group of eager parents that first time, a joy filled me I hadn't known before. Many years later, as I continue to share hope with people, God is still faithful. Is there something too hard for you? Let me encourage you to give your whole self to God—body, soul, and spirit. He will be faithful to show you how good and pleasing his will really is.

Thank you for your Word, which is full of promises that apply to my daily life. Lord, I again give you my life—my regular, walking-around-life. Use me, live through me, love others through me, and accomplish your purposes today as I yield to you.

Cheri

Let us bring what is our own, God will supply the rest.
—ST. JOHN CHRYSOSTOM (ca. 347–407), early church father

30 LOVE BORN OF LOVE

> HE RENEWS MY STRENGTH.
> HE GUIDES ME ALONG RIGHT PATHS,
> BRINGING HONOR TO HIS NAME.
>
> *Psalm 23:3*

AS THE GOOD SHEPHERD, Jesus is ever aware of the weaknesses and needs of his flock. Without the shepherd, sheep would be at a loss to protect themselves or to find pasture or to stay on safe paths. When a flock of sheep comes safely into the sheep pen at day's end, it is a tribute to the shepherding.

God has woven this beautiful promise, framed in the metaphor of sheep and shepherd, throughout his Word. It speaks volumes about the tenderness of his love for us, and the devotion that his love engenders in his sheep.

How is a sheep trained to follow its shepherd's voice? Why does a sheep stay on the path its shepherd leads it on? Because the sheep knows that its shepherd, not the sheep pen or the pastures or the still waters, is his home.

The love that produces love—the shepherd's love for his sheep that creates an answering love in the sheep—is the glue that holds the vulnerable sheep on the right path.

"This is real love—not that we loved God, but that he loved us and sent his Son as a sacrifice to take away our sins" (1 John 4:10).

Here is the miracle of that love born of love. It takes a bunch of sheep and forms them into a flock. All the sheep of a flock are held to the path by their devotion to the same shepherd. Jesus said it this way: "There will be one flock with one shepherd" (John 10:16). His love is so magnetic that it draws diverse sheep and makes them one flock.

To live in the fullness of his promise, we need to be attached to the Shepherd in the bonds of unity "so that the body of Christ may be built up until we all reach unity in the faith and in the knowledge of the Son of God and become mature, attaining to the whole measure of the fullness of Christ" (Ephesians 4:12-13, NIV).

Lord, teach me and fill me with your love for your sheep.

Jennifer

Every converted person becomes "in Christ" at the same time Christ enters into the believer. If I am in Christ and you are in Christ, and if He is in us, then we experience a profound unity in Christ.

—**R. C. SPROUL** (1939–), American theologian, author, and pastor

INSTRUMENTS OF HIS PEACE

LET US THEREFORE MAKE EVERY EFFORT TO DO WHAT LEADS TO PEACE AND TO MUTUAL EDIFICATION.

Romans 14:19 (NIV)

GOD PROMISES that those who make peace will be blessed: "Blessed are the peacemakers" (Matthew 5:9, NIV). But to make peace, a person must be at peace. A person who is filled with turmoil will inject that into relationships and situations. A person who is filled with peace will diffuse peace into relationships and situations. To be a peacemaker, you have to be peaceful.

In Matthew 5, Jesus blesses those who are peacemakers in his Kingdom. In Kingdom peacemaking, the disciple takes the initiative. The disciple lays aside pride, risks rejection or ridicule. In other words, peacemaking is not passive. For example, if a person with the authority to do so ordered you to go carry his load one mile, then going with him or her one mile would avoid conflict. But that is not the same as peace. Don't be satisfied with keeping things on an even keel. Go further.

In order to carry someone's load a second mile, peace has to be in you. It is a peace that has grown out of meekness. A strong, settled, contented person, anchored to eternity's realities, has the courage and the boldness to be outrageous in making peace. "The fruit of righteousness will be peace; the effect of righteousness will be quietness and confidence forever" (Isaiah 32:17, NIV 1984).

Peace comes from the inside and spreads to those around you. Make peace. Create it. Bring peace out of chaos and disorder. Be like your Father. "Blessed are the peacemakers, for they will be called sons of God" (Matthew 5:9, NIV 1984). Radical, outrageous peacemakers are known as sons of God. People who observe them can't help but notice the likeness.

Peace can be costly. It can cost your pride. It can cost your reputation. It cost Jesus his life. But the promise is that peacemakers will live in a state of blessedness. Those who live *in* peace, will live *at* peace.

Father, show me where I am to be your peacemaker, and give me the grace to pay the price.

Jennifer

Lord, make me an instrument of thy peace. Where there is hatred, let me sow love.
—**FRANCIS OF ASSISI** (1181–1226), Italian friar and founder of the Franciscan order

AUGUST

GOD'S PROMISED HOPE

I PRAY THAT GOD, WHO GIVES YOU HOPE, WILL KEEP YOU HAPPY
AND FULL OF PEACE AS YOU BELIEVE IN HIM. MAY YOU OVERFLOW
WITH HOPE THROUGH THE POWER OF THE HOLY SPIRIT.

Romans 15:13

FOR ALMOST every dream, idea, or goal God gives us, there is a delay, a time of difficulty—even a dead end—in which our situation deteriorates from difficult to impossible, and accomplishing the goal looks hopeless. But these times are sent for a special purpose. When Paul and the apostles were overwhelmed in Asia, burdened beyond their strength and even thinking it might be the end, Paul said the calamities happened *so they wouldn't trust or hope in themselves but in God*, who raises the dead. It was this hope that helped them to continue on the mission to which God had called them (see 2 Corinthians 1:8-9).

Even in the midst of overwhelming problems, we, too, can find hope. It all depends on our perspective. Catherine Marshall once described a friend who boarded a plane. As her friend settled into her seat, she noticed that on one side of the plane a sunset filled the sky with glorious color. But out of the window next to her seat, all she could see was a dark, threatening sky.

As the plane began to take off, a gentle Voice spoke within her: *Your life will contain some happy, beautiful times and also some dark shadows. Here's a lesson that will save you much heartache and allow you to abide in me with continual peace and joy: it doesn't matter which window you look through; this plane is still going to Cleveland. You have a choice. You can dwell on the gloomy picture. Or you can focus on the bright things, put your hope in me, and leave the dark, ominous situations to me. I alone can handle them, anyway.*

We have the same choice. We can focus on God's everlasting faithfulness and have hope in him, or we can focus on the dark things and be distressed.

*Jesus, as I continue to believe in you and trust you, fill me with your peace and
let me overflow with hope through the power of your Holy Spirit.*

Cheri

Behind the cloud the starlight lurks,
Through showers the sunbeams fall;
For God, who loveth all his works,
Has left his hope with all!

—**JOHN GREENLEAF WHITTIER** (1807–1892), American poet

2

STRONG AND COURAGEOUS

BE STRONG AND COURAGEOUS! DON'T BE AFRAID OR
DISCOURAGED BECAUSE OF THE KING OF ASSYRIA OR HIS MIGHTY
ARMY, FOR THERE IS A POWER FAR GREATER ON OUR SIDE! HE MAY
HAVE A GREAT ARMY, BUT THEY ARE MERELY MEN. WE HAVE THE
LORD OUR GOD TO HELP US AND TO FIGHT OUR BATTLES FOR US!

2 Chronicles 32:7-8

ARE YOU FACING overwhelming circumstances? Are there situations in your life that look as if they will defeat you? Do you seem small in comparison? Your enemy hopes to keep you focused on his forces and keep you trapped in that perspective. He hopes to call your attention to how you stack up against the circumstances that face you. If he can do that, then your enemy will define your experience.

Today, regroup. Refocus. Let the eyes of your heart come to rest on God. Be strong and courageous, not afraid or discouraged. You can be sure there is good reason for a new perspective: what you see is not the whole picture. You are never in the battle alone. Your battle is God's battle. Every time. You can say to the enemy, "Take it up with him."

A friend of mine faced a scary financial situation. Her husband had lost his job without warning. She was terrified, and every way she looked at their financial situation yielded a bleak outcome. Everything she could see told her that defeat was certain.

But God had been busy laying the groundwork for his provision in ways that weren't part of the picture my friend was focused on. Her husband had owned a fairly worthless piece of land since before she knew him. It had been for sale for years. The week after his layoff, someone called to buy the land. A development was going up. The money was enough to sustain them through the year it took for him to find employment again. While my friend was worrying and stewing, God had been working out the solution.

I don't know what God is doing in your situation, but he is doing something. The fact that you can't see it doesn't mean it isn't in process.

Father, I'm leaving you in charge of my situation.

Jennifer

Every tomorrow has two handles. We can take hold of it by the handle of anxiety, or by the handle of faith.

—HENRY WARD BEECHER (1813–1887), American minister, abolitionist, and author

CLEAN INSIDE

I WASH MY HANDS IN INNOCENCE,
AND GO ABOUT YOUR ALTAR, LORD,
PROCLAIMING ALOUD YOUR PRAISE
AND TELLING ALL OF YOUR WONDERFUL DEEDS.
LORD, I LOVE THE HOUSE WHERE YOU LIVE,
THE PLACE WHERE YOUR GLORY DWELLS.

Psalm 26:6-8 (NIV)

THE CEREMONIAL hand washing of which David speaks illustrates the reality of repentance and cleansing. Hands are the appendages through which we act and work in the world. Hands come into direct contact with objects and substances. They are used symbolically to stand for the point of contact between God's people and sin. That sin might be in thought or attitude or speech, but the hands symbolize where the pollution of sin has intersected our lives: "Who may climb the mountain of the LORD? Who may stand in his holy place? Only those who hands and hearts are pure" (Psalm 24:3-4).

Clean hands can come only from pure hearts. This "hand washing" comes from the inside, not the outside. In today's verse, David says, "I wash my hands in innocence." The word translated "innocence" has a root that means to be poured out or emptied: emptied of sin and purged of sin's poison, to be filled with the fullness of God's Spirit. In that state, David comes to the altar to offer worship.

God promises that sins confessed are sins washed away: "If we confess our sins . . . he is faithful and just to forgive us our sins and to cleanse us from all wickedness" (1 John 1:9). Now we can worship with abandon. Now we can give ourselves over to the joy of his presence.

To be cleansed from the inside out frees us from the toxins of sin and spiritual free radicals that silently wreak havoc. Confessing our sins and receiving the cleansing power of the indwelling life of the Spirit let us experience the state of purity that God has made available to us. We don't have to live in the grime of sin. We can have clean hands and pure hearts and revel in the presence of the Lord, for whose pleasure we were created.

Create in me a clean heart and renew a right spirit within me.

Jennifer

The Pharisees minded what God spoke, but not what He intended. They were busy in the outward work of the hand, but incurious of the affections and choice of the heart.

—**JEREMY TAYLOR** (1613–1667), English cleric

4

ABUNDANT GIFTS

I ALWAYS THANK MY GOD FOR YOU AND FOR THE GRACIOUS GIFTS HE HAS GIVEN YOU, NOW THAT YOU BELONG TO CHRIST JESUS. THROUGH HIM, GOD HAS ENRICHED YOUR CHURCH IN EVERY WAY.

1 Corinthians 1:4-5

GOD HAS GIVEN gifts to each of us, gifts to be used to enrich others. These gifts are from the Spirit of God, and they operate through his power. Each of us was designed in every aspect of our makeup to contain and express the gifts that the Spirit imparts to us. Our personalities, our bents, our talents, our experiences—everything about us is shaped to contain our gifts.

When we are operating in the gifts that we have received from the Spirit, we are at our most productive. We are happiest and most fulfilled. We experience the power of God directly when we are exercising our spiritual gifts. Seeing the Spirit work through the gifts he has given us produces a profound humility and boundless joy. At that moment, we know ourselves to be vessels through which the Spirit is expressing himself. We know what our lives are for.

Acting and living in harmony with our gifts bring us into the abundant life Jesus has for us. Our gifts are for giving. We will never find that abundance and overflowing joy until we start giving away our gifts.

I have a dear friend who dealt with bouts of depression as long as I had known her, until she discovered her great capacity for showing mercy. She started working with a prison Bible study and mentoring program. She had never realized the depth of misery in the lives of other human beings. The kinds of experiences she learned about in mentoring inmates were eye opening to her. She had a knack—a gift—for zeroing in on the very place where a soul was deeply wounded and then offering words and acts of encouragement and mercy. Now my friend seems to have a vitality and purpose that has transformed her. She still has some struggles with depression, but they are fewer, and she has a reason to move through those times: her "girls" need her.

Father, let your gifts flow through me to those around me. Let me be reflective of your generosity and your selfless love.

Jennifer

That we are alive today is proof positive that God has something for us to do today.

—VACHEL LINDSAY (1879–1931), American poet

RESPONDERS

My heart has heard you say, "Come and talk with me."
And my heart responds, "Lord, I am coming."

Psalm 27:8

IN OUR RELATIONSHIP with God, our position is always that of responder. We never have to engage in an activity or a ritual to get his attention because his attention never wanders from any of us. Before time began, he had already settled his heart on you and laid the groundwork for your salvation.

When you and I are drawn in God's direction, we might feel as if that's our own instinct moving us in that direction. When we decide to call to him, it might feel like our idea. When we find ourselves inclined toward him, we might feel as if we are seeking him out. But in reality, every time we have an impulse to pursue the things of God, we are responding to his invitation.

Would it take the burden off you if you knew that you don't have to woo God, because he is wooing you? Would it lessen your anxiety to know that God is calling you to pray and that he is not calling you to pray to air? He is not inviting you to call on him in vain.

The inclination you feel toward God right now, in this very minute, is God calling you. Right now, God's Spirit is saying, *Child, come talk with me. I'm here for you.* All you have to do is respond.

Right now, if you answer yes, you will find his open arms waiting.

When I was a little girl, I loved my grandpa Dick. He lived a few hours' drive from us. When we drove into the driveway of his house, he would always be in the front yard waiting. I would run to him, and he would pick me up and twirl me around in his joy at seeing me.

That's how God responds to you every time you turn his way. Arms outstretched, ready to twirl.

Father, I respond to your love. Here I am.

Jennifer

Turn around and believe that the good news that we are loved is better than we ever dared hope, and that to believe in that good news, to live out of it and toward it, to be in love with that good news, is of all glad things in this world the gladdest thing of all. Amen, and come Lord Jesus.

—FREDERICK BUECHNER (1926–), American minister and author

6 DRAWING ON HIS RICHES

"NO EYE HAS SEEN, NO EAR HAS HEARD,
AND NO MIND HAS IMAGINED
WHAT GOD HAS PREPARED
FOR THOSE WHO LOVE HIM."

BUT IT WAS TO US THAT GOD REVEALED THESE THINGS BY
HIS SPIRIT. FOR HIS SPIRIT SEARCHES OUT EVERYTHING AND
SHOWS US GOD'S DEEP SECRETS. . . . NO ONE CAN KNOW GOD'S
THOUGHTS EXCEPT GOD'S OWN SPIRIT. AND WE HAVE RECEIVED
GOD'S SPIRIT (NOT THE WORLD'S SPIRIT), SO WE CAN KNOW THE
WONDERFUL THINGS GOD HAS FREELY GIVEN US.

1 Corinthians 2:9-12

WHAT WE CANNOT know by seeing, hearing, or imagining, we can know by the Spirit's revelation. The word *revelation* means "uncovering" or "unveiling." The Spirit unveils God's truths to our understanding. When the Spirit gives understanding, we will know what God has ready and waiting as certainly as if we'd seen it with our eyes or heard it with our ears.

We can know God and his deep truths only by receiving them directly from him. Just as no one knows me but me, no one knows God but God. If you want to know his thoughts, he will have to reveal them to you.

God has revealed himself to us. He has given us his Spirit so that we can understand what he has prepared for us and has made freely available to us.

When we know what God has available to us, we will walk in his provision. We will lean on his power. If we don't know what's there, we won't know to avail ourselves of it. Imagine that someone had opened a bank account in your name and made a substantial deposit, but you never accessed the funds. What if you lived as if you had nothing, when in reality you had plenty? That is why God has given us his Spirit to reveal his riches—so we will live in his abundance.

Lord, alert me to your provision so that I can walk daily in it.

Jennifer

We may have as much of God as we will. Christ puts the key of the treasure-chamber into our hand, and bids us take all that we want. If a man is admitted into the bullion vault of a bank, and told to help himself, and comes out with one cent, whose fault is it that he is poor?

—ALEXANDER MACLAREN (1826–1910), British preacher and Bible expositor

THE TRUE LIGHT

THE LORD'S LIGHT PENETRATES THE HUMAN SPIRIT,
EXPOSING EVERY HIDDEN MOTIVE.

Proverbs 20:27

THE GOSPEL of John describes Jesus as "the one who is the true light, who gives light to everyone" (John 1:9). Created light is a copy of True Light. The True Light existed before created light and will continue to exist long after created light is no longer necessary.

When Jesus, the True Light, comes into your life, he brings with him all the power and the attributes of light in its truest form.

Light exposes. It brings hidden motives out of hiding. On the surface, that sounds a bit intimidating. But remember who is exposing your motives. It is Jesus, who loves you so much that he died in your place and rose again to make his home in you. You can feel safe under the scrutiny of his light.

Jeremiah describes our hearts—our inner beings—this way: "The heart is deceitful above all things and beyond cure. Who can understand it? 'I the LORD search the heart and examine the mind, to reward each person according to their conduct, according to what their deeds deserve'" (Jeremiah 17:9-10, NIV).

He is describing the state of our lives apart from salvation; we can easily fool ourselves, and we don't understand our own motives. It is impossible for us to correctly assess our hearts.

Have you ever asked yourself, *Why do I do that? What makes me think like that?* When the revealing Light illuminates your innermost being, you discover the motives—often built on lies—that seem to drive your behavior. Then the True Light goes a step further.

Light heals. It irradiates bacteria, viruses, and fungi. Vitamin D—an essential element for healthy bodies—can be produced only by light. Medicine is continually finding more ways to use light to reduce pain and inflammation and accelerate tissue repair.

The True Light brings into your life his healing power—irradiating sin's toxins, soothing painful soul wounds, and adding power to overcome wrong behaviors.

Light of the World, shine into the deep places of my heart and reveal those hidden motives that have kept me enslaved to fruitless behaviors.

Jennifer

I believe in Christianity as I believe that the sun has risen: not only because I see it, but because by it I see everything else.

—**C. S. LEWIS** (1898–1963), Irish novelist, literary critic, and essayist

8 DO WHAT YOU KNOW

THE KINGDOM OF GOD IS NOT JUST A LOT OF TALK; IT IS LIVING BY GOD'S POWER.

1 Corinthians 4:20

DON'T BE SATISFIED just to know the language of the faith, or even just to understand the doctrines of the faith. It is the doing of the faith that marks you as a true Christ follower. After having taught his disciples, Jesus said, "Now that you know these things, God will bless you for doing them" (John 13:17).

Letting the truth we know transform the way we live translates into blessings—or living in a state of blessedness, living fully supplied, fulfilled.

What if you did everything you know? When I ask myself that question, I have to admit that on many occasions I know things I don't do. Throughout the day as you interact with others, as you make choices, as you walk out the details of life, ask yourself, *What would happen if I did everything I know? Right now, what do I know that I'm not putting into practice?*

This is not a legalistic, rule-following, stress-inducing call to obedience. Rather, it is a call to freedom and safety. Living out the Word is how we put down deep roots. Doing what we know is the strategy for a life with a firm foundation—a life that is not rickety and flimsy and susceptible to the storms of life. It is living in God's power.

Jesus said, "Why do you keep calling me 'Lord, Lord!' when you don't do what I say? I will show you what it's like when someone comes to me, listens to my teaching, and then follows it. It is like a person building a house who digs deep and lays the foundation on solid rock. When the floodwaters rise and break against that house, it stands firm because it is well built" (Luke 6:46-48).

What we put into practice is knowledge. Everything else is just information.

Lord, I want to live in your power. Really live in it. I don't want to be all talk. Nudge me when I'm talking one way and living another.

Jennifer

I have been impressed with the urgency of doing. Knowing is not enough; we must apply. Being willing is not enough; we must do.

—**LEONARDO DA VINCI** (1452–1519), Italian Renaissance artist, inventor, mathematician, engineer

SAFE PASSAGE

YOU ARE MY ROCK AND MY FORTRESS.
FOR THE HONOR OF YOUR NAME, LEAD ME OUT OF
THIS DANGER.
PULL ME FROM THE TRAP MY ENEMIES SET FOR ME,
FOR I FIND PROTECTION IN YOU ALONE.
I ENTRUST MY SPIRIT INTO YOUR HAND.
RESCUE ME, LORD, FOR YOU ARE A FAITHFUL GOD.

Psalm 31:3-5

WE ALL have areas of our lives where we are susceptible to the pull of sin. If we know ourselves and are honest, we know that certain situations or personalities or settings or events play to our weaknesses. We can't avoid these, but we can see them for what they are and cry out to God to lead us through unscathed.

John had a volatile relationship with his mother. He was angry over past hurts and was sensitive to her blunt and controlling ways of interacting with him in the present. It seemed that he could not be around her for any length of time without lashing out or silently spiraling into seething anger that lasted for days afterward.

Then John had an epiphany from the Lord that showed him he was angry with his mother because he could never get the love from her that he felt he should get. He recognized that he was trying to get from her what could come only from God. He recognized that she was acting the only way she knew. And something in him adjusted.

The next time he was to be with his mother, he asked the Lord to walk him safely through the minefield of their relationship. In the past, he would typically have become angry before he even saw her, in anticipation of the hurt to come. This time, he forgave her in advance. He asked the Lord to replace his resentment with compassion.

His new way of responding to his mother proved the power of God to rescue John and brought honor to God's name. The Lord led John in paths of righteousness, and the Lord's name was honored.

Lord, pull me from the traps my enemy sets for me. You are the only one who can. I entrust myself to you for safekeeping.

Jennifer

Anticipate your battles; fight them on your knees before temptation comes, and you will always have victory.

—R. A. TORREY (1856–1928), American evangelist, pastor, and writer

10 MY FUTURE IS IN YOUR HANDS

I AM TRUSTING YOU, O LORD,
SAYING, "YOU ARE MY GOD!"
MY FUTURE IS IN YOUR HANDS.

Psalm 31:14-15

BECAUSE MY PARENTS died relatively young, my father at forty-seven, and Mama at fifty-nine, I've had some issues, some of which are reflected in statements I've made in the past: "I don't worry about being put in a nursing home in my old age. Nobody in our family lives long enough to get there." Or when my friends rushed out to buy half-price decorations the day after Christmas, I'd think, *I don't know if I'll even be here next Christmas. Why buy more stuff?*

The first statement my niece Holly described as downright morbid (although my sisters have said similar things), and after my fortieth and then forty-seventh birthdays, I realized the folly of the second statement, so I gave both those ideas and my fears to the Lord. For truly, only the sovereign Lord who created me knows how many days and years I'll be on this earth before graduating to heaven.

None of us really know how long we're going to live or what our future holds. We are not privy to the personal trials that lie ahead or to information about national or world events that may affect us. In light of record deficits in our nation's economy, wars breaking out around the world, and bad news broadcast daily by the 24–7 news media, it's normal to feel uncertain or even fearful about the future.

Yet the promise in Psalm 31 is that *because* the everlasting Lord is our God, we don't have to worry about the future. He has our future in his loving hands. We don't have to worry that we'll have short lives because of a genetic condition in our family. We don't have to fret about the stock market or tomorrow's trouble. Instead, we can trust God and put our future in his hands today and every day.

Father, I'm trusting my life today and all my tomorrows to you. As I put my future in your hands, I thank you that I don't have to worry because your plans for me can't be thwarted!

Cheri

Thank God for the unknown future. . . . How merciful God is to lift the curtain on today; and as we get strength today to meet tomorrow, then to lift the curtain on the morrow.

—**E. STANLEY JONES** (1884–1973), American missionary and theologian

REBUILDING THE WALLS

THE KING ASKED, "WELL, HOW CAN I HELP YOU?"
WITH A PRAYER TO THE GOD OF HEAVEN, [NEHEMIAH]
REPLIED, "IF IT PLEASE YOUR MAJESTY AND IF YOU ARE PLEASED
WITH ME, YOUR SERVANT, SEND ME TO JUDAH TO REBUILD THE
CITY WHERE MY ANCESTORS ARE BURIED."

Nehemiah 2:4-5

WHILE NEHEMIAH was serving as chief cup bearer to King Artaxerxes in the Persian palace in Susa, he received a report on the tragic situation in Jerusalem. The returned exiles were in constant danger, with no protection; their houses were rubble; the city gates had been burned; and the walls were broken down. Although the Temple had been rebuilt, the city itself and the lives of its people were in ruins.

Upon reading the grim news, Nehemiah sat down and wept. He mourned, fasted, and prayed to God for days and weeks. But he didn't stop there. When the king asked what was wrong, Nehemiah didn't lean on his own understanding. Instead, he again prayed to the God of heaven. Nehemiah had been praying for his people for four months. But now, the original language says that he "breathed" a brief prayer to the Lord and then stated his request.

Nehemiah's prayers continued when he got the go-ahead from the king to leave for Jerusalem. Even with the Lord's favor and help, the Israelites had much hard work ahead. Yet Nehemiah bathed the whole process of rebuilding Jerusalem in prayer. He prayed when they were assailed by enemies from without. He sought God when derailed by problems from within. And when the enormous task of rebuilding the wall of Jerusalem was completed in only fifty-two days, he didn't boast in himself but gave God the glory and credit.

Whether it is a wall, a family, a church, or an individual life that needs rebuilding, it's not too late for God's help. Nothing is impossible when we surrender it into his hands. The same God who responded to Nehemiah's prayers and undergirded him all the way to restoration stands ready to help you succeed.

*Father, I surrender _____ to you. Please come into my life
with your restoring power, and hear my prayers as you did Nehemiah's. As you
prove yourself mighty, may you receive much glory.*

Cheri

Prayer is not flight; prayer is power. Prayer does not deliver a man from some terrible situation; prayer enables a man to face and to master the situation.

—WILLIAM BARCLAY (1907–1978), Scottish author and minister

12 THE GIFT OF FORGIVENESS

Oh, what joy for those
    whose disobedience is forgiven,
    whose sin is put out of sight! . . .
I confessed all my sins to you
    and stopped trying to hide my guilt.
I said to myself, "I will confess my rebellion to
    the Lord."
And you forgave me! All my guilt is gone.

Psalm 32:1, 5

OUTSIDE IT was freezing cold, but inside the small prison chapel, where eighty-five inmates and nine volunteers crowded in, it was warm and cozy. I watched as the women recited Psalm 32 together and then individually got up to say the verses from memory.

Sharon was first and said the first lines of the psalm perfectly. However, when she got to verse five, she choked up and had to wait a moment to collect herself before she continued: "When I refused to confess my sin, I was weak and miserable." Tears ran down her cheeks as she finished the psalm and then shared that she would likely be dead if she hadn't been arrested on drug charges and put in prison. There she was introduced to Jesus Christ and surrendered her life to him.

Sharon had struggled with a profound sense of guilt for the mistakes she'd made, the devastation in her children's lives, and the extra burdens her elderly mother carried having three brokenhearted kids to raise. "But I finally stopped trying to hide my sins, deny them, or numb myself with more drugs," Sharon told us. She had confessed all her sins and years of rebellion to the Lord. And the reality of God's mercy was incredible to her. "And you forgave me! All my guilt is gone."

Her face glowed as she finished her testimony. Hope was alive in her heart and eyes. Though she still had several years to serve on her prison term, she was experiencing the freedom and joy that only Christ's forgiveness can bring.

Father, you are the giver of every good gift, especially the gift of forgiveness through the cross of your Son, Jesus. May we not take for granted your enormous mercy.

Cheri

To the frightened, God is friendly; to the poor in spirit, he is forgiving; to the ignorant, considerate; to the weak, gentle.

—**A. W. TOZER** (1897–1963), American preacher and author

GODSPEAK

THE LORD MERELY SPOKE,
AND THE HEAVENS WERE CREATED.
HE BREATHED THE WORD,
AND ALL THE STARS WERE BORN.

Psalm 33:6

GOD IS not a God who once spoke. He is a God who is now speaking. When he speaks into our lives in present tense, he is speaking the same word that formed the universe.

Speaking requires breath rushing over the vocal chords. Without breath, there are no spoken words. Have you ever been with someone whose breathing is compromised? They can't speak easily. Breath is the transporter of words and without breath, words are imprisoned inside the mind and have no outlet. God's breath is the container of his word. David writes, "He breathed the word, and all the stars were born."

As the creation event unfolds, we see God breathe the breath of life into the human he created on the sixth day—the pinnacle of his creation. The same breath that carried the word of creation in it. When he—in a scene stunning in its intimacy—breathes into the human, life is the result. The man, who was only form, became a living soul when the word of God filled him.

God still breathes his word into his people. He still gives us life through his word. When the living, active word of God dwells richly in us, then we have the life that is truly life. When we are dry, parched, longing for refreshment, it comes from his word. The word he speaks in present tense, breathing it into us and resuscitating us with his life: "I lie in the dust; revive me by your word" (Psalm 119:25).

His promise is that his word is always fresh, always new. He is always speaking that creating, sustaining word, and it always does what he has assigned it to do.

Creator, breathe your word into me in this moment, made sacred by your presence. As you breathe your word out, I breathe it in. May it flow into the deepest recesses of my heart, bringing life.

Jennifer

God is not silent. It is the nature of God to speak. The second person of the Holy Trinity is called The Word.

—A. W. TOZER (1897–1963), American preacher and author

14 GRACE GREATER THAN ALL MY SIN

"Don't be dejected and sad, for the joy of the Lord is your strength!"

And the Levites, too, quieted the people, telling them, "Hush! Don't weep! For this is a sacred day." So the people went away to eat and drink at a festive meal, to share gifts of food, and to celebrate with great joy because they had heard God's words and understood them.

Nehemiah 8:10-12

THE ISRAELITES had returned from seventy years of captivity. They had not heard the Law read in many years. When Ezra read the Word of God and other priests interpreted it so the people understood, the effect was so great that the people began to weep over their sins. Confronted with God's law, their own lawbreaking broke their hearts.

But after allowing an appropriate time of mourning over sin, the leaders reminded the people to rejoice and celebrate.

"God's law was given so that all people could see how sinful they were. But as people sinned more and more, God's wonderful grace became more abundant. So just as sin ruled over all people and brought them to death, now God's wonderful grace rules instead, giving us right standing with God and resulting in eternal life through Jesus Christ our Lord" (Romans 5:20-21).

God shows us our sin so that we can be freed from it through his grace. His grace rules in our lives.

Are you caught in the awareness of your sin but unable to move on to the wonder of God's grace? Do you have the notion that it is very spiritual to remain in constant grief over sin? Jesus died and rose again to set you free from your sin so you could enjoy his grace. Acknowledge sin, turn from it, and move on. The joy of the Lord is your strength.

Lord, I rejoice in the grace you have poured out in my life.

Jennifer

Grace meets the sinner on the spot where he stands; grace approaches him just as he is. Grace does not wait till there is something to attract it nor till a good reason is found in the sinner for its flowing to him. . . . It was free, sovereign grace when it first thought of the sinner; it was free grace when it found and laid hold of him; and it is free grace when it hands him up into glory.

—**HORATIUS BONAR** (1808–1889), Scottish churchman and poet

THE RACE OF A LIFETIME

ALL ATHLETES ARE DISCIPLINED IN THEIR TRAINING. THEY DO
IT TO WIN A PRIZE THAT WILL FADE AWAY, BUT WE DO IT FOR
AN ETERNAL PRIZE. SO I RUN WITH PURPOSE IN EVERY STEP.

1 Corinthians 9:25-26

ONE OF MY DREAMS was to run a marathon. As I watched the runners—including my adult son, Justin, and daughter-in-law, Maggie, and hundreds of others—taking off for the grueling 26.2 miles of the Memorial Marathon in Oklahoma City, something in me leaped for joy. Watching the runners, I was inspired by the discipline it takes to train for a marathon as well as the enormous endurance, self-control, and courage required to complete the race. These athletes had trained hard, yet they also faced obstacles on the course: some suffered with leg cramps or sharp pains in their sides, others were out of breath or exhausted. Yet they kept moving forward and didn't look back. They stayed focused on the prize and finished the race.

Paul uses this athletic analogy in 1 Corinthians 9 to exhort believers not only to run but to run in such a way that we will win the prize. For Paul, there was no place for flaky living and laziness. He had his eyes on the prize and possessed the self-discipline of an elite athlete—and he encourages all disciples to develop these qualities as well.

One of the important things to remember is that the prize waiting for us at the end of our journey is so much more glorious than a gold medal. Philippians tells us that the supreme prize is one that will never fade or tarnish. It's the prize for which God through Christ is calling us up to heaven. In the meantime, here on earth, we're to run with purpose in every step.

> *Jesus, forgive me for getting sloppy and out of condition spiritually. I want to keep my eyes on you and run the race with courage. Grant me your strength and endurance to finish well!*
>
> *Cheri*

When Charlton Heston was concerned about not being able to win the chariot race in the movie *Ben Hur*, Cecil B. DeMille told him, "Your job is to stay on the chariot. It's my job to make sure you win." So too for us—we're just to endure and do what God has asked us to do and leave the winning up to Him.

—UNKNOWN

16 THE LORD HEARS

THE LORD HEARS HIS PEOPLE WHEN THEY CALL TO HIM
FOR HELP.
HE RESCUES THEM FROM ALL THEIR TROUBLES.
THE LORD IS CLOSE TO THE BROKENHEARTED;
HE RESCUES THOSE WHOSE SPIRITS ARE CRUSHED.

Psalm 34:17-18

WE HUMANS tend to grumble about inconveniences like interrupted electricity or a heat wave. Those are definitely *problems*, but when a young woman is waiting for the boat that will take her home to England for a furlough and instead a Japanese ship pulls up and takes her captive, that is *trouble*.

Anne hadn't been home in nine years. Her mother's health was fragile, and Anne longed to see Mama, her little nieces and nephews, and other family. The clatter of the Japanese soldiers shook the deck, and Anne felt a rush of panic. But God spoke to her heart, *Anne, you're not going home. You're going to a Japanese prison camp.*

Lord, how long will this last? Will I ever see my family again?

I will be with you, God assured her. Moments later she and the other missionaries and children began a march of hundreds of miles to a remote prison camp. There she spent three and a half years enduring near-starvation, freezing temperatures in winter, and blazing heat in summer. Cruelty, rats, disease, and death surrounded her, but God heard her prayers to protect the children and mothers from rats and gave her strength to teach Bible studies to the women. As she petitioned God to save the souls of the guards, he even gave her opportunities to share the gospel with several. God's comfort kept her from despair.

After World War II ended, Anne and the surviving missionaries were rescued and released. Although her mother had died during the war, Anne was able to make it home to England to see the rest of her family and gradually recover her health. Then she returned to the mission field, where she served the Lord until old age.

Thank you, Lord, that though we go through many trials in this life, you will sustain and comfort the brokenhearted. You hear us when we call to you for help and are eternally faithful. To him who was and is and is to come, I praise your name.

Cheri

I do not ask to fly above the storm and sing.
Just let me in the tempest feel the covert of your wings!

—ALICE MORTENSON (1934–2010), Christian writer

LIFT UP YOUR EYES

I WILL REJOICE IN THE LORD.
I WILL BE GLAD BECAUSE HE RESCUES ME.
WITH EVERY BONE IN MY BODY I WILL PRAISE HIM:
"LORD, WHO CAN COMPARE WITH YOU?
WHO ELSE RESCUES THE HELPLESS FROM THE STRONG?
WHO ELSE PROTECTS THE HELPLESS AND POOR FROM THOSE WHO
ROB THEM?"

Psalm 35:9-10

DAVID, ONCE AGAIN chased and oppressed by his flesh-and-blood enemies, does what he has learned to do in combat situations. He cries out to the Lord. He has learned that this battle tactic never fails. He knows that though he is in despair right now, victory is just ahead. He doesn't have to wait to see it because he knows it from experience.

David starts by looking around him at his enemies. You and I may not have flesh-and-blood enemies, but we have spiritual enemies. And our spiritual enemies might use flesh-and-blood as weapons. Like David, we might look around and feel ourselves surrounded by circumstances or people who seem to be arrayed against us.

Immediately David turns his attention from the strength of his enemies to the power of God. He moves from worry to worship. His expectation of God's intervention makes him start the celebrating early. Before he sees the rescue with his eyes, he knows it is coming and starts rejoicing in the midst of his difficulty. He grabs on to God's promises like a drowning man grabs hold of a tree branch and hangs on for dear life.

When you look around right now, what do you see? Do you see circumstances aligned against you? Join David's preemptive celebration. Praise sends your enemy into disarray and turns the battle around. With every bone in your body, praise God.

Lord, I choose praise. I choose to celebrate the victory that is in process rather than to wallow in sorrow and declare defeat.

Jennifer

The essence of optimism is that it takes no account of the present, but it is a source of inspiration, of vitality and hope where others have resigned; it enables a man to hold his head high, to claim the future for himself and not to abandon it to his enemy.

—**DIETRICH BONHOEFFER** (1906–1945), German pastor, theologian, and author

18 RECALIBRATING THE HEART

THE LORD WATCHES OVER THOSE WHO FEAR HIM,
THOSE WHO RELY ON HIS UNFAILING LOVE.
HE RESCUES THEM FROM DEATH
AND KEEPS THEM ALIVE IN TIMES OF FAMINE.

Psalm 33:18-19

A FAMINE is an acute shortage or a deprivation. Famines come in every shape, size, and duration. A famine might hit your life in any of several areas: finances, relationships, health, profession.

But like everything else in our lives, famines can serve God's purposes. A famine can change the trajectory of our lives or recalibrate our hearts.

Consider Hannah, the mother of Samuel. Neither Hannah nor Samuel is the primary character in this story. The central, cohesive character is God himself. Everything else— Hannah's barrenness, her prayer, Samuel's birth—is the working out of God's agenda. Our first clear glimpse into what God is doing is found in 1 Samuel: "In those days the word of the LORD was rare; there were not many visions" (3:1, NIV). God had no one through whom to speak to his people, no one whose heart was fully at his disposal.

Do you see how, by withholding the fulfillment of Hannah's desire, God is making Hannah's heart the reservoir of his own desire? God wants a prophet. Hannah wants a son.

During Hannah's famine, God focused her faith. I have to think that, in the beginning of her marriage, Hannah assumed that the biological processes of her body would produce a son. By the time Samuel was born, Hannah had learned that only God could give her a son. Hannah understood that if the Lord gave her a son, that son belonged to the Lord. In the beginning, Hannah had been ready to be the mother of a son. But she had not been ready to be the mother of a prophet. God intended more than Hannah could ask or think, and he had to prepare her heart to receive it. During the famine's prayer process, God recalibrated Hannah's heart to match his own.

Father, in my famine, you are still Lord. Let my famine serve your purposes.

Jennifer

God graciously uses our need and desire for help to educate us for something higher than we were thinking of. We were seeking gifts; He, the Giver, longs to give Himself and to satisfy the soul with His goodness.

—**ANDREW MURRAY** (1828–1917), South African pastor and author

RIGHTEOUSNESS AND UNFAILING LOVE

WHOEVER PURSUES RIGHTEOUSNESS AND UNFAILING LOVE
WILL FIND LIFE, RIGHTEOUSNESS, AND HONOR.

Proverbs 21:21

LIFE, RIGHTEOUSNESS, and honor are the by-products of the right pursuit. When we aim at righteousness and unfailing love, we find that life, righteousness, and honor are the result.

I love the verb *pursue*. It's such a strong word. It has the sense of chase after, hunt down, go after with intention and focus. Put your heart into it.

We are to live our lives *pursuing* righteousness and unfailing love. To boil it down for us, *pursue Jesus*.

He is righteousness, and he is unfailing love. We will find those things only in him. He is the laser-beam focus of our pursuits. Just Jesus.

When we focus on pursuing him, we find that he brings his whole self with him. He expresses himself in us and through us. When we find him, we have found everything.

Where are you expending your emotions? What are you looking to for fulfillment and happiness? What drives your behavior and decisions? Are you pursuing honor for yourself—to be admired and accepted by others? Are you pursuing life on your own—to find the missing piece that will slip into place and complete you? Are you pursuing righteousness as a merit badge—to feel deserving and worthy? Is it an empty pursuit?

Pursue Jesus. When you do, everything else comes as a by-product.

Jesus, I set my heart to seek you. Anything else is a lowered bar of expectation. I want you.

Jennifer

The pursuit of our interest and our happiness is never above God's, but always in God's. The most precious truth in the Bible is that God's greatest interest is to glorify the wealth of His grace by making sinners happy in Him. . . . Therefore Christian Hedonists do not put their happiness above God's glory when they pursue their Happiness in Him.

—JOHN PIPER (1946–), American pastor

20 LOVE IS ALL YOU NEED

LOVE IS PATIENT AND KIND. LOVE IS NOT JEALOUS OR BOASTFUL OR PROUD OR RUDE. IT DOES NOT DEMAND ITS OWN WAY. IT IS NOT IRRITABLE, AND IT KEEPS NO RECORD OF BEING WRONGED. IT DOES NOT REJOICE ABOUT INJUSTICE BUT REJOICES WHENEVER THE TRUTH WINS OUT. LOVE NEVER GIVES UP, NEVER LOSES FAITH, IS ALWAYS HOPEFUL, AND ENDURES THROUGH EVERY CIRCUMSTANCE.

1 Corinthians 13:4-7

THESE VERSES tell us that love has others' best interests at heart rather than our own. The only way to love that way is to be so completely fulfilled in Christ that you are freed from having to be on guard for yourself.

Who is jealous? Those who feel they should have what others have and believe they would be happier if they did. Who is boastful? Those who feel the need to exalt themselves above everyone else. Who demands their own way? Those who feel they have the right to dictate what is best for everyone else and that their happiness should be the deciding factor.

Do you see a pattern? All the descriptions of love in today's verses require that people who are loving be more interested in what others need than in their own desires.

God has poured his own love into our hearts: "We know how dearly God loves us, because he has given us the Holy Spirit to fill our hearts with his love" (Romans 5:5). God's love is the only kind of love that will live up to the standards of today's verses. But he has promised to give us the kind of love—his love—that will be able to function according to Paul's description.

The love of God is a giving love. If we are expressing the love of God, then it looks like Jesus: "Live a life filled with love, following the example of Christ. He loved us and offered himself as a sacrifice for us, a pleasing aroma to God" (Ephesians 5:2).

Jesus, enable me to express your self-giving love to those you have put in my world. Show me ways to love extravagantly, seeking no benefits for myself.

Jennifer

The labor of self-love is a heavy one indeed. Think whether much of your sorrow has not arisen from someone speaking slightingly of you.

—**A. W. TOZER** (1897–1963), American preacher and author

DIRECTED STEPS

THE LORD DIRECTS THE STEPS OF THE GODLY.
HE DELIGHTS IN EVERY DETAIL OF THEIR LIVES.

Psalm 37:23

THE LORD directs us step-by-step, detail by detail. He doesn't give us a map and say, "Here's where you are and here's where you're going. I'll meet you there." Instead, he directs us in such a way that it requires a desperate dependence on the living Lord. Take the example of Abraham.

"Go to a place I'll show you." The call is vague and lacks definition: "Head out that way, and I'll let you know when you're there." He left Abraham in the kind of uncertainty that we resist with all our might. God sends Abraham out to wander on a journey that is unmapped, undefined, marked by its very indeterminacy and, I think, intentionally so.

It's a journey designed to feel like wandering. The way God planned it, if Abraham had any hope of landing on the promise, the journey would require that Abraham be ever alert and listening. Every step mattered because every step was carrying Abraham to the promise and the provision of God. Otherwise, Abraham would never know when the next step would be the one where God says, "You're there!"

Abraham's obedience was to put one foot in front of the other. To take the next small step without trying to project several steps down the road.

Look what happens to small steps when the Holy Spirit is involved. One small step becomes a stride. Your best effort, under his power, becomes his best effort. I think of it like this: have you ever walked on a moving sidewalk? You take a step and you wind up several steps farther because the moving sidewalk carried your small, ordinary step with its forward-moving power. Take that same step on a normal sidewalk, and you have progressed one step. Take it on a moving sidewalk, and that step has been carried and extended by the power beneath it.

Father, direct my steps. I am desperately dependent on your leading.

Jennifer

Have you been holding back from a risky, costly course to which you know in your heart God has called you? Hold back no longer. Your God is faithful to you, and adequate for you. You will never need more than He can supply, and what He supplies, both materially and spiritually, will always be enough for the present.

—**J. I. PACKER** (1926–), Canadian theologian

22 FROM HELPLESS TO HEALED

Do I have the strength of a stone?
Is my body made of bronze?
No, I am utterly helpless,
without any chance of success.

Job 6:12-13

THE STORY is told of Dr. A. B. Simpson, preacher and founder of the Christian and Missionary Alliance, who had extremely poor health. At only thirty-eight he had already experienced two nervous breakdowns and suffered from a serious heart condition. Doctors told him he would never live to see forty. Although he loved to preach God's Word, it took grueling effort. Even climbing a flight of stairs left him breathless and faint.

Eventually this young man's physical weakness and illness drove him to lose heart. Like Job, he felt utterly helpless with no chance of going on to do God's work. Yet he believed the Bible, so he began searching for himself what it said about disease and healing. The more he read the Scriptures, the more he was certain that physical healing and restoration were a part of the gospel.

Soon after this realization, Simpson was taking a stroll in the country. Gasping for air, he could walk only a few steps before having to stop and rest. As he sat down on a log, he poured out his total physical helplessness to Christ and proclaimed that though he was weak and helpless, he still believed in God's healing power. He then humbly asked the Lord Jesus to become his physical life, strength, and energy for everything his body needed to do until his work on earth was completed. A few days later, Simpson climbed a three-thousand-foot mountain, and when he reached the summit, joy unspeakable filled him. From that day on, he never felt exhausted. In the next three years, he preached more than a thousand sermons, at times delivering twenty messages in one week. In his seventy-six years, Simpson produced volumes of literary works and passionately preached the gospel—work that continues to have an impact on countless people today.

Lord, I am helpless in this area of my life: _____. I need your empowering grace, healing, and health. We are inadequate, but you are more than adequate. We are weak, but you are strong! Hallelujah!

Cheri

When we are powerless to do a thing, it is a great joy that we can come and step inside the ability of Jesus.

—**CORRIE TEN BOOM** (1892–1983), Dutch author, speaker, and concentration camp survivor

GOD HEARS MORE THAN WE SAY

YOU KNOW WHAT I LONG FOR, LORD;
YOU HEAR MY EVERY SIGH.

Psalm 38:9

GOD HEARS our sighs as if they were perfectly formed sentences. Our wordlessness is no hindrance to him because he reads our hearts.

My oldest son, Brantley, made up his own language as a toddler. He really didn't have to learn to talk like the rest of us and use words because his "words" accomplished just what he wanted. Because I so intently observed him, I always knew what he meant. For example, his "word" for music was something like "mawk mawk." He would say that phrase, and to everyone else's ears it sounded like gibberish, but I knew exactly what it meant. I responded to it as if he had said, "Dearest Mother, would you mind turning on some music?" Even though the sounds he formed fell far short of actual words, they achieved the same end that a perfectly formed sentence would have.

So it is when you and I speak a ragged and imperfect prayer or have no words to express our groaning. Heaven responds to it as if we had spoken flawlessly.

Psalm 139:4 says, "Before a word is on my tongue you know it completely, O LORD" (NIV, 1984). Before a need or desire has reached the level of conscious understanding so that we could put it into words—while it is still unformed and raw—God already knows it fully. In Romans 8:26-27, we read, "The Spirit himself intercedes for us with groans that words cannot express. And he who searches our hearts knows the mind of the Spirit, because the Spirit intercedes for the saints in accordance with God's will" (NIV, 1984). When our prayer is nothing but an inarticulate moan, the Spirit of God is already communicating it with perfect clarity. By the time we begin to speak our need or desire in prayer, we are simply joining into a flow of prayer that is already in progress: "Before they call I will answer; while they are still speaking I will hear" (Isaiah 65:24, NIV).

Father, hear my sighs and groans as I turn all my longings toward you.

Jennifer

Prayer is not so much an act as it is an attitude—an attitude of dependency, dependency upon God.

—**A. W. PINK** (1886–1952), English evangelist and Bible scholar

24 ABSOLUTELY GOD

NO HUMAN WISDOM OR UNDERSTANDING OR PLAN
CAN STAND AGAINST THE LORD.

Proverbs 21:30

GOD PROMISES that he will triumph over any scheme that is opposed to his plan in our lives. No one can outmaneuver God. If that were not true, he could not reliably make promises, because the outcome of any given situation would be subject to many factors. He would be able to say only, "If all goes well, then such and such will happen."

God can make absolute promises and assurances because he is absolutely God. When you face situations that seem to you as if people are calling the shots, and especially if those people do not care about God's plan, you can be certain that their plans will not override God's.

When Jesus hung on the cross, it seemed that men with godless motives had determined his fate. Nothing could have looked more like a victory for evil and a defeat for God. Yet it was heaven's greatest victory and was the event that had been planned for and promised since before the world began.

When Joseph sat forgotten in Egypt's prison, the victim of false accusations, it seemed that men with godless motives had determined his fate. But it was God's plan to develop a Joseph who had iron in his soul, who would be the salvation of his people when the famine hit Canaan and drove his family to Egypt.

When Moses languished in the desert for forty years after killing a man in Egypt, it seemed that men with godless motives had determined his fate. But God was humbling him and training Moses to trust him so that Moses could rescue God's people.

When the apostle Stephen was being stoned for his powerful preaching of the gospel, it seemed that men with godless motives had determined his fate. But it was part of God's plan for dispersing his people throughout the world, taking with them the message of redemption.

The same God promises that in your life no other plan will succeed against his. No matter what things might seem like right now, God has a plan that is working on your behalf.

Father, I trust your plan, which is higher and deeper than I can perceive.
I believe you.

Jennifer

Prayer is the risen Jesus coming in with His resurrection power, given free rein in our lives, and then using His authority to enter any situation and change things.

—OLE HALLESBY (1879–1961), Norwegian pastor and writer

I TAKE JOY IN DOING YOUR WILL, MY GOD,
FOR YOUR INSTRUCTIONS ARE WRITTEN ON MY HEART.

Psalm 40:8

GOD'S LAWS for living, his instructions for life, are built in, encoded in our DNA. As soon as we allow Jesus into our lives, he brings the law inside us. No longer a set of rules and regulations that we hope to live up to, the law now lives in us, written on our hearts.

The law on the outside could command holiness, but it could not produce holiness. It could control behavior through fear of consequences, but it could not eradicate the inclination toward sinful behavior.

Jesus will do what the law was assigned to do but was inadequate to accomplish. "What the law was powerless to do . . . God did . . . in order that the righteous requirements of the law might be fully met in us" (Romans 8:3-4, NIV). Look at the basic statement Paul made. "What the law was powerless to do"—make us holy, empower our behavior, change our hearts—"God did, in order that the righteous requirements of the law might be fully met." Where are the righteous requirements of the law to be met? "In us."

How did God accomplish in us what the law could not? "I will put my law in their minds and write it on their hearts" (Jeremiah 31:33, NIV).

In the Kingdom of God, all Kingdom dwellers get heart transplants. The new hearts know God, and his law is their heartbeat. The law will not be outside of you, commanding you. The law will be inside you, empowering you.

What the law demands, grace provides. Under the rule of grace, everything that God demands of you, He provides for you. Under the rule of grace, the law that once condemned now empowers.

Jesus, live in me in all your fullness.

Jennifer

The heart in which God gets His way, and writes His law in power, lives only and wholly to carry that writing, and is unchangeably identified with it.

—**ANDREW MURRAY** (1828–1917), South African pastor and author

26 THE SOURCE OF ALL COMFORT

ALL PRAISE TO GOD, THE FATHER OF OUR LORD JESUS CHRIST.
GOD IS OUR MERCIFUL FATHER AND THE SOURCE OF ALL
COMFORT. HE COMFORTS US IN ALL OUR TROUBLES SO THAT WE
CAN COMFORT OTHERS. WHEN THEY ARE TROUBLED, WE WILL BE
ABLE TO GIVE THEM THE SAME COMFORT GOD HAS GIVEN US.

2 Corinthians 1:3-4

I HAVE KNOWN God as many things and in many ways, but when I encountered him as
the Source of all comfort, it came as a surprise. In a matter of seconds—as long as it takes
for a doctor to form the words *no cure*—my world was upended and everything came
crashing down on me. My husband, my partner in both life and ministry, was diagnosed
with aggressive and advanced brain cancer and passed away two months later.

In that shattering moment a blanket of peace descended on us. I know a level of super-
natural comfort from the Father that can't be explained. It has to be experienced. I know
something I can't say in words that has transformed my life and given it a new depth.
I realize that the great wound inflicted on my heart has made me desperately dependent
on God in a way I never would have known otherwise. And I have found him to be exactly
who he promises he is.

I have learned to let strength come out of my weakness. Those moments when I
am overwhelmed with loss and aware that decisions are mine alone to make become
moments when I am brought back to the all-sufficient Jesus, the storehouse of all wisdom and knowledge. I have to trust that the work of my woundedness is showing up
in ministry, though I can't pinpoint it or identify it on a chart.

God is not a burden giver, testing you to see just how much he can pile on you and still
leave you standing. He is the burden bearer. When we learn to hand over burdens in the daily
issues of life, we'll be ready when the big ones come along. We can know him as the Source
of all comfort.

Father, be the strength in my weakness.

Jennifer

Happiness and comfort stream immediately from God himself, as light issues from the sun.
—**JOHN H. AUGHEY** (1828–1911), American minister and author

A GOLDEN PROMISE

HE KNOWS WHERE I AM GOING.
AND WHEN HE TESTS ME, I WILL COME OUT AS PURE AS GOLD.

Job 23:10

HORSES PLODDED along the dusty China road under a hot noon sun, pulling a heavy wagon as Peter, a missionary, brought supplies and money to his fellow missionaries in Yucheng. Before leaving the office that morning, he and his coworkers had prayed, and as they finished, he saw a plaque above the door that read, "He knows the way that I take." As Peter rode along, the words rolled over and over in his thoughts.

At the next village he stopped to water the horses and heard there were bandits on that road. Peter jumped into his wagon and started away from the village. *You know the way that I take, Lord.* Suddenly he heard steps behind him, and in moments he had been captured by bandits who took everything he had. Amazingly, they let him keep the wagon and horses and told him to hurry to the next village or they would shoot him. When he arrived, the villagers opened its gates but wouldn't let him stay. They knew the whole town faced danger if they harbored a foreigner. They led Peter to the far gate and told him to go.

As he headed down the road, the bandits again pursued him. The road turned uphill, and Peter's horses were about to give out. In utter dependence and trust, he cried out, "Oh God, help me *now*, for you know the way I take!"

Suddenly another group of riders poured over the top of the hill. But instead of bandits, Peter saw it was government cavalry. He was safe! God *did* know Peter's path and the bandits that were on it. He met Peter's need in a way that built this missionary's faith and refined it like gold.

Is your path strewn with obstacles or losses that try your faith? No matter where you are going, God knows, and he is with you to the ends of the earth.

All praise to the God and Father of our Lord Jesus Christ, who knows the way that I take. Thank you that when I have been tested, I will come forth as gold. I praise you for your faithfulness that reaches to the skies and all around the world. Amen.

Cheri

God is above, presiding; beneath, sustaining; within, filling.
—**HILDEBERT OF LAVARDIN** (ca. 1056–1133), French medieval poet

28 ONLY JESUS SMELLS LIKE JESUS

THANKS BE TO GOD, WHO ALWAYS LEADS US AS CAPTIVES IN CHRIST'S TRIUMPHAL PROCESSION AND USES US TO SPREAD THE AROMA OF THE KNOWLEDGE OF HIM EVERYWHERE. FOR WE ARE TO GOD THE PLEASING AROMA OF CHRIST AMONG THOSE WHO ARE BEING SAVED AND THOSE WHO ARE PERISHING. TO THE ONE WE ARE AN AROMA THAT BRINGS DEATH; TO THE OTHER, AN AROMA THAT BRINGS LIFE.

2 Corinthians 2:14-16 (NIV)

PAUL WAS drawing on an image from the Roman culture: a procession in which a triumphant general is celebrated as he returns from his campaign. The conquering general is preceded into the city by the captives taken in war and is followed by his triumphant troops. As the troops paraded through the city, they shouted, "Triumph!"

The triumphal procession in which we march is headed by Jesus, our Conqueror. It is one continuous triumphal march that began at the Cross and goes on into eternity. We can march through life with the shout of "Triumph!" on our lips.

Included in the triumphal procession were priests swinging censers filled with incense. When the procession reached its destination, the captives were led away to slavery or execution. The aroma of the procession was a smell that denoted victory for the triumphant and death for those triumphed over. The same smell held differing meanings, depending upon one's position in the procession.

The aroma of Christ is disseminated in the world, both to those who are in the process of being saved and to those who are in the process of dying eternally. To one it is the smell of life; to the other, it is the stench of death. It attracts the one and repels the other.

We are the censers that hold the sweet-smelling incense. Jesus' life is operating on earth in and through us. Only Jesus smells like Jesus.

Father, align my life with Jesus' heart so completely that his beautiful aroma both wafts before me and lingers after me. Let his beauty be the defining adornment of my life, so all who come into contact with me have smelled the fragrance of eternity.

Jennifer

The riches of His free grace cause me daily to triumph over all the temptations of the wicked one, who is very vigilant, and seeks all occasions to disturb me.

—**GEORGE WHITEFIELD** (1714–1770), English evangelist

SHINING FACES

WHENEVER SOMEONE TURNS TO THE LORD, THE VEIL IS TAKEN AWAY. . . . SO ALL OF US WHO HAVE HAD THAT VEIL REMOVED CAN SEE AND REFLECT THE GLORY OF THE LORD. AND THE LORD—WHO IS THE SPIRIT—MAKES US MORE AND MORE LIKE HIM AS WE ARE CHANGED INTO HIS GLORIOUS IMAGE.

2 Corinthians 3:16, 18

IN TODAY'S VERSES, Paul is alluding to the experience of Moses in Exodus 34:29-35. When he came down from Mount Sinai after being in the Lord's presence, he "did not know that the skin of his face shone because of his speaking with Him" (Exodus 34:29, NASB). The presence of the Lord was so radiant that Moses' skin reflected his glory. If the sun's radiance can produce changes in our complexion, then surely the glory that outshines the sun could do so.

The presence of God so marked Moses that he had to wear a veil over his face or the people were afraid to come near him. The glory of the Lord was veiled to them. "But whenever Moses went in before the LORD to speak with Him, he would take off the veil until he came out" (Exodus 34:34, NASB).

Paul has just made the case that the glory of God is still veiled to unbelievers. But whenever someone turns to the Lord, the veil is taken away. We can be in the Lord's presence with unveiled faces. Moses was changed on the outside, but we are changed on the inside. The Lord's presence with us is in us. He so transforms us by his presence in us that we reflect his image more every day.

Do you long for those around you to see God? Just let him reflect himself through your life. Let your life radiate the presence of God.

Lord, let my life mirror yours.

Jennifer

The man who gazes upon and contemplates day by day the face of the Lord Jesus Christ, and who has caught the glow of the reality that the Lord is not a theory but an indwelling power and force in his life, is as a mirror reflecting the glory of the Lord.

—ALAN REDPATH (1907–1989), English evangelist, pastor, and author

30 THE LIGHT OF HIS PRESENCE

GOD, WHO SAID, "LET THERE BE LIGHT IN THE DARKNESS," HAS
MADE THIS LIGHT SHINE IN OUR HEARTS SO WE COULD KNOW
THE GLORY OF GOD THAT IS SEEN IN THE FACE OF JESUS CHRIST.
WE NOW HAVE THIS LIGHT SHINING IN OUR HEARTS, BUT WE
OURSELVES ARE LIKE FRAGILE CLAY JARS CONTAINING THIS GREAT
TREASURE. THIS MAKES IT CLEAR THAT OUR GREAT POWER IS
FROM GOD, NOT FROM OURSELVES.

2 Corinthians 4:6-7

PAUL REMINDS US that the same In-the-Beginning God who spoke light into being has made light to shine in our darkness, the light that has come in the presence—the face— of Jesus Christ.

Imagine a clay pot, all cracked and with pieces broken out of it. Not attractive. Not valuable. Ready for the trash heap.

Now imagine that this clay pot has light inside it. Where does the light show through? At the broken places.

Now imagine water pouring into that clay pot. What happens? The water pours out through the broken places. If water keeps on pouring in, then water will keep flowing out.

If your goal was for the pot to hold the water in, the pot full of cracks would have been a poor choice. But if your goal was for the water to flow out, you couldn't have found a more perfect pot.

Maybe this is what Paul meant when he wrote these words: "'My grace is all you need. My power works best in weakness.' So now I am glad to boast about my weaknesses, so that the power of Christ can work through me" (2 Corinthians 12:9).

Who could have seen that coming? When Jesus made his home in the lives of human beings, he sought out the broken ones: "Healthy people don't need a doctor—sick people do. I have come to call not those who think they are righteous, but those who know they are sinners" (Mark 2:17).

Jesus, shine through my broken places.

Jennifer

He comes to us in the brokenness of our health, in the shipwreck of our family lives, in the loss of all possible peace of mind, even in the very thick of our sins. He saves us in our disasters, not from them. . . . He meets us all in our endless and inescapable losing.

—ROBERT FARRAR CAPON (1925–), American priest and author

SEEING THE UNSEEN

WE DON'T LOOK AT THE TROUBLES WE CAN SEE NOW; RATHER, WE FIX OUR GAZE ON THINGS THAT CANNOT BE SEEN. FOR THE THINGS WE SEE NOW WILL SOON BE GONE, BUT THE THINGS WE CANNOT SEE WILL LAST FOREVER.

2 Corinthians 4:18

OUR YOUNG SON had received all the "big guns" of asthma treatment—oxygen, steroid injections, antibiotics, and everything else the specialist could think of—but his condition worsened steadily. Fear threatened to completely overwhelm me.

I called my neighbor Elaine. When I asked her to pray for our son, she prayed that in the midst of the terrifying circumstances, God would open my spiritual eyes to see the unseen. *What could she mean and what does that have to do with my son's medical condition?* I wondered.

A little while later, my husband insisted I go home, because I was only making our son more nervous. But when I went outside and tried to find the car, it was pouring rain. I couldn't see and went back into the hospital. That was when I saw the sign: "Chapel."

I was drawn to a large, white Bible at the front. As I read the words on the open page, I realized I'd been hoping in the *doctors* to save our son's life and that I needed to release him to the God who had created him. For me as a mother, letting go of a critically ill child was almost impossible. As the lights flickered and thunder boomed, I had a new glimpse of God's grace: *The Creator of the whole universe was in complete control of the thunderstorm and all things, yet I hadn't trusted him with my son's life.*

In this look into the unseen, I sensed God's Spirit saying, "Hope in *me*; trust his life to me totally." As I knelt before the Lord, a peace I'd never experienced swept through me, and I knew my son was safe and cared for.

Lord, forgive us when we cling to who and what is dearest to us. Grant us faith to believe in your faithfulness and help us to see the unseen things that will last forever so that we might release all those we love into your loving hands. Amen.

Cheri

Prayer, even prayer for what God desires, releases power by the operation of a deep spiritual law; and to offer up what one loves may release still more.

—SHELDON VANAUKEN (1914–1996), American author and editor

SEPTEMBER

BATHED IN GRACE'S LIGHT

WE HAVE STOPPED EVALUATING OTHERS FROM A HUMAN POINT OF VIEW. AT ONE TIME WE THOUGHT OF CHRIST MERELY FROM A HUMAN POINT OF VIEW. HOW DIFFERENTLY WE KNOW HIM NOW! THIS MEANS THAT ANYONE WHO BELONGS TO CHRIST HAS BECOME A NEW PERSON. THE OLD LIFE IS GONE; A NEW LIFE HAS BEGUN!

2 Corinthians 5:16-17

THE WORD translated "new" in this passage means something that did not exist previously, or something that has just appeared. Because of Christ, we are brand new. Not patched-up old, not revised, but regenerated. The new you who came into being through Christ is new top to bottom, inside and out. The old you is gone.

Here's the result: now we don't evaluate others according to our old standards. We don't love others based on how they act, or on whether they suit us, or by their ability to be what we want them to be. We have a whole new set of senses that perceive others from Christ's point of view. Rather than seeing others as extras in our own one-man or one-woman show, expecting them to play their roles as we have written them, we begin to see others as God's beautiful creations. Compelled by Christ's love, we seek out ways to build them up and give them opportunities to experience the reality of Christ, who died for them.

Those around us no longer have to dance to our tune. We do not require that others meet our needs and fulfill our expectations. We are free simply to love them.

Paul confessed that at one time he thought of the coming Messiah—the Christ—as merely another human being. He was expecting a Messiah of mere flesh and blood. But he says he knows better now. Discovering the reality of the Messiah Jesus so completely changes people that they are new. As new as if they had just been born.

Father, may I see my world through the prism of the cross, tinged with blood-stained mercy and bathed in grace's light.

Jennifer

He plucks the world out of our hearts, loosening the bonds of attachment. Then He hurls the world into our hearts, where we and He together carry it in infinitely tender love.

—THOMAS R. KELLY (1893–1941), American educator

2 FOR THOSE WHO PLEASE GOD

GOD GIVES WISDOM, KNOWLEDGE, AND JOY TO THOSE WHO PLEASE HIM.

Ecclesiastes 2:26

TODAY'S VERSE holds a great promise, but like many of God's promises, it contains a condition. God gives wisdom, knowledge, and joy to those *who please him*. Wouldn't it be marvelous to have all the wisdom, knowledge, and joy that we would ever need for every situation in life? The key question here is this: What pleases God? Fortunately, he doesn't leave us in the dark to figure out what pleases him! There are many clues throughout God's book, the Bible, and the more we discover and understand these, the more abundant our lives will grow.

Hebrews 11:6 tells us it is *faith* that pleases God: "It is impossible to please God without faith." In 1 Peter 2:19-20, we learn that "God is pleased with you when you do what you know is right and patiently endure unfair treatment." In other words, enduring hardship and suffering patiently pleases God. All through the Psalms it becomes clear that praise glorifies God. For example, Psalm 50:23 says, "Giving thanks is a sacrifice that truly honors me." We especially honor God when we offer thanks to him during difficult times. Thanking God for the blessings in our lives, for his character and nature of faithfulness, mercy, and love honors him. Drawing near to God gives him joy. And one of the significant verses in the book of Romans suggests that presenting our bodies as living sacrifices is pleasing to the Lord (see Romans 12:1).

Oh, to live a life that honors God and makes him smile!

Lord, I want my life to be pleasing to you. Grant me grace to walk in your ways and turn my will, my heart, my mind, and my emotions—in short, my whole being—over to you, the one who loves me with an everlasting love.

Cheri

God makes a promise; faith believes it, hope anticipates it, patience quietly awaits it.
—UNKNOWN

THE GOD
WHO ENCOURAGES

GOD, WHO ENCOURAGES THOSE WHO ARE DISCOURAGED, ENCOURAGED US BY THE ARRIVAL OF TITUS.

2 Corinthians 7:6

PAUL WROTE this letter to the Corinthian believers in a time of conflict and discouragement. He and his followers had endured troubles, hardships, and calamities of every kind. Our trials would not compare to Paul's, but when was one of your most difficult, discouraging times? Mine was when my father died. The six of us children sat around our mother in the black limousine leaving the church where our father's funeral service had been held. We watched the procession of cars behind our vehicle on the slow journey to the cemetery, our cheeks streaked with tears. Eleven years old, I was stunned by our loss and felt as if my world had fallen apart.

In contrast, other cars raced by in the September sunshine. They didn't even glance at our procession. Their lives were going on, while ours had seemed to stop. I felt the heavy weight of loneliness and discouragement as we rode along in silence.

As we turned down a country road toward the cemetery, we passed a farmer in faded overalls, hoeing his garden. When he saw the black hearse and procession, he leaned on his hoe, took off his straw hat, and bowed his head. I took a deep breath and sighed. *Someone cared*. The respect and compassion that man showed breathed into me the courage and hope to get through one of the hardest days of my life. As I look back, I realize that God sent that man across my path to encourage my heart, to lift up my crushed spirit, and to show his love—just as he sent Titus to Paul in a troubled time to lift Paul's burdens and encourage him. The memory of that farmer standing in the Texas field lingered far longer than the sweet scent of the yellow Tyler roses that covered Papa's grave that day, decades ago. Whenever I recall that farmer's concern, I renew my determination to stop my busyness and be a conduit for God's encouragement for someone else—even a stranger.

Father, I thank you and praise you for being the one who lifts up those who are bowed down with discouragement, loss, or grief. Thank you for being the father of the fatherless all these many years of my life.

Cheri

Encouragement is oxygen to the soul.

—**GEORGE M. ADAMS** (1878–1962), American author

4 THE RIGHT TIME AND THE RIGHT WAY

THERE IS A TIME AND A WAY FOR EVERYTHING, EVEN WHEN A
PERSON IS IN TROUBLE.

Ecclesiastes 8:6

THIS VERSE fills me with assurance and confidence. God has promised two things here. First, that in every situation, there is a right time and a right way. And second, that God will reveal to us that right time and right way.

We will never have God's omnipotence (his unlimited power) or his omniscience (his unlimited knowledge). We will never be the source of wisdom. But we do have the Source of all wisdom indwelling us, imparting to us whatever wisdom we need in a given moment: "If you need wisdom, ask our generous God, and he will give it to you. He will not rebuke you for asking" (James 1:5).

God is generous with wisdom; all we need to do is ask for it. When we turn to him for our wisdom—asking to know the right time and the right way—he will deposit it. When we need to act or speak, or to stay out of the way and not speak, we will know what we need to know when we need to know it.

You will never be in a situation in which God is at a loss to know what to do. You will never be in a conversation in which God is at a loss for words—the right words spoken the right way. We have this promise from him that we who are on a mission for our King will have our King's resources immediately accessible.

> *Lord, teach me to step out of my own automatic responses to situations and let
> you reveal what to do and when to do it. Thank you for your promise that you
> not only have that wisdom but also impart it to me.*

Jennifer

Not from without but from within, not in word but in power, in life and truth, the Spirit reveals Christ and all He has for us. He makes the Christ, who has been to us so much only an image, a thought, a Saviour outside and above us, to be truth within us. The Spirit brings the truth into us; and then, having possessed us from within, guides us, as we can bear it, into all the truth.

—**ANDREW MURRAY** (1828–1917), South African pastor and author

THE REWARD OF A GENEROUS GIVER

GIVE GENEROUSLY,
FOR YOUR GIFTS WILL RETURN TO YOU LATER.

Ecclesiastes 11:1

SOMEONE ONCE said, "He who gives is twice blessed," another way of saying that those who take a gift of love to the lives of others cannot keep it from themselves, or that when you give flowers to someone else, the fragrance remains on your hands. That is the promise tucked in today's verse.

Whether the gift is handmade or thoughtfully chosen at a shop, a gift from your garden or your kitchen, quilted or painted, brought from a foreign country or from your own backyard—gifts given in a spirit of love and kindness give grace and encouragement to the person who receives them. The time and care it takes to give a gracious, personal gift speak volumes—and give pleasure to *both* giver and receiver. A steaming pot of chicken soup delivered to a friend who has had surgery says, "Get well soon!" A gift of flowers can say, "I love you" or "You did a great job!" A welcome basket or fresh loaf of bread to newcomers in your neighborhood transforms a lonely experience into a joyful one. Handmade quilts convey friendship; gift baskets personalized to meet the needs of someone we know or love can cheer the body and soul.

People often expect to receive gifts at certain holidays or at birthdays, but the unexpected gift from the heart is perhaps best of all. When giving a gift, we can ponder, *What would make this person happy or lighten her load?* In the process of giving or receiving gracious gifts, kindness blossoms. The fragrance from those gifts radiates out and prompts acts of kindness for still others. Gifts of compassion and simple gifts you make yourself create beautiful memories, warm the heart, and convey loving-kindness to the recipients. Today's verse promises a reward for those who give generously to others. Perhaps the best reward of all is that of pleasing our Lord, for he loves a cheerful giver.

Lord, we confess that often our thoughts are on our own needs and problems. Forgive us for being self-absorbed, and shape us into generous givers who bring joy to others and, most of all, to you.

Cheri

Not what we give, but what we share,
For the gift without the giver is bare.

—JAMES RUSSELL LOWELL (1819–1891), American poet and editor

6 TRUSTING GOD IN TIMES OF TROUBLE

CALL ON ME WHEN YOU ARE IN TROUBLE,
AND I WILL RESCUE YOU,
AND YOU WILL GIVE ME GLORY.

Psalm 50:15

IN 1948, Derek and Lydia Prince and their eight adopted daughters were living in Jerusalem. Although the United Nations had declared the creation of the new independent state of Israel, the countries surrounding Israel were enraged. The 650,000 Jews had little ammunition, food, or supplies and faced fierce attacks by hostile armies who were fifty million in number and had massive military resources.

Having spent twenty years as a missionary in Jerusalem, Lydia Prince had seen battles before, but none as devastating for the Jewish people as this one. Even as their own family was at risk, the couple prayed for the Jewish people. They became convinced that it was God's plan to restore the nation of Israel and were inspired to pray that the Jews would *not* be destroyed by the attacking Arabs—in fact, that God would "paralyze the Arabs."

Since the Israeli army had set up an observation post in the Princes' backyard, the family got to know many of the soldiers. One day during a UN-imposed cease-fire, some of the soldiers talked with them: "There's something we cannot understand. We go into an area where the Arabs are dominating. They outnumber our soldiers ten to one and are much better armed than we are. Yet at times they seem powerless to do anything against us. It's as if they are paralyzed!" they said.

Indeed, God did paralyze the vast Arab forces. And although the battles continued, the invading armies were eventually defeated. The state of Israel became strong and firmly established. The Lord rescued not only Lydia and Derek Prince and their children but also the Jewish people. The Lord used this family's prayers at a crucial time in the life of the nation of Israel, and they gave him all the glory and praise.

Father, I trust your promise that in times of trouble, you will rescue me and those I intercede for. I will give you all the praise, worship, and glory.

Cheri

God is all powerful . . . so he can help you with everything. God is present everywhere . . . He is always with you. God is sovereign. So joyfully submit to his will.

—UNKNOWN

THE JOY OF
A CLEAN HEART

Purify me from my sins, and I will be clean;
     wash me, and I will be whiter than snow.
Oh, give me back my joy again. . . .
     Remove the stain of my guilt.
Create in me a clean heart, O God.
     Renew a loyal spirit within me.

Psalm 51:7-10

ONCE A WOMAN approached me at a café and said, "Cheri, would you forgive me? I've held bitterness against you for a long, long time, and I know now it's wrong. I've learned that in not forgiving you, I'm sinning against God. I'm a cancer survivor, and I've discovered that harboring any unforgiveness is not only displeasing to God but also deadly to my body as well as to my soul."

I hardly knew this precious lady and couldn't remember any negative encounter we'd ever had. Since I had no idea what I could have done to warrant such a long spell of resentment, I asked, "What did I do that offended you?"

"Once in the parking lot at church, you spoke to my friend Debbie but you didn't know or say my name. That really hurt me and made me angry," she responded.

I apologized for ignoring her and having such a hard time remembering names and spoke the forgiveness she asked me for. Then she sat down and told me all about her journey from a diagnosis of cancer through treatment to restored health. After she finished, we hugged, and she swept out the door, seemingly lighter on her feet than she'd been when she arrived.

The truth she learned applies to every one of us: unforgiveness damages our bodies, our souls, and our spirits, but forgiveness brings life and freedom. When we open our hearts and confess our sins, we experience the clean hearts promised in Psalm 51, and the joy of God's salvation is restored to us.

Father, your forgiveness is precious, yet it cost you your only Son's death on the cross that we might be reconciled to you. Grant that I would never take the cleansing blood of Jesus for granted. Create in me a clean heart today, and restore the joy of salvation!

Cheri

God pardons like a mother, who kisses the offense into everlasting forgiveness.
—**HENRY WARD BEECHER** (1813–1887), American minister, abolitionist, and author

8 WEAPONS OF OUR WARFARE

WE DON'T WAGE WAR AS HUMANS DO. WE USE GOD'S MIGHTY WEAPONS, NOT WORLDLY WEAPONS, TO KNOCK DOWN THE STRONGHOLDS OF HUMAN REASONING AND TO DESTROY FALSE ARGUMENTS. WE DESTROY EVERY PROUD OBSTACLE THAT KEEPS PEOPLE FROM KNOWING GOD.

2 Corinthians 10:3-5

THERE ARE TIMES when we lose confidence in our state or national leaders because of laws they pass that adversely affect our lives or our communities. Sometimes parents are anxious or even angry about poor decisions made by the administration at their child's school. They appeal, they rally, they go to the board of education or to their legislators, but nothing changes. What can you do when you "can't fight city hall?"

These verses in 2 Corinthians contain a powerful promise concerning the resources God gives us—the Word of God and prayer, which are "God's mighty weapons." Because the weapons we wield are spiritual, we don't have to depend on the board of education or other authorities to fight our battles. Our arsenal contains weapons that are far more powerful. They can knock down Satan's strategies and open the way for God's Spirit to work. In fact, we can accomplish more on our knees than on our soapboxes! And that applies not just to the big issues but also to the small ones—because the Lord is always willing to work in the ordinary details of life, as well as in the grand scheme of things.

An atheist principal in California once banned anything having to do with Christmas and vetoed every teacher reform. Groups of mothers prayed for this man for ten years, and he eventually came into a life-changing relationship with God. For the rest of his career, he was a positive influence on the county's schools and principals. Oh, that we would turn our hearts to God and wield the weapons he has given us in his Word and in prayer!

May we, Father, use the spiritual weapons you have graciously given us with confidence and trust in your power.

Cheri

It is by prayer that we couple the powers of heaven to our helplessness, the powers which can turn water into wine and remove mountains in our own lives and in the lives of others, the power which can awaken those who sleep in sin and raise up the dead, the power that can raise up strongholds and make the impossible possible.

—OLE HALLESBY (1879–1961), Norwegian pastor and writer

BRANCHING OUT

IN THAT DAY, THE BRANCH OF THE LORD
WILL BE BEAUTIFUL AND GLORIOUS;
THE FRUIT OF THE LAND WILL BE THE PRIDE AND GLORY
OF ALL WHO SURVIVE IN ISRAEL.

Isaiah 4:2

IN TODAY'S READING, God has just described a coming time of tribulation and describes it this way: "The city will be like a ravaged woman, huddled on the ground" (Isaiah 3:36). Desolate, defeated, trampled. But in the middle of it all, God will keep hope alive and will already have restoration blooming.

This shows us a promise we can count on. No matter how bruised and battered we are, the Branch of the Lord is there, beautiful and glorious and fruitful. In the symbols of Scripture there is no question that "the branch" refers to the Messiah: "Listen to me, O Jeshua the high priest, and all you other priests. You are symbols of things to come. Soon I am going to bring my servant, the Branch. . . . And I will remove the sins of this land in a single day" (Zechariah 3:8-9).

When your life is in ruins, look until you see the Branch, blooming and bearing fruit right in the middle of your scorched landscape. Look for the Branch blossoming in the drought: "Out of the stump of David's family will grow a shoot—yes, a new Branch bearing fruit from the old root. And the Spirit of the LORD will rest on him—the Spirit of wisdom and understanding, the Spirit of counsel and might, the Spirit of knowledge and the fear of the LORD" (Isaiah 11:1-2).

Jesus is there. Wherever you are, he is there. When the smoke clears, when the dust settles, he is right where he said he would be. New life is flourishing out of the ruins. Hope is deathless, because Jesus is our hope. Life won't always be sweet and easy, but Jesus will always be there.

Oh Lord, when everything else around me goes up in flames, you are immovable. Train me to look for you and your beautiful and glorious fruit. What you produce in my life out of the ruins is my pride and my glory.

Jennifer

It is not hard for the Lord to turn night into day. He that sends the clouds can as easily clear the skies. Let us be of good cheer.

—**CHARLES HADDON SPURGEON** (1834–1892), English preacher and writer

10 EXPOSED AND CLEANSED

I SAID, "IT'S ALL OVER! I AM DOOMED, FOR I AM A SINFUL MAN.
I HAVE FILTHY LIPS, AND I LIVE AMONG A PEOPLE WITH FILTHY LIPS.
YET I HAVE SEEN THE KING, THE LORD OF HEAVEN'S ARMIES."

Isaiah 6:5

IN GOD'S PRESENCE, we have a twofold revelation: the revelation of who God is and the revelation of who we are.

Isaiah saw the Lord, high and exalted. He saw the glory and the holiness. Instinctively he cried out: "Woe to me! . . . I am ruined! For I am a man of unclean lips, and I live among a people of unclean lips, and my eyes have seen the King, the LORD Almighty" (Isaiah 6:5, NIV).

And Job? "I had only heard about you before, but now I have seen you with my own eyes. I take back everything I said, and I sit in dust and ashes to show my repentance." (Job 42:5-6).

God's holiness exposes our sinfulness. His strength reveals our weakness. His faithfulness lays bare our faithlessness. Only in the light of his presence can we see the truth about ourselves: "In your light we see light" (Psalm 36:9, NIV).

"Everything exposed by the light becomes visible, for it is light that makes everything visible" (Ephesians 5:13-14, NIV 1984).

Until we have a true picture of ourselves, we will be unable to enter into the depths of the Kingdom. The stark contrast between the Holy One in his splendor and us in our filthy rags—the revelation of his worthiness and our unworthiness—compels us to fall on our faces in awe and humility. The awe comes not only from his majesty but also from the fact that he seeks *us* out, that he delights in *us*, that he loves *our* presence. Imagine! In all our weakness. In all our failure. In all our sin. His bloodstained love reaches out and draws us into his presence and brings his presence to reside in us.

Father, thank you for shedding the light of your grace into the darkness of my sin and cleansing me so that I am whiter than snow.

Jennifer

We must have the glory sink into us before it can be reflected from us. In deep inward beholding we must have Christ in our hearts, that He may shine forth from our lives.
—ALEXANDER MACLAREN (1826–1910), British preacher and Bible expositor

THE HEART OF YOUR DESIRE

THREE DIFFERENT TIMES I [PAUL] BEGGED THE LORD TO TAKE [MY THORN IN THE FLESH] AWAY. EACH TIME HE SAID, "MY GRACE IS ALL YOU NEED. MY POWER WORKS BEST IN WEAKNESS." SO NOW I AM GLAD TO BOAST ABOUT MY WEAKNESSES, SO THAT THE POWER OF CHRIST CAN WORK THROUGH ME. THAT'S WHY I TAKE PLEASURE IN MY WEAKNESSES, AND IN THE INSULTS, HARDSHIPS, PERSECUTIONS, AND TROUBLES THAT I SUFFER FOR CHRIST. FOR WHEN I AM WEAK, THEN I AM STRONG.

2 Corinthians 12:8-10

GOD PROMISES to give us the desire of our hearts. He knows the desire of our hearts better than we do. Sometimes what we think of as the desire of our hearts is really the desire of the moment. We can't know the desire of our hearts unless we know the heart of our desire.

Paul's prayer was stated in words that expressed the desire of the moment—to be rid of the thorn in his flesh that seemed to hinder his work. But the Father heard the cry of Paul's heart.

Let's imagine a conversation between God and Paul. God: "Paul, why do you want the thorn in your flesh removed?" Paul: "So I can carry out the ministry you have given me." God: "Why do you want to carry out the ministry I have given you?" Paul: "So I can spread the good news of Jesus the Messiah." God: "Why do you want to spread the good news?" Paul: "So everyone will see that your grace is sufficient." God: "That will require a thorn in your flesh."

What is the heart of Paul's desire? He makes it clear in Philippians 3:10-11: "I want to know Christ and experience the mighty power that raised him from the dead. I want to suffer with him, sharing in his death, so that one way or another I will experience the resurrection from the dead!" It is to know Christ fully. Do you see that God said no to Paul's desire of the moment but said yes to the desire of Paul's heart?

As you surrender yourself fully, God will crystallize for you the one overriding desire—to have more of him.

Father, thank you for loving me enough to say the highest yes.

Jennifer

To fall in love with God is the greatest of all romances; To seek Him, the greatest adventure; To find him, the greatest human achievement.

—**ST. AUGUSTINE** (354–430), Latin North African theologian and philosopher

12 CAN A WOODEN CANE WALK BY ITSELF?

Can the ax boast greater power than the person
who uses it?
Is the saw greater than the person who saws?
Can a rod strike unless a hand moves it?
Can a wooden cane walk by itself?

Isaiah 10:15

ISRAEL, STUBBORN and unresponsive to the prophets' warnings, finally came under God's judgment. The "rod of [his] anger," the instrument he used to bring about judgment, was the pagan nation of Assyria. Isaiah 10 records how God described his activity: "What sorrow awaits Assyria, the rod of my anger. I use it as a club to express my anger. I am sending Assyria against a godless nation, against a people with whom I am angry" (Isaiah 10:5-6).

Assyria is the tool God is using. He is sending the Assyrians for his purposes.

The Assyrians have other plans. Their purpose is to destroy many nations instead of just little Israel, but God says, "The king of Assyria will not understand that he is my tool; his mind does not work that way. His plan is simply to destroy, to cut down nation after nation" (Isaiah 10:7).

In verse 13, the king of Assyria boasts of his victory: "By my own powerful arm I have done this. With my shrewd wisdom I planned it." But in today's verse, God points out how ludicrous it is for Assyria to boast.

God used Assyria for his own purposes. He was in control from beginning to end. Assyria's plans did not come to fruition, but God's plan did.

When the situation you face seems to be controlled by an unbeliever who is taking a wrong, rebellious action, God is in control. Wait it out. Watch. When it all comes together, you will see—what looked wrong in the moment turned out to be necessary to God's purpose.

> *Father, I believe you are in control all the time, under every circumstance. When things look out of control to me, I choose to believe you instead of my own shortsighted perceptions.*
>
> *Jennifer*

The purpose of Christianity is not to avoid difficulty, but to produce a character adequate to meet it when it comes. It does not make life easy; rather it tries to make us great enough for life.

—JAMES L. CHRISTENSEN, contemporary author and minister

LOOK UP

IT WILL ALL HAPPEN AS I HAVE PLANNED.
IT WILL BE AS I HAVE DECIDED. . . .
THE LORD OF HEAVEN'S ARMIES HAS SPOKEN—
    WHO CAN CHANGE HIS PLANS?
WHEN HIS HAND IS RAISED,
    WHO CAN STOP HIM?

Isaiah 14:24, 27

GOD IS ALWAYS working according to a long-term plan. Nothing is willy-nilly or random. Everything is connected. Every part fits together. Everything leads in a positive direction because God knows what he is doing. When things look most chaotic and out of control, God is managing every detail.

If you are in the middle of something right now that has you discouraged and afraid, look up. If it seems as if your life is on a slippery slope with no branch to catch hold of and curtail the slide, look up. If it seems that you have been caught in a cross current and are being tossed around like a rag doll, look up.

You can know that nothing is as it seems at first glance. Wait it out. Let events unfold. Hang on to Jesus for dear life. Whatever the situation is right now, it is not the end of the story.

Remember that it is God's well-documented way to work behind the scenes, using the enemy's own plans to accomplish God's perfect purposes. Don't be surprised when you find yourself in the middle of a storm. You are right where you should be. Right where God can do his best work.

> *Father, forgive me when I fall into self-pity, somehow thinking you should baby me. I want to develop the spiritual muscles to do the heavy lifting. I don't want to be left in the nursery, feeding on only milk. I want meat! So I embrace those things you allow into my life that put me on the front lines. I trust your battle plan.*
>
> *Jennifer*

If I had not felt certain that every additional trial was ordered by infinite love and mercy, I could not have survived my accumulated sufferings.

—**ADONIRAM JUDSON** (1788–1850), American missionary to Burma (now Myanmar)

14 A CONFIDENT HEART

MY HEART IS CONFIDENT IN YOU, O GOD;
my heart is confident.
NO WONDER I CAN SING YOUR PRAISES!
WAKE UP, MY HEART!
WAKE UP, O LYRE AND HARP!
I WILL WAKE THE DAWN WITH MY SONG.

Psalm 57:7-8

THE PSALMIST declares that his heart—the seat of both reason and emotion—is firmly fixed on God. God is his focus. God is his reference point. No wonder he can sing praises, even when the way is fraught with danger and his enemies have laid traps for him and he is weary from distress.

I love the way he bursts out with "No wonder I can sing your praises!" He started cataloging all his problems and seemed suddenly to realize, "And yet, I have confidence and joy! What a surprise!" Then he began to look for the explanation. He realized that his heart had a firm foundation, that his faith had a resting place. "That explains it! No wonder I can sing your praises!"

Isaiah writes: "You will keep in perfect peace all who trust in you, all whose thoughts are fixed on you! Trust in the LORD always, for the LORD GOD is the eternal Rock" (Isaiah 26:3-4).

Using similar phrasing and the same word translated "fixed" in Isaiah 26 and "confident" in Psalm 57, God repeats a promise. When we have our thoughts and emotions rooted in him, we will be surprised by joy in the midst of life's difficulties. When we lean all our weight on the eternal Rock, give all our strength to be at his disposal, and focus all our heart on his word, we find joy gushing in the most unexpected places—like water from a rock.

Eternal Rock, I surrender all of me to all of you.

Jennifer

You will not stroll into Christlikeness with your hands in your pockets, shoving the door open with a careless shoulder. This is no hobby for one's leisure moments, taken up at intervals when we have nothing much to do, and put down and forgotten when our life grows full and interesting. . . . It takes all one's strength, and all one's heart, and all one's mind, and all one's soul, given freely and recklessly and without restraint.

—A. J. GOSSIP (1873–1954), Scottish pastor and college professor

SINGING IN THE RAIN

AS FOR ME, I WILL SING ABOUT YOUR POWER.
EACH MORNING I WILL SING WITH JOY ABOUT YOUR
UNFAILING LOVE.

Psalm 59:16

IN PSALM 59, David is again surrounded by enemies ready to pounce. They are so vicious that he compares them to snarling, vicious dogs and describes their intent to do him harm. But what is David doing while his enemies are plotting against him? Today's verse tells us: he's singing! He starts every day singing with joy.

Our enemies are not flesh and blood; they are invisible forces of Satan's realm. Praise, joy, thanksgiving, and worship are the weapons that will send them running for cover. Against praise they have no defense.

What is it about singing that conveys joy better than any other form of expression? I don't know, but I know that it does. I think God created singing so we would have a way to express emotion that is too big for just talk.

If you are feeling overwhelmed, try singing. You might feel silly at first, but let it flow. No one else can hear you. It's just between you and God. Something about singing releases a flow of deep emotion: "You thrill me, LORD, with all you have done for me! I sing for joy because of what you have done" (Psalm 92:4), and "I will sing to the LORD as long as I live. I will praise my God to my last breath!" (Psalm 104:33).

Are you singing? When you think about the presence and the love of God, can anything other than singing really express what you feel?

Now, think of this: God loves you and takes such delight in you that he, too, bursts into song. "The LORD your God is living among you. He is a mighty savior. He will take delight in you with gladness. . . . He will rejoice over you with joyful songs" (Zephaniah 3:17).

Rest in his presence and let him sing his love song to your heart. Let the promise of his unbridled delight in you calm all your fears.

Lord, I delight in you and in your love for me. I have to sing!

Jennifer

The height of devotion is reached when reverence and contemplation produce passionate worship, which in turn breaks forth in thanksgiving and praise in word and song.

—**R. KENT HUGHES,** contemporary American pastor and author

16 LIVE CRUCIFIED

My old self has been crucified with Christ. It is no longer I who live, but Christ lives in me. So I live in this earthly body by trusting in the Son of God, who loved me and gave himself for me.

Galatians 2:20

GOD'S PROMISE of a complete salvation is the most precious promise of all. Jesus died for me so that he could live *in* me.

In today's verse, Paul is describing the fullness of our salvation. Jesus died for us to pay sin's penalty, but he lives in us to purify us from sin's power. When we accept the gift of salvation, we are not then left on our own to work things out the best we can. We have the promise of his life in us, taking the place of our own feeble efforts.

When Paul paints the picture of being crucified with Christ, clearly he doesn't mean that his physical body hung on the physical cross with Jesus. He means that the part of him that makes him uniquely Paul—his personality, his thought processes, his natural responses to life—have passed through a transformation so radical that the only way to describe it is as a death and a resurrection. "I died, but I live," Paul says.

He goes on to clarify. "Well, it is not I—not the Paul you have always known—who lives. That Paul will never be again. It is Christ who lives in that old Paul's place."

He now lives by faith in the indwelling, present Christ instead of by faith in Paul and his own abilities. He has handed over the reins of his life to Christ—and who better? After all, Christ loved Paul so much that he gave his life for him.

On the cross, Christ's sinlessness for our sin. In life, his strength for our weakness. We can walk in the promise that his life is present in us, and for us, and through us.

Lord Jesus, live big in me. Teach me to live by confidence in you instead of by confidence in me. Let the old ways of my flesh die daily, so that I can find new resurrection life in you.

Jennifer

When Christ bids us come and follow, He bids us come and die.

—**DIETRICH BONHOEFFER** (1906–1945), German pastor, theologian, and author

GOD'S PROMISED PEACE

YOU WILL KEEP IN PERFECT PEACE
ALL WHO TRUST IN YOU,
ALL WHOSE THOUGHTS ARE FIXED ON YOU!

Isaiah 26:3

ONE MORNING during the summer when Cathy's daughter was losing her vision, Cathy was touched by the words of today's verse. Daily she agonized over what her daughter's blindness was causing: Susan couldn't drive, her boyfriend had dropped her, and she was alone because her college roommate had moved out. How would she ever finish the semester, realize her dream of studying in Finland, and become a horse trainer, when blindness was blotting out the light?

Cathy knew that the Bible was the most valuable thing she could own in time of trouble, and she found hers indispensable as she focused on God's promises each morning. When she read Isaiah 26:3, an idea came to her: she wrote down verses from her readings and carried those cards with her everywhere. She intentionally focused her mind on God's promises instead of on her fears for Susan. As she did this, she found not only that it kept her from dwelling on the awful what-ifs, but also that her thoughts were transformed from worry and sadness to a confident sense of peace. Eventually Cathy called her bag of promises her "Peace Packet" and shared it with other women when they were in crisis.

You may not be facing blindness or a serious illness in your loved one today, but all of us face challenges. Perhaps you are worried you'll lose your home. Maybe your teenage son is out of control; you lie in bed at night worrying about what he's going to do next. You're afraid the next crisis may overwhelm you. If you will turn your thoughts to God and his promises as Cathy did, you'll discover grace to trust him. And when you focus on *what he said and promised* in the Bible instead of on *what you feel*, you will find that the Lord will keep your mind and heart in his complete peace, just as Isaiah 26:3 says.

Lord, though my mind and heart are troubled today, I choose to focus on you and believe your Word, pray your Word, and stand on it. Help me to make your promises my foundation for every day of my life.

Cheri

God's Book is packed full of overwhelming riches; they are unsearchable—the more we have the more there is to have.

—**OSWALD CHAMBERS** (1874–1917), Scottish minister and teacher

18 PLOWING TO PLANT

When a farmer plows for planting, does he plow
   continually?
   Does he keep on breaking up and working the soil?
When he has leveled the surface,
   does he not sow caraway and scatter cumin?

Isaiah 28:24-25 (NIV)

SCRIPTURE OFTEN uses the metaphor of plowing to illustrate God's work in our lives to prepare us to produce a harvest: "Plow up the hard ground of your hearts, for now is the time to seek the LORD, that he may come and shower righteousness upon you" (Hosea 10:12).

In the rhythms of our lives, there are seasons of plowing. The topsoil of our lives gets turned over. Things get messy and disheveled as God is getting ready to plant seed in hearts where it will produce a rich harvest.

God doesn't plow ground he is not going to plant. The plowing always has a purpose to it, and in today's verse, we see the promise that the plowing will not last forever. The plowing is only a preparation for planting.

Isaiah goes on to say, "Does he not plant wheat in its place, barley in its plot, and spelt in its field?" (Isaiah 28:25, NIV).

When God plants, he plants the right seed in the right soil. He makes no mistakes. All the preparation has a goal, and God is strategic in his work in our lives.

God may be using circumstances or people to turn over the topsoil of your life. You may feel as though the life you have worked so hard to keep smooth and presentable is being ripped up and destroyed. Maybe you've resisted the process. Maybe you keep trying to smooth it over and make it look like it used to, but to no avail. If you will surrender yourself to the Master Gardener's work, you will see that you are being prepared to produce a harvest.

Father, I surrender to your work in my life as you plow up the ground of my heart. I know that the plowing does not go on forever, and the harvest is just ahead.

Jennifer

God will never plant the seed of his life upon the soil of a hard, unbroken spirit. He will only plant that seed where the conviction of his spirit has brought brokenness, where the soil has been watered with the tears of repentance as well as the tears of joy.

—**ALAN REDPATH** (1907–1989), English evangelist, pastor, and author

HEARING GOD

YOUR OWN EARS WILL HEAR HIM.
RIGHT BEHIND YOU A VOICE WILL SAY,
"THIS IS THE WAY YOU SHOULD GO,"
WHETHER TO THE RIGHT OR TO THE LEFT.

Isaiah 30:21

GOD PROMISES to direct us and guide every step we take. He has set things up so that his guidance comes one step at a time as we listen every moment to him. We don't just meet with him occasionally and get directions to follow until we meet next time; we live our lives attuned to his voice.

Many years ago, at the beginning of my ministry, the Lord clarified for me that we don't *have* a prayer life, but we *live* a praying life. That phrase—*praying life*—has defined my ministry and been the centerpiece of my teaching. We live in a continual flow of God's power and provision. We are in a constant interaction between the needs on earth and the provision in heaven. God's Spirit is speaking to us every nanosecond, in every breath and in every step we take. We are never out of range of his voice, because he lives in us. We are living praying lives.

Scripture is filled with invitations to listen to God. Would God instruct you to do something that it was impossible for you to do? Since God tells you to listen to him, since he promises you that he will instruct and teach you, is not the implied promise that he communicates with you?

In Hebrews 4:7 we read, "Today when you hear his voice, don't harden your hearts." The word translated "hear" means to hear and respond in one action. This seems to teach us that responding is the key to clear hearing. If I hear God's voice and do not respond, a callus begins to form over my heart. The tissue begins to harden. The next time God speaks, it's harder for me to hear him. His voice is less distinct. However, if I hear and do respond, the callus over my heart begins to slough away. The next time God speaks, it is easier for me to hear. Obedience by obedience, my heart softens, and I become more attuned to his voice.

Lord, I'm listening.

Jennifer

God is whispering to us well nigh incessantly.

—FREDERICK WILLIAM FABER (1814–1863), English hymn writer and theologian

20 FRUITFULNESS

THE HOLY SPIRIT PRODUCES THIS KIND OF FRUIT IN OUR LIVES:
LOVE, JOY, PEACE, PATIENCE, KINDNESS, GOODNESS, FAITHFULNESS,
GENTLENESS, AND SELF-CONTROL.

Galatians 5:22-23

A TREE produces fruit of its own kind. An apple tree produces apples; a pear tree produces pears. A tree can be identified by the fruit it produces.

When we are filled and saturated with the Holy Spirit and yielded to him, he reproduces himself through us. Everything that he is, he can express through us to others around us.

The evidence of his presence in our lives is the change he brings. We don't respond the same way we used to. We don't take pleasure in the same things we used to enjoy. We can love others instead of competing with them or judging them. We can have peace in the midst of life's storms. We are gentle where we used to be harsh. We have a new control over our impulsive behaviors.

This is the promise of our salvation: eternal life that starts now producing eternal qualities in us. We can be filled to overflowing with God's very life and presence. He comes to take up residence in us so that he is never far away or out of reach. Rather, he is putting himself on display through the fruit of changed lives. He is giving the world convincing proof of his power through the flowering of new responses in those in whom he dwells.

Are you struggling to change? Try yielding every moment to the Holy Spirit who is in you, ready and available to live through you.

Father, teach me to keep my life cleared of the things that crowd out your Spirit. Train me in the art of yielding.

Jennifer

[At Pentecost] they were not submerged in God, nor did God override them. God was God and they were they; but Person flowed into person, Will into will, Mind into mind, and they could scarcely tell where they ended and God began. He was closer than the blood in their veins and nearer than their own heartbeats. If they should reach out to touch Him, they would reach too far.

—**E. STANLEY JONES** (1884–1973), American missionary and theologian

CAREFUL PLANNING **21**

HAVE YOU NOT HEARD?
    I DECIDED THIS LONG AGO.
LONG AGO I PLANNED IT,
    AND NOW I AM MAKING IT HAPPEN.

Isaiah 37:26

GOD PROMISES us that he is always working according to a plan that has been in place since the beginning. He is never making things up as he goes. Everything has been worked out carefully and is proceeding on schedule. Nothing takes him by surprise.

Things come into our lives that seem to come out of nowhere. We are caught off guard. But God is not. He knew about your situation before it occurred. He filtered out everything about it that he could not use for his purposes. He prepared you in advance and put provision in place.

When things come unexpectedly into our lives, the first thing we need to do is look around for what God has already put into place. We don't have to say, "God, do something!" but instead, "God, what have you already done? How can I position myself to be in the flow of your provision?"

When we know that God has a plan, we can live with confidence. Life is not a conglomeration of disjointed events happening randomly. God's plan flows through generations, from one event to the next, all tied together in an integrated pattern.

If I were to give you one piece of a five-thousand-piece jigsaw puzzle and ask you to look at it and tell me what the picture on the front of the box looks like, you would not be able to do it. But be assured: God knows the picture on the front of the box. Each piece is getting you closer to it. Don't waste your time or emotions trying to figure out the picture from one piece. Let the pieces of God's plan come together. Be patient. Live confidently.

Father, I don't have to know what the big picture is, because you do. I trust that you are moving all things in the direction you have planned.

Jennifer

You find no difficulty in trusting the Lord with the management of the universe and all the outward creation, and can your case be any more complex or difficult than these, that you need to be anxious or troubled about His management of it?

—**HANNAH WHITALL SMITH** (1832–1911), American lay speaker and author

22 THE MASTER GARDENER

A VOICE SAID, "SHOUT!"
 I ASKED, "WHAT SHOULD I SHOUT?"
"SHOUT THAT PEOPLE ARE LIKE THE GRASS. . . .
THE GRASS WITHERS, AND THE FLOWERS FADE,
 BUT THE WORD OF OUR GOD STANDS FOREVER."

Isaiah 40:6, 8

IN THESE VERSES God delivers a message through Isaiah so that his people might know the temporary nature of this life and root their lives in the eternal Word of God, which stands forever. The message is so important that the Lord tells Isaiah to *shout it out* and use creation to demonstrate it: the grass and flowers fade, but the Word of God, the only foundation worth building our lives on, stands firm.

As one who loves to grow flowers, I've learned some great lessons from working in the garden—especially the importance of a strong root system. If I sow my flower seeds around the tangled roots of our large oak tree, they won't develop their own deep roots and grow properly. When the summer's heat rages, the flowers that once were vibrant and gave pleasure will quickly wither and fade.

The Bible gives us many snapshots of the importance of rooting our lives in God's Word. The Lord promises that if we delight in God's Word and deeply root our hearts in it, if we meditate on it and follow it, we will prosper, and our lives will keep producing fruit. It is his Word that will renew our inner strength so we can continue to be productive and bring glory to God. If we turn away from God's Word and do life our own way, we will wither as fast as the flowers that are here one day and gone tomorrow. As we stay rooted in God's Word, we will grow, blossom, and bear fruit wherever we are. The product of our words and deeds can impact people throughout our lifetime and even after our addresses have changed to heaven.

God, your Word is changeless and stands forever true. Thank you, Jesus, for being the living Word and speaking to my heart. May my life be rooted in your eternal Word.

Cheri

God did not write a book and send it by messenger to be read at a distance by unaided minds. He spoke a book and lives in his spoken words . . . causing the power of them to persist across the years.

—A. W. TOZER (1897–1963), American preacher and author

Do not be afraid, for I have ransomed you.
   I have called you by name; you are mine.
When you go through deep waters,
   I will be with you.
When you go through rivers of difficulty,
   you will not drown.
When you walk through the fire of oppression,
   you will not be burned up;
   the flames will not consume you.
For I am the LORD, your God.

Isaiah 43:1-3

HAVE YOU NOTICED that the Scripture repeats its themes? God tells us over and over, in first one picture and then another, that we will go through difficulties but he will always be our Rescuer.

Let the words of this promise get a foothold in your heart. God's love for you is personal and specific. He has ransomed you—purchased your freedom—by the blood of his beloved Son. You did not come cheap.

We are not faces in a crowd. He has called out each of us by name. We belong to him. We are his treasured possession and the apple of his eye.

He tells us that *when* we go through difficulties—not if, but when—he is there. He mitigates the effects: we will not drown; we will not be burned up; we will not be consumed. Because of him, we are indestructible. We will come out of these trials stronger, better, spiritually richer. Our experience will not diminish us; it will strengthen us.

No one gets to avoid life's heartaches. Christian or not, everyone will have troubles. God does not promise us trouble-free lives. He promises us that any troubles we experience have been filtered. He has weighed them in his scales. Only if the glory they produce will outweigh the pain they cause do they reach you. And they never reach you in full force. You have a shelter and a refuge.

Father, in the midst of my deep waters, I hold to you. When I walk through the flames, I keep my eyes on your face. I trust you.

Jennifer

Christianity is not a theory or speculation, but a life; not a philosophy of life, but a living presence.
—**SAMUEL TAYLOR COLERIDGE** (1772–1834), English poet

24 ONE BODY

THERE IS ONE BODY AND ONE SPIRIT, JUST AS YOU HAVE BEEN
CALLED TO ONE GLORIOUS HOPE FOR THE FUTURE.

Ephesians 4:4

I LOVE the truth that we are not alone on our journeys through life. Christ sends people to encourage, speak truth, and be "Jesus with skin on." We are part of the body of Christ and need the other members to survive and thrive.

Just as you and I have many parts to our physical bodies, as Christ's body we are all different parts, but each one of us is necessary to make it complete. We have different gifts, occupations, and callings, but all are from the same Spirit, as today's verse says. God has given you the ability and intelligence to do certain things well, and he's given different abilities to others. We need the prayer support and counsel of trusted people; other members of the body need our hugs, smiles, thoughtful notes and cards that show our appreciation for their gifts or for what God has done through them. We all go through times when we have been battered about in a storm or have lost someone dear to us. Those are times we really need the encouragement and love of others.

God also provides the cloud of witnesses described in Hebrews—real people who have gone before us and have wisdom we can learn from: people like Noah, who believed God and built the ark; Abraham, who left his home and went to the land God promised to give him; Jacob and Joseph; Moses and Joshua; Sarah, Esther, Ruth, Mary, Elizabeth, and other people of great faith. They are all part of that great cloud of witnesses who are cheering us onward and upward. Reach out to others. Read these stories, and remember that you are part of Christ's body on this earth.

Thank you, Father, that you have called all of us who are your children into the same glorious future! May we help others grow, lift others up in their times of need, and be willing to receive their help as well.

Cheri

Christ has no body now but yours, no hands, no feet on earth but yours. Yours are the eyes with which he looks with compassion on this world. Yours are the feet with which he walks to do good. Yours are the hands with which he blesses all the world.

—**SAINT TERESA OF AVILA** (1515–1582), Spanish mystic

I WILL CARE FOR YOU

LISTEN TO ME, DESCENDANTS OF JACOB. . . .
I HAVE CARED FOR YOU SINCE YOU WERE BORN.
  YES, I CARRIED YOU BEFORE YOU WERE BORN.
I WILL BE YOUR GOD THROUGHOUT YOUR LIFETIME—
  UNTIL YOUR HAIR IS WHITE WITH AGE.
I MADE YOU, AND I WILL CARE FOR YOU.
  I WILL CARRY YOU ALONG AND SAVE YOU.

Isaiah 46:3-4

HAVE YOU EVER felt alone or wondered who would care for you in your old age? Has it seemed that when your children grew up and moved across the country, you were left to fend for yourself with no one to care for your soul? Although in this passage Isaiah is speaking to God's people remaining in Israel after many were carried into captivity, this promise has great application for us today.

In this dark time, God wanted his people to know his promise so they would have hope for the years ahead. In verse 3, the people—and we, too—are encouraged to remember God's past faithfulness. So as you reread this passage, consider: *What has the Lord done for me? What evidence do I see of his care in my early life? How did he draw me into relationship, out of darkness into his light?* You might want to jot down some of the ways God has cared for you and worked in your life.

Then you're ready to hear the marvelous assurance in verse 4: "I will be your God throughout your lifetime—until your hair is white with age. I made you, and I will care for you. I will carry you along and save you."

Our Creator has been caring for us all along, through the hands of parents, grandparents, friends, and others who have loved us. No matter what happens in the economy, in Medicare, or in the world around us, our everlastingly faithful God will sustain us even when our hair is white with age. Beloved, believe this promise: The Lord will care for you now and forever!

Our Father and Redeemer, holy is your name. Thank you for caring for me watchfully and faithfully throughout my life.

Cheri

Our all-knowing, ever-present, eternal Father knows the end from the beginning, and thus, in his omniscience, he provides. . . . There is nothing too small to escape his attention. He is a God who is for you, not against you.

—**KAY ARTHUR** (1933–), American Bible teacher and author

26 ALONG THE PATHS

THIS IS WHAT THE LORD SAYS. . . .
I AM THE LORD YOUR GOD,
WHO TEACHES YOU WHAT IS GOOD FOR YOU
AND LEADS YOU ALONG THE PATHS YOU SHOULD FOLLOW.

Isaiah 48:17

A YOUNG WOMAN had been hired by an organization that required staff members to memorize Scripture. Initially she rebelled at the idea, thinking she was old enough to plan her own spiritual disciplines. But after some encouragement, she finally tackled her first verse, Isaiah 48:17.

Around the same time, she decided to apply for a summer mission program in Russia, and the application needed to be postmarked by a certain date. When the deadline arrived, she headed to the post office on her way to work. With everything necessary for the application, including check and envelope, she stopped by a copy shop to print an extra application. When she got back to her car, she realized she'd locked her keys in it. Immediately, the Spirit reminded her of the verse she'd set to memory: "I am the LORD your God, who teaches you what is good for you and leads you along the paths you should follow."

She responded, "Okay, God, I trust you. Either you've got a way to get my car unlocked, or they'll accept my application even if it's late, or I'm not supposed to go."

She walked calmly to her job, leaving her car at the copy shop. A short while later her sister happened to drop by at work—something she'd never done—and produced another set of keys for the young woman's car. She then drove to the post office and mailed her application and soon after was accepted for the mission trip to Russia. Many times since that day, the Lord has brought that promise back to her mind, reminding her that he is leading and teaching her.

Has God brought a verse to your mind to guide you? Are you committed to hiding God's Word in your heart?

We praise you for your eternal Word, Father, and for the way the Holy Spirit uses it to lead and guide us day by day. Amen.

Cheri

We do not understand the intricate pattern of the stars in their courses, but we know that He who created them does, and that just as surely as He guides them, He is charting a safe course for us.

—**BILLY GRAHAM** (1918–), American evangelist and author

THE PROMISE OF HEALING

HE WAS PIERCED FOR OUR REBELLION,
CRUSHED FOR OUR SINS.
HE WAS BEATEN SO WE COULD BE WHOLE.
HE WAS WHIPPED SO WE COULD BE HEALED.

Isaiah 53:5

ONE DAY long ago, two young pastors prayed for our child, and he was restored to health. I discovered that God's healing power isn't locked in the distant past of Bible times but can come through the prayers of compassionate, believing people today. Christ's role as healer was evidenced throughout his mission on earth. Accounts of healing abound in the Gospels.

In witnessing firsthand the Lord's healing power in our own family, I realized that God welcomes us to pray about physical ailments. I also began to discover that Christ can heal people from crippling memories, past hurts, and emotional trauma. When we ask for healing, we aren't asking for something outside the reality of who God is. Healing is part of his manifold grace, the outflow of his never-failing care and love.

As a result of seeing Jesus as the Great Physician, my husband and I began to see praying for others as a normal part of the Christian life. Jesus had a burden for the sick and hurting and wanted his followers to care for those people as well (see Matthew 10:7-8). We've had many opportunities to pray for people who were sick in heart or body. Though we don't know God's timetable or whether the person we pray for will gain wholeness and health on earth or in heaven, we can put our hope in a loving Lord who took our pain, bore our suffering, and healed us because of his wounds.

Lord Jesus, I don't have words to thank you for being the same Great Physician yesterday, today, and forever. Use me as a vehicle for showing your healing mercy to others. Strengthen my faith, and grant me your compassion for people who are hurting.

Cheri

The most eloquent prayer is the prayer through hands that heal and bless.

—BILLY GRAHAM (1918–), American evangelist and author

28 GOD'S WORD DOESN'T RETURN VOID

THE RAIN AND SNOW COME DOWN FROM THE HEAVENS
    AND STAY ON THE GROUND TO WATER THE EARTH.
THEY CAUSE THE GRAIN TO GROW,
    PRODUCING SEED FOR THE FARMER
    AND BREAD FOR THE HUNGRY.
IT IS THE SAME WITH MY WORD.
    I SEND IT OUT, AND IT ALWAYS PRODUCES FRUIT.
IT WILL ACCOMPLISH ALL I WANT IT TO,
    AND IT WILL PROSPER EVERYWHERE I SEND IT.

Isaiah 55:10-11

I WAS a fortunate child; my mother took me and my five siblings to church. We were there often: Sunday morning and evening, girls' mission class, Vacation Bible School in the summer. I had the opportunity to memorize many Bible verses—week after week and year after year. At age six I came upon John 1:1 and was riveted by the words: "In the beginning the Word already existed. The Word was with God, and the Word was God." I loved this chapter so much that I underlined and memorized much of it.

Fast-forward twenty-three years to an afternoon when I was sitting alone in our home in Tulsa, Oklahoma. A few weeks earlier, I had started reading the New Testament, not because I was in a Bible study or particularly spiritual at the time. Instead, I was a lonely, fearful young mother seeking . . . something, and there was nothing else in the house I hadn't read.

As the sun shone in the window that day, I started the first chapter of John. When I read the words *In the beginning the Word already existed. The Word was with God, and the Word was God. He existed in the beginning with God. . . . The Word gave life to everything that was created,* I experienced a life-changing encounter with Christ. All my doubts were swept away as Christ's light filled my heart. The seed planted in my early life took a long time to germinate—but it did at last bring forth fruit and spiritual transformation.

I praise you, Lord of heaven and earth, that your words do not come back empty,
that they do the work you sent them to do and accomplish your purpose. May
I be hungry to read your book, the Bible, valuing your words more than silver,
gold, or anything this world offers.

Cheri

The Bible grows more beautiful as we grow in our understanding of it.
—**JOHANN WOLFGANG VON GOETHE** (1749–1832), German writer

OVERFLOWING LOVE **29**

I PRAY THAT YOUR LOVE WILL OVERFLOW MORE AND MORE, AND THAT YOU WILL KEEP ON GROWING IN KNOWLEDGE AND UNDERSTANDING. FOR I WANT YOU TO UNDERSTAND WHAT REALLY MATTERS, SO THAT YOU MAY LIVE PURE AND BLAMELESS LIVES UNTIL THE DAY OF CHRIST'S RETURN. MAY YOU ALWAYS BE FILLED WITH THE FRUIT OF YOUR SALVATION—THE RIGHTEOUS CHARACTER PRODUCED IN YOUR LIFE BY JESUS CHRIST—FOR THIS WILL BRING MUCH GLORY AND PRAISE TO GOD.

Philippians 1:9-11

THE INFLOW of God's love creates such a volume of love in our hearts that it begins to overflow, to gush out. God has poured his very own love into our hearts. "God's love has been poured out into our hearts through the Holy Spirit, who has been given to us" (Romans 5:5, NIV). When love pours out of us, it is God's love sloshing all over those around us.

As love from God, for God, and for others multiplies until it creates an outgoing current, we need to grow in knowledge of how to express that love in ways that will be productive for the Kingdom. So along with great love, we need great wisdom.

Paul prays the words in today's verses with great confidence, knowing that God promises these things to us. He prays further that the Philippians will understand what really matters. Along with our love and our wisdom we need discernment. We need to be able to distinguish what is superfluous from what is necessary. Otherwise, we'll find ourselves caught up in situations and issues that don't matter.

Finally, Paul prays that the fruit of our salvation—righteous character—will be evident so that God will be glorified.

Do you find yourself in need of love that comes from beyond you? Do you need to know how best to express love to someone you know? Do you need to be able to decide what matters and what doesn't as you actively love a person in your world? Do you need to let God's character shine through your life so that someone you love will see him? Ask God for these things. His answer is most certainly yes!

Father, let me love with wisdom and discernment. Show me the most effective way to express love to each person in my world.

Jennifer

True love is always costly.

—BILLY GRAHAM (1918–), American evangelist and author

30 GOD'S ENERGY

> GOD IS WORKING IN YOU, GIVING YOU THE DESIRE AND THE
> POWER TO DO WHAT PLEASES HIM. . . . LIVE CLEAN, INNOCENT
> LIVES AS CHILDREN OF GOD, SHINING LIKE BRIGHT LIGHTS IN A
> WORLD FULL OF CROOKED AND PERVERSE PEOPLE. HOLD FIRMLY
> TO THE WORD OF LIFE.
>
> *Philippians 2:13, 15-16*

IN THE DEVOTIONAL for September 28 I described the transforming encounter I had with Christ. After that encounter I began to be acutely aware of God's working within me, for at the same time I was experiencing joy and awakening, I also had a sobering sense of conviction. *If this is all true,* I thought, *if every word in the Bible is from God, how should I be living?* Thus God's Spirit in me began the process of repentance.

I had a new desire to know how God wanted me to live. From then on, I read the Bible as if it contained all the treasures of life in its pages—which it does! One day I was driving with my children when a quiet, distinct voice in my spirit answered a question I had had since my father died of a heart attack soon after my grandpa's and aunt's deaths: Is heaven real, or were we just told that to keep us kids in line?

Heaven and hell are real, I sensed the Spirit saying. *Eternal life begins now, for eternal life is an ongoing relationship with me. Which path will you follow and who will you give to your life to?* As I responded, "I'm all yours, Lord, every part of me," God and I began a conversation that has continued to this day. He continues to work within me, and though I'm not in any way a finished product, he keeps patiently drawing me and giving me the energy and desire to do his will.

> *Lord, thank you for the "inside job" you do in your children. I praise you with all my heart and surrender again to your Spirit's direction in my life.*
>
> *Cheri*

To God be the glory, great things he hath done!
So loved he the world that he gave us his Son,
who yielded his life an atonement for sin,
and opened the lifegate that all may go in.

—**"TO GOD BE THE GLORY" BY FANNY J. CROSBY** (1820–1915), American rescue
mission worker, hymn writer, and poet

OCTOBER

WAITING FOR GOD

SINCE THE WORLD BEGAN,
NO EAR HAS HEARD
AND NO EYE HAS SEEN A GOD LIKE YOU,
WHO WORKS FOR THOSE WHO WAIT FOR HIM!

Isaiah 64:4

I WAS ONCE invited to speak in Switzerland to a group of expatriate women from many countries who were there because of their husbands' or their own jobs. The summer before, my friend Leslie and a few other women in the group began praying earnestly that God would touch the hearts of the women through my message. The women had repeatedly asked for a Bible study as one of the options members could choose from, but every year their request had been turned down. They had prayed and waited, seeking God for his timing.

When the decidedly secular leadership realized I was a Christian, they strictly limited what I could speak about. They chose the topic "The Power of Encouragement" but insisted there would be no talk of God, prayer, or Bible verses in the message. Leslie and her friends prayed on and waited expectantly for God to work, and we did as well.

When we arrived that fall day at the group's offices in Geneva, I was introduced and began sharing how the women could encourage their children, friends, and family. All of a sudden, we sensed God's Spirit moving through the room, almost like an ocean tide coming into the shore. As I spoke, the hearts of those very well-dressed, professional, international women were opened, and God's love seemed to flow among the rows of women. Many dabbed away tears and shared how the message had touched their hearts. The night after I spoke, several women called the new president-elect and said they wanted to have a Bible study. Finally, after years of praying and waiting on God, we saw the door open, and a study of Scripture began for the first time. How lovely it was to see God work on behalf of those who had prayed, waited, and persevered.

> *Lord, when you burst forth from the heavens and come down, when we see your work and glory in our lives, we are filled with joy. Help us to wait for you with expectancy and hope.*

Cheri

Teach us, O Lord, the disciplines of patience, for to wait is often harder than to work.

—**PETER MARSHALL** (1902–1949), pastor and chaplain of the U.S. Senate

2 PRESS ON TOWARD THE PRIZE

I PRESS ON TO POSSESS THAT PERFECTION FOR WHICH CHRIST
JESUS FIRST POSSESSED ME. NO, DEAR BROTHERS AND SISTERS,
I HAVE NOT ACHIEVED IT, BUT I FOCUS ON THIS ONE THING:
FORGETTING THE PAST AND LOOKING FORWARD TO WHAT LIES
AHEAD, I PRESS ON TO REACH THE END OF THE RACE AND RECEIVE
THE HEAVENLY PRIZE.

Philippians 3:12-14

JESUS HAS laid claim to us for a purpose. He is perfecting us—bringing us to maturity and completeness. He wants us to live the lives we were created to live. He wants us to live the lives that fit us.

We were designed for him. We were created to be the vessels through which he lives his life in the world. When we step into that relationship and let Jesus be Jesus in our lives, then we begin to possess that for which Christ Jesus first possessed *us*.

Preceding the words in today's verses, Paul had laid out his credentials. He had given his résumé. If anyone ever had reason to be proud and confident in his own accomplishments and pedigree, it was Paul. He was born to be a success.

But he is forgetting all the accolades and awards of the past; he is leaving the past in the past. Once he had had an encounter with the living Christ, everything had been redefined. What he used to value and work toward was now useless to him—garbage, in fact. How did that happen? He had discovered "the infinite value of knowing Christ Jesus my Lord" (Philippians 3:8). Jesus was so much more precious than anything Paul had ever loved or valued that the price tags were switched. The high value was on Jesus, and everything else was junk in the clearance bin.

What from your past do you need to leave behind? Your past may not be filled with glamorous successes like Paul's, but if it still holds your heart captive, you are putting the wrong value on it. Let go of the past, because there is something of great value for you to press toward. Press on to that completeness for which Jesus possessed you. Empty your hands so he can fill them.

Lord Jesus, I am pressing on to you, leaning forward toward your goal for my life.

Jennifer

In Christ we can move out of our past into a meaningful present and a breathtaking future.

—ERWIN W. LUTZER (1941–), North American pastor and author

WHAT DO YOU SAY TO YOURSELF?

FIX YOUR THOUGHTS ON WHAT IS TRUE, AND HONORABLE, AND RIGHT, AND PURE, AND LOVELY, AND ADMIRABLE. THINK ABOUT THINGS THAT ARE EXCELLENT AND WORTHY OF PRAISE.

Philippians 4:8

STUDIES SHOW that we "talk" to ourselves about fifty thousand times a day, and approximately 80 percent of that talk is negative. In Paul's closing letter to the Philippians, written more than two thousand years before any research was done on human thinking, he wisely addressed what healthy thinking looks like. He encouraged those brothers and sisters—and us—to think about things that are true and right, honorable, pure, lovely, and worth admiring. "Think about things that are excellent and worthy of praise," Paul advised. That knocks out gossip, resentful thinking, anxious thoughts, and bad reports about other people right off the bat.

Yet it also refers to that 80 percent of our thinking that is not about other people but is negative self-talk that says we've failed and aren't good enough. This same research discovered that these kinds of negative thoughts have a profound effect on people: they control our behavior and attitudes and even cause destructive physiological changes in our bodies.

Paul's words remind us we have a choice. We don't have to be so wrapped in negativity that we fail to see the blessings and gifts in our lives. We can acknowledge the reality of sad memories and disappointments and yet learn to manage our thought life. These verses give us a great start. What if for just one day we banned negative thinking and purposed to fill our minds with what is listed in today's verse, the things worthy of praise rather than things to complain about? What if we focused on the best about people, not the worst or weakest things; the beautiful creation around us instead of the dark, even ugly, situations in the world? If we can change our way of thinking, we will gain a fresh perspective and experience a deeper sense of Christ's peace and presence.

Holy Spirit, take my thoughts and let them be pure and holy, gracious and thankful. Cleanse me of negative thinking, and help me to celebrate the Lord Jesus moment by moment—for he is excellent and worthy of praise!

Cheri

Occupy your mind with good thoughts, or the enemy will fill it with bad ones: unoccupied it cannot be.

—SIR THOMAS MORE (1478–1535), English lawyer, philosopher, and statesman

4

ALL IN ALL

[CHRIST] EXISTED BEFORE ANYTHING WAS CREATED AND IS
SUPREME OVER ALL CREATION,
FOR THROUGH HIM GOD CREATED EVERYTHING
IN THE HEAVENLY REALMS AND ON EARTH. . . .
EVERYTHING WAS CREATED THROUGH HIM AND FOR HIM.
HE EXISTED BEFORE ANYTHING ELSE,
AND HE HOLDS ALL CREATION TOGETHER.

Colossians 1:15-17

JESUS IS the fulfillment and the embodiment of every promise. Second Corinthians 1:20 says, "All of God's promises have been fulfilled in Christ with a resounding 'Yes!'"

Today, let Jesus be your focus. Think on the supremacy and surpassing worth of Christ. Join Paul in his outburst of wonder and adoration. You have Jesus as your own, and so everything about him is fully at work in your life, on your behalf.

Paul reminds us that everything in existence came into being through Christ. Everything visible and invisible exists because he created it. It remains in existence because he sustains it—holds it all together. Everything is at his command: "Through the Son he created the universe. The Son radiates God's own glory and expresses the very character of God, and he sustains everything by the mighty power of his command" (Hebrews 1:2-3).

Everything was created *through* him, but also *for* him. Everything that exists, exists for his use in accomplishing his purposes: "Your regulations remain true to this day, for everything serves your plans" (Psalm 119:91). He designed our minds so that we could receive his enlightenment and comprehend "how wide, how long, how high, and how deep his love is" (Ephesians 3:18).

This Jesus—Creator and Sustainer of everything that exists—loves you so personally that he numbers the hairs on your head. He knows your heart better than you do. He works without intermission on your behalf and for your good. You are in good hands.

Lord Jesus, I adore you. When I stop to think that you have condescended to live in me and through me, I can barely contain the wonder. Thank you.

Jennifer

He, who counts the very hairs of our heads and suffers not a sparrow to fall without him, takes note of the minutest matters that can affect the lives of his children, and regulates them all according to his perfect will, let their origin be what they may.

—HANNAH WHITALL SMITH (1832–1911), American lay speaker and author

GOD'S WAYS

YOUR ROAD LED THROUGH THE SEA,
YOUR PATHWAY THROUGH THE MIGHTY WATERS—
A PATHWAY NO ONE KNEW WAS THERE!

Psalm 77:19

YOU PROBABLY know the event to which the psalmist is referring. You may have learned the story in Sunday school or seen it depicted in movies. A dramatic, climactic moment. The Israelites flee Egypt only to reach an impasse at the Red Sea, with no way around it and no way through it, and their enemy in hot pursuit.

Following God's specific instructions, Moses had led the people to this very location. Exodus 14:1-4 reports, "The LORD gave these instructions to Moses: 'Order the Israelites to turn back and camp by Pi-hahiroth between Migdol and the sea. Camp there along the shore, across from Baal-zephon. Then Pharaoh will think, "The Israelites are confused. They are trapped in the wilderness!" And once again I will harden Pharaoh's heart, and he will chase after you.' . . . So the Israelites camped there as they were told."

God led the Israelites into an impossible situation, with no hope of escape—on purpose. When they looked around, all they could see was hopelessness. All the empirical evidence that met their eyes told them that they were trapped and there was no way out. "As Pharaoh approached, the people of Israel looked up and panicked when they saw the Egyptians overtaking them. They cried out to the LORD, and they said to Moses, 'Why did you bring us out here to die in the wilderness?'" (Exodus 14:10-11).

Why would God deliberately lead his people into a trap? He explained it to Moses when he told Moses what route to take: "I have planned this in order to display my glory through Pharaoh and his whole army" (Exodus 14:4). God was creating a platform for displaying his power.

Does a situation you are in look like a dead end? Does it look as if things have hit a wall? There is a way out. Maybe you can't see it yet, but God will reveal it. He will open a path through the sea, and you will know that he did it and no one else.

Lord, open my eyes to your provision. I thank you in advance for the pathway that no one knew was there.

Jennifer

God will make a way where there seems to be no way.

—DON MOEN (1950–), American pastor, singer-songwriter, and producer of Christian worship music

6

LIVING MANNA

HE COMMANDED THE SKIES TO OPEN;
HE OPENED THE DOORS OF HEAVEN.
HE RAINED DOWN MANNA FOR THEM TO EAT;
HE GAVE THEM BREAD FROM HEAVEN.
THEY ATE THE FOOD OF ANGELS!
GOD GAVE THEM ALL THEY COULD HOLD.

Psalm 78:23-25

HAVE YOU ever become so focused on some need or desire that it consumed you, and all you could see was what you didn't have? That's what happened to the Israelites. They were in the wilderness and provision was scarce, when God opened the skies and rained down manna.

The provision of manna came in just the right amount for the day. When an Israelite went to bed for the night, no manna was in sight. If he walked around looking for tomorrow's manna, he would have found no hint of manna, no evidence that it was available. He might have gone to bed and said to his wife, "Things look bleak. We're manna-less. I looked and looked and saw nothing to give me hope."

But the next morning the picture would have changed dramatically. While the Israelite slept, provision fell. And he walked out and collected all the manna he could hold, for himself and his household.

Where was that manna the night before, when he was scouring the ground looking for any evidence of it? The Israelites called manna "bread that came from heaven." It was in the spiritual end of the spectrum, the heavenlies. Manna was a substance that was in heaven and moved into the environment of earth. Jesus claimed that he is the Living Manna. He is the substance of heaven moved into the environment of earth. He brought the power of heaven into the circumstances of earth.

He is the Promise. Even when you don't see any hope on the horizon, you can rest assured. The provision will be there when you need it. Jesus, I believe you even when I don't see your provision.

Jennifer

Those who do not hope cannot wait; but if we hope for that we see not, then do we with patience wait for it.

—**CHARLES HADDON SPURGEON** (1834–1892), English preacher and writer

SHAKE, SHAKE, SHAKE

THOSE WHO WISH TO BOAST
SHOULD BOAST IN THIS ALONE:
THAT THEY TRULY KNOW ME AND UNDERSTAND THAT I AM
THE LORD
WHO DEMONSTRATES UNFAILING LOVE
AND WHO BRINGS JUSTICE AND RIGHTEOUSNESS TO THE EARTH.

Jeremiah 9:24

GOD REMINDS us that nothing we possess on our own is able to hold us up in times of trouble and distress. We can't put our confidence in anything other than God himself.

We have evidence everywhere we look that the resources of humanity—or governments or commerce or intelligence—are shaky and weak and not up to the task. Everything our societies have placed confidence in has been revealed as fallible and uncertain. Everything that can be shaken is being shaken: "When God spoke from Mount Sinai his voice shook the earth, but now he makes another promise: 'Once again I will shake not only the earth but the heavens also.' This means that all of creation will be shaken and removed, so that only unshakable things will remain. Since we are receiving a Kingdom that is unshakable, let us be thankful and please God by worshiping him with holy fear and awe. For our God is a devouring fire" (Hebrews 12:26-29).

Is it possible that God shakes things up so that what is shakable will be exposed and what is unshakable will be evident? I am often surprised to discover that things I considered unshakable have shown themselves to be imminently shakable. Institutions and governments that seemed unassailable have been assailed and breached and left naked, their inadequacy exposed. And it shakes me.

I embrace these days of shake-ups. Let them remind me that I am receiving the unshakable Kingdom and that anything that has proven vulnerable is not of that Kingdom. If I have foolishly transferred trust to anything that is on shaky ground, then I am glad to have that silliness exposed. I choose to embrace the promise of the unshakable Kingdom, and there to invest my hope.

King of kings, show me where I have placed my trust in someone or something other than you, and teach me to transfer it to the one who is unshakable.

Jennifer

O slow of heart to believe and trust in the constant presence and overruling agency of our almighty Saviour!

—ADONIRAM JUDSON (1788–1850), American missionary to Burma (now Myanmar)

8

PRAYER STREAMING

DEVOTE YOURSELVES TO PRAYER WITH AN ALERT MIND AND A
THANKFUL HEART.

Colossians 4:2

DOES DEVOTING yourself to prayer—giving constant, unremitting attention to prayer—seem like an unreasonable command? Paul says, "Never stop praying" (1 Thessalonians 5:17). Does God not understand that we have other things we have to do?

If we are defining prayer as words sandwiched between "Dear God" and "Amen," then this command sounds almost ridiculous. If we think that prayer requires always saying words in God's direction, then this command cannot be obeyed.

But what if prayer is more than that? What if prayer is a heart's consistent orientation toward the Father? What if we could define prayer as the undercurrent of our lives, always active? What if prayer doesn't always have to be articulated in sentences, with nouns and verbs and modifiers? What if it's not a prayer life we're called to but a *praying* life?

We can live our lives in such a way that we are always oriented toward the spiritual realm. Our minds are designed to multitask. We can be thinking on many levels at one time. Some of those levels are top tier at a given moment, and others more in the background. We switch those levels around as the moment requires it. At some level, the living, indwelling Jesus is always reproducing his praying life in you. At some level, you are always praying.

The key to everything is that the life of Jesus is flowing through you by means of his Spirit. It is Jesus' prayers that are the content of your prayers. The Spirit is reproducing the intercession of Jesus in you. Jesus is the praying life, and his life is in you.

Lord, teach me to pray.

Jennifer

The life in Him and in us is one and the same. His life in heaven is an ever-praying life. When it descends and takes possession of us, it does not lose its character; in us too it is the ever-praying life—a life that without ceasing asks and receives from God. . . . As we know that Jesus communicates His whole life in us, He also, out of that prayerfulness which is His alone, breathes into us our praying.

—ANDREW MURRAY (1828–1917), South African pastor and author

SHORTHAND PRAYER

WE ALWAYS THANK GOD FOR ALL OF YOU AND PRAY FOR YOU
CONSTANTLY.

1 Thessalonians 1:2

PAUL KNOWS the power that prayer holds does not reside in much speaking. He knows that a shorthand prayer—simply mentioning the object of our request—releases heaven's power for earth's circumstances. We can speak shorthand prayers.

Sometimes what keeps us from prayer is the belief that prayer has to be long, involved, and complicated. When we learn that God promises us that shorthand prayers have power too, we find ourselves living praying lives.

Relationship changes the way we communicate. Long intimacy, shared history, entwined lives—this kind of relationship colors conversation. For example, I have two sisters. Sometimes when we are talking, one of us will say a single word or phrase that sends us into gales of laughter. To an outsider listening in, nothing that was said would have seemed funny. However, because of our long history, a word between us says volumes.

As you live in intimacy with God, you will find the same thing playing out. A mere word may be all the prayer you need to voice in some circumstances. That one word speaks it all. As intimacy grows, the act of praying, in many circumstances, becomes simpler.

The kind of intimacy that leads to verbal shorthand between you and God is the result of prolonged, intense interaction. Because of the time invested in intimate communion, an easy and loving familiarity develops. The relationship deepens through focused and deliberate time with him and then flows naturally through the circumstances of life with an uncontrived delight in each other's company.

Father, thank you for hearing my heart in every word I speak. Teach me to be on the alert for everything and everyone I can bless through prayer with just a word or two.

Jennifer

This power is so rich and so mobile that all we have to do when we pray is to point to the persons or things to which we desire to have this power applied, and He, the Lord of this power, will direct the necessary power to the desired place at once.

—OLE HALLESBY (1879–1961), Norwegian pastor and writer

10 FAITH REBOOT

CAN ANY OF THE WORTHLESS FOREIGN GODS SEND US RAIN?
DOES IT FALL FROM THE SKY BY ITSELF?
NO, YOU ARE THE ONE, O LORD OUR GOD!
ONLY YOU CAN DO SUCH THINGS.
SO WE WILL WAIT FOR YOU TO HELP US.

Jeremiah 14:22

SOMETIMES OUR FAITH needs a reboot. It is easy to let our faith begin to wander to things or people other than God. I don't mean we think someone else can secure our salvation or that we start consciously worshiping some different god; the problem is more subtle than that. But some circumstances cause us to recognize that we have been counting on something else to do for us what only God can do.

My friend had been unemployed for a while. She was successful in her career, and her field has always been stable, so being laid off was not on her radar screen. With a generous severance package and great qualifications, she felt her finances would be secure until she found employment again, which surely would happen quickly. Time passed, with no job offers. She was overqualified. Her salary had been too high. Her money began to run short.

She realized that although she trusted God, she had put her faith in her severance package, her abilities, her network of professionals, and her reputation in her industry. She had to reboot. She had no choice but to wait on God. As I write this, the story is still in progress. But my friend is gaining a new and deeper realization of what it means to look only to God. Her goal is to use the time during which God is calling her to wait in a way that makes this time productive.

Do you recognize little ways you have put your faith in things or people other than in God himself? Is it time to reboot?

> *Lord, keep my faith fastened on you. Call to my attention anything my faith has come to rest on other than you.*

Jennifer

So long as we are quietly at rest amid favourable and undisturbed surroundings, faith sleeps as an undeveloped sinew within us; a thread, a germ, an idea. But when we are pushed out from all these surroundings, with nothing but God to look to, then faith grows suddenly into a cable, a monarch oak, a master-principle of the life.

—F. B. MEYER (1847–1929), English pastor and evangelist

FRUITFULNESS INTO OLD AGE

BLESSED ARE THOSE WHO TRUST IN THE LORD
AND HAVE MADE THE LORD THEIR HOPE AND CONFIDENCE. . . .
THEIR LEAVES STAY GREEN,
AND THEY NEVER STOP PRODUCING FRUIT.

Jeremiah 17:7-8

SOME OF THE most inspiring women I've known are those who, in spite of old age, widowhood, or severe health problems, have produced abundant fruit. My friend Cathy, whose husband died more than ten years ago, is in her eighties and has had health problems, yet she still teaches Bible studies and just had her first book published. She recently went to Africa to keynote a women's conference. Although she misses her husband, she doesn't focus on what she's lost; instead, she keeps trusting the Lord and making him her hope and confidence. I'm amazed at the spiritual fruit her life is producing. Of course, fruit bearing has no retirement age.

Ruth is in her seventh decade of life. She and her team of women have been taking a Bible study into a maximum-security women's prison in Oklahoma for eighteen years. Even when her own sons got into trouble with the law and were sent to prison, Ruth didn't let her sorrow stop her from responding to God's call. In fact, her passion for teaching women in prison is the result of this very difficult life experience. I've seen firsthand the scores of women, young and old, in prison for five years to life without parole, who have come to know Christ and are being discipled and finding new purpose and hope.

What is the secret of these friends of mine? The key is trusting not in themselves or other "mere humans," as Jeremiah 17:5 describes, but in receiving the promise and living it out day by day. God pledges that if our trust is in him, he *will* make us like trees planted along the riverbank that receive their sustenance from the deep water of his love and provision.

Thank you for your promise, Father. Grant that my roots would go even deeper, so that as I trust you more day by day, I'll grow in confidence and experience life abundant, even producing fruit into old age. In Christ's name, amen.

Cheri

Feed on Christ, and then go and live your life, and it is Christ in you that lives your life, helps the poor, that fights the battle, and that wins the crown.

—**PHILLIPS BROOKS** (1835–1893), American minister and author

12 I'VE GOT THE JOY, JOY, JOY, JOY DOWN IN MY HEART

Always be joyful. Never stop praying. Be thankful in all circumstances, for this is God's will for you who belong to Christ Jesus.

1 Thessalonians 5:16-18

PAUL STATES this in the form of a command: Always be joyful. When God gives us a command, it includes an implied promise: whatever he commands us to do, he enables us to do. We can choose joy.

God is not calling us to pretend everything is great when it isn't. He is not calling us to pretense but to reality, the reality of God who is in control all the time. The reality of God who is working out everything for our good and his glory. The reality of God who loves us, and protects us, and rescues us.

Look at the commands that go hand in hand with this call to choose joy: "Never stop praying. Be thankful in all circumstances." How do you choose joy when despair makes more sense? How do you choose joy when your heart is broken and your world is shattered? You let the Spirit of God in you have control and choose him over and over. You discipline the direction of your thoughts. You keep your thoughts flowing Godward. You set your heart on those things that are eternal realities, not on the things of this world that are passing away.

Choose to remember who God is, and call it out into the abyss of your sorrow. Choose to cling to him, and if you can't, remember that he is clinging to you. All of this is possible because he has given you his Spirit, who can bring to remembrance all that you know about the Father and his love. The Spirit can reveal the enemy's lies and lead you into all truth. A deep undercurrent of joy can be flowing, even when sadness and sorrow are your lot.

I choose you, every moment of every day. I choose joy and hope. Right here, right now.

Jennifer

Begin to rejoice in the Lord, and your bones will flourish like an herb, and your cheeks will glow with the bloom of health and freshness. Worry, fear, distrust, care—all are poisonous! Joy is balm and healing, and if you will but rejoice, God will give power.

—A. B. SIMPSON (1843–1919), Canadian preacher, theologian, and author

WEIGHING IN

WE KEEP ON PRAYING FOR YOU, ASKING OUR GOD TO ENABLE
YOU TO LIVE A LIFE WORTHY OF HIS CALL. MAY HE GIVE YOU
THE POWER TO ACCOMPLISH ALL THE GOOD THINGS YOUR FAITH
PROMPTS YOU TO DO. THEN THE NAME OF OUR LORD JESUS WILL
BE HONORED BECAUSE OF THE WAY YOU LIVE, AND YOU WILL BE
HONORED ALONG WITH HIM. THIS IS ALL MADE POSSIBLE BECAUSE
OF THE GRACE OF OUR GOD AND LORD, JESUS CHRIST.

2 Thessalonians 1:11-12

PAUL USES an interesting word in verse 11: *worthy*. The *Theological Dictionary of the New Testament* defines it as "bringing up the other beam of the scales" or "bringing into equilibrium." God's call is weighty—valuable, precious. Now imagine a set of balancing scales with God's call on one side and your life on the other. God will enable you to live a life of such quality that it balances out the scales. Your life = God's call.

What does that look like? God's Spirit empowers you to accomplish all the good things your faith prompts you to do. What does your faith prompt you to do? Your faith in God prompts you to live in such a way that God's power is evident in you. Your faith in God prompts you to live and act beyond your own power or personality. God calls you to the impossible. If it were possible for you in your own power, then it would be a task rather than a call, an assignment rather than a mission. But the Spirit compels you to live up to God's call.

When you live at that level, then Jesus is honored. He is the only explanation for a life worthy of the call. He is the only worthy one, so he has to be the source for any worthy life.

How is your life balancing the scales? Are you living a life for which Jesus is the only explanation? What is your faith prompting you to do right now?

Lord, may your power weight my life toward your glory.

Jennifer

When godliness is produced in you from the life that is deep within you—then that godliness is real, lasting and the genuine essence of the Lord.

—MADAME JEANNE GUYON (1648–1717), French Christian mystic

14 LOVE'S PROOF

> THE LORD GOD IS OUR SUN AND OUR SHIELD.
> HE GIVES US GRACE AND GLORY.
> THE LORD WILL WITHHOLD NO GOOD THING
> FROM THOSE WHO DO WHAT IS RIGHT.

Psalm 84:11

GOD DOES NOT withhold good. He is not a stingy God from whom we need to wrest carefully hoarded riches. He is a lavish giver. He doesn't sprinkle blessing or dribble it. He *pours* it out in abundance: "He generously poured out the Spirit upon us through Jesus Christ our Savior" (Titus 3:6). He offers us "the riches of God's grace that he lavished on us" (Ephesians 1:7-8, NIV 1984). "How great is the love the Father has lavished on us, that we should be called children of God!" (1 John 3:1, NIV 1984).

He loves you so much that he makes available to you all his riches. *All.* He has no desire to withhold anything from you. "What's mine is yours," he says to you. "Since he did not spare even his own Son but gave him up for us all, won't he also give us everything else?" (Romans 8:32).

Paul makes this compelling case for God's generosity, saying in essence, "He did not even hold his own Son in reserve, but gave him up as an offering for you. Is that not proof that all he has is available to you?" Do you see? If he loves you so completely that he did not even spare his own Son, could he possibly be reluctant to give you any other thing? "God showed how much he loved us by sending his one and only Son into the world so that we might have eternal life through him. This is real love—not that we loved God, but that he loved us and sent his Son as a sacrifice to take away our sins" (1 John 4:9-10). Is there anything left for him to prove?

> *Father, I know that you are not holding anything back. I thank you that you are pouring out a tsunami of blessings.*
>
> *Jennifer*

A wrong view of God leads inevitably to a failure to enjoy and grow in His grace. Failure to appreciate His love, His kindness and generous heart leads eventually to a life which bears no fruit and makes no progress. The lesson is clear: if you would grow in grace, learn what grace is. Taste and see that the Lord is good.

—**SINCLAIR B. FERGUSON** (1948–), Scottish preacher and theologian

UNDERSTANDING AND EXPRESSING

MAY THE LORD LEAD YOUR HEARTS INTO A FULL UNDER-
STANDING AND EXPRESSION OF THE LOVE OF GOD AND THE
PATIENT ENDURANCE THAT COMES FROM CHRIST.

2 Thessalonians 3:5

AS A LEFT-BRAIN person who loves logic, I delight that God promises to lead us to understanding. To understanding, followed by expression. We don't have a "because I said so" kind of God. He wants to lead our hearts into a full understanding. Until we understand, we obey because he said so, but he is always moving us forward into all the understanding our minds can accommodate.

Look at Paul's prayer recorded in the book of Colossians: "I want them to be encouraged and knit together by strong ties of love. I want them to have complete confidence that they understand God's mysterious plan, which is Christ himself. In him lie hidden all the treasures of wisdom and knowledge" (Colossians 2:2-3). Once you have Christ and have come to understand God's plan—his revealed mystery of Christ in you—you have access to the wisdom and knowledge of God, because God's love is embodied in Jesus. You have the storehouse of all the resources of God. Your salvation is not just what happens to you after your body dies. God wants you to have as much understanding as possible here on earth.

God wants us to understand his ways. He has given his Spirit "so we can know the wonderful things God has freely given us" (1 Corinthians 2:12). Jesus "has come, and he has given us understanding so that we can know the true God" (1 John 5:20). He wants to "give you complete knowledge of his will and to give you spiritual wisdom and understanding" (Colossians 1:9). He wants us to "understand and experience all the good things we have in Christ" (Philemon 1:6).

God progressively brings understanding through his Spirit in us so that our lives will express the love of God and the endurance that comes from Christ. He promises us unfolding and ever-increasing understanding.

Lord, lead my heart into fuller understanding so you can express your love through me.

Jennifer

If you do not understand a book by a departed writer you are unable to ask him his meaning, but the Spirit, who inspired Holy Scripture, lives forever, and He delights to open the Word to those who seek His instruction.

—CHARLES HADDON SPURGEON (1834–1892), English preacher and writer

16 IT'S ALL IN THE PLANNING

"I KNOW THE PLANS I HAVE FOR YOU," SAYS THE LORD. "THEY ARE PLANS FOR GOOD AND NOT FOR DISASTER, TO GIVE YOU A FUTURE AND A HOPE. IN THOSE DAYS WHEN YOU PRAY, I WILL LISTEN. IF YOU LOOK FOR ME WHOLEHEARTEDLY, YOU WILL FIND ME. I WILL BE FOUND BY YOU," SAYS THE LORD.

Jeremiah 29:11-14

THE CONTEXT of this great promise is that God is talking about prophets who speak in his name but have not heard from him. These false prophets are telling the people what they want to hear. God says of them: "They offer superficial treatments for my people's mortal wound. They give assurances of peace when there is no peace" (Jeremiah 6:14).

Then God promises that his plans are for our *shalom*—our completeness and prosperity. He knows his plans. We can listen to him. He has a future filled with hope planned for us. David wrote of God in Psalm 119:68, "You are good and do only good."

God is a planner. By the time any situation comes into your life, he has already had a plan in place. It will move you forward, not backward. His plan will enrich you, not diminish you. God stands ready to provide everything you need at any moment in your life. When you look for him, there he is.

Have you ever noticed how often God's response to your question is not an answer but a person? God doesn't promise to explain himself, but he does promise to reveal himself. His ways are impossible for us to understand (see Romans 11:33) and are higher than our ways (see Isaiah 55:9). He may hide his ways, but he never hides himself.

> *Thank you, Father, that you always have a plan and always work the plan you have. Thank you that I don't need to know every detail of your plan because the Planner is my God, to whom I look wholeheartedly.*

Jennifer

God, of Your goodness, give me Yourself; for You are sufficient for me. I cannot properly ask anything less to be worthy of You. If I were to ask less, I should always be in want. In You alone do I have all.

—JULIAN OF NORWICH (c. 1342–after 1413), English Christian mystic and writer

GOD'S UNFAILING, EVERLASTING LOVE

LONG AGO THE LORD SAID TO ISRAEL:
"I HAVE LOVED YOU, MY PEOPLE, WITH AN EVERLASTING LOVE.
WITH UNFAILING LOVE I HAVE DRAWN YOU TO MYSELF."

Jeremiah 31:3

WHEN JEREMIAH SPOKE this promise to God's people, they were in captivity in Babylon. Because they had repeatedly turned from the Lord, they were now slaves in the hands of a foreign power. They had lost their lands and possessions, and some of them would never see their homeland again. They had seen the destruction of Jerusalem and the Temple, and countless families had been separated by their oppressors. As Psalm 137 describes, beside the rivers of Babylon, the Israelites sat and wept as they thought of their beloved Jerusalem. Hanging up their harps of praise, they cried out to God.

In the midst of their great distress, God let them know their captivity would be a long one, but he sent them comfort and promises through the prophet Jeremiah. One of the best is today's verse, which speaks of the kind of love God has for his people: an everlasting love that *never goes away*. Just think: with all their apostasy and rebellion, he drew them to himself with unfailing love—just as he draws each of us to himself.

Whether the bottom drops out of our jobs, our marriages, our health, our finances, or other areas of our lives, nothing can take away God's love or snatch us out of his hand. Regardless of whether you find success or failure by the world's standards, no matter what difficulties happen on the journey of life or how long they last—God couldn't love you any more than he loves you right now. He'll never stop loving you. He loved you so much he gave himself totally to you and asks that you respond to his love. When you commit yourself to living in his love, your life will be woven into the Lord's plan not only on this earth but also for all eternity.

Lord, I want your love to be my anchor, and I'm willing to say yes to whatever your plan is. Forgive me for resisting your love and being blind to your faithful working in my life.

Cheri

Every character has an inward spring; let Christ be that spring. Every action has a keynote. Let Christ be that note to which your whole life is attuned.

—**HENRY DRUMMOND** (1851–1897), Scottish evangelist and writer

18 A NEW HEART

I WILL PUT MY INSTRUCTIONS DEEP WITHIN THEM, AND I WILL WRITE THEM ON THEIR HEARTS. I WILL BE THEIR GOD, AND THEY WILL BE MY PEOPLE.

Jeremiah 31:33

GOD PROMISES a new covenant for a new Kingdom. The new covenant is inscribed not on tablets of stone but on human hearts. Pay particular attention to the words from Ezekiel 36:26: "I will take out your stony, stubborn heart and give you a tender, responsive heart." The finger of God engraved the original law on stone tablets. When a stone is engraved, the markings are cut into the stone and become one with it. When God engraves his law on your heart, his law becomes one with your heart. Your heart changes. It is set apart for his purpose: to contain God's law.

Now look at the words of Jeremiah 24:7: "I will give them hearts that recognize me as the LORD. They will be my people, and I will be their God, for they will return to me wholeheartedly." In the new covenant for the new Kingdom, he will give his people hearts that know him.

In the Kingdom of God, all Kingdom dwellers get heart transplants. The new hearts know God, and his law is their heartbeat. Look what God says will change: "I will put my Spirit in you and *move you* to follow my decrees and be careful to keep my laws" (Ezekiel 36:27, NIV 1984, emphasis added). He will be the power moving you to follow his decrees and to be careful to keep his law.

We live in the new Kingdom under the new covenant. God's law is not foreign to us. It fits us. He promises that if we will seek him, he will teach us to follow his ways.

Father, lead me in your ways, and teach me your commands.

Jennifer

The heart in which God gets His way, and writes His law in power, lives only and wholly to carry that writing, and is unchangeably identified with it.

—**ANDREW MURRAY** (1828–1917), South African pastor and author

GOD'S PRIVATE TELEPHONE NUMBER

THIS IS WHAT THE LORD SAYS—THE LORD WHO MADE THE EARTH, WHO FORMED IT AND ESTABLISHED IT, WHOSE NAME IS THE LORD: ASK ME AND I WILL TELL YOU REMARKABLE SECRETS YOU DO NOT KNOW ABOUT THINGS TO COME.

Jeremiah 33:2-3

MANY OF US find it challenging enough to listen to those we interact with on a daily basis, let alone to God, who is invisible. Throughout the Bible, God implores us to listen, to consult him and to hear his voice, not because he is a cruel taskmaster, but because he wants to share with us great and mighty things we can know only if we listen to him.

Corrie ten Boom called Jeremiah 33:3 "God's private telephone number" and encouraged us to call him day and night, for he never slumbers or sleeps. Following this suggestion may take us out of our comfort zones, but our lives will never be boring. No matter what age you are, it's never too late to start listening to and obeying the Lord.

Lois, a Seattle woman, sensed as a young woman that she was being called to overseas mission. But she wanted to get married and live near her family. After her children were grown and she was a widow, she again asked for guidance and heard God tell her to go to the Philippines. Seventy-six by then, she told him, "I'm too old to go." But eventually Lois sold all she had and embarked on the biggest adventure of her life, becoming the lifeline for countless orphans in the Philippines and building an orphanage called "King's Garden" that has had an impact on hundreds of children's lives.

Just as God had a remarkable plan for Lois, he has good plans for you—marvelous things he wants to show you if you will listen. If we seek God and listen for his voice, he will guide us every step of the way.

Father, to be honest, I'm not the best listener, and I often go in so many directions that I do all the talking and don't wait to hear what you have to say. Teach me to hear your voice, and grant me the faith to trust and obey.

Cheri

A man prayed and at first he thought prayer lies in talking. But he became more and more quiet until in the end he realized prayer is listening.

—**SØREN KIERKEGAARD** (1813–1855), Danish theologian, philosopher, and writer

20 FACE UP

HAPPY ARE THOSE WHO HEAR THE JOYFUL CALL TO WORSHIP,
FOR THEY WILL WALK IN THE LIGHT OF YOUR PRESENCE,
LORD.
THEY REJOICE ALL DAY LONG IN YOUR WONDERFUL REPUTATION.
THEY EXULT IN YOUR RIGHTEOUSNESS.
YOU ARE THEIR GLORIOUS STRENGTH.
IT PLEASES YOU TO MAKE US STRONG.

Psalm 89:15-17

DAVID USES exultant language to describe the person who lives in an awareness of God's presence: *happy, rejoice, exult, glorious*. He pulls out all the stops, piling word upon word to put together sentences that might at least hint at the megajoy of walking in the light of the Lord's presence.

The Hebrew word most often translated "presence" is the word for face. It is the word used in the second line of today's verses. It means intimate presence, being face-to-face.

The light in the Kingdom is Jesus. Paul writes that the light "is seen in the face of Jesus Christ" (2 Corinthians 4:6). God gives us the light of his glory in the face of Jesus.

An emerging science is the study of facial communication, or what you might call "seeing the voice." Studies done on infants eighteen to twenty weeks old show that even at a prelinguistic age, babies read facial expressions to understand speech. A thought or emotion registers on the face before any words that are spoken. In others words, a face registers the true emotion, even if the words are meant to mask the emotion. Facial Action Coding System, a highly specific science that maps the facial muscles, allows specialists to read a person's face and know his or her thoughts. Even though the subject can learn to rearrange his face quickly to mask emotion, the true emotion always registers on the face, even if only fleetingly.

A person's face speaks without words. The most intimate communication is facial communication. And God promises us his presence—his face.

Oh Father! Let me walk in your presence. Let me live my life face-to-face with you, knowing you so intimately that just a look can communicate.

Jennifer

Christianity is not a theory or speculation, but a life; not a philosophy of life, but a living presence.
—**SAMUEL TAYLOR COLERIDGE** (1772-1834), English poet

ENOUGH IS ENOUGH

TRUE GODLINESS WITH CONTENTMENT IS ITSELF GREAT WEALTH.
AFTER ALL, WE BROUGHT NOTHING WITH US WHEN WE CAME
INTO THE WORLD, AND WE CAN'T TAKE ANYTHING WITH US
WHEN WE LEAVE IT. SO IF WE HAVE ENOUGH FOOD AND
CLOTHING, LET US BE CONTENT.

1 Timothy 6:6-8

CONTENTMENT MEANS a state of satisfaction. Paul says that godliness, expressed in contentment, is great wealth. It puts us way ahead. He explained in Philippians 4:11-12: "I have learned how to be content with whatever I have. I know how to live on almost nothing or with everything. I have learned the secret of living in every situation, whether it is with a full stomach or empty, with plenty or little."

Paul had learned a secret. This secret caused him to live every moment of every day in a state of contentment. He learned it by experience, not through theoretical study. He learned that the unchanging presence of God satisfied him. It was the same whether God allowed adversity in Paul's life or supernaturally intervened to circumvent difficulties. Either way, God was enough.

Let me explain what I think Paul discovered. It starts with realizing how our human nature works. We are all busy trying to arrange outward events in such a way that they will produce inner contentment—a sense of safety, of being loved, of satisfaction. If this would happen, or if that would go away, or if this would change, or if that would stay the same, then we would have inner contentment. Or so we think.

Paul learned that it's not what God does but *who God is* that produces contentment. What happened on the outside of him did not add to or subtract from his inner rest. How did he know such a wonderful thing? He learned it. How did he learn it? He learned how to be content when he was in need by being in need. He learned how to be content when he was hungry by being hungry.

Contentment keeps its eyes on God, who is bringing to completion a good and loving work. When he allows difficulties to come into your experience, you can be sure that he is doing something beneficial by means of them.

Lord, teach me contentment. Thank you for what I have.

Fretting springs from a determination to get our own way!
—**OSWALD CHAMBERS** (1874–1917), Scottish minister and teacher

22 ANGELIC PROTECTION

IF YOU MAKE THE LORD YOUR REFUGE,
   IF YOU MAKE THE MOST HIGH YOUR SHELTER,
NO EVIL WILL CONQUER YOU;
   NO PLAGUE WILL COME NEAR YOUR HOME.

Psalm 91:9-11

EVERY TWO WEEKS a missionary made a two-day journey on his bicycle to purchase medicine and supplies for the small African field hospital where he served. One day when he was in the city to go to the bank and the supply store, he saw two men. One of them was injured, so the missionary treated his injuries and shared God's love with him. After finishing his business, the missionary started back home, stopping to camp that night in the jungle.

Two weeks later, when the missionary arrived back in the city, the young man he'd bandaged up on the previous trip approached him.

"My friends and I knew you carried money and medicine, so we followed you to your campsite in the jungle, planning to steal everything you had and kill you. But just as we were about to attack you, we saw twenty-six armed guards surrounding you."

"You must be mistaken; I was all alone that night," the missionary answered.

"Oh no," the young man said. "All of us saw the guards. That's the only reason we didn't kill you."

Months later, the missionary shared this story with his home church, and a man in the congregation interrupted him: "What was the specific month and day this happened?"

When the missionary told him, the man explained, "At the time of this incident, I was on the golf course for some morning practice. I was about to putt when I was struck by a sudden urge to pray for you. It was so strong I left the course and called some men at our church to join me in praying for you. Would all you men who prayed that day stand up?" One by one the missionary counted the men. There were twenty-six—the exact number of "armed guards" the thwarted assailants had seen.

> *Lord, in your mysterious, powerful ways, you send your angels around us to protect us in all our journeys through life. Thank you! May I always look to you as my shelter and live in freedom, not fear, no matter what I face.*
>
> *Cheri*

Make yourself familiar with the angels and behold them frequently in spirit; for without being seen, they are present with you.

—ST. FRANCIS DE SALES (1567–1622), bishop of Geneva

VITAL AND GREEN

THE GODLY WILL FLOURISH LIKE PALM TREES
AND GROW STRONG LIKE THE CEDARS OF LEBANON.
FOR THEY ARE TRANSPLANTED INTO THE LORD'S OWN HOUSE.
THEY FLOURISH IN THE COURTS OF OUR GOD.
EVEN IN OLD AGE THEY WILL STILL PRODUCE FRUIT;
THEY WILL REMAIN VITAL AND GREEN.

Psalm 92:12-14

PROMISES LIKE these verses inspire me more each year that as we continue sinking our roots deep into God, we will flourish and our faith will grow strong. Even in old age—not just during our youth and twenty-, thirty-, and forty-something years—we can remain vital and productive. I'm not quite to old age yet, but I'm definitely heading in that direction!

These verses remind me of older women who have served as examples of how God can sustain his people into their elder years with the vitality to be about his work. Flo Perkins, despite the pain and physical limitation of multiple back surgeries, mentored many younger women like me in prayer. A group of us mothers met in her home at six in the morning to pray for our children and husbands. Flo had been coming to the throne of grace for over fifty years, and as she took us on her wings into God's presence, we learned to pray. Even to the last days of her life, Flo flourished in intercession, and her heart remained young and open to the Lord.

These verses also remind me of my friend Patty Johnston, whose wisdom has blessed me (and many other women) and whose prayers have sustained my ministry and my family. Though her body is getting older, her spirit is young; her mind is intellectually curious and interested in big world issues as well as the Spirit's whispers.

When we are transplanted into God's garden by committing our lives to him, he promises to give us the strength we need to stay "green," to keep serving and living for and with him.

Lord, I want my roots to grow deep in you and my faith to grow tall. Grant me the grace to keep trusting you and believing you can produce fruit from my life—even into old age. For Christ's sake, amen.

Cheri

Strength has ever to be made perfect in weakness, and old age is one of the weaknesses in which it is perfected.

—**GEORGE MACDONALD** (1824–1905), Scottish author and minister

24 SHAPED BY THE WORD

ALL SCRIPTURE IS INSPIRED BY GOD AND IS USEFUL TO TEACH US
WHAT IS TRUE AND TO MAKE US REALIZE WHAT IS WRONG IN OUR
LIVES. IT STRAIGHTENS US OUT AND TEACHES US TO DO WHAT IS
RIGHT. IT IS GOD'S WAY OF PREPARING US IN EVERY WAY, FULLY
EQUIPPED FOR EVERY GOOD THING GOD WANTS US TO DO.

2 Timothy 3:16-17

A WISE MAN once said that today the Bible is often used not as God intended but as the authority for pop psychology or to undergird a personal philosophy of life. His Word is adapted to fit our way of thinking rather than the way it was intended: to reveal God and how we need to live in personal relationship with him.

Today's verses give us a picture of the origin and purpose of Scripture as the Lord intended. Though written by human hands and given through men, it is God-breathed, inerrant, and authored by the Holy Spirit.

Having underscored this indisputable fact, Paul gives Timothy a charge to keep his confidence in Scripture and let it be his anchor and guide for life. Practically speaking, Scripture instructs us in the truth and convicts us of sin; it will bring us into a vital, personal relationship with God through the Spirit. His Word corrects us when we need straightening out or are off the path of right living. God promises us that Scripture will also guide us, correct our mistakes, and prepare us for every good work he has planned for us to do.

How grateful I am that the Lord doesn't just give us a job or ministry and then say, "Do well, now, and I'll see you in heaven." Instead, through his powerful, eternal Word we are equipped for every task and challenge we face. His Word will keep inspiring and empowering us, illuminating our prayers and shaping our lives for the purposes prepared before the foundation of the earth. Join me in thanking God for the wonders of his Word.

Father, in your written Word you have shown us the way to salvation through faith in your Son, Jesus Christ. You have given us love letters that reveal your heart and guide our lives. Thank you for the inspired Word of God, more precious than silver or gold!

Cheri

The Bible redirects my will, cleanses my emotions, enlightens my mind, and quickens my total being.

—**E. STANLEY JONES** (1884–1973), American theologian and missionary to India

POURED OUT

MOAB HAS BEEN AT REST FROM YOUTH,
    LIKE WINE LEFT ON ITS DREGS,
NOT POURED FROM ONE JAR TO ANOTHER. . . .
SO SHE TASTES AS SHE DID,
    AND HER AROMA IS UNCHANGED.

Jeremiah 48:11 (NIV)

GOD IS working in you a process that goes beyond simple obedience down to the roots of unrighteousness that produce disobedience. He is cleansing you moment by moment, moving you from one level to the next and never leaving you to "sit on your dregs."

Jeremiah is describing Moab as people who have never been challenged and forced to face disappointment or disruption of their lives. They are like wine on its dregs, which becomes bitter and harsh.

Wine making involves different stages and vessels of different size, shape, and construction. A wine must be moved from vessel to vessel. Each stage accomplishes something different for the final product—the wine that it is becoming. At each stage, the dregs settle to the bottom and must be strained out. Only the winemake can tell the stage at which a wine must be emptied from one vessel to another

God, the great Winemaker, is fermenting a rich and perfect wine in you. Do you feel yourself being emptied from vessel to vessel? Just as you get used to the shape and feel of your life as it is, you find yourself being emptied out. It is disorienting. Then you find yourself poured into a life of a completely different shape and size.

Don't be frightened when the shape of your life seems to be changing. God will not let you sit on your dregs. You will not be locked into your immaturity, retaining the same aroma as in your youth. God is ripening you, fermenting you, enriching you. Embrace his transitions, because God moves only forward.

> *Father, you are the Winemaker—fermenting my life until it is a perfect vintage
> with beautiful aroma. I trust you and thank you for all the stages of my journey.
> With you, nothing is wasted or capricious but is part of a beautiful process.
> I yield myself to you.*

Jennifer

Faith is to believe what you do not yet see; the reward for this faith is to see what you believe.

—**ST. AUGUSTINE** (354–430), Latin North African theologian and philosopher,

26 FREE AT LAST

THE PEOPLE OF ISRAEL WILL RETURN HOME
   TOGETHER WITH THE PEOPLE OF JUDAH.
THEY WILL COME WEEPING
   AND SEEKING THE LORD THEIR GOD.
THEY WILL ASK THE WAY TO JERUSALEM
   AND WILL START BACK HOME AGAIN.
THEY WILL BIND THEMSELVES TO THE LORD
   WITH AN ETERNAL COVENANT THAT WILL
   NEVER BE FORGOTTEN.

Jeremiah 50:4-5

JEREMIAH'S PROPHECY describes the joy of freedom after the Lord's people have lived 70 years in captivity.

Have you experienced what it is like to be set free? There are tears of joy, tears of repentance, the overwhelming emotion of a real and deep turning of the heart toward God. The released captives ask the way to Jerusalem—where the Lord dwells. For us, Jerusalem is the Lord's presence. We start learning from others.

The people of Israel and Judah return home together. Broken relationships are healed. Unity is restored. Old disagreements fade away. This is evidence of the Lord's action in our lives. On our own, we will never let go of grudges and move toward unity.

The people bind themselves to the Lord. Bind—fasten, link, attach. They cling to the Lord with an unbreakable covenant. At this moment of sudden restoration, we are extremely aware of how dependent we are on the Lord. Having just passed through a time when our bondage and oppression seemed to have no end, we now find ourselves dancing in the light, and we know that this is the Lord's work and we are helpless without him.

God's promise is that seasons of oppression end. He knows the last day of our captivity, and he can already see the triumphal procession. Let him show you.

Father, my season of struggle is made bearable by your presence. I know there is an end, and I will begin to celebrate that release even before I see it in my experience.

Jennifer

Our life is full of brokenness—broken relationships, broken promises, broken expectations. How can we live with that brokenness without becoming bitter and resentful except by returning again and again to God's faithful presence in our lives.

—**HENRI NOUWEN** (1932–1996), Dutch writer and priest

FREE TO SERVE **27**

[JESUS] GAVE HIS LIFE TO FREE US FROM EVERY KIND OF SIN, TO CLEANSE US, AND TO MAKE US HIS VERY OWN PEOPLE, TOTALLY COMMITTED TO DOING GOOD DEEDS.

Titus 2:14

CHRIST'S AIM was to redeem us not merely from the penalty of sin but also from the practice of sin. He was so zealous for our salvation that he paid for it by giving his own life. He did not consider his life too high a price for ours.

The promise of our salvation includes the penalty paid for our sins but also the power to keep us from sinning. Jesus cleanses us inside and out. He forgives us in one fell swoop by dying for our sins. But now, as he lives in us, his Spirit progressively cleanses us from the unrighteousness that causes us to commit sins.

By redeeming us, he has brought us into an intimate relationship with him. We are his very own people. We are precious to him. His love for us is beyond our comprehension. We are his, and he is ours.

After he has freed us from sin's penalty, he then begins to free us from sin's power. The more we experience that inner cleansing that results in freedom, the more we find ourselves committed to living out that inner transformation through doing good for others. Good deeds become the natural and exuberant expression of the one who is inside us. When we are free of the inner corruption that keeps us bound to our old, self-serving, self-involved ways, then we can express the new being we are becoming. Our new nature is self-giving and other-focused. We learn that giving is better than receiving. Joy is found in being generous instead of demanding.

The promise of our salvation is comprehensive. It is for all eternity, and all eternity starts now.

Lord Jesus, thank you for paying the price to set me free. I want to honor that act of love by embracing everything about my salvation. Forgive me when I ignore the great privilege of demonstrating your love to others. Bring me many opportunities to love in your name, even when it interrupts my self-centered tendencies.

Jennifer

Genuine love is so contrary to human nature that its presence bears witness to an extraordinary power.
—**JOHN PIPER** (1946–), American pastor

28 FROM WORTHLESS TO WORTHY

AT ONE TIME WE TOO WERE FOOLISH, DISOBEDIENT, DECEIVED AND ENSLAVED BY ALL KINDS OF PASSIONS AND PLEASURES. WE LIVED IN MALICE AND ENVY, BEING HATED AND HATING ONE ANOTHER. BUT WHEN THE KINDNESS AND LOVE OF GOD OUR SAVIOR APPEARED, HE SAVED US, NOT BECAUSE OF RIGHTEOUS THINGS WE HAD DONE, BUT BECAUSE OF HIS MERCY.

Titus 3:3-5 (NIV)

WHEN JESUS wrapped himself in flesh and left heaven for earth, it was not as a reward to those who were saintly and deserving but as a Redeemer for those who were fallen and completely undeserving. He came taking the servant's role, not demanding to be treated as the King he is: "The Son of Man came not to be served but to serve others and to give his life as a ransom for many" (Matthew 20:28). Heaven's highest work was aimed at earth's lowliest inhabitants.

The incarnate Word came to set my captive thoughts free and to captivate my restless mind and anchor it in him. Without him, my thoughts were entangled by the dictates of my flesh. They poisoned and polluted my life. My thoughts were infused with the stench of corruption and decay, marching steadily toward the grave. The power of death spread to cover every pursuit, every relationship, every dream.

Then Christ came. Barely a ripple in the course of humankind's doings, yet one that reverberated through the heavenly realms. With a battle cry that sounded to earthly ears like a newborn baby's whimper, he set in motion our redemption. The sound heard in the heavens that first Christmas moment was a victory shout that rattled the enemy's forces and ensured their defeat.

Jesus, thank you for recasting my thoughts into the mold of yours. Teach me how to receive that gift in its fullness. Make me so moldable that you can transform my heart completely, until its thoughts and intents are reflective of your life in me.

Jennifer

Non-Christians seem to think that the Incarnation implies some particular merit or excellence in humanity. But of course it implies just the reverse: a particular demerit and depravity. No creature that deserved Redemption would need to be redeemed. They that are whole need not the physician. Christ died for men precisely because men are not worth dying for; to make them worth it.

—**C. S. LEWIS** (1898–1963), Irish novelist, literary critic, and essayist

I WILL LEAD A LIFE OF INTEGRITY
IN MY OWN HOME.

Psalm 101:2

YOU'VE HEARD the phrase "big fish in a small pond." In smaller settings, actions are amplified. In the microcosm of our families and homes, our true selves are on display.

Some time ago I spoke at my father's memorial service. My father had lived a public life and was widely admired for his wisdom and kindness. He was known to be generous and honest and a man of integrity. In my tribute to him, I was so pleased to be able to say, "As his daughter, I can tell you that he was just exactly what you thought he was." He led a life of integrity in his own home—the proving ground.

When we let down our guard, who are we? That is the reality. What God promises is a transformation so real that it holds up, even in our own homes.

Integrity means "of one piece." From the same root, we get the word *integer*, meaning whole, undivided. A person of integrity is not one person in public and another in private.

When I was growing up, my parents had several guidelines to regulate our behavior at mealtimes. I don't know about your household, but in ours, mealtimes could become chaotic quickly. One rule was that during mealtime we were to treat one another as if the other person were a guest in our house for the evening. That really demonstrated how differently we treat people in our own families. My dad once instituted a rule that we could say any unkind words we wanted to another family member, but we had to *sing* them. Are you laughing? That's just what happened to us.

Showing kindness in our homes is one of the most significant experiences for the recipients. Those closest to us have the power to cut us most deeply or to bring the most healing. Jesus living *in* you can be Jesus living through you.

Lord, I will walk with integrity in my own home.

Jennifer

The only humility that is really ours is not that which we try to show before God in prayer, but that which we carry with us in our daily conduct.

—**ANDREW MURRAY** (1828–1917), South African pastor and author

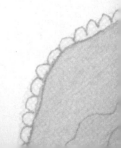

30 GOD'S ASTONISHING FAITHFULNESS

THE FAITHFUL LOVE OF THE LORD NEVER ENDS!
HIS MERCIES NEVER CEASE.
GREAT IS HIS FAITHFULNESS;
HIS MERCIES BEGIN AFRESH EACH MORNING.

Lamentations 3:22-23

FROM CHILDHOOD and throughout adulthood I've sung the hymn "Great Is Thy Faithfulness" countless times. But only recently did I learn the story of the man who wrote the lyrics. Thomas Chisholm, born in Kentucky in a log cabin in 1866, became a Christian at age twenty-seven. He had only an elementary school education, yet as a young man he worked as an editor of a local newspaper and also as the business manager and editor of a Christian publication. Later he became an ordained Methodist minister, but after only a year in the pulpit he had to resign because of failing health. He eventually became an insurance agent, but his health prevented him from making a good income.

Throughout his trials, Chisholm didn't become embittered toward God. Instead, he discovered the Lord's faithfulness so often that he was compelled to record the "wonderful displays of his providential care" which filled him with "astonishing gratefulness." Though he wrote more than twelve hundred poems, many of which became hymns, his most famous is based on today's verses from Lamentations. "Great Is Thy Faithfulness" has inspired millions of people in church services, revival meetings, and—as my mom requested—at memorial services.

Though Thomas Chisholm lived with hardship and ill health much of his life, he encourages us through the words of this hymn to lift up our hearts and focus on God's goodness and unfailing love. Choosing to root our lives in the unfailing faithfulness of our Lord will help us walk in victory no matter what we face.

Lord, help me to triumph over my adversities by focusing on your great faithfulness and on your mercies, which are new every morning. May hope in you bear me up so that I'll praise you until my last breath.

Cheri

Summer and winter and springtime and harvest,
Sun, moon and stars in their courses above.
Join with all nature in manifold witness
To Thy great faithfulness, mercy and love.

—"GREAT IS THY FAITHFULNESS" BY

THOMAS O. CHISHOLM (1866–1960),
American poet and hymn writer

MERCY

HE DOES NOT PUNISH US FOR ALL OUR SINS;
    HE DOES NOT DEAL HARSHLY WITH US, AS WE DESERVE. . . .
HE HAS REMOVED OUR SINS AS FAR FROM US
    AS THE EAST IS FROM THE WEST.
THE LORD IS LIKE A FATHER TO HIS CHILDREN,
    TENDER AND COMPASSIONATE TO THOSE WHO FEAR HIM.
FOR HE KNOWS HOW WEAK WE ARE;
    HE REMEMBERS WE ARE ONLY DUST.

Psalm 103:10, 12-14

GOD IS not fair. Aren't you glad? We don't get what we deserve. Jesus took what we deserve: "He was pierced for our rebellion, crushed for our sins. He was beaten so we could be whole. He was whipped so we could be healed. . . . Yet the LORD laid on him the sins of us all" (Isaiah 53:5-6).

He disciplines us for our own good, but not as retribution for our actions. Discipline is corrective. In Hebrews 12:5-6 we read, "My child, don't make light of the LORD's discipline, and don't give up when he corrects you. For the LORD disciplines those he loves, and he punishes each one he accepts as his child."

Though the word for discipline is translated "punishment" in this passage, the *Theological Dictionary of the New Testament* indicates that it means "to show someone his sin and to summon him to repentance." Discipline is loving and productive.

God promises that he does not deal with us as we deserve. The enemy likes to make use of guilt and shame to keep us from experiencing the love God has for us. This promise robs the enemy of one of his most potent weapons.

> *Lord, sometimes it is so hard for me to believe that you aren't waiting to scold me. But I know the truth. All my sins are covered by the blood of the Lamb. They have been removed from me as far as the east is from the west. I accept your gentle tenderness.*

Jennifer

He remembers our frame and knows that we are dust. He may sometimes chasten us, it is true, but even this He does with a smile, the proud, tender smile of a Father who is bursting with pleasure over an imperfect but promising son who is coming every day to look more and more like the One whose child he is.

—A. W. TOZER (1897–1963), American preacher and author

NOVEMBER

NOURISHED

THE VOICE SAID TO ME, "SON OF MAN, EAT WHAT I AM GIVING YOU—EAT THIS SCROLL! THEN GO AND GIVE ITS MESSAGE TO THE PEOPLE OF ISRAEL." SO I OPENED MY MOUTH, AND HE FED ME THE SCROLL. "FILL YOUR STOMACH WITH THIS," HE SAID. AND WHEN I ATE IT, IT TASTED AS SWEET AS HONEY IN MY MOUTH. . . . THEN HE ADDED, "SON OF MAN, LET ALL MY WORDS SINK DEEP INTO YOUR OWN HEART FIRST. LISTEN TO THEM CAREFULLY FOR YOURSELF. THEN GO TO YOUR PEOPLE IN EXILE AND SAY TO THEM, 'THIS IS WHAT THE SOVEREIGN LORD SAYS!' DO THIS WHETHER THEY LISTEN TO YOU OR NOT.'"

Ezekiel 3:1-3, 10-11

EZEKIEL'S VISION carries a theme that is repeated throughout Scripture. God's Word is food that nourishes our spiritual lives in the same way physical food nourishes us physically.

Just as my body requires a daily, consistent intake of food, my spirit requires a daily, consistent intake of God's Word, so that I will progressively mature and so that my spiritual immune system will be strong.

Physically, when we eat food, its nutrients are absorbed into our bloodstream and delivered to our cells. All of our food enters our bodies the same way, and yet the specific nutrients and vitamins get to the right cells.

This reflects the amazingly complex digestive system, which "clicks on" when we eat. First the process changes food into a form our bodies can use. Then the food is delivered to the cells.

Amazing, isn't it? You have billions of cells in your body, each drawing from your bloodstream exactly what it needs, and it happens without your effort. You eat; your body does the rest. The nutrients in your food literally are "life to those who find them, and healing to their whole body," which is exactly how Proverbs 4:22 describes the Word of God.

Nourishing your spirit works the same way. You feast on the Word of God and the Spirit of God applies his truth to your life. When you engage in the discipline of taking in the Word of God on a regular basis, your spiritual digestive system does the rest.

Father, feed me your Word. Let me digest it and assimilate it and then live it out.

Jennifer

We may be certain that whatever God has made prominent in his Word, he intended to be conspicuous in our lives.

—CHARLES HADDON SPURGEON (1834–1892), English preacherr

2 CONFIDENT IN GOD'S PRESENCE

LET US COME BOLDLY TO THE THRONE OF OUR GRACIOUS GOD.
THERE WE WILL RECEIVE HIS MERCY, AND WE WILL FIND GRACE
TO HELP US WHEN WE NEED IT.

Hebrews 4:16

THERE IS nothing like coming to the throne of grace, fearlessly and confidently, knowing that our heavenly Father welcomes us. An image that helped me relate to this verse comes from the example of John F. Kennedy Jr., the son of President John F. Kennedy. I'll never forget the photographs of "John John" securely and happily sitting under his dad's presidential desk or rushing into his arms for a big hug between his father's meetings with national and international leaders. The child didn't shrink back in fear or run in the other direction when he saw his father. Even though his father was the leader of the free world, the highest-ranking official in our nation, to his son he was just Daddy.

We, too, have a loving Father. Though some might find him intimidating to approach, for all those who have put their trust in Christ and become God's children, he invites them to call him *Abba* (the Aramaic word for "Daddy"). Because of Christ, we can poke our heads around the door to his throne room anytime we want. Ephesians 3:12 says, "Because of Christ and our faith in him, we can now come boldly and confidently into God's presence." We can bring others to meet him or just enter by ourselves for a heart-to-heart conversation.

Do you ever feel distant from God or find it difficult to pray? Even when your life is a mess, he invites you to climb into his lap and tell him all about your struggles. That feeling of distance will melt away as your Father replaces your fears with a deep feeling of his love—and you'll receive the mercy, grace, and help you need.

> *All thanks and praise to you, Father, who sits on heaven's mercy seat. What a privilege it is to be invited into your presence. Thank you for loving us! It's so good to experience the amazing grace of being your children and having a heavenly Father! In Jesus' name, amen.*

Cheri

We need to let it soak in that there is nothing we can do to make God love us more . . . and nothing we can do to make God love us less. God is love.

—PHILIP YANCEY (1949–), American writer and preacher

SHOW OFF

GIVE THANKS TO THE LORD AND PROCLAIM HIS GREATNESS.
LET THE WHOLE WORLD KNOW WHAT HE HAS DONE.
SING TO HIM; YES, SING HIS PRAISES.
TELL EVERYONE ABOUT HIS WONDERFUL DEEDS.
EXULT IN HIS HOLY NAME;
REJOICE, YOU WHO WORSHIP THE LORD.
SEARCH FOR THE LORD AND FOR HIS STRENGTH;
CONTINUALLY SEEK HIM.

Psalm 105:1-4

GOD WANTS to work in our lives in such a way that his power and provision are evident to others. He wants us to be branches that display the Vine's fruit. He wants us to let the whole world know what he has done.

When something wonderful happens to you, isn't your first impulse to tell someone else about it? Something great happens, and your first thought is, *I can't wait to tell so-and-so.* The person we choose to tell is someone we know will rejoice with us. It doubles our own joy, and the experience is not complete until you have told the other person about it. In today's verses, David encourages us to "tell everyone about [God's] wonderful deeds."

When we have known and experienced the Lord's great work in our lives, it overflows to others. Others who worship the Lord will be overjoyed. The joy will be contagious. The person who is in a valley at that time will be encouraged by hearing about God's work in your life. When we are so intimately in tune with one another, our joys are multiplied. We get not only our own God adventures but also the God adventures of our fellow worshipers.

Then David's thought flows to the next admonition. Be always, continuously seeking God—deliberately and attentively pursuing him. Keep your life lined up with his. On purpose. There you will find his strength that strengthens you.

God promises that in seeking him, you will find him and his strength.

Father, teach me to seek you continually, just as you seek me. Let my life put you on display.

Jennifer

God, I pray Thee, light these idle sticks of my life, that I may burn for Thee. Consume my life, my God, for it is Thine. I seek not a long life, but a full one, like You, Lord Jesus.

—**JIM ELLIOT** (1927–1956), American missionary and martyr

4

SANCTUARY

TELL THE EXILES, "THIS IS WHAT THE SOVEREIGN LORD SAYS:
ALTHOUGH I HAVE SCATTERED YOU IN THE COUNTRIES OF THE
WORLD, I WILL BE A SANCTUARY TO YOU DURING YOUR TIME
IN EXILE."

Ezekiel 11:16

NO MATTER where life takes us, God is our sanctuary. A place of refuge as well as of worship. A place to dwell and be at home: "Lord, through all the generations you have been our home!" (Psalm 90:1) and "If you make the LORD your refuge, if you make the Most High your shelter, no evil will conquer you; no plague will come near your home" (Psalm 91:9-10).

God comes back to this theme over and over, driving home the point. You can't find a location on earth where God is not your refuge and home. You are always at home because home is where your heart is. Even if you are trying to escape him, you can't find a place where God is not fully present. Maybe someone you love is away from you. Maybe you don't even know where that one is, and your heart aches with the pain of separation and uncertainty. Let these words bring comfort to you. God is where you cannot be:

> I CAN NEVER ESCAPE FROM YOUR SPIRIT!
>   I CAN NEVER GET AWAY FROM YOUR PRESENCE! . . .
> IF I RIDE THE WINGS OF THE MORNING,
>   IF I DWELL BY THE FARTHEST OCEANS,
> EVEN THERE YOUR HAND WILL GUIDE ME,
>   AND YOUR STRENGTH WILL SUPPORT ME.

Psalm 139:7, 9-10

You are never out of God's presence, and those you love and long to protect are never out of his presence either.

Thank you, Father, that you are always my home and my refuge. Thank you that those I love and for whose restoration I pray cannot find a place on the planet where you are not.

Jennifer

We may ignore, but we can nowhere evade, the presence of God.
—C. S. LEWIS (1898–1963), Irish novelist, literary critic, and essayist

BLOOD FROM A TURNIP, WATER FROM A ROCK

THE LORD SPREAD A CLOUD ABOVE THEM AS A COVERING
AND GAVE THEM A GREAT FIRE TO LIGHT THE DARKNESS.
THEY ASKED FOR MEAT, AND HE SENT THEM QUAIL;
HE SATISFIED THEIR HUNGER WITH MANNA. . . .
HE SPLIT OPEN A ROCK, AND WATER GUSHED OUT
TO FORM A RIVER THROUGH THE DRY WASTELAND.

Psalm 105:39-41

THESE VERSES describe how God demonstrated his promise to take care of his people.

His presence changed forms to become what the Israelites needed at any given moment. During the day, a cloud was their covering. As they walked through scorching desert, God provided a cloud to provide shade and protect them from the heat of the sun. Perhaps the covering cloud also hid them from enemies, a common use of the cloud metaphor. The cloud hid God's people under God's active presence.

At night, God's presence appeared as a pillar of fire. Lighting the way, warming the air around them, intimidating their enemies. Whatever the people needed, God was: "He guided them during the day with a pillar of cloud, and he provided light at night with a pillar of fire. This allowed them to travel by day or by night. And the LORD did not remove the pillar of cloud or pillar of fire from its place in front of the people" (Exodus 13:21-22).

God also fed them, not merely to meet their needs but even with the delicacy of quail. The people never went without nourishment. God's provision never failed even one day of their forty-year journey.

Have you heard the expression "You can't get blood from a turnip"? You might just as well say, "You can't get water from a rock." Except when you can: "[God] split open the rocks in the wilderness to give them water, as from a gushing spring. He made streams pour from the rock, making the waters flow down like a river!" (Psalm 78:15-16). God made water gush from a rock, and his provision was so abundant that the millions of Israelites and their livestock drank their fill!

We may walk through deserts, but the provision of the Lord will always be ours.

Father, you are my provider. Your provision never fails. I look to you.

Jennifer

The vision of the Divine Presence ever takes the form which our circumstances most require.

—**ALEXANDER MACLAREN** (1826–1910), British preacher and Bible expositor

6 ALWAYS AND FOREVER

THERE WERE MANY PRIESTS UNDER THE OLD SYSTEM, FOR DEATH
PREVENTED THEM FROM REMAINING IN OFFICE. BUT BECAUSE JESUS
LIVES FOREVER, HIS PRIESTHOOD LASTS FOREVER. THEREFORE HE
IS ABLE, ONCE AND FOREVER, TO SAVE THOSE WHO COME TO GOD
THROUGH HIM. HE LIVES FOREVER TO INTERCEDE WITH GOD ON
THEIR BEHALF.

Hebrews 7:23-25

THE WRITER of Hebrews makes the case that the high priest of the old system, a human,
was able to effect only a temporary and partial salvation. The priest himself had sins that had
to be atoned for before he could then offer the prescribed sacrifices to atone for the sins of
the people. Because the blood was that of goats and bulls and could not make eternal atonement, the ritual had to be repeated daily. A second problem was that no priest could serve
permanently because he would die and be replaced. So the old system was a placeholder,
waiting for the eternal High Priest and the eternal sacrifice to appear and bring a complete
and eternal salvation.

That is the point of the discussion when the writer inserts this wonderful promise.
Jesus, the real High Priest, has neither of the weaknesses of the old system. Because he has
no sins of his own to atone for, he can pour out his whole life for *our* sins. It costs that High
Priest a whole life to pay for all our sins, but he can save once and for always. And because
he lives forever, his priesthood has the power of his indestructible life. He is a priest forever and can save completely.

He is the High Priest, and also the sacrifice. He offered himself. The perfect Priest
offered the perfect sacrifice and now lives forever in the Father's presence, making unending intercession on our behalf. Jesus is our Advocate in the throne room, and his work on
our behalf is without intermission.

*Jesus, thank you for being my eternal High Priest as well as the complete sacrifice
for my sins. I rest in the fact that you are always interceding for me in the power of
your indestructible eternal life.*

Jennifer

In his life, Christ is an example, showing us how to live; in his death, he is a sacrifice,
satisfying for our sins; in his resurrection, a conqueror; in his ascension, a king;
in his intercession, a high priest.

—**MARTIN LUTHER** (1483–1546), German theologian and reformer

UNCLAIMED RICHES

THE PEOPLE REFUSED TO ENTER THE PLEASANT LAND,
FOR THEY WOULDN'T BELIEVE HIS PROMISE TO CARE
FOR THEM.
INSTEAD, THEY GRUMBLED IN THEIR TENTS
AND REFUSED TO OBEY THE LORD.

Psalm 106:24-25

AS THE ISRAELITES arrived at the border of the land God had promised them, Moses sent in twelve men to get a feel for the situation. When they returned, ten of the twelve reported that there were giants in the land and that the Israelites would be like grasshoppers to them. The people decided to let their fear direct their decisions. The Israelites did not wonder whether or not God had led them to the land or whether or not God was telling them to go into the land. That was a given. But they did not have faith *in God*.

Listen to them whine: "The whole community began weeping aloud, and they cried all night. Their voices rose in a great chorus of protest against Moses and Aaron. 'If only we had died in Egypt, or even here in the wilderness!' they complained. 'Why is the LORD taking us to this country only to have us die in battle? Our wives and our little ones will be carried off as plunder!'" (Numbers 14:1-3). Here is unbelief—choosing to believe their own perceptions and intentionally choosing not to trust God. Refusing, intentionally and rebelliously, to obey God because they did not have faith in him. They aligned themselves with the enemy's lies and agreed with fear. They had faith—but not in God. They put their faith in fear and trusted that failure would be the result of obeying God.

Unbelief will cause you to intentionally dismiss God's power in favor of your own abilities. Read in Hebrews 3:19 the effect of unbelief: "We see that they were not able to enter, because of their unbelief" (NIV).

God promises that when we line ourselves up with him and his truth, no giant will stand in our way.

Lord, I believe. I will not choose to believe what I perceive with my senses over what you have promised.

Jennifer

Surely scripture is right when it makes the sin of sins that unbelief, which is at bottom nothing else than a refusal to take the cup of salvation. Surely no sharper grief can be inflicted upon the Spirit of God than when we leave His gifts neglected and unappropriated.

—ALEXANDER MACLAREN (1826–1910), British preacher and Bible expositor

8

A NEW AND LIVING WAY

BY THESE REGULATIONS THE HOLY SPIRIT REVEALED THAT THE
ENTRANCE TO THE MOST HOLY PLACE WAS NOT FREELY OPEN
AS LONG AS THE TABERNACLE AND THE SYSTEM IT REPRESENTED
WERE STILL IN USE. . . . THE GIFTS AND SACRIFICES THAT THE
PRIESTS OFFER ARE NOT ABLE TO CLEANSE THE CONSCIENCES OF
THE PEOPLE WHO BRING THEM.

Hebrews 9:8-9

THE OLD TESTAMENT systems for worship and sacrifice were promises of what—or who—was to come. They pointed to the time when all the promises of God would be fleshed out in Jesus. Today we live in the fulfillment of that promise.

In today's verses the writer is describing the portion of the Tabernacle called the Most Holy Place, or Holy of Holies. The high priest entered the Most Holy Place once a year on the Day of Atonement to offer sacrifices, first for his own sins and then for the sins of the people. The Most Holy Place—the presence of God—was not freely open until the shadow version—the Tabernacle made by human hands and of earthly materials—was replaced by the real Way into God's presence, Jesus himself.

The sacrifices offered by the priests could not finish the job. They had to be repeated in an endless cycle. The sacrifices could not cleanse people's consciences. Though God had extended his grace and mercy through a system that would temporarily *cover* sins and restore the relationship between God and his people, the real remedy would not just cover sin but wash it away.

Jesus, our High Priest, has entered the eternal Most Holy Place with his own blood. His blood washes us clean inside. His blood takes the guilt and shame of our sin that stains our consciences and scrubs us whiter than snow. The veil that hid the Holy of Holies is gone, and we can enter freely into the Most Holy Place—the place of his presence.

*Jesus, thank you that your blood flows in a cleansing fountain through my life,
paying for my sins and making me pure. You have opened the way for me to live
in your presence.*

Jennifer

I am as sure as I live that nothing is so near to me as God. God is nearer to me than I am to
myself; my existence depends on the nearness and the presence of God.

—MEISTER ECKHART (c. 1260 – c. 1327), German theologian and philosopher

RECALL AND REPORT

THOSE WHO ARE WISE WILL TAKE ALL THIS TO HEART;
THEY WILL SEE IN OUR HISTORY THE FAITHFUL LOVE OF
THE LORD.

Psalm 107:43

IN PSALM 107, the psalmist gives a rundown of God's dealings with his people. The psalm opens with exhilarated praise: "Give thanks to the LORD, for he is good! His faithful love endures forever. Has the LORD redeemed you? Then speak out!" (Psalm 107:1-2).

Then he goes through a list of the ways that God has made his presence known to his people. We see in this litany two things about God's dealings. He brings and allows difficulties meant to correct and redirect. But he is always there. When his people call out to him, he snatches them to safety. Over and over his faithfulness is evident in their lives. The psalmist is calling the people to review and remember and celebrate.

The Lord calls us to remember and to report. Remembering God's faithfulness in our lives builds our faith. It gives birth to praise and celebration. When I am struggling with present circumstances, I get out old prayer journals and review the many times God has proven true to his promises. It brings faith back to life. When I talk to a prayer partner about it and report God's past faithfulness, I find my faith growing bolder. Something about sharing God's faithfulness with another solidifies my faith further.

The history the psalmist recounted in Psalm 107 includes what happened when the people were not faithful. It incorporates the times when God proved himself true because what he had said would happen if the people rebelled did indeed happen. Going their own way took them off course every time. But merciful, gracious God was always there, ready to rescue.

God promises that he will be faithful to us, and that his Word is true. When we recall his work, that promise takes firm hold in our hearts. Respond to him in the present in light of all he has proved in the past.

Lord, I recall all the ways that you have been faithful and gracious to me. Remind me when I forget. Call your work to my attention, and then anchor it in my memory. I will recall and report.

Jennifer

Religion . . . is in essence the response of the created personalities to the Creating Personality, God.

—A. W. TOZER (1897–1963), American preacher and author

10 GOD'S GLORY

I WILL THANK YOU, LORD, AMONG ALL THE PEOPLE.
I WILL SING YOUR PRAISES AMONG THE NATIONS.
FOR YOUR UNFAILING LOVE IS HIGHER THAN THE HEAVENS.
YOUR FAITHFULNESS REACHES TO THE CLOUDS.

Psalm 108:3-4

DURING WORLD WAR II, missionary Gladys Aylward was making a dangerous journey from Yangcheng over the mountains toward free China, leading more than a hundred orphans whose parents had been slaughtered by the Japanese. If she could get the children to an orphanage in free China, they would be safe, but there were hundreds of miles to go—on foot.

To keep the children walking, the missionary led them in singing hymns of God's unfailing love. Mile by mile they continued to praise the Lord . . . until they reached the Yellow River, so vast that no one had ever swum across and survived. The Japanese had closed the river, and Gladys was afraid they would die there. Weary, starving, and with no hope of reaching safety, Gladys spent a sleepless night. Her thirteen-year-old adopted daughter saw how distressed she was and reminded her of Moses and how God had parted the Red Sea so the Israelites could cross.

"But I am not Moses!" Gladys cried in desperation.

"Of course you aren't," the young girl said. "But Jehovah is still God!"

These few hope-filled words turned Gladys's focus from the impossibility of their situation to the God whose unfailing love reaches to the clouds. She led the children in thanking God, and they began singing praises once again. Before long a Chinese nationalist down the river heard what he thought might be an Allied helicopter. When he saw it was a woman and children singing, he risked his life to carry boatloads of orphans across the river. Gladys and the children made it safely through the mountains to the orphanage, not only proving God's faithfulness to them but also bringing God glory as other believers heard the story.

God, just as you were faithful to this missionary, you promise to be for me.
I surrender my fears and trust in you to see me through. Grant me grace to
praise and thank you this day and to see your glory, no matter what!

Cheri

In God's faithfulness lies eternal security.

—**CORRIE TEN BOOM** (1892–1983), Dutch author, speaker, and concentration camp survivor

THE MOST HOLY PLACE

WE CAN BOLDLY ENTER HEAVEN'S MOST HOLY PLACE BECAUSE
OF THE BLOOD OF JESUS. BY HIS DEATH, JESUS OPENED A NEW AND
LIFE-GIVING WAY THROUGH THE CURTAIN INTO THE MOST HOLY
PLACE.

Hebrews 10:19-20

MANY FOLKS see prayer as a duty or obligation, but to really gain a perspective of the value and gift of prayer, we need to look to the Old Testament when God's people had no direct access to the Lord. They had to stand in the outer court of the Temple, away from God's presence, while once a year the high priest went into the Most Holy Place (on the other side of the sixty-by-twenty-foot-by-four—inch curtain so heavy it took three hundred men to move it) to minister to the Lord with sacrifices and intercede for the people.

But when Jesus cried out on the cross, "It is finished!" and yielded his spirit to the Father (see John 19:30), in that instant the curtain in the Holy of Holies tore from top to bottom. Because of Christ's death on the cross, fallen humanity was no longer separated from God, and a new, life-giving way was opened for us. Now we (not just high priests or ministers) are welcomed into God's throne room, to be in relationship with our Father and to pray directly to him 24–7 every day of our lives!

Many people try to reach God, especially when there are hurricanes, accidents, financial calamity, or other disasters that touch us or our loved ones. Thousands of faxes and e-mails are sent to God weekly in care of the Wailing Wall in Jerusalem. Countless people search for God on the Internet. But the remarkable news is that we *can* reach God; he has already provided a way through the life, death, and resurrection of his Son.

*Blessed be your name, oh Lord, for providing a way into intimate relationship
with you. Words can't express my gratefulness and awe!*

Cheri

When I am in trouble, and when I go to my friend, I don't want anything from him except himself. I just want to be with him . . . to feel his comradeship, his concern, his caring . . . and then to go out to a world warmer because I spent an hour with him. It must be that way with me and God. I must go to him simply for himself.

—**WILLIAM BARCLAY** (1907–1978), Scottish author and minister

12 THE REWARD OF CONFIDENT FAITH

FAITH IS THE CONFIDENCE THAT WHAT WE HOPE FOR WILL
ACTUALLY HAPPEN; IT GIVES US ASSURANCE ABOUT THINGS WE
CANNOT SEE. THROUGH THEIR FAITH, THE PEOPLE IN DAYS OF
OLD EARNED A GOOD REPUTATION.

Hebrews 11:1-2

I LOVE Hebrews 11, where the "Hall of Faith" lists those who obeyed God: Abel, Enoch, and Noah, Abraham and Sarah—faithful ones who believed and welcomed the promises of God. The Lord set his favor and approval on them because they believed things they couldn't see and hoped for what was going to happen with confident assurance.

This passage also reminds me of a little boy I knew who was diagnosed with leukemia and endured aggressive chemotherapy, radiation, and a bone marrow transplant—all before he was a year old. But after treatment and five years of remission, Michael faced a new challenge: a large mass had formed on the bone. Facing tests and possible surgery, seven-year-old Michael prayed and put "Mr. Lump," his name for the mass, in Jesus' hand. Every night at bedtime prayers with his family, Michael asked Jesus to take Mr. Lump away. As he prayed, he possessed a confident, simple trust that enabled him to leave his lump with Jesus. Where most of us are tempted to pick up our "lumps," take them back again and try to carry them ourselves, Michael trusted his lump to God.

A week later, Michael had a series of tests, including a bone scan, an MRI, and an ultrasound. From the results of those tests, the doctors told the family they believed the lump was a benign mass produced by previous chemo and nothing to worry about. But Michael already knew not to worry; he trusted God and had faith in God's ability to heal—and his faith was rewarded.

*Lord, grant me the faith of a child, the assurance that you are good and you
are in control, and the grace to believe and welcome your promises into my life.
Amen.*

Cheri

We need to learn to know [God] so well that we feel safe when we have left our difficulties with him. To know Jesus in that way is a prerequisite of all true prayer.

—OLE HALLESBY (1879–1961), Norwegian pastor and writer

GLORY AND MAJESTY

How amazing are the deeds of the LORD!
All who delight in him should ponder them.
Everything he does reveals his glory and majesty.

Psalm 111:2-3

ONE SUNDAY morning I sat with our young children at church. As I joined the congregation in singing, a fountain of thanksgiving flowed through me to our glorious Savior, who had done something amazing in our lives earlier that morning.

Our son, who had suffered with severe asthma since he was four, had begun an asthma attack on Saturday and had worsened steadily through the day. We gave him his usual medicine but felt there a missing puzzle piece, something we didn't know to help our son.

In our bookshelf, we found a little workbook on what the Bible says about healing and wholeness. By bedtime, we had filled our coffee cups and tucked the two younger kids in bed. With our son on the couch so we could watch over him, we began looking up verses and writing them in the workbook. At three that morning we read a passage from James 5 that said when someone is sick to call the church elders to pray over him and anoint him with oil in Christ's name. Although we'd never noticed that verse before or seen that kind of prayer practiced in the church we attended, our motivation soared when we read the next verse, "Such a prayer offered in faith will heal the sick, and the Lord will make you well" (James 5:15).

We called two young pastors, who came at daybreak and prayed for our son. They anointed him with oil, as the Bible says to do. Within moments, his bronchial tubes cleared and his breathing returned to normal. He sat up with a rosy color back in his cheeks and his blue eyes shining brightly as God's glory and presence filled the room and our hearts.

What has God done in your life or loved ones that has revealed his glory? This passage calls us to remember, to ponder those deeds, and to give the Lord praise.

Lord, may we never forget your amazing deeds. Grant us faith and grace to share them with others, and fill us with praise. For Jesus' sake, amen.

Cheri

God joyfully employs an infinite variety of means to bring health and well-being to his people. We are glad for God's friends, the doctors. . . . We also celebrate the growing army of women and men and children who are learning how to bring the healing power of Christ to others for the glory of God and the good of all concerned.

—RICHARD FOSTER (1942–), American minister and author

14 KEEPING OUR EYES ON JESUS

LET US RUN WITH ENDURANCE THE RACE GOD HAS SET BEFORE US. WE DO THIS BY KEEPING OUR EYES ON JESUS, THE CHAMPION WHO INITIATES AND PERFECTS OUR FAITH.

Hebrews 12:1-2

THERE ARE so many things that can hinder our spiritual progress, so many weights that slow us down and derail us from God's purpose for our lives. Yet inherent in this passage from Hebrews is a precious promise that assures us we can run the race God marked out for each of us *if* we keep our eyes on Jesus. How important is this? It means the difference between victory and defeat, living in faith or living in doubt, accomplishing our purpose on earth or giving up.

Amy Carmichael, missionary to India and founder of the Dohnavur Fellowship, found that the more we know of the person we're looking at, the more we see, and the more our eyes are able to see of the Lord Jesus, the more we can keep our eyes on him. Even this great woman of faith, who rescued countless Indian children from temple abuse for fifty-five years, experienced times when she was caught in the crush of life, pushed down, and tempted to lose her focus. She learned it takes a very intentional effort to look up to the Lord and turn her attention to him. But when she did, she was able to keep going no matter what happened—in times of physical suffering, when funds were lacking, and through waves of other difficulties.

When you and I turn from focusing on ourselves to keeping our eyes on the Author and Finisher of our faith, we, too, will be filled with life, joy, and peace.

Father, I want to keep my eyes on Jesus. Help me and give me grace to consciously turn my eyes away from my problems and the things of this world to the one upon whom my faith depends from start to finish. In the name above all names, amen.

Cheri

Keep looking in the right direction in everything you do; this is so important. Keep looking up and kneeling down.

—**CORRIE TEN BOOM** (1892–1983), Dutch author, speaker, and concentration camp survivor

GOD'S PROMISE

WHEN GOD SPOKE FROM MOUNT SINAI HIS VOICE SHOOK THE
EARTH, BUT NOW HE MAKES ANOTHER PROMISE: "ONCE AGAIN I
WILL SHAKE NOT ONLY THE EARTH BUT THE HEAVENS ALSO." THIS
MEANS THAT THE THINGS ON EARTH WILL BE SHAKEN, SO THAT
ONLY ETERNAL THINGS WILL BE LEFT.

Hebrews 12:26-27

THE SCRIPTURES describe the Lord's voice as so powerful that when he speaks, the
mighty cedars are split and shattered. His voice strikes with lightning bolts and makes the
desert quake (see Psalm 29) and shakes everything that can be shaken. When God acts,
nothing can thwart his purposes or will, and he never breaks a promise. This passage from
Hebrews describes an important promise: the voice of God will ultimately shake not only
the earth but also the heavens. When this final shaking takes place, God will recreate the
heavens and the earth. As one scholar said, "What remains after this cataclysmic event will
be eternal."

However, when things start shaking here on earth, it may not be a pretty picture; it
can, in fact, cause great anxiety and fear in us. When the stock market falls hundreds of
points, businesses, investors, and the whole economic system experience a great financial
shaking. When a devastating, terminal disease strikes us personally, our plans are shaken,
and our faith may be tested. When disasters such as tsunamis, earthquakes, or hurricanes
hit, whole communities and countries are shaken to the core.

Yet during apparent chaos and cataclysmic events, we are to remember that God is still
on his throne. There is absolutely no panic in heaven! These are the times when his mercies
are on display. As Psalm 113:4 declares, "The LORD is high above the nations; his glory is
higher than the heavens." When all that can be shaken on earth and in our personal lives is
shaken, in whom will we trust and hope?

> Oh Lord our God, you are higher than the heavens and your voice shakes the
> earth. When all around me are dazed by the surprising shakings, help me trust
> in you and your eternal plan. Only you are worthy of trust, praise, honor, and
> glory.
>
> *Cheri*

God is never in a panic, nothing can be done that he is not absolutely Master of. . . . God
alters the inevitable when we get in touch with him.

—**OSWALD CHAMBERS** (1874–1917), Scottish minister and teacher

16 GOD NEVER FAILS

God has said,

"I will never fail you.
I will never abandon you."

So we can say with confidence,

"The Lord is my helper,
so I will have no fear."

Hebrews 13:5-6

A WOMAN who survived the 1995 bombing of the Murrah Federal Building in Oklahoma City struggled terribly at the memorial services. She was still dealing with physical and emotional trauma herself and was in constant pain. Seated in a wheelchair, she wrestled with God about why he hadn't rescued her dear friends and coworkers, who were dedicated Christians.

Then she recalled how God's presence had been so real to her when she had fallen nine stories and was buried under concrete. When the rescuer held her hand until they could get her out, it was like Jesus' hand. His Spirit spoke through her thoughts, reminding her to breathe slowly and keep calm so she could get oxygen in the small space. Wherever she was, Jesus was *with her*.

In the hospital and through the comfort of friends and strangers, Jesus' presence surrounded her. She knew God was with her friends who died. She also knew that when it's time for her to join those precious friends, she won't fear, for Jesus will be with her. This knowledge and continuing experience of God's presence sustained her during months of pain and grieving, bringing her into more freedom than she had ever known before.

From the time we surrender our lives to God, his care for us is secure. He does not break his promise that he'll be with us and never abandon us. He will never forsake us or relax his hold on us. What a Savior!

Thank you, Lord our God, that you promise us to be with us, to help us, and never to fail or forsake us! We can take refuge in you and count on your goodness and mercy all the days of our lives. With all my heart I praise you!

Cheri

Dear Lord, never let me be afraid to pray for the impossible.
—DOROTHY SHELLENBERGER (1918–), American writer

EVERYDAY WISDOM

IF YOU NEED WISDOM, ASK OUR GENEROUS GOD, AND HE WILL
GIVE IT TO YOU. HE WILL NOT REBUKE YOU FOR ASKING. BUT
WHEN YOU ASK HIM, BE SURE THAT YOUR FAITH IS IN GOD ALONE.
DO NOT WAVER, FOR A PERSON WITH DIVIDED LOYALTY IS AS
UNSETTLED AS A WAVE OF THE SEA THAT IS BLOWN AND TOSSED BY
THE WIND.

James 1:5-6

ONCE ONE of our children and I were going head-to-head. He was mad that we wouldn't buy him a certain kind of trendy pants and irritated with reminders to clean his room and stop bugging his sister. I wanted him to talk with me, at least a little, but he clammed up. I wanted him to know how much I loved him, yet irritations pushed us further apart. Despite my efforts, nothing changed.

So I began to pray for our relationship, believing God's promise in today's verses. The Lord Almighty doesn't mind our lack of wisdom if we ask for his—in fact, he delights in sharing his divine wisdom with his children (even if we are parents).

One morning in a quiet time, I heard his Spirit whisper, *You're the one who needs to change. Accept your son just as he is, enjoy and appreciate him, ten-year-old quirks and all.* That message prompted me to humbly pray, "Lord, change *me*! Make me a more loving, understanding mom who sees my precious son through your eyes. Give me your wisdom in relating to him."

As God worked in my heart, I realized I needed to overlook the "minors" and focus on the "majors" and spend more time doing things he enjoyed. I asked him if he'd like to shoot hoops with me after school, and as we did, my usually quiet son began to share his thoughts: things happening at school, what he was frustrated about, what his hopes and dreams were. Closeness grew between us as I found new ways to encourage him with notes in his lunch bag and on his mirror. The everyday wisdom God supplied made all the difference for this mom!

Lord, thank you for caring about all the details in our lives and for supplying the wisdom we need to do life, parenting, work, and relationships. Thank you that long before we loved you, you loved us!

Cheri

Wisdom is oftentimes nearer when we stoop than when we soar.
—**WILLIAM WORDSWORTH** (1770–1850), English poet

18 HEAR AND DO

IF YOU LISTEN TO THE WORD AND DON'T OBEY, IT IS LIKE
GLANCING AT YOUR FACE IN A MIRROR. YOU SEE YOURSELF,
WALK AWAY, AND FORGET WHAT YOU LOOK LIKE. BUT IF YOU
LOOK CAREFULLY INTO THE PERFECT LAW THAT SETS YOU FREE,
AND IF YOU DO WHAT IT SAYS AND DON'T FORGET WHAT YOU
HEARD, THEN GOD WILL BLESS YOU FOR DOING IT.

James 1:23-25

JAMES COMPARES God's Word to a mirror. We see our true selves reflected in it, warts and all.

What if a person looked intently into a mirror, noticed that he had a smear on his cheek or that his hair was standing on end, then went away and forgot what he saw that he could have corrected? I think James is making a joke.

But the Word of God has the same effect on a spiritual level. It shows us how to make corrections in our lives. We gaze into the perfect law—the law that will set us free from our sins and entangling patterns of behavior—and let it change us. We hear it, and then we do it. We make the changes and adjustments the Word shows us we need.

This is not a new problem. God addressed it with Ezekiel generations before James wrote his epistle: "My people come pretending to be sincere and sit before you. They listen to your words, but they have no intention of doing what you say. . . . You are very entertaining to them, like someone who sings love songs with a beautiful voice or plays fine music on an instrument. They hear what you say, but they don't act on it!" (Ezekiel 33:31-32).

God promises that his Word will reveal you. The saying goes, "You don't read the Word of God so much as the Word of God reads you." Respond to what the Word reveals about you, and find the blessed life God means for you to have.

Living Word of God, speak to me and reveal the hidden places of my heart.
Empower me to take the steps your Word points me to, so I can live in your blessing.

Jennifer

A readiness to believe every promise implicitly, to obey every command unhesitatingly, to stand perfect and complete in all the will of God, is the only true spirit of Bible study.

—**ANDREW MURRAY** (1828–1917), South African pastor and author

THE POWER OF WORDS

> THE TONGUE IS A SMALL PART OF THE BODY, BUT IT MAKES GREAT BOASTS. CONSIDER WHAT A GREAT FOREST IS SET ON FIRE BY A SMALL SPARK. THE TONGUE ALSO IS A FIRE, A WORLD OF EVIL AMONG THE PARTS OF THE BODY. IT CORRUPTS THE WHOLE BODY, SETS THE WHOLE COURSE OF ONE'S LIFE ON FIRE, AND IS ITSELF SET ON FIRE BY HELL.
>
> *James 3:5-6* (NIV)

THE OLD ADAGE, "Sticks and stones may break my bones, but words will never hurt me" doesn't hold up. Words can cause wounds that are deep and crippling, though unseen. These wounds, left untended, can be like an ulcer on the soul—spilling poisonous bile a little at a time until the cumulative effect is disabling.

God created words, of course, and designed them to be powerful. Our words are modeled after his. Our words are a scaled down version, to be sure, but still we were created by a speaking God who made us in his image. His words created the earth. His words ordered cells and molecules into alignment. His words sustain the earth and keep the planets in their orderly rotation.

He gave us words. Our tongues deliver those words into the lives of others. Because God does not command us to do what he cannot empower us to do, I believe we can take James 3:5-6 as a promise that our tongues can be put at the Spirit's disposal to be his instruments of hope and encouragement.

Words, once spoken, live on. Those words you speak to your teenager, thinking they are going in one ear and out the other? They are landing and making themselves a home. The words you thought you could throw out in a huff and apologize for later? They've carved out a nook and settled in. The words of kindness and encouragement that seemed to be ignored? They are fertilizing dreams.

Make it your goal to speak into others' lives such a preponderance of uplifting, encouraging words that they will eventually tip the balance and move a life from discouragement to hope.

Father, change my heart so profoundly that the words that flow from it are your healing, uplifting words.

 Jennifer

Kind words do not cost much. Yet they accomplish much.
—**BLAISE PASCAL** (1623–1662), French mathematician and philosopher

20 AN END TO QUARRELS

WHAT IS CAUSING THE QUARRELS AND FIGHTS AMONG YOU?
DON'T THEY COME FROM THE EVIL DESIRES AT WAR WITHIN
YOU? . . . WHEN YOU ASK, YOU DON'T GET IT BECAUSE YOUR
MOTIVES ARE ALL WRONG—YOU WANT ONLY WHAT WILL
GIVE YOU PLEASURE.

James 4:1, 3

FEW THINGS can distract us from the Lord's voice like being at odds with those around us. In today's verses, James pinpoints the reason behind quarreling and contention. He isolates evil desires at war within a person as the crux of the problem. The word translated "evil desires" simply means strong, intense desires. The word is neutral as to good or bad. In this case, those desires have become misdirected. They probably started out as legitimate desires, but we try to get them met outside of God's provision, so they get warped, and instead of drawing us toward God, they put a wedge between us and others.

For example, our desire for love and acceptance is built in by the Creator and is meant to be his entry point into our lives. When we turn that desire outward and expect others to love us as we want to be loved, it backfires. No one can fill that role. That sloshes over into the desire for possessions and position as we try to feel loved and valued.

James says we should turn that desire to God to find fulfillment of our longings. Otherwise that same desire will put us into conflict with those around us.

He concludes by saying that when we do ask God for something, we tend want to spend it on our own desires. It's not that God never wants our desires to be fulfilled, but in this situation he withholds fulfillment because we are trying to acquire something that will fill the space in our hearts reserved for him. Getting what we asked for in this case would diminish us instead of enhancing us.

God promises not only to protect us from our misdirected desires but also to give us all good things.

Father, I trust your decisions about how you want to fulfill the needs and desires in my life.

Jennifer

Nothing is won by force. I choose to be gentle. If I raise my voice may it be only in praise. If I clench my fist, may it be only in prayer. If I make a demand, may it be only of myself.

—**MAX LUCADO** (1955–), American pastor and author

POWER PRAYING 21

THE EARNEST PRAYER OF A RIGHTEOUS PERSON HAS GREAT
POWER AND PRODUCES WONDERFUL RESULTS. ELIJAH WAS AS
HUMAN AS WE ARE, AND YET WHEN HE PRAYED EARNESTLY THAT
NO RAIN WOULD FALL, NONE FELL FOR THREE AND A HALF YEARS!
THEN, WHEN HE PRAYED AGAIN, THE SKY SENT DOWN RAIN AND
THE EARTH BEGAN TO YIELD ITS CROPS.

James 5:16-18

PRAYER HAS POWER, and prayer produces an effect. Prayer is the means by which the power of heaven is moved into the circumstances of earth.

James expects his readers to know the story of Elijah. He expects his readers to see that this is a synopsis of the story, not two sentences that stand alone. If you were to read these two sentences without putting them in their bigger setting, it might sound as if Elijah one day decided that a drought would be a good idea and began to ask God for it. This was not the case.

The story to which James is referring is found in 1 Kings 17, where a prophet named Elijah first comes on the scene. He presents himself before wicked King Ahab and pronounces himself the ambassador coming from his King—the Lord God. He gives Ahab his King's pronouncement. It will not rain on the land until Elijah's King says it will.

James says that Elijah prayed that it would not rain. Was Elijah trying to convince God? Trying to influence God to carry out Elijah's plan? No, Elijah prayed because he knew that prayer is the conduit through which God's power flows. God, having revealed his intention to Elijah, was calling Elijah to pray.

Then, James says, Elijah prayed for the drought to end. God revealed to Elijah that he was ready to end the drought, and Elijah cooperated with God by praying—again bringing the power of heaven to bear on the circumstances of earth.

God promises that our prayers are not in vain. He promises that our praying, in cooperation with his work on the earth, has great power and produces wonderful results.

Father, may the Spirit of prayer move in me, aligning my heart with yours.

Jennifer

In the first place, it is not our prayers that move the Lord Jesus, but the Lord Jesus who moves us to pray.

—OLE HALLESBY (1879–1961), Norwegian pastor and writer

22 UNFOLDING TRUTH

OPEN MY EYES TO SEE
THE WONDERFUL TRUTHS IN YOUR INSTRUCTIONS.

Psalm 119:18

JESUS ASKED the Father to reveal truth to us: "Make them holy by your truth; teach them your word, which is truth" (John 17:17). He prayed that the Father would use the truth hidden in his Word to make us holy. The Father always hears and answers the Son (see John 11:41). So we are experiencing the Father's work in response to the Son's words.

Is the truth in God's Word sitting on the surface to be skimmed off by the casual reader? No. The Scriptures make it clear that the treasures of the Word are hidden: "In him lie hidden all the treasures of wisdom and knowledge" (Colossians 2:3). They are hidden in the written Word and in the living Word. The wonderful, rich, consecrating truth is buried. It must be mined, like gold or silver (see Proverbs 2:3-4).

God has deliberately hidden deep truth so that the Holy Spirit, the Spirit of truth, can disclose it. The Spirit, working directly in our minds and understanding, reveals truth. First Corinthians 2:12 tells us that God has given us his Spirit for this purpose: "We have received God's Spirit (not the world's spirit), so we can know the wonderful things God has freely given us." Because we have the Holy Spirit, we can understand what the human intellect alone is unable to comprehend. The truths of God's Word are buried for one purpose—so that you and I can find them.

In the process of revealing "deep and hidden things," God anchors in his children the knowledge that we are totally dependent upon him. Even our understanding of the truth comes directly and only from him. Left to our own devices, we would never see any deeper than the surface. But as we learn directly from him, our intimacy with him is strengthened and enriched.

Father, show me your deep and hidden truths.

Jennifer

It may be indispensable that Our Lord's teaching, by its elusiveness (to our systematising intellect), should demand a response from the whole man, should make it so clear that there is no question of learning a subject but of steeping ourselves in a Personality.

—**C. S. LEWIS** (1898–1963), Irish novelist, literary critic, and essayist

PRICELESS

YOU KNOW THAT GOD PAID A RANSOM TO SAVE YOU FROM
THE EMPTY LIFE YOU INHERITED FROM YOUR ANCESTORS. AND
THE RANSOM HE PAID WAS NOT MERE GOLD OR SILVER. IT WAS
THE PRECIOUS BLOOD OF CHRIST, THE SINLESS, SPOTLESS LAMB
OF GOD. GOD CHOSE HIM AS YOUR RANSOM LONG BEFORE
THE WORLD BEGAN, BUT HE HAS NOW REVEALED HIM TO YOU
IN THESE LAST DAYS.

1 Peter 1:18-20

THE LOVE of God is unfathomable. He paid for our freedom with the precious blood of
the spotless Lamb of God.

How do you decide what something is worth? When you list your possessions for
insurance purposes, how do you establish their value? One element is what you paid for
them. Another is what someone else would be willing to pay. By either measure, we are
precious to the Father.

Among your possessions, are you particularly protective of those with a high value?
People have been known to spend almost as much on protecting a valuable possession as
the possession itself cost: dust-free environments, special lighting, burglar alarms, maybe
even armed guards. All these are evidence of how valued and precious the protected possession is to its owner.

You cost everything the Father had to give. There was no higher price to be paid.
Heaven's most valued asset—the precious blood of Christ—was poured out unstintingly
to ransom you from the emptiness of life and to provide for you the abundant life.

> *God's love is a promise. He would not pay the ultimate price for you and then
> be careless about your life. You can be sure that every precaution has been
> taken. Every protection is in place. You are shielded and sheltered under his
> hand. Father, show me when I dishonor the precious blood of the Lamb by which
> I was redeemed. Teach me to live as one bought with heaven's greatest treasure.*

Jennifer

I have seen the marks of the cross upon Him, and by His grace the marks of the cross have
been put upon me and I am no longer my own; I am bought with a price, redeemed by His
precious blood. Yes, I have seen Him—not in the outward physical sense only, but in
the inward sense of a deep spiritual reality. I have had a clear view of Jesus and
my life will never be the same again.

—ALAN REDPATH (1907–1989), English evangelist, pastor, and author

24 LET THE RIVER FLOW

LIFE WILL FLOURISH WHEREVER THIS WATER FLOWS.

Ezekiel 47:9

IN JOHN'S REVELATION of heaven, he saw exactly what Ezekiel had seen in Ezekiel 47:3-5. "The angel showed me a river with the water of life, clear as crystal, flowing from the throne of God and of the Lamb" (Revelation 22:1).

Jesus defined the river for us: "'Anyone who believes in me may come and drink! For the Scriptures declare, "Rivers of living water will flow from his heart."' (When he said 'living water,' he was speaking of the Spirit)" (John 7:38-39).

Water is nearly always a symbol of the Spirit of God. Ezekiel learned that you can wade on the fringes where the water is ankle deep, or you can plunge into the depths. Where would you like to be?

Let your imagination loose. You've been hiking rough terrain. You are thirsty and wasted and desperate. Listen! Rushing water? Hope turns to anticipation as you run toward the sound and glimpse a river. Cool, fresh, sparkling water rushing in torrents through the landscape. Inviting you. Offering refreshment and relief. All you have to do is immerse yourself in it.

As you peel your shoes and your socks from your tortured feet, already you can feel the water's spray touching you with the offer of renewal. Feel the water as it wraps your feet—your hot, tired, swollen feet. Ahh! Sit still and let the healing waters do their work.

The water courses around you, and you become more aware of its power. Now wade deeper. Walk out until the water is waist high. Not only do you experience the reenergizing effects of the river, but the deeper you go, the more you encounter its power and strength. Now you have to work harder to walk through the water. The river has a path and an agenda of its own, and it pulls at you. Hardest of all is to stand still in the mighty, rushing waters.

Deeper still. Now you have only one option: give yourself to the river's flow. Surrender. God promises that life will flourish in the deep places.

Father, let me drown in you.

Jennifer

As rivers, the nearer they come to the ocean whither they tend, the more they increase their waters, and speed their streams; so will grace flow more fully and freely in its near approaches to the ocean of glory.

—JOHN OWEN (1616–1683), English theologian

DEEP AND HIDDEN THINGS

PRAISE THE NAME OF GOD FOREVER AND EVER,
FOR HE HAS ALL WISDOM AND POWER.
HE CONTROLS THE COURSE OF WORLD EVENTS;
HE REMOVES KINGS AND SETS UP OTHER KINGS.
HE GIVES WISDOM TO THE WISE
AND KNOWLEDGE TO THE SCHOLARS.
HE REVEALS DEEP AND MYSTERIOUS THINGS
AND KNOWS WHAT LIES HIDDEN IN DARKNESS,
THOUGH HE IS SURROUNDED BY LIGHT.
I THANK AND PRAISE YOU, GOD OF MY ANCESTORS,
FOR YOU HAVE GIVEN ME WISDOM AND STRENGTH.
YOU HAVE TOLD ME WHAT WE ASKED OF YOU
AND REVEALED TO US WHAT THE KING DEMANDED.

Daniel 2:20-23

GOD WANTS to work in our lives in such a way that he is the only explanation. He has all wisdom and power and is controlling world events, setting up and removing governments, dispensing wisdom and knowledge.

He reveals the things that we can't know any other way. Things we can't know—by seeing, hearing, or even by imagining—are fully known by God, and he is willing to reveal them to us: "'No eye has seen, no ear has heard, and no mind has imagined what God has prepared for those who love him.' But it was to us that God revealed these things by his Spirit. For his Spirit searches out everything and shows us God's deep secrets" (1 Corinthians 2:9-10).

God promises to reveal what we need to know when we need to know it: "Ask me and I will tell you remarkable secrets you do not know" (Jeremiah 33:3). Where do you need wisdom beyond knowledge or training or skill? Ask him. Nothing is a puzzle or mystery to him, so just ask.

Lord, I surrender to your Spirit in me. I am not leaning on my own understanding or insight. I look to you for understanding and wisdom. Reveal to me those things of which only you are custodian.

Jennifer

God does not reveal information by communication: He reveals Himself by communion. Revelation is a personal meeting of God with man. It is a meeting of mind with mind or person with person.

—SAM STORMS (1951–), American pastor and educator

26 CASTING YOUR ANXIETY

HUMBLE YOURSELVES UNDER THE MIGHTY POWER OF GOD, AND
AT THE RIGHT TIME HE WILL LIFT YOU UP IN HONOR. GIVE ALL
YOUR WORRIES AND CARES TO GOD, FOR HE CARES ABOUT YOU.

1 Peter 5:6-7

RESPONDING TO God's invitation to cast our worries on him takes a good deal of humility. When people can handle things by themselves and have experienced a high degree of success, they can easily become prideful. But humbling ourselves can be very freeing to our souls.

The flip side is this: if we don't follow the advice in today's verses, we can become too burdened down to press on in our calling. God wants us to soar like the eagles and run without fainting, but we won't have the spiritual or physical energy to do this if we're carrying a fifty-pound burden of worry on our backs.

Carol came out of an abusive marriage a number of years ago and was left with no money. Fearful and anxious, she was constantly in crisis-management mode. She worried the tires were going to fall off her old car. She dreaded the first of the month, afraid she couldn't pay her bills. When she heard sirens, she feared her teenage daughter had been in a wreck.

Finally, exhausted and at the end of her rope, Carol cried out to God and slowly realized that he wanted her to give her worries and cares to him because he loved and cared about her deeply. She began to roll her burdens onto God in prayer, and as she did, her energy was renewed. She started her own business and eventually was able to support herself and her daughter, send her daughter to college, and even help others.

You and I are given the same invitation today from the God who holds all power and authority: cast all your worries and cares upon the one who promises to care for you.

Lord, I am prone to be anxious with the unbearable weight of myself and my problems. Yet your Word says you don't want your children to be anxious about anything but to pray about everything. Grant me deep humility and renewed dependence on you to do this day by day.

Cheri

Talk to [God] in prayer of all your wants, your troubles, even of the weariness you feel in serving him. You cannot speak too freely, too trustfully to him.

— **FRANÇOIS FÉNELON** (1651–1715), French theologian, priest, and poet

GOD'S GOODNESS

MAY GOD GIVE YOU MORE AND MORE GRACE AND PEACE AS
YOU GROW IN YOUR KNOWLEDGE OF GOD AND JESUS OUR
LORD. BY HIS DIVINE POWER, GOD HAS GIVEN US EVERYTHING
WE NEED FOR LIVING A GODLY LIFE. WE HAVE RECEIVED ALL OF
THIS BY COMING TO KNOW HIM, THE ONE WHO CALLED US TO
HIMSELF BY MEANS OF HIS MARVELOUS GLORY AND EXCELLENCE.
AND BECAUSE OF HIS GLORY AND EXCELLENCE, HE HAS GIVEN US
GREAT AND PRECIOUS PROMISES.

2 Peter 1:2-4

WHEN JANICE'S husband's law firm went bankrupt, they faced many financial consequences, including not being able to replace their ancient cars. Janice's parents were chronically ill in a neighboring state, and she made recurring trips to help them. After several breakdowns, a more reliable car became a real need.

Janice began to pray about the situation specifically: "Please, Lord, provide a car for our family." Over time, her sense of God's ability to provide for their needs grew. Months went by, and she began to thank God for the vehicle he was going to provide—in his timing.

While taking her girls to swim at a local water park that summer, Janice filled out an entry for a car giveaway.

Two months later she got a call—she was a finalist. "A finalist for what?" she asked, having forgotten about the entry she had filled out. She was invited to the big drawing but was reminded that *out of one million people* who had entered and out of one hundred finalists, *only one* would win.

A week later, Janice stood with the ninety-nine other nervous, excited finalists. When it was her turn, she pulled a key from the basket and inserted it into the car door, and it opened! The car was hers!

Although the example is a dramatic one, the principle remains: our gracious God is intimately involved in the details of our lives, and he delights to show his goodness to his children. Not always on our timetable or the way we expect, but always faithfully.

*Lord, for you nothing is impossible. Thank you for reminding us today of your
grace and mercy and that sometimes you do more than we could ask or imagine.*

Cheri

Think of how good God is! He gives us the physical, mental, and spiritual ability to work in his kingdom, and then he rewards us for doing it!

—ERWIN W. LUTZER (1941–), North American pastor and author

28 GOD'S WAITING ROOM

MY EYES STRAIN TO SEE YOUR RESCUE,
TO SEE THE TRUTH OF YOUR PROMISE FULFILLED.
I AM YOUR SERVANT; DEAL WITH ME IN UNFAILING LOVE,
AND TEACH ME YOUR DECREES.

Psalm 119:123-124

IF YOU ARE straining to see God's promise fulfilled, you are not alone. The Scripture is clear: God ordains waiting periods.

The most difficult part of the process of prayer can be waiting on God. When we fail to recognize the waiting time as an indispensable ingredient in the process, it becomes a time of discouragement and frustration. At those times, many people drop out of the school of prayer. Not receiving their answers as they expected, many conclude that prayer doesn't work, at least not for them.

While the waiting time is the most difficult part of the process, it is also the most important. Our waiting time gives God the opportunity to redefine our desires and align our purpose and vision with his. What appears from the earthly perspective to be a delay on God's part is really the time when God is working in the spiritual realm, beyond our senses. "Faith . . . gives us assurance about things we cannot see" (Hebrews 11:1). During the waiting time, we are operating by faith.

Even though it sometimes appears that prayer isn't working, that God is delaying, the truth is that God is acting in "fulfilled time." God does not act in elapsed time but in fulfilled time. "The time is fulfilled, and the kingdom of God is at hand" (Mark 1:15, NASB). The word "fulfilled" means "filled full." God says, "I am filling your waiting period full. When I have filled it full—when I have done all that I need to do with it—your wait will be over and my Kingdom will be revealed." When the time is ripe, when all the pieces have been put in place, God's answer will be revealed. His concern is not time but timing. Everything has a ripe moment: "For everything there is a season, a time for every activity under heaven" (Ecclesiastes 3:1). God's timing is perfect.

Father, I settle in to this waiting time, trusting your work in realms that I can't see. Thank you for the times you schedule for me to walk by faith.

Jennifer

The prayer that begins with trustfulness, and passes on into waiting, will always end in thankfulness, triumph, and praise.

—ALEXANDER MACLAREN (1826–1910), British preacher and Bible expositor

FROM SACRIFICE TO PRIVILEGE **29**

I RISE EARLY, BEFORE THE SUN IS UP;
   I CRY OUT FOR HELP AND PUT MY HOPE IN YOUR WORDS.
I STAY AWAKE THROUGH THE NIGHT,
   THINKING ABOUT YOUR PROMISE.

Psalm 119:147-148

FOR THE PRACTICES that we know have effect, we will make the time. We have time for what matters to us.

Are you convinced that time spent focused on God makes a difference? If you are, then you will probably get up as early as necessary to have time with him before the day begins and will even focus on him as you wake through the night.

Though I have been teaching about a praying life—a continual flow of prayer—for most of my life, that praying life has to be nourished and undergirded by disciplined times of prayer.

The pursuit of any goal requires a narrowed focus. To hold fast to one goal means to dismiss many others. The pursuit of any goal demands a single-minded diligence.

The more you see the power of God released in response to your prayers, the more excitement you have about prayer. You life's focus will be to see God work in every situation with tremendous power. You will welcome God's purifying work because you know it is freeing you of encumbrances. Choosing to live a praying life—a life through which the power of God is free to flow—involves sacrifice. In this, it is no different from any other rock-solid commitment. Whatever you choose to pursue will require that you sacrifice something else. The key is this: if the goal is sufficiently attractive, the sacrifice necessary will be irrelevant. In fact, the more focused on your goal you are, the less you will perceive the requirements as "sacrifices." What once seemed a sacrifice will soon feel like a privilege. What once was a duty will become a delight.

Father, create in me such a longing for you that sleep is no competition.

Jennifer

We must face the fact that many today are notoriously careless in their living. This attitude finds its way into the church. We have liberty, we have money, we live in comparative luxury. As a result, discipline practically has disappeared. What would a violin solo sound like if the strings on the musician's instrument were all hanging loose, not stretched tight, not "disciplined"?

—A. W. TOZER (1897–1963), American preacher and author

30 STANDING TALL

THOSE WHO LOVE YOUR INSTRUCTIONS HAVE GREAT PEACE AND
DO NOT STUMBLE.

Psalm 119:165

GOD HAS WRITTEN his law on our hearts—encoded it in our DNA. It is not imposed on us. It is built into us. "I will walk in freedom, for I have devoted myself to your commandments" (Psalm 119:45). God's law fits us. We are at home there. There we find contentment, rest, pleasure. "Make me walk along the path of your commands, for that is where my happiness is found" (Psalm 119:35).

When we embrace God's Word and make it our compass, we discover a steadiness and balance that keep us upright even when we are walking treacherous paths. Our steps are sure no matter what. "The LORD directs the steps of the godly. He delights in every detail of their lives. Though they stumble, they will never fall, for the LORD holds them by the hand" (Psalm 37:23-24).

Life is littered with stumbling blocks. Troubled relationships, disappointing circumstances, illness, financial setbacks . . . the list is inexhaustible. God's promise is that none of these will make you fall utterly, without hope of getting up. He does not promise that none of life's difficulties will touch you but that none of them will destroy you. When you are finding your footing in God's law, you are indestructible.

Outward circumstances will never be static or even. Turbulence will always find you eventually. Sorrow will certainly make its appearance in your life, sometimes many times. People will disappoint you. But you don't have to be sucked in to the vortex of life's chaos. You can stand tall and strong when all around you the storms of life roil and rage. Your stability is anchored in God and his ways. You carry your peace inside you, where the stuff of life has no access.

Are circumstances in your life pummeling you and threatening to overwhelm you? Turn your attention to that inward place where the Lawgiver and his law stand strong. Nothing can destroy you.

*Father, thank you for not leaving me at the mercy of circumstances. Thank you
for giving me your law so that I can find traction even when the way is slippery.*

Jennifer

Those that love the world have great vexation, for it does not answer their expectation;
those that love God's word have great peace, for it outdoes their expectation, and in
it they have sure footing.

—MATTHEW HENRY (1662–1714), English pastor and Bible commentator

DECEMBER

LIVING LOVE

I AM NOT WRITING A NEW COMMANDMENT FOR YOU; RATHER IT IS AN OLD ONE YOU HAVE HAD FROM THE VERY BEGINNING. THIS OLD COMMANDMENT—TO LOVE ONE ANOTHER—IS THE SAME MESSAGE YOU HEARD BEFORE. YET IT IS ALSO NEW. JESUS LIVED THE TRUTH OF THIS COMMANDMENT, AND YOU ALSO ARE LIVING IT.

1 John 2:7-8

THE DEFINITIONS of words changed when the living Word fleshed them out in real time on planet earth. The flat, one-dimensional words became multidimensional, real-life, flesh-and-blood realities.

Take the word *love*. It might mean one thing to me and something different to you. We define it as we know it.

Now comes the Word made flesh, *love* made flesh, living out love in daily encounters with both friends and enemies, and saying, "This is my commandment: Love each other in the same way I have loved you. There is no greater love than to lay down one's life for one's friends" (John 15:12-13). Jesus described the highest expression of love: "to lay down one's life for one's friends." Forgive-them-even-while-they're-pounding-nails-in-your-flesh love. Die-for-them-while-they're-still-your-enemies love. Lay-down-your-life-for-them love.

With these altogether new and radical examples, the command took on a whole new complexion: love not just when I feel loving. Love not the way *I* want to love. Love not in the most convenient way, but love to the uttermost, without limit. It's the "in the same way I have loved you" addendum that seals it.

That's a big call, but we live it out in small moments.

Time and time again Jesus calls us to lay down our lives. Not always our physical lives, but our own self-interests, our own schedules, our own comfort. The love to which God calls us is specific and active. It nearly always means setting aside our own interests, even if only momentarily. Rarely is it convenient. It will almost never fit into our schedules where we have a break. It will mean lots of rearranging. Calls to love those around us as Christ loves us come daily. To lay down our daily lives and their self-focused vision. To love others with the love Christ produces in us. If he commands it, then he supplies it. Promise.

Lord, here is my life. I lay it down for you.

Jennifer

Love gives itself. It is not bought.
—HENRY WADSWORTH LONGFELLOW (1807–1882), American poet and educator

2

CLIMBING INTO DADDY'S ARMS

SEE HOW VERY MUCH OUR FATHER LOVES US, FOR HE CALLS US HIS CHILDREN, AND THAT IS WHAT WE ARE! BUT THE PEOPLE WHO BELONG TO THIS WORLD DON'T RECOGNIZE THAT WE ARE GOD'S CHILDREN BECAUSE THEY DON'T KNOW HIM.

1 John 3:1

ONE SUNDAY in church we were singing, "There's no place I'd rather be than in your arms of love, in your arms of love, holding me still, holding me near in your arms of love." As I pondered the words, I noticed Bonnie, a little girl I taught in Sunday school, going up and down the aisles. She had a bewildered look on her face as she passed each row, persistently searching each pew.

Finally she arrived at our aisle and saw her daddy a few seats down from me. She climbed over me, my husband, and several other people and literally leaped up into her father's arms and rested her head on his shoulder. As the song continued, he held her small hand in his, and the biggest smile I've ever seen lit her face. She was home!

This picture of what we were singing about struck me: God wants us to experience the same kind of daddy-love from him that Bonnie did with her father, only much more.

God doesn't ask us to come to him just to make us better, more successful businesspeople or more effective parents. He invites us to climb into his lap by faith and to rest our heads on his loving shoulder. He created us for relationship—first and foremost—with him, our Abba Daddy. What a great opportunity we have to let everything drive us into the arms of our heavenly Father, where he has promised us rest in his everlasting, always-available love.

Abba Daddy, I humbly come to you with all my needs. Thank you for loving me, for having your arms open to me, and for drawing me near to you so I can rest in your great love. In Christ's name, amen.

Cheri

Accustom yourself to the wonderful thought that God loves you with a tenderness, a generosity, and an intimacy which surpasses all your dreams. Give yourself up with joy to a loving confidence in God and have courage to believe firmly that God's action toward you is a masterpiece of partiality and love.

—ABBE HENRI DE TOURVILLE (1842–1903), French priest

LOVE'S SLAVE

DEAR CHILDREN, LET'S NOT MERELY SAY THAT WE LOVE EACH OTHER; LET US SHOW THE TRUTH BY OUR ACTIONS.

1 John 3:18

PAUL WAS CONVINCED that because Christ died for him, he was to live for Christ. Christ's love rules our lives. "Live a life filled with love, following the example of Christ. He loved us and offered himself as a sacrifice for us, a pleasing aroma to God" (Ephesians 5:2). A life of love is made up of small acts of love. Small ways every day that we set aside our own agendas to become fragrant offerings to God, to love our friends, our enemies, even people we don't know personally.

We were created to love—made in the image of God, who is love. The promise is that instead of taking away from our lives, loving others adds to our lives.

Are there things you do for those you love but inwardly harbor feelings of irritation or resentment? Do you pick up your husband's dirty socks, sighing and thinking irritably how many times you've asked him to pick up his own socks? Husband, do you run an errand for your wife feeling resentful that she forgot to make time for it? Do you do the daily chores your role demands for a family that you love but feel put upon because you are the only one who takes the time? Can you identify with scenarios like these?

What if you instead did those mundane, routine, blah, repetitive jobs as if you were offering worship to the Lord? What if you said, "Thank you, Lord, for giving me this avenue to love"? What if you decided to take joy in the acts?

Love as a grand idea or lofty concept boils down to small acts of love. Love in the small things adds up to a life lived in love.

Lord, teach me to live a life of love.

Jennifer

You can give without loving, but you can't love without giving.

—**AMY CARMICHAEL** (1867–1951), Irish missionary to India

4 QUIET IN THE MIDST OF ALARM

SUCH LOVE HAS NO FEAR BECAUSE PERFECT LOVE EXPELS ALL FEAR.

1 John 4:18

WHEN WE were first married, I nearly drove my husband, Holmes, crazy when we were in the car. I was the worst backseat driver ever because of a car accident in my childhood. If Holmes got too close to the car in front of us or was driving on rainy streets, I was sure we were going to have an accident.

But the late April night we were driving through western Oklahoma on the way to Denver with our three children asleep, I was more frightened than I'd ever been. Without warning, blinding snow streamed toward our windshield. The highway was slippery, and we couldn't see the stripes on the two-lane road or anything else because of the blizzard.

Fear rose in me and tension gripped my body. Several times I asked Holmes to slow down, pull over, or stop. He didn't think that was a good idea because we might freeze out there in the cold. My hand gripped the armrest, hoping for some semblance of control. I began to silently pray, *Please help me with this, Lord. I know your love casts out all fear. So I ask you to fill me with your perfect love so I can somehow relax.*

As I continued to pray, a song with a melody I'd never heard came to my consciousness. "When I am afraid, I will trust in you," the words played in my mind. "In God whose word I praise, in God I have put my trust. I will not be afraid, no, I will not be afraid." I started singing it, first in my head and then quietly aloud. As I sang, my fears diminished and my mind quieted. Wrapped in God's presence, I felt the fear being washed away, and my whole body relaxed. Later I found the words of the song were from Psalm 56:3-4. The Spirit brought to my mind verses that I read weeks before just when I needed to be remember them.

Lord, often we humans are fearful about the events swirling about us. Let your perfect love fill us and quiet our hearts.

Cheri

God incarnate is the end of fear; and the heart that realizes that he is in the midst . . . will be quiet in the midst of alarm.

—**F. B. MEYER** (1847–1929), English pastor and evangelist

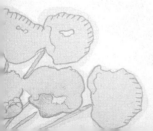

THE HEDGE OF THORNS

I WILL FENCE HER IN WITH THORNBUSHES.
   I WILL BLOCK HER PATH WITH A WALL
   TO MAKE HER LOSE HER WAY.
WHEN SHE RUNS AFTER HER LOVERS,
   SHE WON'T BE ABLE TO CATCH THEM.
SHE WILL SEARCH FOR THEM
   BUT NOT FIND THEM.

Hosea 2:6-7

MAYBE YOU'VE felt like the woman I met at a retreat who tearfully told me, "I've run out of ways to pray for my prodigal, and she is still running away from God and head-long toward destruction." Perhaps the person you are concerned about is your spouse or nephew. Although the story of Hosea's experience with his wife, Gomer, happened thousands of years ago, a prayer inherent in today's passage holds promise for times when we feel at the end of our rope with someone we care about.

Gomer, Hosea's adulterous wife, was constantly running after other lovers. So Hosea pledged to block her path with thornbushes so she couldn't find her way. She would look everywhere but not be able to find her lovers. She would chase after them and not catch them. Hosea hoped that Gomer would then return to him.

When a young person doesn't have the wisdom to see the destructive or deceptive path he or she is on, we can pray, "Lord, I ask you to build a hedge of thorns around (name) to separate this dear one from any influence not ordained by you. I pray that those who would lure my loved one into evil will lose interest and flee. Please place a hedge so she won't be able to contact those who are outside your will." Just as Hosea's actions caused Gomer's lovers to depart, praying this prayer with faith and perseverance can form a double hedge by which God can block wrong influences. Then we can pray that in their frustration our dear ones will turn to God!

Oh Lord my God, teach me to pray with perseverance and faith, knowing that nothing is impossible to you. Help me to wait in trusting expectation for the breakthrough I long for.

Cheri

Prayer must often be "heaped up" until God sees that its measure is full. Then the answer comes. Just as each of ten thousand seeds is a part of the final harvest, frequently repeated, persevering prayer is necessary to acquire a desired blessing.

—ANDREW MURRAY (1828–1917), South African pastor and author

6 LIVING IN THE TRUTH

HOW HAPPY I WAS TO MEET SOME OF YOUR CHILDREN AND FIND THEM LIVING ACCORDING TO THE TRUTH, JUST AS THE FATHER COMMANDED.

2 John 1:4

I WAS READING 2 John with a group of mothers who gathered each week to pray for our college-age children. This verse caused us to think how truly happy each of us would be if we met one another's children someday and found them living in the truth, walking with Christ in their own lives. But just as surely as we discussed how glad we would be, we were reminded of the reality that several of our kids weren't living for Christ and that even if we desired it with all our hearts, we couldn't *make them* live in the truth. We can teach our children well, take them to a good church and school, and build solid foundations of faith in their young lives in every way possible. But only God can change a heart to be fully his!

Only the Lord can shape our children into people who want to follow his commands instead of following the moral downslide in the culture around them. This is an inside job, and we can't do it. The good news, the wonderful promise, is that every time we pray, the Spirit is activated and God's heart-changing power is released. Will it take a lifetime or only a season of prayer? Only God knows.

You may not see the transformation this week or next year, but with each prayer you are building a spiritual legacy that will keep blessing your children, grandchildren, and every generation after them until Christ comes. Long after your sons or daughters are on their own, your prayers will continue to have an impact on them. As you continue to pray, may their lives be covered by the grace and love of Christ and may your heart be filled with peace.

Lord, may my prayers lay the track on which your power comes into my loved ones' lives. Help me to keep praying and not lose heart!

Cheri

The shower of answers to prayer will continue to your dying hour. Nor will it cease then. And when you pass out from beneath the shower, your dear ones will step into it.

—OLE HALLESBY (1879–1961), Norwegian pastor and writer

KNOWING GOD

[GOD SAYS,] "I WANT YOU TO KNOW ME MORE THAN I WANT BURNT OFFERINGS."

Hosea 6:6

ONE SUNDAY I was teaching the prayer class I led for five years. It was an optional Sunday school class taught to nine children who chose to faithfully attend. That morning, some parents dropped off their three children in our room just as I was explaining that we were going to pray for missionaries and other people in a flooded village in Honduras. Then I explained to the new kids why we were learning and practicing prayer—so they would know God instead of just knowing about him and hear God instead of just hearing about him. All I got was puzzled stares, as if I were speaking Greek.

"But where are the worksheets? Why aren't we doing regular stuff?" the children wanted to know. As I pondered about a word picture to share with the children, Andrew, an eight-year-old, raised his hand.

"Ms. Cheri, could I explain to the kids?" he asked. When I gave the go-ahead, he turned to the newcomers and began. "It's kind of like me and President Bush," he said. "I've seen him lots of time on the TV news. I've read newspaper articles about him and even did a report about him for social studies class. And I hear his radio address sometimes. But I have never had a conversation with President Bush. So I don't really know him, do I?"

"No, you don't!" the new children said as the lightbulb went on in their minds. What Andrew said is so true. We can read all kinds of doctrines about God and even watch a religious "expert" expound on theological theories. But until we have our own conversations and experiences with the Lord, we don't really know him. And if we don't truly know him, how can we love him? How can we possibly know the love he has for us?

God, I want to know you. Teach me to pray! For Christ's sake, amen.

Cheri

We look upon prayer as a means of getting things for ourselves. The Bible idea of prayer is that we may get to know God himself.

—**OSWALD CHAMBERS** (1874–1917), Scottish minister and teacher

8 GOD IS ABLE

ALL GLORY TO GOD, WHO IS ABLE TO KEEP YOU FROM FALLING
AWAY AND WILL BRING YOU WITH GREAT JOY INTO HIS GLORIOUS
PRESENCE WITHOUT A SINGLE FAULT.

Jude 1:24

LONG AGO when I was a new Christian, I picked up J. B. Phillips' book *Your God Is Too Small*. Reading it made me ponder the small views of God I had heard in sermons and people's opinions, even those of religion professors. On the first day of my Religion 101 class, the learned professor had held up a Bible and said, "Students, these are all good stories but they are only myths. Furthermore, God may have set the world in space, but he isn't able to intervene in it." Phillips' book was describing men like this professor, who suffer from a very limited view of God. Though they have many academic degrees or titles, they haven't discovered the God big enough for the complex troubles we face today.

Scripture gives us an entirely different picture of the Lord, and today's verse from Jude 1 is a good example. God is so powerful, so loving, that he can keep us flawed, broken human beings from stumbling. Or, as *The Message* says, he can "keep you on your feet, standing tall in his bright presence, fresh and celebrating." He is the God who not only calls us and saves us but also never leaves us or forsakes us. He will lead us step by step until he brings us into his glorious presence in heaven.

This God, who is absolutely sovereign, knows everything, and listens to the prayers of little children and grandmas, kings and presidents all at the same time, is *able* to make all grace abound. He is *able* to bring good out of evil and to keep everything that we have committed to him until the day when we see him face-to-face. This is a God whose promises we can count on!

Heavenly Father, let us see your glory. Give us spiritual eyesight to see what our natural eyes cannot. Hallowed be your name.

Cheri

Only to sit and think of God,
Oh what a joy it is!
To think the thought, to breathe the Name,
   Earth has no higher bliss.

— "MY GOD, HOW WONDERFUL THOU ART" BY

FREDERICK WILLIAM FABER (1814–1863),

English hymn writer and theologian

ALL PRAISE TO JESUS

ALL PRAISE TO HIM WHO LOVES US AND HAS FREED US FROM OUR
SINS BY SHEDDING HIS BLOOD FOR US.

Revelation 1:5

THIS CALL to praise holds one of the most important truths of the Bible: that through Christ's sacrifice on the cross we have been set free from our sins. To a person who has sat in church and heard sermons week after week, month after month, from infancy to adulthood, those words might elicit a ho-hum response. But today's verse gives us the opportunity to pause and think about the immensity of this truth: because of the extravagant, boundless love the Father has for us, he gave his only Son so that anyone who believes in him will experience complete forgiveness.

Think of it: God absolutely and completely loves you. Not because of your performance or achievements, not just when you are doing the right thing, but when you've failed or are crushed by life. Before you ever thought of him, the Father deeply loved you and made a way through the life, death, and resurrection of his Son to include you in his forever family. He takes great delight in you! He has creatively and uniquely drawn you to himself and exerts limitless patience because he doesn't want anyone to perish but to gain eternal life.

Most of all, God the Father has freed you from guilt and condemnation; your shame has been swallowed up in Christ's loving presence. And he invites you to enter his rest and *enjoy*, even bask in, his love for you. What a great God we belong to! How should we respond to this amazing love? By giving the Lord our worship, praise, and thanks. As Revelation 1:6 proclaims, "All glory and power to him forever and ever! Amen."

God, just the thought of the sacrifice you made fills me with praise. Make my life one that brings glory to you and makes you smile.

Cheri

The Resurrection is at its very essence the ultimate victory over sin, death, and hell. All the forces of evil spent their best efforts to permanently ground their Archenemy behind a massive, immovable stone—guarded by imperial guards from the most powerful empire on earth. And then, with a word from God—the merest breath—death was defeated, and sin and the forces of hell no longer held sway. Jesus lives and in Him the power of sin is rendered weak and ineffective.

—**JOSEPH STOWELL** (1944–), American university president

10 LOVE AGAIN

I HAVE SEEN YOUR HARD WORK AND YOUR PATIENT ENDURANCE.
. . . YOU HAVE PATIENTLY SUFFERED FOR ME WITHOUT QUITTING.
BUT I HAVE THIS COMPLAINT AGAINST YOU. YOU DON'T LOVE ME
OR EACH OTHER AS YOU DID AT FIRST! LOOK HOW FAR YOU HAVE
FALLEN FROM YOUR FIRST LOVE! TURN BACK TO ME AGAIN AND
WORK AS YOU DID AT FIRST.

Revelation 2:2-5

IN REVELATION 2, the Lord exhorts his church at Ephesus to recover their first love—a deep devotion to Christ that supersedes everything else.

The Ephesian believers were not slackers! They had worked hard, patiently endured, refused to quit even with great adversity, and had been courageous in suffering—and Jesus commended them for this. Yet they had fallen so far that the Lord was on the verge of removing their "lampstand," which represents their church's influence in God's Kingdom.

Maybe you can relate to earnest people like this who pursued their ministry vigorously but became so immersed in working for God that they lost the simple devotion of loving him and one another. In his faithfulness, the Lord called the Ephesians back—as he calls us today through these words of Scripture—to recover the level of love and devotion to Christ they had when they first came to know him.

What did Jesus not want them to miss? First, his desire was clear: that they would listen to the Holy Spirit (see Revelation 2:7). Second, that in returning to their first love of Christ, they wouldn't miss the blessing stored up for those who abide in simple, loving devotion to him, despite all obstacles and trials. These verses end with a promise we can bank our hopes on: that *everyone* who is victorious will eat from the tree of life in God's paradise and experience eternal joy in his presence.

> Lord, I confess I've gotten pulled away from you and lost my first love. Thank you
> for continuing to love me and for calling me back to a more focused devotion
> to you. You've created me for something far better than a life of scheduled
> hyperactivity: an abundant life in your loving presence.

Jennifer

Give me a pure heart—that I may see thee,
A humble heart—that I may hear thee,
  A heart of love—that I may serve thee,
    A heart of faith—that I may abide in thee.

—DAG HAMMARSKJOLD (1905–1961), Swedish diplomat, economist, and author

WATCHMEN IN WAIT

I AM COUNTING ON THE LORD;
    YES, I AM COUNTING ON HIM.
    I HAVE PUT MY HOPE IN HIS WORD.
I LONG FOR THE LORD
    MORE THAN SENTRIES LONG FOR THE DAWN,
    YES, MORE THAN SENTRIES LONG FOR THE DAWN.

Psalm 130:5-6

WE KNOW we can count on the Lord because he has made promises.

The Hebrew word translated "counting on" can also be translated "wait for." It can even be used to mean "wait in ambush." It has the sense of watching and being alert. That means it also hints at expectation and certainty.

The psalmist compares this kind of waiting to the longing sentries have as they look for the arrival of dawn. And like the coming of dawn, the Lord's intervention in our lives is a certainty. It will come. Our hope lies in his Word, where his promises are abundant and as sure as the dawn of a new day.

What do we mean when we say, "I'm counting on it"? We mean we consider it done. It is a sure thing. Our watching is not so we can see *if* God will rescue but only to see *how* he will rescue.

Just as we know a new morning has arrived when we see the first faint rays of dawn, we know God's provision has arrived even when we see only the first evidence of his intervention. "The path of those who do what is right is like the first gleam of dawn. It shines brighter and brighter until the full light of day" (Proverbs 4:18, NIrV). When we see the first gleam, we know that it will get progressively brighter. At the first hint, the wait is over.

Are you waiting for something? You can wait expectantly. You can wait with certainty. You can count on God's promises as you count on the sunrise.

Lord, I'm counting on you. In everything, for everything, I wait expectantly for you. I wait for you like watchmen waiting for the dawn.

Jennifer

Never think that God's delays are God's denials. Hold on; hold fast; hold out. Patience is genius.
—COMTE GEORGES-LOUIS LECLERC DE BUFFON (1707–1788), French naturalist

12 COME IN

> Look! I stand at the door and knock. If you hear my voice and open the door, I will come in, and we will share a meal together as friends.
>
> *Revelation 3:20*

I LOVE THIS portrait of Jesus. He is always the one making the approach. Always the one seeking us out. Always the one initiating relationship.

We are the responders. All we have to do is open the door to him. Let him in to our needs. Welcome him into our struggles and our challenges.

Here is the promise of the Savior's love: "I am always right there, ready to come in and put my power to work on your behalf. I am always ready to enter your life in friendship and intimacy, to be fully involved in every detail of your life. Just say yes."

We sometimes have the feeling that we have to convince him to work. We have to chase him down and bring our need to his attention and then persuade him to take up our cause. We often develop elaborate rituals meant to get his attention. We look for ways to win his favor.

All of this is wasted effort. What a revelation it is to discover that our inclination to seek him is a response to his seeking us. We are in relationship with a God who is determined that we will find him. Infinite God that he is, he has placed himself within our small reach. He pulls at our hearts and stubbornly refuses to give up on us. In today's verse, the verbs *stand* and *knock* are in present tense. The action is happening now. He is knocking in the ever-present.

He is reaching out to you in this moment. Wherever you are, whatever is happening in your life right now, he is reaching out to you and offering himself in your struggle. Just say yes.

Yes, Lord Jesus.

Jennifer

Love in regard to men emptied (humbled) God; for He does not remain in His place and call to Himself the servant whom He loved, but He comes down Himself to seek him, and He who is all-rich arrives at the lodging of the pauper, and with His own voice intimates His yearning love, and seeks a similar return, and withdraws not when disowned, and is not impatient at insult, and when persecuted still waits at the doors.

—NICOLAUS CABASILAS (1322– c. 1392), Byzantine theological writer and mystic

CROWN HIM 13

YOU ARE WORTHY, O LORD OUR GOD,
TO RECEIVE GLORY AND HONOR AND POWER.
FOR YOU CREATED ALL THINGS,
AND THEY EXIST BECAUSE YOU CREATED WHAT YOU PLEASED.

Revelation 4:11

THE SIGHT of our exalted God and resurrected, glorified Christ must be so overwhelming that the only logical response is extravagant praise and worship. A glimpse into the throne room pulls from the heart unrestrained worship and adoration.

The biggest, most flamboyant words language can produce —*worthy, glory, honor, power*— don't give full expression. The elders around the throne throw their crowns at the feet of the Lord God Almighty, as if nothing they could have accomplished or that might honor them belongs to them. Every position or success has no worth other than to be offered as a gift to the King.

Today's verse states that the King created all things, and those things are in existence still because he created what he pleased. Translate that into your heart this way: You exist because you are a pleasure to God. He created what he pleased, and he pleased to create you.

Isn't it beautiful, this scene that only our hearts can see? Does it sweep you away in its pageantry and splendor? And yet the glorious, all-powerful, eternal God at his most exquisite is mindful of you. He is not aloof from the adoration poured out on him, but he returns boundless love in equal measure.

Let your heart meditate on this scene. In the sanctuary of your own soul, worship with abandon. Let the wonder that you are precious to God, known by him, in existence because that pleases him—let it all wash over you and capture you in the great wave of love flowing from him and drawing you in.

> *King of kings, Lord of lords, Creator, Sustainer, only God, I pour out my life at your feet. May it be a sweet-smelling offering of worship. May it please you and give you some small echo of the joy you give me.*

Jennifer

Ordinary human motives will appeal in vain to the ears which have heard the tones of the heavenly music; and all the pomp of life will show poor and tawdry to the sight that has gazed on the vision of the great white throne and the crystal sea.

—**ALEXANDER MACLAREN** (1826–1910), British preacher and Bible expositor

14 LET MERCY RULE

Jonah prayed to the Lord his God from inside the fish.
He said,

"I cried out to the Lord in my great trouble,
 and he answered me.
I called to you from the land of the dead,
 and Lord, you heard me!
You threw me into the ocean depths,
 and I sank down to the heart of the sea.
The mighty waters engulfed me;
 I was buried beneath your wild and stormy waves."

Jonah 2:1-3

JONAH'S CONDITION could be blamed entirely on his own choices and actions. He had failed God, failed the mission, failed himself. Anyone who knew of Jonah's time in the fish's belly could rightly have said, "Well, he brought it all on himself."

I breathe a sigh of relief when I see that God heard and responded to Jonah from the pit of his self-made abyss. God didn't say, "You got yourself into this, so you can just get yourself out. You made your bed; now lie in it."

It's a good thing God's mercy does not stop at messes I get myself into. Most of them can be traced to something I did or didn't do, or said or didn't say. I deserve most of my messes.

So I am very grateful for the mercy God has shown me over and over. If I want to be the vessel through which Jesus works in my world, surely mercy will flow freely from me. Withholding the judgment that comes so easily when I see someone else's mess, and instead pouring on the very mercy I have received, should be what God's mercy produces in me.

I need to ask, *Am I short on mercy when someone else brings on his own problems?* If so, I need to remember that God's intervention and rescue in my life are not mine because I deserve them but rather because of God's great mercy.

Let his kindness and mercy be evident in you and through you. Let mercy rule.

Father, thank you for opportunities to show your mercy—the kind of forgiveness that responds like a heat-seeking missile to the pain of another's plight.

Jennifer

God's way of forgiving is thorough and hearty—both to forgive and to forget; and if thine be not so, thou hast no portion of His.

—**ROBERT LEIGHTON** (1611–1684), Scottish preacher and scholar

HOME AT LAST

EVERYONE WILL LIVE IN PEACE AND PROSPERITY,
ENJOYING THEIR OWN GRAPEVINES AND FIG TREES,
FOR THERE WILL BE NOTHING TO FEAR.
THE LORD OF HEAVEN'S ARMIES
HAS MADE THIS PROMISE!

Micah 4:4

WE ARE not yet in our homeland. We are aliens and strangers passing through this world, living in tents, not putting down roots. Every now and then, the Lord reminds us what home will be like when we get there.

We don't need to be surprised that things are never perfect here in the land of our sojourning. We were made for another world. And one day we will be home.

Our journey seems long, and it is hard to keep in mind that we are headed some-where—to a land he will bring us in to. When we lose a loved one, we grieve for the many years we will live without that person, and it seems long in our estimation. It's hard to keep perspective when we are trapped for the moment in time and space. Eternity is beyond our experience, and we have to take the Lord's word for it.

Do you remember when you were a child and the time from one Christmas to another seemed like an eternity? But as you have lived more years, it now seems that the next Christmas is here before the trappings of the previous Christmas are cleaned up and put away. *Time flies* is the cliché we often use to express it.

When it comes to things eternal, we are still little children. Our only context is time. But the Lord promises that time is flying by. Eternity is closer every day. When we step into eternity, time will seem to have been something less than the blink of an eye.

Whatever we are going through here, in the land where we are itinerant travelers, it has an end. A glorious end. God promises his presence and his provision while we are on the journey—as he did for the Israelites when they were strangers in the land. We are in his care here and now, in time and space. But this is not our home.

Oh Lord, my heart longs for home.

Jennifer

My home is in Heaven. I'm just traveling through this world.
—**BILLY GRAHAM** (1918–), American evangelist and author

16 SMALL BEGINNINGS

You, O Bethlehem Ephrathah,
   are only a small village among all the people
   of Judah.
Yet a ruler of Israel will come from you,
   one whose origins are from the distant past.

Micah 5:2

THE ACCOUNT of the Incarnation, when the King of kings shed his kingly grandeur and donned mere clay, is packed with God's attention to detail. The little village of Bethlehem was singled out and marked as the location for Messiah's birth—the opening act of redemption. Pretty big stuff.

The location was so important that God revealed it through his prophets generations in advance. Bethlehem was no accident. It was a key element in the unfolding of events.

The coming of Christ into the world was heaven's sole occupation. Every act, every event, everything was moving toward that one grand moment. Can you imagine that even one single detail was left to chance?

Heaven planned every component of the birth of the Savior. The location was specific, not random. Though the Incarnation narrative can seem to indicate that Mary and Joseph found themselves in Bethlehem by chance, the big picture says otherwise. When the one whose "origins are from the distant past" (Micah 5:2) transitioned from heaven's throne to little planet earth, Bethlehem was the portal.

God has always been big on small beginnings. A tiny acorn becomes a towering oak. A pebble thrown into the water produces a ripple effect that multiplies the impact for miles. Every human being has his or her beginning in a seed too small to see with the human eye.

Nothing can become big without first being small. That is the immutable law that governs the created world. If a manger, hidden from the view of all but a few, can become the birthplace of the King, then nothing God calls us to is servile. Rather, it is a privilege, and our lives are elevated by the call. God is in the details.

Father, I embrace the adventure of living in your details, where the seemingly small and insignificant are actually eternal and exalted.

Jennifer

In the infinite wisdom of the Lord of all the earth, each event falls with exact precision into its proper place in the unfolding of His divine plan. Nothing, however small, however strange, occurs without His ordering, or without its particular fitness for its place in the working out of His purpose.

—B. B. WARFIELD (1851–1921), American minister and theologian

PRAYERS THAT OUTLIVE OUR LIVES

ANOTHER ANGEL WITH A GOLD INCENSE BURNER CAME AND STOOD AT THE ALTAR. AND A GREAT AMOUNT OF INCENSE WAS GIVEN TO HIM TO MIX WITH THE PRAYERS OF GOD'S PEOPLE AS AN OFFERING ON THE GOLD ALTAR BEFORE THE THRONE. THE SMOKE OF THE INCENSE, MIXED WITH THE PRAYERS OF GOD'S HOLY PEOPLE, ASCENDED UP TO GOD FROM THE ALTAR WHERE THE ANGEL HAD POURED THEM OUT.

Revelation 8:3-4

WHEN THE VEIL is pulled back, we are given a glimpse into heaven, where we discover "gold bowls filled with incense, which are the prayers of God's people" (Revelation 5:8). Bowls full of prayers. We see that every prayer we have prayed, every petition we have offered, is held safely in heaven's throne room. They didn't evaporate into the air. They are a vital part of heaven's energy. In today's verses we see the angel pouring prayers out on the altar before the throne.

What do you think that pictures? I think it is telling us that our prayers are living. They are vital. Perhaps the prayers—held in a golden bowl and mixed with the incense of worship—were offered generations before, or perhaps just minutes earlier. Prayers live.

Prayer is not limited to linear time because God is not limited to linear time. God speaks of the past, the present, and the future as one. "I will answer them before they even call to me. While they are still talking about their needs, I will go ahead and answer their prayers!" (Isaiah 65:24). His name is I Am. The Eternal Now. Always in the present tense.

The prayers you pray today will be answered in the lives of your descendants at the right time. Those prayers will be working in their lives as if you had just prayed them.

Father, I pray for the salvation and righteousness of my every descendant until the end of time.

Jennifer

God shapes the world by prayer. Prayers are deathless. The lips that uttered them may be closed in death, the heart that felt them may have ceased to beat, but the prayers live before God, and God's heart is set on them, and prayers outlive the lives of those who uttered them; outlive a generation, outlive an age, outlive a world.

—**E. M. BOUNDS** (1835–1913), American minister and writer

18 EVERY WINTER COMES TO AN END

THOUGH THE FIG TREES HAVE NO BLOSSOMS,
    AND THERE ARE NO GRAPES ON THE VINES;
EVEN THOUGH THE OLIVE CROP FAILS,
    AND THE FIELDS LIE EMPTY AND BARREN . . .
YET I WILL REJOICE IN THE LORD!
    I WILL BE JOYFUL IN THE GOD OF MY SALVATION!
THE SOVEREIGN LORD IS MY STRENGTH!

Habakkuk 3:17-19

AS I TRUDGED down the lane near our rented house in Maine, everything was frozen and the bare trees stood stark against the white, snow-covered fields. The sky was a steel gray *again*. In all of April there had been only twenty-four hours of sunshine. My soul felt as dull and gray as the sky.

Then I noticed a rosebush that had been harshly cut back. It reminded me of our family. The stock market had crashed and with it my husband's building projects. Our savings was gone, and money was so tight we didn't know how we'd get back to Oklahoma.

Into my thoughts God seemed to whisper, *This rosebush wasn't cut back by accident; the gardener pruned it so there would be abundant blooms next summer. Trust me in the winters too, my child.*

Just as that rosebush bloomed gloriously a few months later, God brought us through that long winter too. We saw him provide over and over, and each time our trust in him enlarged. We grew a hardy endurance as Holmes worked an all-night job at a printing press and I substitute-taught by day and wrote magazine articles at night.

By the next spring we were back in Oklahoma. The Lord brought us through the mountains of problems and deepened our faith. As surely as God had promised, spring eventually did come again—in our marriage, our careers, and our family's life together.

What in your life seems like a never-ending winter? The barren fields and the seed that seems to be dead in the ground hold the promise of spring. Trust God in this season and for the resurrection that he has coming for you in times ahead.

> *Father, may the same Spirit that raised Jesus from the dead give us life and strength to make it through all the dark winters we face and to bear much fruit in your perfect time and season.*

Cheri

After winter comes summer. After night comes the dawn. And after every storm, there comes clear, open skies.

—AMY CARMICHAEL (1867–1951), Irish missionary to India

THE NAME ABOVE ALL NAMES

I BOW BEFORE YOUR HOLY TEMPLE AS I WORSHIP.
I PRAISE YOUR NAME FOR YOUR UNFAILING LOVE
AND FAITHFULNESS;
FOR YOUR PROMISES ARE BACKED
BY ALL THE HONOR OF YOUR NAME.

Psalm 138:2

PEOPLE MAKE lots of promises. Some are reliable; others are worthless. What is the difference? The difference is the person who makes the promise. Every promise is backed by the character of the promiser. A promise is only as good as the person who makes it.

God's promises are backed by the honor of his name. A name stands for a person's entire being and character. So we don't have to say, "The man who is trustworthy and deals honestly and has proven himself to be competent and was born in 1953 and . . ." We just say "Jim," and the facts of his life and character are compacted into that name.

God's name is so big that a single word can't say it all. Through his dealings with his people, he revealed aspects of his name, showing who he is by what he does. All the many versions of his one name converge in the name of Jesus—who made God fully known. He has the name above all names because it was bestowed on him by the Father.

Jesus revealed the glorious name by fleshing it out in real time. Through the Gospel of John, we see Jesus laying claim to the eternal I AM name.

- I am the bread of life. (John 6:35)
- I am the light of the world. (John 8:12)
- I am the good shepherd. (John 10:14)
- I am the resurrection and the life. (John 11:25)
- I am the way, the truth, and the life. (John 14:6)

Each time he claimed the name, he lived it out in his dealings with people. Show and tell.

Jesus, I revere the name above all names, and declare my confidence in your promises that are backed by your great name.

Jennifer

My dear Jesus, my Savior, is so deeply written in my heart, that I feel confident, that if my heart were to be cut open and chopped to pieces, the name of Jesus would be found written on every piece.

—IGNATIUS OF ANTIOCH (c. 35–c. 108), bishop of Antioch and early Christian martyr

20 GOD'S WILL, GOD'S WAY, GOD'S TIME

THE WORLD HAS NOW BECOME THE KINGDOM OF OUR LORD
AND OF HIS CHRIST,
AND HE WILL REIGN FOREVER AND EVER.

Revelation 11:15

ULTIMATELY EVERY kingdom on earth will be the Kingdom of our Lord and his Christ. That is God's plan and has been from the beginning. He has been working out that plan since the world began, and it is a foregone conclusion.

Did the enemy know this when he offered Jesus the kingdoms of the world? "The devil took him to the peak of a very high mountain and showed him all the kingdoms of the world and their glory. 'I will give it all to you,' he said, 'if you will kneel down and worship me'" (Matthew 4:8-9).

I see it like this. Satan was genuinely tempting Jesus. A person can't be tempted to do something that holds no appeal. For example, no one could ever tempt me to bungee jump. No one could ever make that sound appealing enough to tempt me to do it.

Jesus had no desire outside God's will. He had no agenda except to do the will of the Father who sent him. He had no self-aggrandizing desires. The only thing that Satan could tempt Jesus with was to do his Father's will in his own power. Since the only way to do God's work and accomplish his will in Jesus' own power would be to hand over to another the allegiance that belonged only to the Father, it held no allure. So Satan—who knows his tempting business—knew the only shot he had was to appeal to Jesus' desire to see God's plan in effect. Satan knew that God wanted Jesus to be fed when hungry. He knew that God wanted Jesus recognized by his people as Messiah. And he knew God wanted all the kingdoms of the earth to be the Kingdom of our Lord and of his Christ.

Sometimes temptation aims at eliciting wrong execution of legitimate desires. Jesus was willing to wait to see God's will accomplished in God's way and at God's time. God ensures that everything he has promised us will be fulfilled. He will do it. Our part is to wait patiently and let God work it out all the way to its conclusion.

Father, I surrender to your timing and to your ways.

Jennifer

What Thou wilt; as Thou wilt; when Thou wilt.
—**THOMAS À KEMPIS** (c. 1380–1471) German monk and writer

OVERCOME

THEY HAVE DEFEATED HIM BY THE BLOOD OF THE LAMB
AND BY THEIR TESTIMONY.

Revelation 12:11

TODAY WE get a glimpse of the final defeat of the our enemy Satan and see how he has been overcome: by the blood of the Lamb and the testimony of those whose lives are living proof that God is victor.

When we are living out the promises of God, our testimony is that he is faithful. When we are following God's call on our lives, our testimony is that he is trustworthy. When we keep our eyes on him, not on earthly circumstances, our testimony is that he is worthy.

If we are not living what we believe, our testimony has holes in it, places where the enemy can create doubt and uncertainty.

Let's say that I believe that a certain chair will hold me up but I have never sat in it. My adversary can say, "That chair will never hold you up."

"Of course it will. I believe it will," I reply.

"How do you know?" my adversary taunts.

"Because it is constructed of sturdy materials. I can see where the center of gravity would be. I'm sure it would hold me up."

Then my adversary could say, "There may be a hidden flaw you don't know about."

My only answer could be, "Well, yes, there could be."

Belief can be shaken. Faith cannot.

Now suppose that I sit in the chair. My adversary can say, "That chair will never hold you up." To which I can reply, "Of course it will."

My adversary will say, "How do you know?"

And I will reply, "Because it is." Faith that comes from firsthand experience cannot be shaken. It is anchored in the blood of the Lamb, through which flow all life and power. When the enemy encounters the blood of the Lamb, the fight is over.

*Father, I rest all my expectations on you and take you at your word. May my
every moment stand as proof that you are utterly faithful.*

Jennifer

When we feel the need of a power by which to overcome the world, how often do we not seek to generate it within ourselves by some forced process, some fresh girding of the will, some strained activity which only leaves the soul in further exhaustion?

—HENRY DRUMMOND (1851–1897), Scottish evangelist and writer

22 MOUTH GUARD

TAKE CONTROL OF WHAT I SAY, O LORD,
  AND GUARD MY LIPS.
DON'T LET ME DRIFT TOWARD EVIL
  OR TAKE PART IN ACTS OF WICKEDNESS.
DON'T LET ME SHARE IN THE DELICACIES
  OF THOSE WHO DO WRONG.

Psalm 141:3-4

DAVID PRAYS fervently that the Lord will guard his words. The New International Version (1984) translates it like this: "Set a guard over my mouth, O LORD; keep watch over the door of my lips."

David's prayer progresses along these lines: first, guard my lips so that wrong words don't escape. The first step toward wrong actions is often wrong words. We take the restraints off our mouths and say whatever comes into our minds without the filter of the Holy Spirit, and often actions follow. If we can catch the thought or attitude before it takes shape in words, then we have cut it off at the pass.

Second, David says, don't let me drift toward evil. Drifting is often how we get there. We begin by giving voice to thought, solidifying it and legitimizing it. Then we drift. We lean in the direction of wrong action and, finally, take part in acts of wickedness. Our words get us into conversation—an interchange of ideas—with others who lean toward sin.

Third, keep me away from the delicacies of those who do wrong. Delicacies often look pretty but have no substance. They entice the eyes, taste good going down, but are empty of value. That's the way sin is. It has a momentary, fleeting pleasure to it. In Hebrews 11:25 we read that Moses chose to obey God "instead of enjoying the fleeting pleasures of sin."

David believed that God had the power to station a guard at his lips and stop evil at its genesis. He felt certain that he could ask God for that power. I think we can take it as God's promise to us that he is willing and able to station a guard at the doors of our lips. How much difficulty or disruption might we avoid by letting the Holy Spirit manage our mouths?

Lord, let my words be your captives, managed by your power and freed only at your command.

Jennifer

The true test of a man's spirituality is not his ability to speak, as we are apt to think, but rather his ability to bridle his tongue.

—R. KENT HUGHES, contemporary American pastor and author

CRADLED IN HIS LOVE

> I cry to you, Lord;
> I say, "You are my refuge,
> my portion in the land of the living."
>
> *Psalm 142:5* (NIV)

THESE WORDS follow David's lament that he has no one on his side: "Look and see, there is no one at my right hand; no one is concerned for me. I have no refuge; no one cares for my life" (v. 4, NIV).

David has experienced betrayal by those he trusted. He finds himself abandoned by his friends in his time of need. He must be mourning the loss of companionship and the death of friendships. He is lonely and afraid and hurt.

Then he speaks the words above, declaring that the Lord is there for him. The Lord is his safe place. The Lord is his portion. When everything is divvied up, he gets the lion's share because he gets the Lord as his portion. He comes out sitting pretty.

A friend of mine was abandoned by friends and coworkers when she took a stand against a wrong she had discovered. She was dismissed from her job, and her whole family was rebuffed. She discovered that she could not count on the love or loyalty of any human being. Her greatest shock was to be left out by people she had considered close friends for many years. Later the truth of the situation was revealed, and most of those friends have come back into her life. But the lesson she learned is that the Lord is her portion, and he is more than enough.

Have you been betrayed? Has a friend or loved one abandoned you? Do you feel left alone in your time of vulnerability? If you feel alone right now, you're not. You have the Lord as your portion. He will never leave you or forsake you. Nothing can separate you from his love. It is is wrapped around you like a warm blanket, and he will not let you go. He is your refuge and your portion.

Lord, wrap your love around me and remind me that you are always, always my portion.

Jennifer

Snuggle in God's arms. When you are hurting, when you feel lonely, left out. Let Him cradle you, comfort you, reassure you of His all-sufficient power and love.

—**KAY ARTHUR** (1933–), American Bible teacher and author

24 LIVING WATER

I LIFT MY HANDS TO YOU IN PRAYER;
I THIRST FOR YOU AS PARCHED LAND THIRSTS FOR RAIN.

Psalm 143:6

DAVID DESCRIBES his soul-deep thirst for God. He thirsts for God like a parched land—a land that has been denied water for so long that it is dried out, cracked open, dead.

Why does land thirst for water? Because without it the land has no life. It was not designed to be dry. It was designed to be drenched with life-giving water. Without water, nothing can grow. Without water, any life that may have one time had some footing has long since withered.

We are not designed to live apart from God. We need to be drenched in a downpour of his Spirit. Flooded with his presence. We need living water—a continual flow of it.

Living water that flows into us becomes living water that flows out of us. Imagine a clear glass. Imagine that glass filled with nasty, contaminated water. Scum floating on the top. Sediment sitting on the bottom. Unidentified particles throughout. Do you see it? Now, take that glass and turn it upside down and empty it. Is the glass clean?

If you pour more water in, will the new water be clean? No, it will pick up the grunge left on the inside of the glass and immediately become dirty.

Now, see the glass of dirty water again in your mind's eye. This time, take the glass of dirty water and put it under a faucet flowing with fresh water. Let the water continue to flow into the glass. The flow of fresh water displaces the dirty water. It disrupts the sediment on the bottom. It progressively changes the inside of the glass until it is clean and the water it is holding is clean and the water splashing over the edges is clean.

The secret is the continual fresh flow of clean water on the inside. The life of Christ flowing freely in you, flowing freely from you.

Our souls thirst for the Living Water. Without him, we are parched and lifeless. But he promises that we can be drenched in and filled to overflowing with the Living Water himself.

Living Water, pour yourself out in me, and then pour yourself out through me.

Jennifer

The soul's deepest thirst is for God Himself, who has made us so that we can never be satisfied without Him.

—**F. F. BRUCE** (1910–1990), Scottish Bible scholar and writer

MAY OUR SONS FLOURISH IN THEIR YOUTH
   LIKE WELL-NURTURED PLANTS.
MAY OUR DAUGHTERS BE LIKE GRACEFUL PILLARS,
   CARVED TO BEAUTIFY A PALACE.

Psalm 144:12

THIS HAS been a favorite prayer of mine for my sons, their wives, and their descendants. I have prayed this from the time my three sons were babies, and for the wives they would one day have.

David prays for sons to be mature beyond their years. We need to pray for our sons during their youth, when immaturity and lack of experience can sidetrack them.

David prays for our daughters to be like graceful pillars, using a word that describes the corner pillar—the load-bearing pillar that causes the palace to stand. Isn't it interesting that God views women as strong and sturdy and able to bear the weight of life? Pray that our daughters would be crafted, polished, and perfected so they display the beauty of holiness and adorn their homes with grace.

Start praying now for your descendants, whether they are spiritual or biological ones. Ask God to work in the lives of generations. You can reach into the future through prayer this very day. You can sit in your living room or on the airplane or in the doctor's office and have an impact on the world for generations to come.

It is beyond our imaginations what prayer can effect on the earth. When God's name and his renown are the desire of our hearts (see Isaiah 26:8), our prayers for our children, grandchildren, and further descendants can be the catalysts that will cause his fame to spread to all the corners of the earth: "Let this be recorded for future generations, so that a people not yet born will praise the Lord" (Psalm 102:18).

Father, I pray that all the generations of my descendants will be fruitful for you.

Jennifer

Remember how the psalmist described children? He said that they were as an heritage from the Lord, and that every man should be happy who had his quiver full of them. And what is a quiver full of but arrows? And what are arrows for but to shoot? So, with the strong arms of prayer, draw the bowstring back and let the arrows fly—all of them, straight at the Enemy's hosts.

—JIM ELLIOT (1927–1956), American missionary and martyr

26 HELP FOR THE FALLEN

THE LORD HELPS THE FALLEN
AND LIFTS THOSE BENT BENEATH THEIR LOADS.

Psalm 145:14

IT DIDN'T look as if God was being gracious to the homeschooling mother who was six months pregnant when her husband disappeared. At first everyone thought he was dead. Overwhelming grief threatened to sink the woman and her children. Her pregnancy became high risk, and she was left with no income. Detectives in the city he had traveled to found no trace of him except clothes and a suitcase left in his hotel room.

A year later the husband was arrested in another state, posing as a widower, and faced felony charges for abandoning minor children. His wife asked that the charges be dropped, but she faced even greater grief when her husband said he had no desire to be reunited with his wife and children.

As the horror of what had happened sank in, feelings of abandonment and betrayal hit the mother in waves. *Why do you declare yourself to be good when you dropped this in my lap?* she asked God. Then a wise Bible study teacher encouraged her to read aloud Psalms 144–150 every day as her prayer. Reading these psalms told her more about God, and she began to feel him lift her up and give her hope. Over the next decade she came to experience God as her faithful husband and see small glimpses of how he was a father to her fatherless children.

Are you bent beneath a load? Whether you are caring for an elderly parent, working multiple jobs, or dealing with medical problems, the Lord will give you the strength and hope to carry on. Take Psalms 144–150 and pray all of them aloud each day. God will bless you in ways you can't imagine.

> *God, I ask your Holy Spirit to bridge the gap between my head and my heart
> so the truth will sink in and bring sweeping transformation. In Christ's name,
> amen.*

Cheri

Christ is full and sufficient for all his people. . . . He is a garment of righteousness to cover and adorn them; a physician to heal them . . . ; a counsellor to advise them . . . ; a captain to defend them . . . ; a husband to protect; a father to provide; . . . a foundation to support.

—EDWARD REYNOLDS (1599–1676), English bishop and author

TURNING TO GOD

ASK THE LORD FOR RAIN IN THE SPRING,
FOR HE MAKES THE STORM CLOUDS.
AND HE WILL SEND SHOWERS OF RAIN
SO EVERY FIELD BECOMES A LUSH PASTURE.

Zechariah 10:1

TODAY'S VERSE contains a theme that runs throughout Scripture, and the wonderful promise that accompanies it: ask the Lord . . . and he will give it. Zechariah tells the people to ask God to water the earth in the spring, because the Lord is the rainmaker. He is the creator of the clouds that drop the showers to nourish the fields so they become fruitful; he "sends his orders to the world" and "snow like white wool" (Psalm 147:15-16). He set the stars in the heavens and knows each of them by name. Yet God encourages his people to ask for what they need.

Throughout the pages of the Bible and in the history of humanity, the Lord seeks people who will give themselves to earnest, persevering prayer. If we could provide everything ourselves, we could be independent of God's provision. If we could simply wish for something we want and instantly get the desired results, we wouldn't need prayer. Yet God had in mind that we would have an intimate relationship with him. How do we come into that kind of communion? By prayer: asking God for the provision we need, seeking and knocking persistently, and then trusting him to answer in his time and way.

Is there something that you sense God wants you to pray for until the answer comes? Is it a need so great it seems impossible to you? There is no impossible with God. He is the one who keeps every promise forever. Let me encourage you to write your prayer down and seek God today and every day until you see the answer.

Thank you for your great promises in the Bible that those who ask will receive;
that when we pray, you hear and answer. Grant me faith and hope to believe
your Word and put it into action. For Christ's sake, amen.

Cheri

The reason we must ask God for things he already intends to give us is that he wants to teach us dependence, especially our need for himself

—ERWIN W. LUTZER (1941–), North American pastor and author

28 A FLOWING FOUNTAIN

ON THAT DAY A FOUNTAIN WILL BE OPENED FOR THE DYNASTY OF DAVID AND FOR THE PEOPLE OF JERUSALEM, A FOUNTAIN TO CLEANSE THEM FROM ALL THEIR SINS AND IMPURITY.

Zechariah 13:1

THE PROMISED fountain is the fountain of Messiah's atoning blood. The verses preceding this refer to the one who is pierced, and the prophet continues on, pointing to the day when the great fountain of cleansing is opened.

In the Old Testament sacrificial system, the blood of the sacrifice pooled at the altar's base. It was stagnant and decaying and had to be washed away daily. That sacrificial system pointed toward the day when the eternal sacrifice would be offered. The blood of the eternal sacrifice flows as a fountain of cleansing. It is active, not stagnant. It is forever new because it is eternal.

The fountain flows for our cleansing, washing away the guilt of the sins we have committed and the impurity that causes us to sin. The word translated "sins" means to miss the mark—in other words, an action or behavior that fell short of the target. The word translated "impurity" means pollution or filthiness. It refers to a condition. The fountain cleanses us of both sin and impurity. In 1 John 1:9 we read, "If we confess our sins to him, he is faithful and just to *forgive us our sins* and to *cleanse us from all wickedness*" (emphasis added). John clarified that it is Christ's blood that cleanses: "the blood of Jesus, [God's] Son, cleanses us from all sin" (v. 7).

We live in the day of the fountain that cleanses completely, inside and out: "Under the old system, the blood of goats and bulls and the ashes of a young cow could cleanse people's bodies from ceremonial impurity. Just think how much more the blood of Christ will purify our consciences from sinful deeds so that we can worship the living God" (Hebrews 9:13-14).

Accept the promise that your sins are forgiven and Jesus is cleansing you. Every moment you can be cleaner than the moment before.

Lord Jesus, thank you for such a complete salvation. I receive the forgiveness for which you paid so great a price, and also the cleansing that is ongoing from moment to moment.

Jennifer

I thought I could have leaped from earth to heaven at one spring when I first saw my sins drowned in the Redeemer's blood.

—**CHARLES HADDON SPURGEON** (1834–1892), English preacher and writer

THE VICTORY IS WON

THEN I [JOHN] SAW AN ANGEL COMING DOWN FROM HEAVEN
WITH THE KEY TO THE BOTTOMLESS PIT AND A HEAVY CHAIN IN
HIS HAND. HE SEIZED THE DRAGON—THAT OLD SERPENT, WHO
IS THE DEVIL, SATAN—AND BOUND HIM IN CHAINS.

Revelation 20:1-2

IT IS GOOD to know not only that our Father God knows the end from the beginning but also that the victory has already been won. No matter how dark things get on this earth or how challenging the times we face in our own lives, the Lord has already written the end of the story, and it is a glorious culmination of his plan.

Satan's game plan has always been to detour and destroy God's children, to keep them from their destiny. Since he can't be God, he consistently opposes all those who are precious to the Father and tries to thwart God's plans and purposes. He endeavors to blind unbelievers to the truth. He aims to distort the focus of Christians by bringing such tribulation and sorrow that it throws them off their game and they lose hope. Satan has only a limited amount of time before the buzzer sounds, so he plays hard. Perhaps he has brought spiritual opposition or injury to you. No matter how many times Satan strikes, remember: the final score is already flashing on the board. God wins!

As this passage in Revelation describes, one day Satan will be thrown out of the game altogether, but until then, how we play is critical. Souls are at stake. If we work together and pray for one another, we are all strengthened as we depend on our victorious Lord and King. Let me encourage you to understand that your true opponent is not people or circumstances but rather an enemy who knows he is already defeated. Don't let him get the best of you! Shoot for the goal; keep focused on the prize, all the while rejoicing that God has secured the victory.

Father, I give you praise because you are still on the throne and have already overcome the enemy. Grant me courage and heart to press on, to fix my eyes on Jesus, and to rejoice in you today and in days ahead.

Cheri

Have plenty of courage. God is stronger than the devil. We are on the winning side.
—**JOHN JAY CHAPMAN** (1862–1933), American essayist and poet

30 LIVING OFFERING

"How I wish one of you would shut the Temple doors so that these worthless sacrifices could not be offered! I am not pleased with you," says the LORD of Heaven's Armies, "and I will not accept your offerings. But my name is honored by people of other nations from morning till night. All around the world they offer sweet incense and pure offerings in honor of my name. For my name is great among the nations," says the LORD of Heaven's Armies.

Malachi 1:10-11

THESE WORDS were written in the days before the eternal sacrifice was offered, perfect and acceptable to the Lord, on our behalf. When your sacrifice is examined, the Lord pronounces him unblemished, pure, faultless, spotless. Therefore, you have full access into heaven's throne room and the very presence of the Lord of hosts.

We have the opportunity to live our lives as offerings to the Lord. In Romans 12:1 we read, "I plead with you to give your bodies to God because of all he has done for you. Let them be a living and holy sacrifice—the kind he will find acceptable. This is truly the way to worship him."

The world in which we live becomes our altar, and we become living sacrifices, or offerings. We are not offering sacrifices to atone for our sins. We are giving ourselves to him as offerings of love and gratitude.

When we live with our lives laid on his altar, a sweet incense is spread throughout the world. Paul wrote, "Now he uses us to spread the knowledge of Christ everywhere, like a sweet perfume. Our lives are a Christ-like fragrance rising up to God" (2 Corinthians 2:14-15).

What a wonderful promise—that our sins are covered in a once-for-all perfect sacrifice so that we can worship him with our lives and find our altar in the world—the place where we live as the aroma of Christ.

Lord Jesus, let my life be worship—an offering to you.

Jennifer

Even our bodies must not be made the instruments of sin and uncleanness, but set apart for God, and put to holy uses, as the vessels of the tabernacle were holy, being devoted to God's service.

—MATTHEW HENRY (1662–1714), English pastor and Bible commentator

REFINED

WHO WILL BE ABLE TO ENDURE IT WHEN HE COMES? WHO
WILL BE ABLE TO STAND AND FACE HIM WHEN HE APPEARS? FOR
HE WILL BE LIKE A BLAZING FIRE THAT REFINES METAL, OR LIKE
A STRONG SOAP THAT BLEACHES CLOTHES. HE WILL SIT LIKE A
REFINER OF SILVER, BURNING AWAY THE DROSS.

Malachi 3:2-3

Oh, Lord, who can stand when You appear?
The splendor of Your presence near
Then knee shall bow and tongue proclaim
The pow'r of Your majestic name.

My hungry heart cries out for You.
No earthly substitute will do.
Refiner's Fire, come near to me
Your unveiled glory, let me see.

A heart like Yours, my one desire.
Do Your work, Refiner's Fire.

Your holy Fire now burns within
And purges every secret sin.
My life the bush, Your life the Flame
That leaves me nevermore the same.

Your life in me ignites the Fire
That now fulfills my heart's desire.
The Spirit's work, my life made new,
Transformed within, ablaze with You.

A heart like Yours, my one desire.
Do Your work, Refiner's Fire.
(© Jennifer Kennedy Dean 1990)

When we come face-to-face with him, we find a desire to be holy is suddenly ignited.
Nothing proves his presence more completely than a longing for purity—something our
human nature on its own would never crave. He promises to create that desire in us and
then to fulfill that desire for us.

Refiner's Fire, burn in my life.

Jennifer

May God so fill us today with the heart of Christ that we may glow with the divine fire of
holy desire.

—**A. B. SIMPSON** (1843–1919), Canadian preacher, theologian, and author

SCRIPTURE INDEX

Psalm 34:17-18	August 16	Psalm 102:28	May 1
Psalm 35:9-10	August 17	Psalm 103:10, 12-14	October 31
Psalm 36:8	February 17	Psalm 103:13-14	May 2
Psalm 37:4	January 24, February 18	Psalm 105:1-4	November 3
Psalm 37:23	August 21	Psalm 105:16-17	May 6
Psalm 38:9	August 23	Psalm 105:39-41	November 5
Psalm 39:7	February 22	Psalm 106:24-25	November 7
Psalm 40:8	August 25	Psalm 107:43	November 9
Psalm 40:16	February 24	Psalm 108:3-4	November 10
Psalm 41:1	February 25	Psalm 111:2-3	November 13
Psalm 44:5-7	February 28	Psalm 112:4	May 16
Psalm 46:1-3	March 3	Psalm 118:15-16	July 14
Psalm 48:10	March 5	Psalm 118:24	May 22
Psalm 50:9, 14-15	March 7	Psalm 119:1-2	May 23
Psalm 50:15	September 6	Psalm 119:18	May 24, November 22
Psalm 51:7-10	September 7	Psalm 119:49-50	May 26
Psalm 55:22	March 1, 12	Psalm 119:103	May 29
Psalm 57:7-8	September 14	Psalm 119:123	May 30
Psalm 59:16	September 15	Psalm 119:123-124	November 28
Psalm 60:12	March 17	Psalm 119:140	May 31
Psalm 61:3-4	March 18	Psalm 119:147-148	November 29
Psalm 62:1-2	March 9	Psalm 119:162	June 1
Psalm 62:5-6	March 19	Psalm 119:165	November 30
Psalm 63:5	March 20	Psalm 120:1	June 2
Psalm 65:3	March 22	Psalm 126:1-3	June 8
Psalm 68:4	March 25	Psalm 127:3-5	June 9
Psalm 69:13-14	March 27	Psalm 130:5-6	December 11
Psalm 70:4	March 29	Psalm 132:9	June 14
Psalm 72:18-19	March 31	Psalm 133:1	June 15
Psalm 75:1	April 3	Psalm 138:2	December 19
Psalm 77:19	October 5	Psalm 138:6	June 20
Psalm 78:23-25	October 6	Psalm 139:5, 13-16	June 21
Psalm 84:5-6	April 15	Psalm 141:3-4	December 22
Psalm 84:11	October 14	Psalm 142:5	December 23
Psalm 89:5-6	April 20	Psalm 143:6	December 24
Psalm 89:15-17	April 21, October 20	Psalm 144:12	December 25
Psalm 91:9-11	October 22	Psalm 145:14	December 26
Psalm 91:11-12	April 23	Psalm 145:18-19	June 27
Psalm 92:1-2	April 24	Psalm 146:6	June 28
Psalm 92:12-14	October 23	Psalm 147:1-3, 5	June 29
Psalm 94:18-19	April 25	Psalm 148:1-2, 4-5	June 30
Psalm 98:1	April 27	Psalm 149:4	July 1
Psalm 101:2	October 29	Proverbs 1:7	February 14

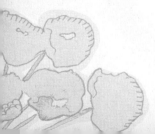

ABOUT THE AUTHORS

CHERI FULLER is a gifted speaker and award-winning author of more than forty books, including *The One Year Women's Friendship Devotional*, the bestselling *When Mothers Pray*, and *A Busy Woman's Guide to Prayer*. Her books have been translated into many languages, and her speaking ministry has provided encouragement to people throughout the U.S. and abroad. A former Oklahoma Mother of the Year, Cheri has been a frequent guest on national TV and radio programs. Her articles on family, spiritual growth, relationships, and prayer have appeared in *Family Circle, Focus on the Family, Guideposts*, and many other publications. Cheri holds a master's degree in English literature and is executive director of the nonprofit organization Redeeming the Family. She and her husband, Holmes, live in Oklahoma and have three grown children and six wonderful grandchildren. Cheri's books, Bible studies, and other resources can be found at www.cherifuller.com along with information on her speaking topics and how to schedule Cheri for events. To find out more about the ministry, visit www.redeemingthefamily.org.

JENNIFER KENNEDY DEAN is a respected author and speaker and the executive director of The Praying Life Foundation. Widely recognized as an unusually gifted communicator of the deep truths of God's Word, Jennifer speaks throughout the United States, calling God's people to discover the difference between "a prayer life" and "a praying life." She has spoken in such venues as the Billy Graham Training Center at The Cove and at Focus on the Family. She is a member of Advanced Writers and Speakers Association, a member of America's National Prayer Committee, a board member and national prayer director for Women in Christian Media, and a broadcaster on Salem Network's internet radio and TV sites.

Jennifer is the author of numerous books and studies focusing on prayer and spiritual formation. Among her books are *Live a Praying Life, Heart's Cry, Fueled by Faith, The Life-Changing Power in the Name of Jesus*, and *Secrets Jesus Shared*. Jennifer also writes for magazines such as *Pray!* and *SpiritLed Woman*.

Jennifer was widowed in 2005 after twenty-six years of marriage to Wayne Dean, her partner both in life and ministry. They are the parents of three grown sons. Jennifer makes her home in Marion, Kentucky.

MORE RESOURCES *for* PRAYING *the* PROMISES *of* GOD

Find extra helps like questions for small-group discussion or journaling, Retreat-in-a-Box, and other resources to encourage you to pray God's promises at www.prayingthepromises.com.

Do-able. Daily. Devotions.

START ANY DAY THE ONE YEAR WAY.

Do-able.
Every One Year book is designed for people who live busy, active lives. Just pick one up and start on today's date.

Daily.
Daily routine doesn't have to be drudgery. One Year devotionals help you form positive habits that connect you to what's most important.

Devotions.
Discover a natural rhythm for drawing near to God in an extremely personal way. One Year devotionals provide daily focus essential to your spiritual growth.

For Women

The One Year® Devotions for Women on the Go

The One Year® Devotions for Women

The One Year® Devotions for Moms

The One Year® Women of the Bible

The One Year® Coffee with God

For Women
(continued)

The One Year®
Devotional of Joy
and Laughter

The One Year®
Women's
Friendship
Devotional

For Men

The One Year®
Devotions for
Men on the Go

The One Year®
Devotions for
Men

For Families

The One Year®
Family
Devotions, Vol. 1

For Couples

The One Year®
Devotions for
Couples

The One Year®
Love Language
Minute Devotional

The One Year®
Love Talk
Devotional for
Couples

For Teens

The One Year®
Devos for Teens

The One Year®
Devos for Sports
Fans

For Personal Growth

The One Year®
at His Feet
Devotional

The One Year®
Walk with God
Devotional

The One Year®
Daily Insights
with Zig Ziglar

For Bible Study

The One Year®
Praying through
the Bible

The One Year®
Through the
Bible Devotional

It's convenient and easy to grow
with God the One Year way.
TheOneYear.com

CP0145

Also available from
Cheri Fuller

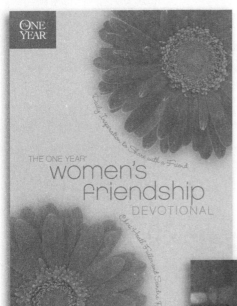

The One Year Women's
Friendship Devotional

ISBN 978-1-4143-1458-7

Connect with
Your Grandkids

ISBN 978-1-58997-536-1